Guido Liebermann

THE ORIGINS OF
PSYCHOANALYSIS
IN ISRAEL

*The Freudian Movement
in Mandatory Palestine
1918-1948*

Translation to English by
Merav Datan

Preface by
Élisabeth Roudinesco

THE ORIGINS OF PSYCHOANALYSIS IN ISRAEL

The Freudian Movement
in Mandatory Palestine 1918-1948

Guido Liebermann

Translation to English by Merav Datan

Published by ISRAEL ACADEMIC PRESS, New York
(A subsidiary of MultiEducator, Inc.)
553 North Avenue • New Rochelle, NY 10801
Email: nhkobrin@Israelacademicpress.com

ISBN # 978-1-885881-72-4
© 2019 Israel Academic Press

First published as La psychanalyse en Palestine 1918-1948.
Aux origines du mouvement analytique israélien
© Campagne Première / 2012
All rights reserved

To Leonor, Demian, and Anaïs
For their valuable support
and patient accompaniment

To my parents, in memory

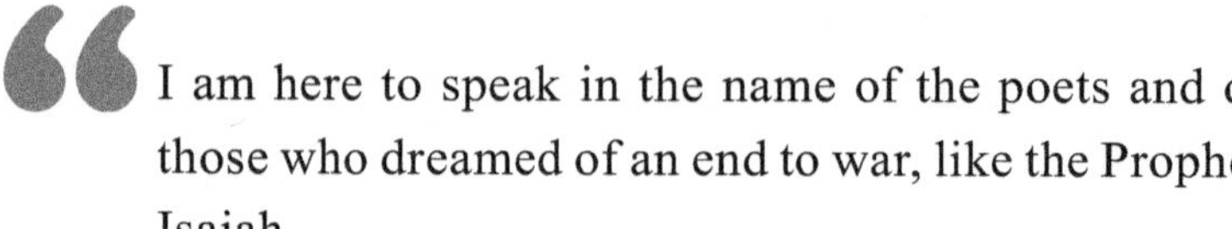 I am here to speak in the name of the poets and of those who dreamed of an end to war, like the Prophet Isaiah.

I am also here to speak in the names of sons of the Jewish people like Albert Einstein and Baruch Spinoza, like Maimonides, Sigmund Freud and Franz Kafka.

And I am the emissary of millions who perished in the Holocaust, among whom were surely many Einsteins and Freuds who were lost to us, and to humanity, in the flames of the crematoria.

… I stand here as the emissary of the soaring hopes of a people which has endured the worst that history has to offer and nevertheless made its mark – not just on the chronicles of the Jewish people but on all mankind. 

Excerpts from the speech by Yitzhak Rabin
at the Nobel Peace Prize ceremony,
December 10, 1994, Oslo

Acknowledgements

To Élisabeth Roudinesco, for her enthusiasm and support; Professor André Gueslin, Director of the Department of Geography/History and Social Science at the University of Paris 7 – Denis Diderot; Professor Patrick Guyomard of the University of Paris 7 – Denis Diderot, President of the Société de psychanalyse freudienne, for his decisive assistance; Dominique Bourel and Jacques Le Rider, for their pertinent remarks and suggestions; the late Shlomo Dunour, my friend and first teacher of Jewish history in Jerusalem; and to Silvio Yeschua for his advice and encouragement.

To my sister Claudia Liebermann and my brother Dario Liebermann; my friend and colleague Jean Szpirko; Marcelle, Arthur, Anne-Marie, and Monique Kasparian; Ferida Meurin; Ivan Denis; Marc Melka; and Roseline Dery.

To Naomi Belsitzmann of Tel Aviv and Lou Seinfeld of New York, for opening their personal archives and providing me with important biographical information about their fathers, Ariel and Dorian Feigenbaum; Raphael Friedjung of Haifa, for opening his personal archives and providing me with important documentation about his grandfather; Nava Aizen and Uri Nardi, at the Archives of the History of Jewish Education at Tel Aviv University, for their invaluable assistance in finding the documents relevant to my research; Nelly Varsariewsky, at the Archives of the Municipality of Tel Aviv; Josepha Fecher, at the Archives of Yad Ya'ari – HaShomer HaTza'ir Research and Documentation Center at Kibbutz Giv'at Haviva; and Jean Delaite, for his editorial work.

In producing this English edition, I wish first of all to acknowledge and express my very deep gratitude to Prof. Yitzhak Reiter, Editor in Chief of Israel Academic Press, and Dr. Nancy Hartevelt Kobrin, Director of Communication, for inviting and encouraging me to publish this book through their publishing house.

I am particularly grateful to Merav Datan, the translator, for her valuable work and efforts to produce a faithful text in English by translating from Hebrew with attention to the original French, preserving the essence of the Hebrew source documents as well as the style of the author.

Thanks to the authorities of the Archives of the Sigmund Freud Museum in London, the Archives of the British Psychoanalytic Society, the Sigmund Freud Archives at the Library of Congress, the Archives of the A.A. Brill Library of the New York Psychoanalytic Society and Institute, and the YIVO Institute for Jewish Research in New York, for their permission to consult and access material for this research.

Thanks to all those individuals, each of whom helped me, supported me, and encouraged me in a different way from the outset and along the way, in this lengthy but impassioned historical and intellectual undertaking:

To Dr. Saul Malosowski and his wife Claudia (Washington), and to Dr. Daniel Benveniste (Seattle, formerly San Francisco) for their help and their loyal support.

To Prof. Martin Bergmann (New York), Dr. Frank Lachman (New York), Prof. Peter Paret), Nelly Thompson (New York), Lou Seinfeld (New York), Josephine Shapiro (New York), Michael Molnar (London), Dr. Riccardo Steiner (London), Pr. Malcolm Pines (London), Huguette Elhaddad-Charbit (Tel Aviv), Gideon Remez and Isabella Ginor (Jerusalem), Annie Milgram (Paris), Hélène Oppenheim (Paris), and Hélène Potter (New York).

A very special acknowledgement and heartfelt appreciation go to Professor Rubén Gallo, who not only was the first to invite me to present aspects of my book at Princeton University, but also strongly encouraged me and provided me help and support in producing this book in English, and to Mrs. Paola Mieli, President of Après-Coup Psychoanalytic Association, New York, for inviting me to present aspects of my research before the psychoanalysts members of this institution.

Table of Contents

Preface

ÉLISABETH ROUDINESCO

This book has its origins in a doctoral thesis defended in 2006 at the University of Paris 7.[1] The thesis spanned a broader period and explored Freud's relationship with Zionism as well as status of psychoanalysis in Germany during 1933-1945, including the differences of opinion between Max Eitingon and Ernest Jones regarding the possibility of rescuing psychoanalysis under Nazism. It also addressed the collaboration of certain Berlin Freudians with Hitler's regime.[2]

In consultation with the author, the publisher of the original French edition of this book chose to retain from this thesis only those portions that address the establishment of psychoanalysis in Mandatory Palestine until the founding of the State of Israel, with a few forays into the origins of medicine and psychiatry in the Ottoman Empire, the early waves of Jewish immigration before 1918, and the evolution of the Israeli psychoanalytic movement after 1950.

I met Guido Liebermann in 1997. It was a difficult period for him, having participated in an unsuccessful project to establish a school for doctoral studies in Jerusalem under the auspices of the University of Paris 7. The project was piloted by Benny Levy with the support of several prominent French intellectuals, including Jean-Claude Milner, Alain Finkielkraut, and Bernard-Henri Lévy. Guido then considered undertaking a study on the works of Jacques Lacan, with the assistance of our mutual friend Jean Szpirko. I suggested that he undertake a study on the history of psychoanalysis in Israel, as the subject had never been explored and I was in a position to serve as his thesis advisor as well as refer him to an excellent historian engaged in his own research in Jerusalem, who could provide assistance: Dominique Bourel. I soon discovered that Guido was a passionate student of the history of psychoanalysis, and that with his knowledge of several languages – German, French, Spanish, English, and Hebrew – he was the best possible candidate to dive first-hand into unpublished archival sources, particularly the writings of Max Eitingon, the second founder alongside Moshe Wulff of the Palestine Psychoanalytic Society, which was inaugurated in 1934.

Guido Liebermann spent years exploring all the archives that contained potentially useful material, first in Israel and later in Germany, United States, Britain, and Switzerland, and meeting with many witnesses who provided new information. In 2000 I traveled to Israel for the first time, where I met with many psychoanalysts across the professional spectrum and realized how little they, like psychoanalysts everywhere, knew about the history of their movement. Worse yet, it became evident that Freud's writings were of no interest to Israeli clinicians, whose work drew primarily on Anglophone or Francophone psychoanalytic literature. They were happy to discuss child psychology, Melanie Klein, Lacan, Winnicott, or Maud Mannoni, and above all neuroscience and psychopharmacology. But they had little to say about Freud and his Jewishness, his relationship with Zionism,[3] or Vienna, and they knew next to nothing about the adventures of their movement's founders, the Nazi era, and the destruction of psychoanalysis in Europe.

In fact, as Edward Said on the one hand and Yosef Haim Yerushalmi on the other have elucidated,[4] the State of Israel had repressed Freud's work and language in its historical memory, although eventually, in 1977, in repentance, the Hebrew University established a Sigmund Freud Chair, inaugurated by his daughter Anna under dramatic circumstances: her assertion that psychoanalysis should be identified as a "Jewish science" sparked a massive outcry. Although many of the practitioners I met mentioned Freud's name, it was only has an academic reference that had little to do with historical origins. For these reasons I encouraged Guido to publish his archival discoveries without delay, especially as other works were already in progress: a thesis by Alex Liban, cited in this work, and a study by Eran Rolnik on the same subject.[5]

Born in 1961, Guido Liebermann is in many ways heir to the history he loved so much and reinvented so well. Like the heroes of this adventure, he belongs to a family of Jewish immigrants: his father emigrated from Germany to Argentina and his mother came from a family of second-generation Ukrainian emigrants who settled in Argentina. He took an early interest in psychoanalysis in a country where Freud was venerated. At a very young age he had his first experience of analysis with Luis Kancyper while planning a career as a top-level athlete. But he also dreamt of becoming a physician and soon a psychoanalyst, when General Videla's bloody dictatorship took hold

Argentina and resulted in his going into exile. Just as his parents had fled Europe to escape the "brown plague," so too he left Buenos Aires in 1979 and immigrated to Israel, convinced that the history of Zionism was linked with that of Freudianism. These were happy years for him. After learning Hebrew at a kibbutz, he continued his studies at David Yellin College of Education, where he deepened his understanding of the Hebrew language, Hebrew literature, and Jewish history with an exceptional teacher – Shlomo Dunour.

Dunour, a Polish, Zionist, secular Jew, had gone into exile and immigrated to Palestine during the inter-war period. In 2000 I had the privilege, thanks to Guido, of discovering Jerusalem with him during a long walk. He knew every site, every building, every piece of land, every name, every alley, every piece of wall, and every Jewish or Arab resident. His words brought to life the lost world of Old Europe that had seen the emergence of Freud and his disciples. And he told me how, as a soldier in the British Army with a Star of David on his uniform, he had participated in the liberation of an extermination camp, to the astonishment of the survivors of this hell – who also wore the Star, that yellow symbol of horror – and how they welcomed him as their brother.

And now, fifty-five years later, in the midst of a people he saw as his own, knowing they were united by eternal memory, he worried about the future of this land of Zion that had become his only homeland. Emotion, nostalgia, hope, humor: I have never met a man so capable of conveying, within a few hours and with infinite lucidity, the tragic subjectivity of European Jews. He spoke admirable French and possessed the sweet voice of those who, after painful exile, were still able to convey the mournful tones so characteristic of Yiddish as well as the aristocratic elegance so distinctive to the Polish language.

Determined to train in psychoanalysis, Guido Liebermann traveled to Europe and was finally able to realize his dream in Paris, where many Argentinians had taken refuge. In 1981 he enrolled in the psycho-pedagogy program of the psychology department at the University of Paris 8 and later transferred to the University of Rennes II. Through his studies and internships in clinical psychology, he became familiar with Lacan's work, while also undergoing analysis with Leopoldo Bleger, son of the renowned Argentinian psychoanalyst José Bleger, who had immigrated to France. After the fall the dictatorship, he returned to Argentina and in 1992 decided to settle in Israel as a psychologist and psychoanalyst. Meanwhile, he married and attended Patrick Guyomard's seminars in Paris. In the years that followed he organized several conferences with French Lacanian psychoanalysts and became a member of the Société de psychanalyse freudienne (SPF – Freudian Psychoanalytic Society). During this period he also embarked on the research that led first to his doctoral thesis and later to this book – fifteen years of work.

This book therefore focuses on the internal history of psychoanalysis in Mandatory Palestine and that of its pioneers from Europe, far more than on an analysis of the international context relevant to the psychoanalytic movement. Beginning with the institutionalization of rational medicine in the mid-nineteenth century, Liebermann demonstrates that one of the characteristics of the history of psychoanalysis in Palestine stems from the recurring quasi-structural rivalry between the local religious community, which depended on the Khalukah (donations from Jews across the world) and adhered to an ultra-Orthodox lifestyle based on Jewish law, on the one hand, and secular Jews from Europe or the United States who were followers of the Haskalah (Jewish Enlightenment) movement, on the other. He describes how the difficult fate of the great physician Simon Frankel, a Polish Jew who came to Palestine in the mid-nineteenth century and who throughout his life was accused of disrespecting Judaism, pre-shadowed the accusations leveled a century later at the pioneers of Freudianism. He also relates how psychiatry was born in 1894, with the establishment of Ezrat Nashim as an asylum for Jews and non-Jews.

In the aftermath of the Balfour Declaration, which called for the establishment of a national Jewish homeland in Palestine, Chaim Weizmann, the English representatives of the World Zionist Organization and a devoted admirer of Freud, entrusted Montague David Eder with the task of promoting the immigration of psychiatrists to Palestine. Eder, a Jewish English psychoanalyst of Lithuanian heritage, a physician who treated the poor, and a socialist Zionist activist, encouraged immigration by those who were to establish the psychoanalytic movement in the future Jewish state. Thanks to him, Freud was elected to the Board of Governors of the Hebrew University.

It was during this period, with the arrival of Henrietta Szold from Baltimore, that systematic care for orphans and other children in distress was instituted in Palestine. The two Feigenbaum brothers – Aryeh and Dorian – who came from Galicia, were convinced that Freudianism could promote a new form of emancipation from human subjectivity, and they introduced modern educational methods into the field of teacher training. Yet they too encountered religious opposition, and Dorian was accused of conspiracy and collaboration with Bolshevism. It seemed as though from the moment anything related to Freudianism was raised, the ultra-Orthodox, who resisted anything novel, could not help but resort to accusations worthy of the Protocols of the Elders of Zion. Some even went so far as to charge Freudian Zionists with "profaning the holy places."

Liebermann's account includes some beautiful portraits of these pioneers: Grete Obernik, born in Brno and a friend of Kafka, who underwent analysis with Anna Freud in Vienna and later went mad; and Siegfried Zadock van Vriesland, Hebrew scholar and immigrant from the Netherlands, a melancholic Zionist who committed suicide in 1939.

Thus, without a mentor to mediate, there emerged an elite group of activists who sought not only to promote the establishment of a Jewish homeland but also the emancipation of the Arabs of Palestine. They were imbued with a universalist ideal and were remarkably similar to the early disciples of Freud who gathered in Vienna at the beginning of the twentieth century, determined to found a Platonic school – a Republic of the elect – that would introduce self-knowledge based on exploration of the unconscious into the Western world.

In 1934 they were joined by Max Eitingon, who was to play the most prominent role in the consolidation of this movement. Born in 1881 in Mohilev, Belarus, he was the son of a wealthy fur trader. After studying psychiatry in Zurich, he traveled to Vienna in 1907 and there he met Freud, who became his analyst during their evening walks. In February 1921, after the collapse of the Central European empires, and out of love for psychoanalysis, he saw the fruition in Berlin of his life's work: the Berlin Psychoanalytic Institute, the first training institute, which would serve as a model for all the institutes founded later throughout the world and were integrated into the International Psychoanalytical Association (IPA) founded in 1910. On the basis of this experience, Eitingon established the rules of a curriculum that is still in force today: didactic analysis, (also known as Supervision), theoretical instruction, and the like. As a sign of gratitude, Freud gave him the gold ring reserved for the initiated. Over the years Eitingon used his fortune in the service of his Institute and, within the framework of a polyclinic, instituted free treatment for indigent patients and treatment by payment for others. By 1930 he alone represented, in Jones's words, "the heart of the international psychoanalytic movement." Aside from psychoanalysis, Eitingon (who, although a socialist and atheist, was concerned about Jewish heritage) had two additional passions: the Zionist cause and his wife Mirra, a theater actress with a fragile temperament. Averse to Jones's politics, he left Germany and settled in Jerusalem, where he met the writer Arnold Zweig and laid the foundations for the future Israeli psychoanalytic movement. He was assisted in this task by Moshe Wulff, an exceptional clinician from Odessa.

Liebermann takes great care in describing the personality of Eitingon, who was often the victim of slander throughout his life. Forty years after Eitingon's death, a former CIA employee claimed that he had been a Soviet agent involved in Trotsky's assassination, sponsored by Colonel Nahum Leonid Eitingon of the NKVD (predecessor to the KGB) – allegedly his brother. That claim, reiterated in 1993 by Alexander Etkind,[6] a Russian historian who conducted no archival research, is thoroughly refuted in this book.

Aside from the ultra-Orthodox opposition to psychoanalysis (which was, after all, secular), Freud's work was, surprisingly, rejected by two of the greatest scholars in Jewish history – Martin Buber and Gershom Scholem. The former, who proposed the establishment of a chair in experimental psychology at the Hebrew University, supported the appointment of Kurt Lewin over a disciple of Freud. The latter preferred Carl Gustav Jung – whom he viewed as more serious and who appeared all the more "Zionist" as his anti-Semitism increased[7] – over Freud. Jung, who had admired Nazi ideology until 1936, abhorred diaspora Jews (whom he regarded as too intellectual and detached from their "roots") and wanted them expelled from Germany to Palestine. In his view, the only way they would be able to regenerate was if they finally had a territory of their own.

Freud himself was never a Zionist, even if he ardently hoped that his doctrine would be taught in Jerusalem and even if, on numerous occasions, he voiced support for colonization in Eretz Israel (the Land of Israel). He regarded the creation of a state for Jews as a perilous idea. Although he never denied his Jewishness, he in no way shared the views of his Viennese contemporary, Theodor Herzl, and did not believe that a return to the ancestral land possibly resolve the issue of European anti-Semitism. A universalist Jew, he sought to explore the territory of the unconscious; a Jewish seeker of knowledge, in the sense of Jewishness rather than Judaism, he aspired to be heir to Spinoza and the German cultural tradition. As such, the religious Jews of Eretz Israel saw him sometimes as a heretic and sometimes as a Prussian of sorts, detached entirely from the Hebrew tradition and lacking any empathy for the grand dream of a return to the Promised Land. Moreover, even after the Holocaust his work was not fully accepted, as I could see during my first visits to Jerusalem and Tel Aviv.

For these reasons, Freud's great work, and in effect bequest, *Moses and Monotheism*, was received in Palestine with remarkable animosity. Although the book certainly served as a standard for many intellectuals who opposed obscurantism (which, incidentally, indicates that resistance to a doctrine might be a symptom of its progress in action), Freud was still accused of being a bad Jew, liberal, assimilationist, rationalist, westernized, and therefore diabolical. Some even argued that he was simply anti-Semitic because he dared to put forward the hypothesis that Moses was Egyptian and had evidently been murdered by his own people. Aharon Kaminka challenged Freud's claim that the University of Vienna authorities had discriminated against him, going so far as to assert that it was Freud's own fault that he had been rejected: "[Freud] did not realize and did not want to recognize that his science was a source of shame and an abomination for intellectuals, and that the Hebrew University, which respects itself and the great spiritual strength that gave rise to everything exalted and sublime in Jewish culture, would not accept as a professor a man who from the outset dismisses all the positive and creative influence of the human spirit and denies the very foundation of belief and the divinity in human beings."[8]

Guido Liebermann deserves our thanks for having retraced this little-known history, which reveals that – despite the endeavors of his Zionist disciples and many leftist intellectuals who saw him as a "hero of the Jewish People" – Freud encountered mistreatment precisely where one would have imagined a completely different reception for him and his work.

Introduction

Anyone seeking to trace the history of psychoanalysis in Ottoman and Mandatory Palestine, and later in Israel, must take into account the tragic background of concurrent Jewish history: pogroms, anti-Semitism, the rise of Nazism, and the consequent exile of psychoanalysts from Vienna, Berlin, and Russia to Palestine during the early decades of the twentieth century. After a difficult period of introduction and transition in Mandatory Palestine, psychoanalysis then had to cope with the construction of a new state – the culmination of the Zionist vision. As a result, the pursuit and evolution of psychoanalysis were intertwined with the Zionist enterprise.

This point of view is, in general, shared by other authors who have carried out research on the origins of psychoanalysis in Israel: first by Alex Liban, author of a doctoral thesis defended in Berlin in 1999, then by Eran Rolnik, who after defending his thesis in Tel Aviv in 2004 published the original version of his book in Hebrew in 2007 and later in other languages.

These three studies – Liban's, Rolnik's, and mine – offer three different perspectives on the history of psychoanalysis, which sometimes overlap and often contradict one another.

Alex Liban focuses his investigation of the introduction of Freudianism into Jewish Palestine on four clearly distinguishable points, which are: 1) resistance to the introduction of Freudian doctrine in the halls of the Hebrew University, where it was opposed by such influential intellectuals as Martin Buber, Hugo Bergmann, Gershon Sholem and Ernst Simon; 2) the reception of Freudianism within the Zionist left, and in particular within the Zionist and Marxist movement HaShomer HaTza'ir; 3) the reception of Freud's ideas in the circles of the Hebrew literary world, 4) and finally the implementation of psychoanalysis as a practice introduced by Freud's immigrant disciples in the country.

This research includes important developments concerning the first and second points mentioned above. The pages dedicated by the author to the influence of psychoanalysis in the world of Hebrew literature are, however insufficient to shed light on this vast field. Likewise, those dedicated to the implementation and institutionalization of psychoanalysis in Palestine and Israel remain fragmented and incomplete. This thesis has not reached the publishable stage.

Eran Rolnik, in his book, argues that the process by which Freud's ideas permeated modern Hebrew culture was a synthesis of what he calls a "German" Freud, known for his individualistic, critical, and pessimistic conceptions, and a "Russian" Freud, understood in a constructivist and collectivist sense. He maintains, in fact, that "The encounter between psychoanalysis and the society of the Yishuv was, first, in part, a repetition of the one between psychoanalytic theory and Russian Marxism and, in another part, an extension of the one between the youth movements of Central Europe and German Neo-Romanticism." If the last assertion of this sentence seems admissible to us, the parallel that the author draws between the conditions of reception of Freudian doctrine in Jewish Palestine and that of Russian Marxism seems very unjustified to us.

On the other hand, Rolnik attributes to the process of institutionalization and definitive establishment of the practice of psychoanalysis in Mandatory Palestine a psychoanalytical heritage of Berlin pedigree, and considers Max Eitingon the best candidate to accomplish this mission, being both a Freudian and a Zionist.

For our purposes, we situate the reception of Freud's ideas in a modern Hebrew culture that is heir to the Haskalah, that is, in a vast Zionist ideological and cultural project embodying the rational, universal, and secular values of the modern era, with psychoanalysis as one of its vectors, and Freud, this Galician Jew of genius, as one of its most worthy representatives.

The pages we devote in this book to the transmission of Freudian doctrine in Palestinian Jewish society unfold, as we shall see, in the shadow of the Zionist movement's milestones. Among them was Lord Balfour's famous speech of April 1, 1925, at the opening ceremony of the Hebrew University of Jerusalem, when he named Freud among the Jewish giants of universal thought, alongside Einstein and Bergson. We regard this memorable day as one of the major events in the history of Freudianism: it marks the starting point for the introduction of Freud's work into the new Hebrew culture and into the Zionist world in general.

Also, in a much more pronounced way than with other authors, the pages of this book devote a more important place to the singular journeys of Zionist intellectuals and practitioners won over to Freudianism, the "precursors of Freudianism in Eretz Israel," and those of immigrant psychoanalysts, starting with Max Eitingon and Moshe Wulff.

It should henceforth be underscored that, in contrast to Rolnik's theses in particular, we attribute to Moshe Wulff a predominant role in the advent of psychoanalysis in Israel and to the Freudians who came from Austria. The immense, rich, and vast work of Moshe Wulff in the Hebrew world, as well as his actions in support of the Freudian cause in Mandatory Palestine and Israel, have for a very long time been hidden behind the image of an idealized Max Eitingon, still evoked today, wrongly, as the founding father of psychoanalysis in Israel.

This book aims to pay tribute to Max Eitingon's work, while at the same time providing evidence of and doing justice to the immeasurable achievements of this other great figure in the history of international psychoanalysis, Moshe Wulff.

The first part of this book poses the critical question: Are the institutions of psychoanalysis transferrable from one place to another? Moreover, the singularity of the institutionalization process that psychoanalysis underwent in Palestine requires that first we review the history of medicine in this region, and specifically of psychiatry, before addressing the establishment of the Psychoanalytic Society of Palestine (1934).

The second part examines how psychoanalysis was, perhaps unwillingly, interwoven with revolutionary experiments, especially in the area of education. Palestine was then a laboratory bubbling with new ideas, and the psychoanalysis of those years deviated from its traditional framework. Clinics focused entirely on the treatment of thousands of immigrant children who had survived the war and pogroms, or on the care of kibbutz children. Leaders of the Yishuv (the Jewish community in Palestine), concerned about the extraordinary scope of the problem, enlisted the assistance of psychoanalysts and pedagogues trained in Freudian theory to formulate the terms of a new education system.

The third part addresses resistance to Freudian theories. As we shall discover, the Hebrew University rejected psychoanalysis (during 1925-1948), in particular because of religious and traditional opposition. But we shall also learn about the enthusiastic reception of Freud's writings in the Yishuv, where his many followers termed him the "great Jewish genius." Next we will address the question of translation, for as we know, the history of psychoanalysis is that which is written down, that which leaves traces. And Freud's work – a "Jewish science" – poses the delicate problem of post-Holocaust reception of a body of work composed in German.

PART I

The Institutional Foundation
of Psychoanalysis
in Palestine

CHAPTER 1

A Brief History of Medicine in Palestine (1799-1894)

The History of Jewish Immigration to Palestine

The institutions, science, and culture of the Yishuv remained subject to religious control until relatively late, after a painful period of transition that began in 1881 with the arrival of the first Zionists and concluded with the founding of Israel, in 1948. These early settlers are known in Hebrew and in Israeli history as pioneers (*halutzim*).

Even after the destruction of the Second Temple and failure of the Bar-Kochva rebellion, many Jews still remained in Palestine, as evidenced by the multitude of synagogues such as the famous one in Beit Alpha. Over the generations, however, the Jewish population declined, and in recent centuries it consisted of only a few small religious communities, primarily in Jerusalem, Safed, and Tiberius. The immigrants who arrived during those years were primarily religious Jews who wanted to spend their remaining years in Eretz Yisrael[9] (alternative spelling of "Eretz Israel" – the historical "Land of Israel" and for our purposes, Jewish Palestine).

The major waves of immigration only began to take place towards the end of the nineteenth century. All of these immigrants shared the same tragic history: the rise of anti-Semitism in Europe, discriminatory laws that foiled Jewish efforts to fit into or integrate with non-Jewish society, persecution, and pogroms. During this period Zionist organizations emerged in Eastern, Western, and Central Europe, inspiring the first waves of Jewish immigration (Aliyah).

Five major waves of Aliyah left their mark on the history of Israel. The First Aliyah (1882-1904) took place with the encouragement and assistance of the first Zionist associations that appeared in Europe. Many young Jews fled Russia (as it became intolerable for them under the laws of Tsar Nicolai II), seeking to join the ancient religious community in Eretz Israel, which enjoyed the protection of the Ottoman sultan in Constantinople (today Istanbul). During this period Jews from Yemen and North Africa also arrived in Palestine and settled there.

The Second Aliyah (1905-1914) primarily comprised East European Jews. Many had been long-time activists or leaders of socialist movements that emerged in the Russian Empire, and they became key figures in the political landscape of Palestine. They founded important Yishuv institutions, such as the General Federation of Workers in the Land of Israel (the Histadrut, Israel's association of labor unions) in 1920, and later the Haganah (Mandate-era Jewish paramilitary) and Solel Boneh (a major construction company to this day), among others.

The Third Aliyah (1919-1923) included enthusiastic leftist Zionist activists from Galicia and Russia, who established the *kibbutz* (cooperative settlement) and *moshav* (communal agricultural village) movements.

The Fourth Aliyah (1924-1929) comprised mainly Jews from Poland who had been driven out by anti-Semitic laws that restricted their commercial and financial activity. They were joined by Jews from Russia, Lithuania, Romania, Yemen, and Iraq. Most of these immigrants settled in urban areas, many in Tel Aviv.

The Fifth Aliyah (1931-1939) increased over time with Hitler's rise to power in 1933. For several years, there was a nearly continuous flow of Jews fleeing Nazi persecution. This wave of immigrants, the largest one before Israel attained statehood in 1948, played a supremely important part in the history of psychoanalysis in Mandatory Palestine and later in Israel.

The Haskalah (Jewish Enlightenment) and the Pioneers of the Second Aliyah

Most pioneers of the First Aliyah, like the longstanding Jewish communities, depended on the support of foreign philanthropists (namely, the Khalukah, an institution that collected funds from Jews across the world for Palestine's Jewish community) for the construction and maintenance of agricultural settlements and the development of commercial activities, among other enterprises.

Members of the Second Aliyah transformed the character of the Yishuv. Beginning in 1905, with the onset of this wave of *olim* (immigrants), dramatic changes began to take place across all spheres of life: political, demographic, social, educational, and cultural. The socialist Zionist activists, who were humanists and completely secular, challenged the privileged status and extensive influence of the religious institutions that had been the main beneficiaries of foreign philanthropy and direct aid. These workers, socialist leaders, writers, teachers, physicians, playwrights, journalists, and intellectuals, most of whom came from tsarist Russia, Poland, or Austro-Hungarian Galicia, were proud representatives of the Haskalah (Jewish Enlightenment) movement. They were infused with a singular enthusiasm and a single vision: to establish a new homeland in Palestine with the strength of their conviction, the power of their pen, their own hands and ideas, and a firm commitment to universal, secular values. The pioneers of the Second Aliyah, on whom anti-Semitism and persecution had left their mark, devoted themselves entirely to secular Jewish settlement in Palestine on the basis of socialist values and the new Hebrew culture they sought to forge. Before the arrival of the Third Aliyah, which supported and continued their enterprise, they put all their efforts into establishing new agricultural settlements, although not without clashing with the religious communities and other ethnic groups that had been living together in Palestine relatively peacefully for nearly four centuries under Ottoman rule. The communities of the old Yishuv fiercely defended the philanthropic institution of the Khalukah, and any perceived threat to their steady income or their share of donations sparked animosity and fierce opposition.

This was a painful period for the Jewish community: the pioneers of the Second Aliyah, who had made it their mission to save the Yishuv from its backwardness, now had to struggle against the social, linguistic, and cultural order promoted by foreign Jewish philanthropists. Until then most children had been educated in Yiddish, Ladino, German, or French – that is, in the languages of the donors or foreign organizations that funded their communities. The pioneers waged a merciless war against Khalukah representatives, who in turn viewed these Russian and Galician "pork eaters" as enemies, despicable and dangerous in equal measure.

Thanks to this very same obstinacy, psychoanalytic theory and practice were eventually able to take root in Palestine: Jewish immigrants who had trained at Europe's great universities, and whom Freud's work had influenced in diverse and individual ways, arrived in Jewish Palestine ardently determined to instill the universal values of the Haskalah into the new society.

On November 2, 1917, at the height of the struggle between supporters of the Khalukah and adherent of the Haskalah and just before British forces entered Jerusalem, Britain's then foreign secretary, Lord Balfour, announced the establishment of a Jewish national home in Palestine. The British government, which was confident of an Ottoman victory, assigned the task of constructing this national home to the World Zionist Organization, which was based in London at the time.

In the spring of 1918, a civilian delegation accompanied one of the military convoys. Among its primary missions was to assess the situation of the Jewish community in Palestine and establish a Jewish administration that could oversee the affairs of the Yishuv. The delegation was led, naturally, by Chaim Weizmann, head of the Zionist Organization then residing in London, alongside his right-hand man, Montague David Eder, a longtime Zionist leader and a psychoanalyst. But let us not get ahead of ourselves.

A Brief History of Medicine in Palestine

Before examining the history of psychoanalysis in Palestine, let us briefly review the history of medicine and the medical establishment, initially in Ottoman Palestine and later under the British Mandate.

Jewish Physicians in the Courts of Arab Rulers

Many Jewish as well as Arab physicians practiced medicine throughout the Islamic world. Caliphs, viziers, and other Arab dignitaries frequently praised the Jewish physicians who, like their Arab colleagues, were often renowned doctors of theology, philosophy, or science as well. From Masardijs of Basra (622-683?) to Maimonides (1161-1241), through Rabbi Nathanael (known as "the Prince" who, in the eleventh century, authored a textbook on the body and the mind),[10] physicians such as Ibn Sina or Avicenna (980-1037) and Ibn Rushd or Averroes (1198-1126) contributed to the advancement of culture, thought, and science, and to the development of fields related to medicine, such as botany and especially pharmacy. During the Golden Age of Islam, the only constraint imposed on them was that they never mix their faith with their practice or use prayer or religious ritual in treating their patients. Moreover, as faithful Jews they were forbidden from using spells or popular customs based on superstition, as Judaism prohibits any practices anchored in other belief systems.

Thus, dissociated from religious authority, Jewish medicine was able to explore other spheres of knowledge and investigate other powers that affect the body and mind. Be they locals or immigrants, the Jewish physicians were always sought after in the courts of Ottoman rulers. Towards the end of the fifteenth century, many Jewish physicians who had been expelled from Spain arrived in the Ottoman Empire, where they found ample opportunities to establish and advance themselves. There are many testimonies of their activities in Constantinople, the seat of the Empire, as well as elsewhere, including Thessaloniki, Rhodes, North Africa, and Asia.

The Birth of Modern Medicine[11]

Paradoxically, it was Napoleon's campaign in Egypt that marked the first attempt to introduce modern medicine to Palestine. Let us briefly review the history: towards the end of the eighteenth century, the French Directory (a directorial government that existed from 1795 to 1799) decided on March 1798 to send Napoleon Bonaparte to seize Egypt. Napoleon embarked on this conquest with 38,000 soldiers and a large number of scholars, particularly in the field of medicine. Napoleon's forces achieved a stunning victory, and in early 1799 the first major hospital opened in Cairo, where physicians conducted extensive research and treated common as well as tropical diseases.

On February 8, 1799, intent on conquering Palestine, Napoleon departed Egypt with a force of 12,000 men. He captured the coastal cities of El Arish, Gaza, and Jaffa, but was stopped at the gates of Acre. The fierce resistance of the Ottomans, aided by British forces, compelled him to abandon any plans of delivering Palestine and the Tomb of Christ to France and the Catholic Church. After a siege of sixty days, he retreated to Egypt.

In Palestine Napoleon encountered a different type of enemy, no less determined than the Ottoman army: the plague. In order to fight this enemy, treat the war wounded, and provide care for local populations, Napoleon delegated extensive authority to Dr. Dominique Larrey, a renowned surgeon in his company. Larrey first opened a large hospital in Jaffa and then, with the help of the Carmelite Order, established a rural hospital with six hundred beds near the village of Shefar'am in the north. He also sought to replicate the mobile units that he had successfully introduced in Egypt: horse- or camel-drawn carts operated by military medical teams that would cross the desert and, when necessary, provide care for local residents using medicine and equipment intended for the war wounded. Yet even though the geographical conditions were identical, these mobile units were unsuccessful in Palestine: the "ambulance drivers" were robbed, injured, or murdered by local gangs, or forced to slaughter their own animals to avoid starvation. Thus, unlike in Egypt, no trace of this modern medical practice remained in Ottoman Palestine.

Missionary Physicians in Jerusalem

Meanwhile, the French Revolution was a continuing source of concern for the British and for religious circles. In 1799, French forces arrived in Egypt and Palestine, where Napoleon intended to instill secular principles (including freedom of worship), on the one hand, while capturing the Church of the Holy Sepulcher so as to appease the Catholics, on the other hand. That same year, the British government decided to support a plan promoted by London-based evangelists, to convert the Jews. Their objective was to bring the Jewish People back to the "path of righteousness" by confessing their sin of not having recognized Christ as the Messiah. They believed that Christ's Second Coming required that Jews convert to Christianity and return to their ancestral homeland. They were as determined as their mission was challenging. Their organization, the London Society for Promoting Christianity amongst the Jews, grew rapidly, attracting new followers among the ruling authorities and wealthy families of London. Thanks to its supporters' generous donations, the organization under its new name (the London Jews' Society, or in its shorter version, the Jews' Society) had many successes. By offering financial contributions and various forms of assistance, this group of Protestants managed to convert many poor Jews. As the group's reputation and power steadily grew, they decided to take their missionary work a step closer towards ensuring the Second Coming: they set out to convert the Jews of Palestine to Christianity.

The Catholics and Muslims viewed this Protestant delegation as a genuine threat to their community and reacted as such, but the missionaries were interested first and foremost in the Jews of Palestine. Their arrival in the Holy Land sparked the wrath of the ultra-Orthodox (Haredi) community, which regarded conversion in the gravest of terms. Any Jew who chose to covert would be excommunicated and forever ostracized from the community. The

British evangelists, however, discovered a way to cope with ultra-Orthodox opposition: they realized that Palestine lacked proper medical institutions and that there was no attempt to address issues of hygiene, so they launched a competition with the other religious communities of Palestine to "outbid" each other in the provision of medical services. As a consequence of their work, it is customary today to attribute the introduction of modern medical practices in Palestine to the London Jews' Society. Because of these bidding wars with the various religious communities and the effort to provide healthcare for Jews who would otherwise go to missionary facilities, healthcare facilities soon emerged across Jerusalem and throughout the country.

In 1824, Dr. George Edward Dalton was appointed to examine the state of affairs in Palestine and identify the conditions necessary for the London Jews' Society to be successful. Late that year he set out to Beirut, where he met another Protestant, William Lewis, and together they travelled to Jerusalem.

With John Nicolayson, a Dane, they rented a Greek monastery known as the "Theodoros Monastery" to house the first Protestant hospital for the Jewish population. Believing they could thereby gain the support of the community, they conducted negotiations with the city's Ottoman authorities for the release of an imprisoned rabbi, Menachem Mandel, but were categorically unsuccessful. The Holy City of Jerusalem turned out to be cursed. And when Dalton died, on January 25, 1826, evidently of malaria, one could count the number of Jews who had converted to Protestant Christianity on one hand. The Jews of Palestine – some 10,000 in total, half of whom resided in Jerusalem[12] – then had a period of respite, as the London Jews' Society now had to wait until it could send another physician as the entire region was already experiencing upheavals. In 1825, the forces of Muhammed Ali, ruler of Egypt, had invaded the Ottoman-ruled Peloponnese in Greece. Later, in 1827, Muhammed Ali proposed to Sultan Ibrahim Pasha that this land be released in exchange for Syria and Palestine. The sultan rejected this offer, however, and Muhammed Ali invaded both countries in the summer of 1832.

In 1839, with a new mood in the air, the British government considered turning Palestine into a buffer state as well as a Jewish state so as to ease tensions between the Ottomans and Egyptians, who would no longer have a common border. Persecuted Jews could then have a place to welcome them, and Britain would reinforce its rule over Palestine. On March 26, 1839, Henry Temple, Britain's then foreign secretary, sent Vice-Consul William Turner Young to Jerusalem with a twofold mission: to protect the Jews of the city and to take the measures needed to enable mass immigration of persecuted Jews into Palestine. At the same time, the British government continued to support Protestant missionaries by funding the London Jews' Society. In so doing, Britain sought to thwart the two powers that had in the past fought for control over the Holy Sepulcher in Jerusalem and were now vying for control over Palestine: France, which continued to defend Vatican interests, and tsarist Russia, which wanted to protect the interests of the Orthodox Church.

Some decades would pass before Britain could correct this serious political mistake: as a result of those efforts to convert them, the Jews of Palestine came to see Britain as an ally of its bitter and most detested enemies. The London Jews' Society would have to wait until Palestine, alongside Syria, returned to Ottoman rule and enjoyed relative quiet once again, before it could send the leading authority, Dr. Albert Gerstmann, in 1841. With the support of another Brit, Melville Bergheim, as well as the Dane Nicolayson, who was still working at the facility he had established with Dalton, Gerstmann began practicing in the Protestant hospital in Jerusalem, earning the respect of several Jews who became his patients. But his fate was the same as that of his predecessor, and even before the year came to an end, he died in Constantinople while on his way to Britain to receive medical treatment.

Edward MacGown, a prominent physician and devoted follower of the London Jews' Society, then tried his luck in Palestine. He received a royal welcome in Jerusalem, entering the gates of the city in the company of an entourage led by the senior representative of the Anglican Church in the Holy Land, Archbishop Williams. He was then received by representatives of the Turkish pasha and the consuls of France, Prussia, and Sardinia. He could not have dreamt of a better beginning. Much more significant than British and local support, however, his proven medical skills and personal determination enabled him to establish excellent medical services in Jerusalem quickly and successfully. He offered services of a quality that Palestine had not seen since the time of Dominique Larrey. The city's ultra-Orthodox Jewish community was, naturally, concerned: having suffered the successes of Gerstmann, MacGown's steadily growing reputation generated ever-increasing fears. The rabbis of Jerusalem therefore turned to the greatest supporter of the Jewish community, "Minister" Moshe Haim Montefiore.

When he learned of the threat to his fellow Jews in Palestine posed by the excellent medical services of Protestant proselytizers, Montefiore employed all means at his disposal to undermine them. He sent Shimon Frankel, a Polish Jewish doctor trained in Germany, to Palestine to serve the community and, like MacGown, provide its members with quality medical treatment free of charge. For this reason, upon his arrival in Jerusalem on April 14, 1843, he was immediately hailed "the anti-missionary doctor" (*Antimissionärarzt*).

With the arrival of Giovanni Assouani, a Greek physician trained in Pavia, northern Italy, Jerusalem now had three very skilled practitioners, and the mutual competition among them worked wonders. On December 1, 1844, just a few days before the London Jews' Society inaugurated their own hospital, Frankel opened the city's first hospital – the Jewish Hospital of Jerusalem.

In 1848, however, this small facility closed for lack of funds, and Frankel began working with MacGown. Their cooperation was unacceptable to ultra-Orthodox leaders, especially as Frankel agreed to treat excommunicated and ostracized former community members. When he showed a keen interest in the wages offered him by a hospital that Protestant Deaconesses[13] had founded, the rabbis of Jerusalem, determined to oust him, spread the rumor, initially in the city's synagogues and then beyond Palestine, that the "anti-missionary doctor" was mistreating his patients. The Jewish press in Britain described Frankel as "arrogant, contemptuous, and dangerous to his patients." The Orthodox Jews of Jerusalem urged Montefiore to prohibit Frankel from practicing medicine in Palestine. Initially Frankel resisted: he loved this land and wanted to continue helping his fellow Jews in Eretz Israel. But no Jewish medical institution would accept him. Ironically, those who received him as a hero later also destroyed his career and even tried to erase his name from the annals of the Old Yishuv. No one knows when he left Jerusalem. He died in Jaffa on January 10, 1880, at the age of seventy-one, humiliated and rejected by the ultra-Orthodox Jews of Palestine.

The tragic story of the first Jewish physician of Jewish Palestine demonstrates the fierce resistance of the Yishuv's religious establishment to followers of the Haskalah movement and, through them, to modernity. A similar fate befell the pioneers of medicine and psychoanalysis in Jerusalem: Shimon Frankel, Dorian Feigenbaum, and Martin Pappenheim were foiled, one way or another, by their own people. They were prevented from offering their skills in the service of their community, and the latter in fact spread vile rumors about them. Seventy years after ousting Frankel for collaborating with enemy missionaries, Jerusalem's religious dignitaries sought to destroy the career of Dorian Feigenbaum, the first psychoanalyst to arrive in Palestine, by accusing him of collaborating with the Bolsheviks! And in 1933, they tried to dissuade the Tel Aviv Municipality from appointing the highly renowned Viennese neuropsychiatrist Martin Pappenheim – a close associate of Freud's and member of the Viennese Psychoanalytic Society – as administrator of the city's first psychiatric hospital. They claimed he had converted to Christianity and was in contact with an agent of Soviet Union's communist regime.

First Medical Services:
Competition among the Various Religious Communities

In the mid-nineteenth century, medicine in Palestine became, for all intents and purposes, a battlefield. The warring parties were the religious communities and the foreign powers funding them. Medical institutions served as weapons to attain influence and power, and their establishment was intended to attract new followers or protect community members from rivals in any other community or small congregation.

The Crimean War had significant implications for the future of the country. In the mid-nineteenth century Russia, which saw itself as the successor to the Byzantine Empire, demanded custodianship and administrative rights over the Orthodox Christians of the Ottoman Empire. The Russian tsar coveted the Straits of Bosphorus and the Dardanelles, which control passage between the Black Sea and the Mediterranean Sea. In 1853 he sent his army to invade the principalities of Moldavia and Wallachia (in today's Romania), marking the opening shot of the Crimean War. France, Britain, and Italy united to support the Ottomans, launching a counter-attack on March 12, 1854. When the war ended in March of 1856, the Ottoman Empire granted the victorious powers custodianship over the holy sites and their own nationals residing in Jerusalem.

Thus, at the end of the nineteenth century, there emerged the first medical services for the various religious communities that enjoyed the patronage of the victorious foreign powers: Britain assisted the Protestant missionaries, France supported the Catholic missionaries, Russia spread its patronage over the Orthodox Church, and Prussia and the Austro-Hungarian Empire helped the Jews, who also received philanthropic support. Over the decades a fierce competition developed among these parties. After the Crimean War, a series of religious orders – Dominicans, Franciscans, Carmelites, Copts, Lutherans, Presbyterians, and others – further contributed to the establishment of hospitals in Jerusalem and the development of medical services throughout the country.

France dispatched Émile Botta as its first consul to Jerusalem, with the aim of impeding the progress of Protestant missionaries and converting the Arab population to Catholicism. It also financed construction of the Saint Louis Hospital, which opened in 1852.

In 1858 Russia provided the Orthodox Church with the means to construct the largest hospital in Palestine. At the time of its inauguration, its seventy-five beds were occupied by large numbers of Russian pilgrims, about a dozen Greek and Armenian pilgrims, and roughly the same number of Arab patients. Jews would never receive medical treatment there.

The Deaconesses' hospital was also built with overseas funding, in this case the Prussian government. But in contrast to the previous facilities, this institution aimed exclusively to treat the ill. The German Protestant nuns who ran the hospital did not seek to convert patients. In fact, they enlisted Jewish doctors so as to provide patients with proper medical care in line with religious practice and the laws of *kashrut* (on handling food).

In the mid-nineteenth century an important shift took place within the Jewish community in Jerusalem, led mostly by Sephardic dignitaries who maintained good relations with the Ottoman bureaucracy and the local Arab population, thanks largely to their familiarity with language and customs. From this period onwards, the Jewish community (which received no direct support from a foreign power) could rely on the support of Jewish philanthropists from the US and Europe, as well as the support of organizations established to meet the needs of poor Jewish communities throughout the world, until the start of the Mandate era. In the 1850s, long before the First Aliyah, large numbers of Ashkenazi Jews had begun to arrive in Palestine, mostly from Russia or the eastern provinces of the Austro-Hungarian Empire. These religious Jews, some of whom came to spend their final years and be buried in Eretz Israel, maintained the *kollel* structure. They recognized only the authority of their rabbis, established their own synagogues, held their own courts, and ran their own schools and *yeshivot* (plural of *yeshiva*, place of religious study). Each *kollel* was responsible for the management and allocation of the donations received from its overseas community of origin.

With the aid of these diverse donors, many *kollel*s established their own medical facilities. The result was a vast range of hospitals and medical centers, each aimed at providing care for their own community members. From the 1880s onwards, curbing missionary activity and competing with hospitals funded by foreign powers were no longer the only priorities: institutions began multiplying so as to meet the demands of receiving Jewish immigrants who were fleeing the escalating anti-Semitism and pogroms in the Russian Empire and Central Europe, arriving in Palestine in ever-growing numbers. Only insanity, mental illness in its various forms, escaped this competition and remained for some time in the realm of superstition and dark magic.

On July 26, 1854, a decade after Shimon Frankel's inauguration of the Jewish Hospital, the Rothschild Hospital opened its doors, under the directorship of the German physician Bernhard Neumann. It would later be renovated, in 1888, and become one of the leading hospitals in Palestine. Baron Rothschild, who followed in the footsteps of Baron Montefiore, had the necessary medicines, as well as the most modern equipment available in major European hospitals at the time, imported into Palestine. He also channeled the funds necessary to establish additional medical centers in Jaffa, Safed, Tiberias, and Rishon LeZion. Similarly, in 1867, with the support of the Prussian government, religious Jews from Vilna founded Bikur Holim Hospital, which was opened to all. In 1879, the Sephardic dignitaries of Palestine established Misgav Ladach in the Old City. This hospital maintained the tradition of cooperation and tolerance among the various ethnic and religious communities of Jerusalem, accepting any resident of Jerusalem regardless of ethnic origin or religious belief. In 1890, religious Jews from Germany, members of the Society for Zion, opened Shaare Zedek Medical Center in Jerusalem.

The hospitals and medical centers of Jerusalem grace its panorama, cresting the ridges of the city's hills and nestling in its heart. Like the domes of Jerusalem's synagogues, the bell towers of its churches, and the minarets of its mosques, they inspire yearnings. Their gables carry lettered engravings in gold, invoking God as well as the names of prophets and saints, alongside the symbols and images of philanthropists and rulers from far and wide. The Swedish author and 1908 Noble Laureate in Literature, Selma Lagerlof, visited Egypt and Palestine during 1899-1900. She described the atmosphere of late nineteenth-century Jerusalem, when missionaries were competing for the hearts and minds of the city's residents amid ever-escalating inter-communal violence:

> Here is the Jerusalem of desolation, pain, torment, and atonement…. Here are monks and nuns, nurses and deaconesses, popes and missionaries…. Here are the great missionary schools that provide instruction, lodging, food, and clothing free of charge in the hope of winning the souls of their pupils. The hospitals of the missionaries are open to all, pleading for the sick to come and seek medical care, so as to convert them…. Here during religious worship and prayer services, the faithful fight over a person's soul.
>
> Here the Catholic rejects the Protestants, the Methodist rejects the Quaker, the Lutheran rejects the Reformed, the Russian rejects the Armenian. Here envy and jealousy slither along. Here the delusional are suspicious of the exalted, here orthodoxy fights heresy, here there is no mercy or forgiveness, and for the greater glory of God, they hate each other.
>
> And here the visitor finally finds what he seeks. Here is the Jerusalem that hunts souls. Here is the Jerusalem of falsehood, calumny, and slander. Here is the unceasing pursuit and weaponless killing. Here is the Jerusalem that kills.[14]

Jerusalem would soon, however, have no cause to fear the English Protestants: their hospital beds, which had been prepared only for the sake of saving Jewish souls, remained empty. By the 1880s, realizing the mistake it had made in supporting the London Jews' Society, Britain began to set up medical facilities across Palestine that were open to all and devoid of any proselytizing. One such example was the St. John Ophthalmologic Hospital, designed to treat trachoma and many other ophthalmological diseases that were quite widespread at the time because of the lack of water and unsanitary conditions affecting large segments of the population.

One way or another, on the eve of the twentieth century – despite concerted efforts by all communities to eliminate the most common diseases in the country, and despite the marked improvement in medical services – malaria, typhoid, cholera and cirrhosis continued to claim many victims, especially in rural areas.

1894: Ezrat Nashim, the First Asylum

Little was known at that time about the treatment of mental illness. Surprisingly, the rather inefficient Ottoman administration actually issued a law on the matter in 1892, with the following provisions: In cases of mild mental illness, the family could treat the patient at home, provided they submit a request to the hospital administration with two medical certificates signed by two specialists and the approval of the local representative of the Turkish government; the costs of securing these certificates fell to the family. Regarding patients perceived as "dangerous," only legal officials had authorization to decide on hospitalization. However, for the patients to receive medical treatment, their families had to provide government authorities with a written request for hospitalization, a certificate signed by a physician, and approval from the religious community to which the patient belonged. It is quite likely that the low numbers of hospitalized patients was due to these cumbersome bureaucratic procedures and corruption among Turkish officials.

Apparently the treatment of mental illness long remained the exclusive domain of the clergy, healers, and mystics. Many viewed mental illness as the effect of divine action or the influence of evil spirits and therefore within the purview of God's representatives on earth or, alternatively, of healers and witch doctors. Within their own community, all could, if not recover from their illness, at least find a place to endure their suffering and the "agony" of existence. Prayers, blessings, confessions, rituals, and rites, in accordance with religious faith and the beliefs of each healer, allowed the patients to endure their sometimes unbearable suffering.

In the Muslim community, if a family member seemed insane or possessed, it was customary for the family to approach the *mukhtar* or imam of the local mosque. In the Jewish community many would consult with rabbis or kabbalists and various mystics. A good reputation would draw the followers of all faiths as well as secular visitors from all walks of life, some having despaired of the medical professionals or possibly seeking discretion so as to avoid any documentation that might jeopardize the personal and professional future of the patient or family. In some circles,[15] mental illness is seen as a blow to family honor, tarnishing the name of the family or clan.

The treatment for "agitated" patients in monasteries was horrific: at the monastery of St. George, for example, on the road from Bethlehem to Hebron, they were chained to the doors of building, sometimes waiting entire weeks for St. George the Dragon Slayer to release their miserable souls from the demonic spirits that had possessed them. St. John's Monastery in Bethlehem provided comparable treatment. In 1922, with the opening of the first public psychiatric asylum in the Bethlehem neighborhood of Beit Jalla, the British government in Palestine officially banned these barbaric practices.

Similar practices existed across the Jewish community, and to this day there is no shortage of healers, Kabbalists, and ritual sites with a reputation for curing suffering and spiritual illness. In the nineteenth century, Rabbi Mohaliver, an early follower of the movement Hibat Zion (Love of Zion) and the founder of religious Zionism, was noted for his "excellent treatment of inflammation, toothache, and especially the art of releasing his patients from the *dybbuk* [evil spirit]."[16] During the same period, the disabled, sterile women, unmarried men, and the madmen of the Yishuv were sent to pray in the caves or tombs of the great *tzadikim* (righteous men). Elisha's Cave on Mount Carmel was considered to have unique qualities in this regard; accordingly, with hands and feet bound, a patient would spend the night with a family member who had to recite certain prayers until the patient recovered. To this day, the Tomb of Rabbi Shimon bar Yochai on Mount Meron and Rachel's Tomb remain gathering sites for sufferers in search of a cure for their ailments.

It was not until December 1894 that an association of Jewish women, the wives of prominent Ashkenazi and Sephardic men of Jerusalem, established a place that would welcome the lost Jews of Jerusalem. The name they chose, Ezrat Nashim, has a twofold meaning: the women's section of a synagogue, and "women's help" – the aid that women provide. Initially the founders intended to devote themselves to the *klita* (absorption into society) of destitute immigrants from the First Aliyah, who were arriving at Jaffa Port from Eastern Europe.

But from 1894 their main objective became the provision of care for Palestine's mentally ill. Indeed, for about three decades, Ezrat Nashim was the only place in the Middle East dedicated to treating the mentally ill. The hospital soon developed a reputation beyond the borders of Palestine, where many still relied on the Khalukah for their livelihood. Ezrat Nashim's founder managed to secure large foreign donations, allowing her to expand the facility and reinforce its standing in the Jewish community. The institution, run by prominent members of the Jewish community, soon became a true stronghold of the Khalukah. Moreover, during this period – the decline of the Ottoman Empire – the Turkish rulers of Jerusalem had in effect abdicated all authority.

In 1905 Ezrat Nashim was opened to all, regardless of religion, race, or ethnic origin. It became the leading and most important psychiatric institution not only in Palestine but throughout the Middle East as well and would remain so a long time. By the end of WWI it would have a medical board, following the recommendations of the World Zionist Organization, which the British government tasked with overseeing the affairs of the Jewish community in Palestine. It was at Ezrat Nashim that the word psychoanalysis was first heard publicly, and it was here that the analytical method was first tested.

It was a source of pride for these prominent Sephardic and Ashkenazi families that they had jointly founded the first mental asylum in Palestine and the Middle East. It was an even greater source of pride that Ezrat Nashim was the first medical center to bring members of their two communities together under one roof. This was an unprecedented event in the history of the Yishuv. It was also the first time that an important institution was in the hands of women within the Jewish community, where until then control had rested exclusively in the hands of religious men.

At the outset of WWII, Ottoman authorities seized most of the hospitals. When the officer assigned to commandeer Ezrat Nashim arrived at the hospital gates, Ita Yellin, the director and daughter of former director Tzippa Pines, threw the keys at his feet and shouted contemptuously, "Here, pick them up!" Although the Turks did not take over Ezrat Nashim, Ita Yellin and her husband, David Yellin, were sentenced to house arrest in Damascus. Ita, however, did not stop directing hospital affairs, and throughout the war she would send instructions to her sister Margalit, who remained in Jerusalem.

Undoubtedly the Jewish community deserves recognition for having removed the issue of mental illness and suffering from the realm of superstition and witch doctors, bringing it into the field of science and modern medicine. Still, the directors of Ezrat Nashim managed the hospital's affairs in accordance with the strict terms of the Khalukah. Towards the end of WWI, when the British government and leaders of the Zionist General Council, tasked with overseeing the affairs of the Jewish community in Palestine, tried to establish a new administration and formulate a new framework, they ran into stubborn resistance on the part of the hospital's directors. Although the latter were eventually compelled to hire a new medical director, they remained one of final strongholds of the Khalukah regime and its supporters, who opposed any British or Zionist interference into the affairs of Jerusalem's longstanding traditional community.

With the start of the First Aliyah, after the early days of missionary medicine, came the era of "pioneer doctors." Among the first immigrants to arrive in this wave, fleeing anti-Semitic persecution in Central and Eastern Europe (especially Russia and the eastern provinces of Austro-Hungarian Galicia), were large numbers of physicians whose training spanned nearly all areas of medicine. Between 1918 and 1933, at the initiative of the British government and the Zionist General Council, medical institutions and services emerged throughout the country. This marked the fourth and most important period in the history of medicine in Palestine. With the Fifth Aliyah (1933-1939), which ended with the outbreak of WWII, thousands of immigrants started arriving from Central Europe, fleeing Nazi persecution in Central European countries, Germany in particular. During this time, Moshe Wulff, Max Eitingon, and many other European psychoanalysts arrived in Palestine with the intent of establishing themselves professionally.

In 1920, when the British government was granted the Mandate over Palestine, it established a range of new medical institutions alongside its administrative, educational, and legal ones. Thus a large number of organizations and institutions that had previously been accountable to private religious communities now became secular, public entities.

CHAPTER 2

The Pioneers of Psychoanalysis in Palestine and the Psychoanalytic Study Group in Jerusalem (1922)

The Pioneers (Halutzim) of Psychoanalysis in Mandatory Palestine (1918-1922)

As World War I drew to a close, General Edmund Allenby, commander of the British forces stationed in Egypt, invaded Palestine in early April 1917. On October 28, Allenby's forces entered Jerusalem, where the Ottoman army surrendered without a struggle. On November 8 the British press published an announcement that elated Jews across the world. Lord Balfour, the foreign secretary, had declared as follows on November 2: "His Majesty's Government view with favour the establishment in Palestine of a national home for the Jewish people." With few exceptions, the International Jewish community as well as intellectual and political figures received the Balfour Declaration enthusiastically and expressed a desire to contribute to the establishment of the Jewish homeland.

Chaim Weizmann, as representative of the World Zionist Organization[17] (WZO), was placed in charge of this project. Towards this end, he formed a "Committee of Delegates" (the Zionist Commission for Palestine), tasked with traveling to Palestine and paving the way for the establishment of the national homeland. It would liaise between the WZO and Yishuv, on the one hand, and the British authorities in Palestine, on the other. The Committee of Delegates comprised political figures from the British Zionist movement and field specialists – mostly physicians, economists, and engineers, but also . . . psychoanalysts. The Committee of Delegates arrived in Palestine in 1918, with Eder as Weizmann's representative. He worked in Jewish Palestine for five years and, after returning to London in 1923, continued his work with institutions and individuals based in Palestine. He strove tirelessly on behalf of the Jewish homeland until his death in 1936.

Weizmann could not have chosen a better representative than this perfect diplomat, skilled statesman, and experienced military leader. Eder had proved his abilities when he organized the deployment of Jewish forces to support the British army against the Turks. Let us take a look at this unique figure.

Montague David Eder: Diplomat and Psychoanalyst

Montague David Eder was born in London on August 12, 1868, to a wealthy assimilated family that had immigrated to Britain from Lithuania a century earlier. He began to study medicine in his native city, then continued in Germany and later in Belgium. He was enchanted by the writers and philosophers of his time, especially Pyotr Alexeyevich Kropotkin (1842-1921), who believed that the medical profession's mission was to treat "social pathology," that is, the people in the margins, the insane. This Russian anarchist, a former member of the First International (the International Workingmen's Association), sought to establish a "scientific anarchism" to struggle against individualism by relying on "man's natural social instincts," and to promote "permanent revolution through speech, writing, sword, gun, and dynamite." He also argued that the fall of capitalism and assimilation of the Jews would put an end to anti-Semitism, and here Eder disagreed: like many other Jews born during the latter nineteenth century, he had read Pinsker's highly influential *Auto-Emancipation* and adopted its theses. Leon Pinsker, a Zionist from Tomaszów Lubelski (in today's Poland) regarded anti-Semitism as a mental pathology (for which he coined the term *Judeophobia*) and believed that the only way to put an end to the centuries of discrimination, deprivation, and persecution was to let the Jews establish a national homeland, preferably in Eretz Israel, but elsewhere if that turned out to be impossible.

Following his cousin Israel Zangwill, Eder often met with a group of young English intellectuals that included D.H. Lawrence and George Bernard Shaw. He discovered socialist theories at an early age and, after joining the Fabian Society, became secretary of the Bloomsbury Socialist Society.

Along with his supporters, Zangwill (who would establish the Jewish Territorial Organization (JTO) in 1905) believed that the Jewish problem could be resolved in any territory that agreed to accept the Jews, not only in Palestine. Around this time, Eder, greatly concerned about the fate of Russian Jews in light of ever-increasing pogroms, had been searching for a safe haven. His travels took him first to Colombia, where one of his uncles had made a fortune from coffee plantations. He taught medicine at the University of Bogota but had to flee when rioting erupted across the country towards the end of the century, and he returned empty-handed. At the Fourth Zionist Congress, in Vienna in 1903, he naturally supported Herzl and the Uganda Plan. Most WZO members, however, believed that Eretz Israel was the only suitable land for the return of the Jews, and that a Jewish homeland could not emerge anywhere but in Eretz Israel. Herzl's support for the British Colonial Office proposal, to settle the Jews in Uganda, scandalized them. This was the first time Eder publicly supported Herzl.

Eder worked within the Jewish Territorial Organization alongside Zangwill, its leader, until he resigned from it in 1915. Zangwill, meanwhile, continued even after the Balfour Declaration to oppose any relationship between his organization and the Zionist Organization, which called for Jewish settlement in Eretz Israel. Eder eventually changed sides, joining Weizmann's camp within the World Zionist Organization. His many contributions to Zionism and the Yishuv are well known, but his work in the field of psychoanalysis, in both Jewish Palestine and Britain, is largely overlooked. Eder maintained an interest in the discipline throughout his life. His many duties prevented him from treating patients in Palestine, but he supported and guided many initiatives: with Dorian Feigenbaum he founded and coordinated the first psychoanalytic studies group in Palestine; he interceded on behalf of Freud's appointment to the Hebrew University's Board of Governors; he made sure that Jewish psychoanalysts fleeing Nazi Germany were welcomed and settled in Palestine; from London he worked to finance construction of the first psychiatric hospital in Tel Aviv; and alongside Eitingon, he raised funds for the publication and dissemination of the journal *Folia Medica Orientalia*. In 1934, more than a decade after he had left Palestine, psychoanalysts who had settled there granted him honorary membership in the newly founded Palestine Psychoanalytic Society (Chevra Psychoanalitit BeEretz Israel – CPEI). After Eder's death in 1936, the psychoanalyst Moshe Wulff and his followers founded a new institute devoted to child psychoanalysis, which they named after Eder – HaMachon HaPsychoanalyti al Shem Doctor Eder (the Doctor Eder Psychoanalytic Institute), in Tel Aviv.

Eder was very familiar with Freud's work, thanks to his fellow student Ernest Jones, a faithful disciple of the Viennese psychoanalyst from early days. He became active in the psychoanalytic movement in 1909, and in 1911 made his mark in the Freudian world with a presentation before the Edinburgh Medical Society, where he described a case of neurosis that he treated using the Freudian approach. This was the first time that Freudian theories about infantile sexuality were openly discussed and defended within British medical circles. Audience members rose and left in indignation. But Eder did not despair, and when Jones returned to England, having helped introduce psychoanalysis into the US and Canada, the two jointly founded the London Psychoanalytic Society. The Society's first members were young intellectuals from Cambridge, who were more receptive to Freud's innovative ideas than physicians and psychiatrists. The latter suffered at the time from what British psychoanalyst Edward Glover described as true "atrophy of the imagination" and only a handful were open to Freud's theories.

Before long, however, a rift developed between these two pioneers of psychoanalysis in Britain. In his memoirs, which are filled with complaints about Eder, Jones accused his former colleague of having introduced into the London Psychoanalytic Society questionable personalities who challenged the validity of Freud's theories about infantile sexuality,[18] and of being "obstinate" and "incredibly stupid."[19] Jones disbanded the Society in February 1919 and in the same year, along with other colleagues, founded the British Psychoanalytic Society, which is still active.[20]

In fact, Eder long resisted coming to terms with the incompatibility of Freud's and Jung's theories. He sided with Freud's approach but was also drawn to Jung's theory of archetypes[21] (his wife Edith had undergone analysis with Jung). Enchanted by the various cultures he encountered on his many travels, he found they resonated somewhat with this theory. He helped disseminate Jung's writings in England and maintained close relations until he departed for Palestine. Ultimately he became disappointed with Jung's theories, aligned himself with Freud's orthodoxy in 1920,[22] and renewed his ties with the psychoanalytic movement before setting out for Europe.

During WWII Eder joined the British army, and in 1916 he was stationed in Malta as supervisor of the psycho-neurological unit at the military hospital there. His experience treating soldiers led to the publication of his first book, which addressed "war shock" and its therapeutic treatments:

hypnosis, the cathartic method, and psychotherapeutic techniques inspired by psychoanalysis. He relied on psychoanalysis to describe certain psychological mechanisms and explained how he had treated "shell-shocked" soldiers after the Ottoman victory over the Allied forces at Gallipoli, using the same techniques he had applied with other war-wounded at a neurological clinic in London, and with similar success.[23] He hastened to publish his observations for the benefit of other physicians stationed on the frontline, and a letter from his cousin Zangwill informed him that his book enjoyed a very favorable reception immediately upon its publication in London.[24] He was discharged from military service in 1917.

Montague David Eder – The "Freudian Physician of the Poor"

Upon his return from Malta, Eder joined the World Zionist Organization, to the great satisfaction of Chaim Weizmann, who had finally succeeded in convincing the British authorities of the merits of his project – namely, the establishment of a Jewish homeland in Palestine. As noted, British Foreign Secretary Balfour had issued his famous declaration on November 2, 1917, the British government had appointed Weizmann to head the Committee of Delegates that was tasked with advising the British government in Palestine, and Eder served as Weizmann's representative on this committee.

Eder arrived in Palestine in the spring of 1918, after spending some time in Egypt, and immediately ran into difficulties. The local pioneers (*halutzim*) remembered his past support for the Uganda Plan – which they had fiercely resisted – and deeply mistrusted him. Although known in London as the "Freudian Physician of the Poor," among the pioneers he became "the bourgeois doctor from London."

In 1918 the British government began reorganizing the public services in Palestine and establishing suitable institutions in the fields of medicine, education, and transportation. Nevertheless, upon his arrival in Jerusalem and the Zionist delegation and British military authorities, he discovered a city in distress. Famine and epidemics stemming from the lack of potable water were having a devastating effect on the population, and the child mortality rates were shocking. All the officials responsible for providing public services under Ottoman rule had abandoned their posts and left Palestine. The Ottomans viewed citizens of their enemy countries as traitors and expelled them from the city. Those who had acquired Ottoman citizenship were forcibly conscripted to the Turkish military, and many fell in battle. Jerusalem's population was decimated. Of the city's 50,000 pre-war residents, fewer than 30,000 remained after four years of fighting, inhabiting a ruined and desolate city. The war had hurt all of Jerusalem's communities, but the ultra-Orthodox Jewish population, which had been weak even before hostilities broke out, was particularly desperate: ties between Eretz Israel and overseas communities were almost completely severed, and the Khalukah funds that sustained this population group had been cut off.

Montague David Eder and the War Orphans

Jerusalem and all the other cities in Palestine were filled with abandoned children, thousands of whom wandered the streets, left to their own devices, starving and sickly. Some were unable to see to their most basic needs, while others had resorted to prostitution in order to survive. Very few were receiving adequate care. Too often the men who oversaw those few facilities that were still operating pocketed the incoming donations and failed to provide even minimal care or education for these destitute children. Corruption was rampant.

In 1919 Eder published a detailed analysis of this situation in the newsletter of the teachers' union, *HaKhinukh*. Weizmann, among others, was deeply distraught by the findings: of Jerusalem 27,000 residents at the time, 2,974 were war orphans; only 32 were receiving care under the auspices of the one suitable facility that existed, run by a Mrs. Silverschmidt; 400 were housed in orphanages of dubious repute; and others had been adopted by family members who were also facing hardship, or by Orthodox Jews who were dependent on Khalukah funds. Eder was disturbed by this state of affairs and bluntly asserted that many were profiting from orphans and orphanages, regarding themselves as great experts, but that only a few were worthy of such responsibility. In his view only the children under Mrs. Silverschmidt's care were in relatively good shape, while all the others were suffering or even exhibiting pathological behavior. Eder attributed the situation to their environment: "These children were infants when they entered these institutions, and they will remain infants after leaving and throughout their adulthood."[25]

There was a precedent for the care of orphans, which deserves a brief mention here. In 1903 Israel Belkind (1861-1929), a founder of the Bilu movement (whose goal was the agricultural settlement of Eretz Israel) and a pioneer of the First Aliyah, brought fifty orphans who had survived the Kishinev pogrom to Palestine. To preserve their Jewish culture and educate them in the spirit of the First Aliyah, he founded the agricultural school Meir Shfeya near Zichron Yaakov, where he placed these children. The school closed in 1909 for lack of funding, but Belkind reopened it in 1920 and brought more war orphans from the Ukraine.

The care for orphans in Jewish Palestine was strongly influenced by Freudian psychoanalysis – a unique and unprecedented phenomenon. Prominent psychoanalysts contributed to this endeavor: besides David Eder, the list includes Siegfried Bernfeld (another notable Zionist and psychoanalyst who led a similar struggle in Vienna); Moshe Wulff, who worked in Tel Aviv; and Fanny Lowtzky, Shmuel Nagler, Max Eitingon, and Josef Friedjung, who operated in Jerusalem and Haifa. Psychiatrists such as Martin Pappenheim in Tel Aviv and Mordechai Brachyahu (who was responsible for child services) also contributed. Participating pedagogues included David Idelsohn from the "Children's Society" of Kibbutz Beit Alpha as well as educators from the kibbutz movement HaShomer HaTza'ir, such as Shmuel Golan and Zvi Sohar. And lest we forget, there was Henrietta Szold, a social worker by training, who founded Hadassah Hospital and oversaw Aliyat HaNo'ar (Youth Aliyah – an organization that rescued Jewish children from the Nazis). We will return to these figures in the second part of the book.

In order to save Eretz Israel from poverty and backwardness, David Eder, like Henrietta Szold and many others, had to dive into the dirty waters of domestic politics and navigate his way among the various factions of the Zionist Organization that were fighting one another both locally and abroad. He was soon swept up in one of these disputes: local Zionists, especially Second Aliyah immigrants from Russia and Poland, accused him and Chaim Weizmann of pro-British leanings within the Zionist Executive.

Palestine was plagued by endless rioting. The Arabs sought Arab governance, and in the course of their struggle against Jewish immigration, bloody clashes broke out in 1921, after which the British commitment to the

Balfour Declaration began to wane. Britain tried to restrict Jewish immigration, triggering fierce opposition by Yishuv leaders, who argued that the British were not doing enough to defend Jews against the violence being perpetrated by Arab nationalists. Eder found himself in the eye of the storm, a target of fury on the part of other Zionist leaders in the Yishuv.

After returning to London, he resumed the post of chairman of the Zionist Federation of Great Britain (the British chapter of the WZO). During 1921-1923 he served as a member of the Zionist Executive, and in 1927 was again elected as the chairman. In April 1925 he returned to Palestine. Eder had always believed that the Hebrew University would symbolize the new Eretz Israel, and alongside Weizmann and Einstein he was an active member of the Friends of the Hebrew University of Jerusalem. Naturally, therefore, he could not miss the opening ceremony, but the event marked his last visit to Palestine. When his friend Henrietta Szold, who had assisted him greatly in establishing an effective healthcare system in Palestine, offered him the post of director of the Hadassah Medical Organization in Palestine, he declined.

His two passions converged once again when the opportunity to include Freud in the Hebrew University's Board of Governors fell into his hands. Eder had never abandoned the field of analysis, and even in 1920, after breaking with Jung and reconciling with Jones, he took advantage of his travels to England in order to attend the meetings of Britain's new psychoanalytic society. When he returned to London after five trying years in Palestine, he intended to resume his psychoanalytic training by going to Karl Abraham. Abraham, however, could not receive him for analysis (for reasons unknown), so he underwent his final "chapter" of analysis with Sandor Ferenczi in Budapest, in 1924. According to Edward Glover, this chapter allowed him to resolve tensions between Zionism and psychoanalysis: "The rival claims of Zionism and psychoanalysis had not yet been settled for him. To judge, not only by his own account, but by the subsequent course of his life, he did find with Ferenczi the solution [for] his main problems"[26]

A Haven for Psychoanalysis: Hadassah

In 1910, Henrietta Szold – along with a group of Zionist American women who, like her, responded to the WZO call – decided to found an organization whose prime objective would be to set up autonomous socio-medical services throughout Palestine. The services would be run by professional nurses who would train additional nurses, so as to provide adequate care for disadvantaged population groups across all communities. In 1912, after long months of preparation, they founded Hadassah, the Women's Zionist Organization of America, named after Queen Esther (whose name in Hebrew was Hadassah).

Only after arriving in Palestine a year later did Henrietta Szold confront the full scale of misery that plagued the residents of the land. Upon returning to New York, she revised her plan in order to prepare her so-named American Zionist Medical Unit for what was to come. But the war delayed these plans, and Szold was unable to return to Palestine until the cessation of hostilities in 1918. She arrived with a team of twenty eminent specialists from various disciplines: pediatricians, ophthalmologists, obstetricians, gynecologists, epidemiologists, and others, and a comparable number of highly qualified nurses, including Rose Kaplan and Rachel Lantry – in short, all the forms of medical care that war-torn Palestine needed at the time. With its exceptional financial resources, the American Zionist Medical Unit, led by the American Zionist physician Isaac Rubinow, was able to establish a presence across Palestine in its effort to aid a population decimated by disease and deprivation. Henrietta Szold was able to enlist several physicians from the Yishuv to join her medical unit, which became the Hadassah Medical Organization in 1918.[27]

Born in Baltimore in 1860, Henrietta Szold ranks among the leading and most prominent Zionists who helped bring Palestine out of its post-WWI state of misery and backwardness. Like the activists and supporters of Brit Shalom, a movement Szold joined upon its establishment in 1925, she never stopped working for both the Jewish and the Arab communities of Palestine in the hope that they jointly define their respective modes of co-existence on the basis of equal political rights. Brit Shalom was an initiative of Joseph Horowitz, a renowned orientalist from Frankfurt University, who conceived the idea of establishing a body to defend and advance the goal of co-existence. He persuaded many Zionist figures, with different perspectives, to support his movement, which called for the creation of a bi-national state in Palestine with equal rights for both peoples. The riots of 1929 dashed these hopes and marked the end of this enterprise.

Henrietta Szold cultivated ties with the psychoanalysts of Palestine. She sought their help in implementing her socio-medical program and aided them in pursuing their own plans. David Eder, Dorian Feigenbaum, and, later, Max Eitingon and Josef Friedjung benefited from her respect and support. In 1925 she offered Eder the post of director of Hadassah in Palestine, but he declined. In any event, Hadassah Hospital provided a prestigious home for psychoanalysts and psychoanalysis for years after Israel achieved independence, and in 1954 it created a psychiatry department within its medical school. The department was run by practitioners – members of the American Psychoanalytic Association who came from the United States or the Psychoanalytic Institute in Jerusalem.

When she arrived in Palestine in 1922, Henrietta Szold enlisted psychoanalyst Dorian Feigenbaum to instruct the students of the nursing school she had founded in the discipline of psychopathology. She referred many children who suffered from mental illness to his care. Later she also recruited Viennese psychoanalyst Josef Karl Friedjung to provide training in psychoanalysis for the educators and counsellors treating the children and adolescents who arrived in Palestine through the Youth Aliyah project (which Szold headed from 1933 until her death in 1945).

The Feigenbaum Brothers and the Psychoanalytic Study Group

Dorian Feigenbaum, with the assistance of Eder and invaluable support of his brother Aryeh, established the Psychoanalytic Study Group of Jerusalem, which I regard as the true foundation of the Freudian movement in Palestine. This small group had an enormous impact on the pedagogical circles of the Zionist Left, mainly thanks to the active participation of Grete Obernik, Yichiel Heilperin, and David Idelsohn, whom we shall encounter again later. To shed light on this formative moment in the history of psychoanalysis – often termed "psychology of the depths" at the time – in Palestine, I plunged into the files of Aryeh Feigenbaum at the Municipal Archives of Jerusalem. But only thanks to his daughter Nomi Belsitzmann, in Tel Aviv, and Dorian's daughter Lou Seinfeld, in New York, was I able to assemble the pieces of this puzzle.

Dorian Feigenbaum was born in 1887 in Lvov (or Lemberg in German) in Austro-Hungarian Galicia, where he began his medical studies. He went on to specialize in psychiatry, first in Munich with Emil Kraepelin, the already-renowned founder of psychiatric nosography, and later in Vienna with Julius Wagner-Jauregg, one of the grand masters of neuro-psychiatry at the time. During his medical specialization in 1910-1911 at the University of Vienna, he heard lectures by Freud and thus discovered the man and his theories. The person who drew his attention to this profession was Victor Tausk, whom Feigenbaum met during his final year of studies and subsequently befriended. Feigenbaum received a degree in neuro-psychiatry in 1914. He was working as an epidemiologist at the Red Cross hospital in Vienna when the First World War broke out. In 1916 he was appointed as an assistant in the neurology department of the leading reserves hospital in Lvov. In 1919 he wrote to Freud, seeking permission to present himself as a disciple. Freud acquiesced and even recommended him to his colleague Emil Oberholtzer. In the autumn of that year he settled in Lugano and began practicing psychoanalysis, while also undergoing analysis with Otto Gross (1877-1920). The following spring he began working at the Mendrisio asylum some twenty kilometers from Lugano, which was run by Dr. Bruno Manzonni.

In 1920 Feigenbaum was invited to Jerusalem to assume the post of medical director of Ezrat Nashim, which as noted had opened in 1894. He was offered the position thanks to his brother and, presumably, the efforts of Eder. Among other responsibilities, Eder oversaw the affairs of the Jewish community in Palestine within the framework of the British Mandate (initially through the Committee of Delegates, later as a member of the Zionist Commission, and from 1921 as a member of the Zionist Executive). He also supervised the establishment of a healthcare infrastructure for the Yishuv. Aryeh Feigenbaum, for his part, was a Zionist, an ophthalmologist, and a Freudian – an important figure in the local medical arena. He was an established member of the most influential circles in Jerusalem's Jewish community and had close ties with Ezrat Nashim's board of directors, given that he was married to Rachel Meyouchas, the daughter of Margalit Pines-Meyouchas and granddaughter of Chaya Tzippa Pines.

Thus Dorian Feigenbaum, a psychiatrist and psychoanalyst, became the first medical director and a loyal representative of what was then the only psychiatric institution in Palestine and one of the oldest institutions of the Khalukah era – namely, Ezrat Nashim Hospital. But Ita Yellin maintained her hold over the institution, and Dorian was helpless when she concluded that he was adhering too closely to Freudian theories and decided to dismiss him.

1921-1923: Psychiatry and Psychoanalysis at Ezrat Nashim

In 1924 Dorian Feigenbaum published a report[28] in the *International Journal of Psychoanalysis* that proved to be highly valuable. In it he surveyed the early psychoanalytic endeavors in Palestine and described in detail the many successes that psychoanalysis achieved in Jerusalem. In the article Feigenbaum comes across as both a psychoanalyst and a psychiatrist, and a review of his various publications paints a picture of him as "very psychoanalytic" in his approach to illnesses termed psychiatric. His own notes from the time he spent at the Mendrisio asylum also attest that even then he was already examining cases of psychosis through a Freudian lens.

At the time Ezrat Nashim was the only psychiatric institute in the entire Middle East that treated the mentally will regardless of race, ethnicity, or religion. It was not until January 1922 that, in accordance with a Mandate government decision, a second institution of this kind was opened in the Bethlehem neighborhood of Beit Jala, in an abandoned hospital whose Swedish administrators had been expelled by the Ottoman authorities in 1914.

Dorian Feigenbaum worked at Ezrat Nashim with the same enthusiasm that characterized the leading actors of the time in psychiatric clinics across Europe. Those were the fruitful days of collaboration between psychoanalysis and psychiatry – the days of Eugen Bleuler, Carl Jung, and Hermann Rorschach, who had discovered Freud and brought his theories into their daily practice. Despite the brevity of his time in a leadership position, Feigenbaum introduced modern methods of treatment based on Freudian theory. He proposed that the patients of Ezrat Nashim paint and draw pictures, and that the clinical staff analyze these works of "art" because he believed that staff attention was important in itself: the drawings, paintings, and sketches provided a wealth of insights into the patients' psychoses and helped advance the research in this field. To his great satisfaction, he also succeeded in introducing the Rorschach test[29] (which psychoanalysts still viewed as a window into unconscious psychological mechanisms) into the diagnostic toolkit. Like many of his colleagues, he resorted to this test primarily with patients who had difficulty engaging in the process of transference.

In the spring of 1922, when he was spending his mornings treating Ezrat Nashim inpatients and other outpatients using Freudian methods, and the later hours making house calls, Feigenbaum along with David Eder convened a small group of Jewish intellectuals to study the works of Freud. Eder and Feigenbaum were devoted followers of the father of psychoanalysis. Moreover, the former had spent time on Tausk's analytic couch and the latter was Tausk's friend. This study group, which had a "promising future" according to Feigenbaum's report, was particularly interested in the analysis of dreams and parapraxis (a "faulty act" or "slip of the tongue" – an error in speech or action, presumably representing an unconscious wish or train of thought). The colleagues who joined Eder and Feigenbaum in this endeavor played a crucial role in introducing psychoanalysis into Palestine and disseminating Freud's work. They included Aryeh Feigenbaum; Hugo Shmuel Bergmann, a philosopher born in Prague and serving as director of the National Library of Jerusalem (who, although critical of psychoanalysis, deeply respected Freud); Bergmann's friend and fellow countrywoman, the pedagogue Grete Obernik; and the jurist and Zionist leader Siegfried Tzadok van Vriesland, who hosted the small group at his home in the neighborhood of Talbieh.

Conflict between Hadassah and Ezrat Nashim: Resistance to Psychoanalysis

Dorian Feigenbaum's efforts, however, triggered the hostility of the old Yishuv, in the form of Ezrat Nashim's directorship. This antipathy was directed at what some were calling the "analytical plague" or the "arrogance of those American Zionists" and their intentions. Ita Yellin governed Ezrat Nashim with an iron fist. Dorian Feigenbaum's lectures received a lukewarm response, which he attributed to the novelty of his ideas but also, and primarily, to the "scornful fanaticism" of the old Yishuv's conservatives. Before long, the Khalukah dignitaries took a stand against him for reasons that remain unclear but accurately reflect the state of affairs in Palestine of the 1920s. He was reproached, among other reasons, for hosting his nephew Leopold Weiss (1900-1992), who was interested not only in psychoanalysis but also in Islam. According to historian Florence Heymann, Dorian had "undoubtedly" met with his sister Dora's son in Europe.[30] In the spring Leopold received a letter from his uncle, who wrote, "I invite you to spend a few months with me. I will pay for your travel here and back. You may return to Berlin whenever you like. While here, you will live in a pleasant Arab house built of stone, which is cool in the summer (and freezing in the winter). We shall spend time together. I have an enormous quantity of books, and you can read as much as you like." But the young journalist, who was enchanted by Arab culture and Islam, clashed with the Zionist leaders and British authorities immediately upon arriving in Jerusalem, and found himself imprisoned on more than one occasion. Feigenbaum was angry with his nephew but did not cut ties with him. Some years later, speaking of the "misunderstandings" and disagreements they had experienced, Leopold Weiss thanked his uncle for the latter's assistance and unconditional support. He also explained that their time together had sealed his fate.[31] Upon returning to Vienna in late 1913, he became the Arab affairs and Middle East correspondent for *Frankfurter Zeitung*. In this capacity, he traveled extensively under the pseudonym Muhammad Talal Asad, returning to Palestine in 1924, after his uncle had departed. His unique career, escapades, and conversion to Islam attracted a great deal of press until the late twentieth century and sparked the curiosity of many researchers. During the early 1920s, the names of Dorian and Aryeh Feigenbaum often surfaced in association with his story. And as if that were not enough, a rumor spread in Jerusalem that Dorian was a Bolshevik spy. Amidst the violence and unrest that characterized Palestine in 1923, rumors abounded that communists agents sent by the Comintern in Moscow were fomenting the riots that erupted against the British authorities and Jewish immigration.[32] Jerusalem's governor, Colonel Storrs, with the assistance of West Jerusalem's chief of police, David Tidhar (a Haganah member and officer in the British police force) led the British security services in pursuing the rioters relentlessly, and they kept a close eye on immigrants from Eastern Europe. The "Histadrut Bolsheviks" and, in particular, the activists of Po'alei Zion Smol – the left wing of Po'alei Zion – as well as those of the Labor-oriented Gdud HaAvodah, who were even closer to Russian communists, were all suspected of supporting the Kremlin's agents.[33]

In May 1923, following his final lecture and immediately after the violent Arab riots that raged across Jerusalem, Dorian Feigenbaum was interrogated by the police for the first time. In July he was summoned to the British police station at Jaffa Gate and questioned about his ties with a man named Aisner, with whom he and his brother shared a mailbox.[34] The British secret service had discovered that this mailbox, number 241, contained a package sent from Egypt and filled with many documents in English and Arabic. According to David Tidhar (who had led them to the mailbox), the material comprised Bolshevik propaganda in support of communist agitators operating against the British in Palestine.[35] This Aisner was none other than Yitzhak Berger-Barzilai ("Aisner" in German, like "Barzilai" in Hebrew, means "iron merchant"), the Middle East representative of Russia's Communist Party, where he was known by the pseudonym Tchlesnik. He had disguised himself as an ultra-Orthodox Jew, infiltrated the movement HaPoel HaMizrahi, and even managed to secure the position of secretary. He operated among Jerusalem's upper echelons, particularly the respected Yellin and Hecker families, without arousing the slightest suspicion until David Tidhar discovered his true identity.[36]

Dorian Feigenbaum knew nothing about this employee of the Hecker family, who was also a well-known figure in the Yishuv. When Norman Bentwitch, the attorney general of the Mandate government, summoned him early in the summer of 1923 "to discuss very important affairs,"[37] he hastened to reply. The following are excerpts from his letter:

> I further assure you, that I have never in my life been interested in politics and have never participated in acts or writing in any political movements. But I limited myself always to psychiatric interests. Though I have not heard anymore of the matter since May I am now informed that certain rumours are current in town hinting at my connection with Bolshevism which rumours are used by different people to damage my career.[38]

Feigenbaum requested that Bentwitch launch an immediate investigation to clear him from any suspicion and help him "dispel these rumors, which are intended to destroy my future in this country."[39] The rumors indeed ceased, but it was now evident to Feigenbaum that in this still-provincial city, deeply rooted as it was in the mentality of the Khalukah, his own future was in doubt.

Dorian Feigenbaum's experience in Palestine was, therefore, as brief as it was painful: like Frankel before him, he was accused of desecrating the sanctity of the city, and he soon became a target for hate and persecution through no fault of his own. This period of history, with a Jewish community torn between the old Yishuv and the new Yishuv, as religion was losing its hold on the city's governance, was evidently not conducive to the spread of psychoanalysis. In truth, Mandatory Jerusalem of the 1920s was still in the grip of the medieval administration and mentality of the Khalukah regime, which infuriated Eder and other Zionist leaders. Given that the elite of the old Yishuv still held a great deal of sway in Jerusalem, that slander of the worst kind still abounded, and that he had become the focus of hatred on the part of Ita Yellin and her supporters, Dorian Feigenbaum remained with no choice but to leave Ezrat Nashim in the summer of 1923.

He set his sights on America,[40] but two failed attempts to secure sea passage[41] delayed his departure until the spring of 1924. In the meantime he continued to provide judicial expertise for the British authorities while simultaneously assuming new responsibilities. Upon his resignation from Ezrat Nashim, the Histadrut appointed him as the chief medical officer of a polyclinic that had just opened in Jerusalem. Having the unconditional support of Henrietta Szold, he was also able to continue to provide training in psychoanalysis and psychopathology for the staff of Hadassah, the largest and most prestigious medical organization in the Middle East. During January 4-6, 1924, he delivered his three final lectures at Hadassah's nursing school – Experimental Psychology and Freud's Depth Psychology; The Unconscious; and Hypnosis, Sleep, and Dream[42] – quite the introduction to psychoanalytic theory for lay people.

Grete Obernik, the main spokesperson for Bernfeld[43] in Palestine, had participated in the Psychoanalytic Study Group in Jerusalem and subsequently invited Feigenbaum to give his first psychoanalytic lectures in April 1923. Thus it was she who introduced him – and psychoanalysis – into the professional circles that focused on pedagogy and child psychology. The socialist pedagogues of Jerusalem flocked to his lectures, and their interest in psychoanalysis and its "potential applications" (in his words) as well as child psychology and education grew when Deborah Kallen,[44] director of a new liberal school named the School of the Parents Education Association (where Grete Obernik worked), offered to exhibit his patients' drawings and paintings at her school.[45]

Thus, Dorian Feigenbaum drew the attention of educators to the unconscious relations – namely, the effects of transference – between educators and children that color any educational situation. He also showed them how to identify unique psychological conflicts in a child's drawings. This initiative had some resonance and, indeed, received mention in a Jerusalem newspaper as well as the *International Journal of Psycho-Analysis*.

Feigenbaum also met Yichiel Heilperin, the supervisor of Hebrew-language preschools in Palestine (1920-1926), at Deborah Kallen's school, again thanks to Grete Obernik. A pioneer of progressive education in Palestine, Heilperin had, in 1918, begun publishing a magazine, *HaGina* (The Garden), for preschool teachers as well as parents of young children and infants. Heilperin was born in the Ukraine in 1880 to a Lubavitcher Hasidic family of rabbinic lineage, but he left home at an early age, studied abroad, and entered the field of education. In 1909 he emigrated to Warsaw, where he founded the first Hebrew-language nursery school and, some months later, the first seminary for preschool teachers. He came to Palestine in 1920, and that autumn, with his wife Pnina (who had arrived a year earlier with their children) as well as David Idelsohn and Yehuda Ron-Polani, he founded the first preschool for children of workers and an elementary school, both of which were run by the Histadrut.

Heilperin asked Feigenbaum to lecture educators and bring the issue of infantile sexuality to their attention. Consequently the latter discovered a new world of enthusiasts who were eager to build the Eretz Israel of which the pioneers had dreamt. This was to be a country whose people – its workers – would be freed from the neuroses of the ghetto through a new educational approach, which in turn would replace the Khalukah regime and the traditional religious education system that jealously guarded its authority and was preoccupied mainly with performance and ratings.

Feigenbaum delivered two lectures that met with great success: participants responded enthusiastically to the research methods of psychoanalysis and its potential future breakthroughs. His lecture on childhood masturbation raised so many questions and comments that he proposed convening a seminar devoted to the issue.

Socialist and progressive pedagogues began to view psychoanalysis as an extraordinary praxis rather than yet another theory among many. They realized its potential for exploring various modalities of education, providing tools to address all forms of child behavior, and formulating simple solutions to a range of problems. Many types of behavior previously considered indecent, inappropriate, or pathological could now be regarded as normal stages of psychosexual development.

Dorian Feigenbaum's views reflected the theoretical perspective of many other psychoanalysts of his time, who attributed a decisive role to infantile sexuality in the development of one's psyche and love life. Psychoanalysis did indeed shed light on the manifestations of infantile sexuality, which, though often evident even in the school environment, still gave rise to discomfort and uncertainty regarding treatment, particularly when it became clear that repression or appeals to morality were ineffective.

Dorian left Palestine in February 1924. He traveled by way of Vienna, where he attended the Congress of Salzburg as a delegate from Jerusalem. From there he embarked to America, where he settled in New York. Perhaps he still intended to return to Jerusalem, but he soon found himself immersed in the elite psychoanalytic circles of the United States. His first major success came when he organized a seminar with the Hungarian psychoanalyst Sandor Ferenczi in New York during March-April 1927.[46]

Along with other colleagues form the New York Psychoanalytic Society, he launched a second psychoanalytic journal in English, *The Psychoanalytic Quarterly*. As his social status rose and his fortune increased, he was able to hire a personal assistant, and his family traveled in a chauffeured limousine when in New York or on vacation. He consistently took advantage of any important opportunity to reconnect with European psychoanalysts for substantive exchange, and during the 1934 psychoanalytic congress in Lucerne, he met Max Eitingon, a delegate from Jerusalem. The two maintained close ties through a trans-Atlantic dialogue between Jerusalem and New York.

Dorian Feigenbaum continued to support his European colleagues. He hosted his friends Felix and Helen Deutsch, who had fled the rising anti-

Semitism in Vienna, and he organized an evening event in their honor at his home. He also responded affirmatively to a request by Abraham Arden Brill, head of the American psychoanalytic movement, to help his German Jewish colleagues. In November 1935, upon hearing that the Gestapo had arrested a German psychoanalyst and murdered one of his patients, Brill proposed that a committee be established to support German Jewish psychoanalysts, by raising funds to finance their exit visas and help them find employment in the United States. A committee was immediately set up, with Dorian Feigenbaum as chairman. Its members included Bertram Lewin, Karen Horney, Frankwood Williams, and Emanuel Klein, among others.

On January 2, 1937, at the height of his brilliant and still promising career, Dorian Feigenbaum died of pneumonia within three days of taking ill. He had not even reached the age of fifty.

Aryeh Feigenbaum: An Activist Ahead of His Time

Aryeh Feigenbaum was born in Lvov in 1885. Like other Zionist intellectuals who faced anti-Semitism, he had always believed that the only way for Jews to be free of anti-Semitic dictates and the threat of pogroms was to return to Eretz Israel. In their ancient homeland, Jews could live freely and build a Jewish nation-state based on the humanistic and universal values of Hebrew culture. He belonged to the generation of German-speaking Galician Jews who passionately adhered to the rationalist thinking of the nineteenth century and denounced any form of assimilation or religious interference in civil affairs, particularly education.

From the mid-nineteenth century, the question of assimilation had become increasingly acute in both Western and Eastern European discourse. A growing number of Jews in Britain, Germany, France, and Austria, hoping to distance themselves from anything reminiscent of ghetto life, from its humiliation and oppression, and seeking the same rights as other citizens, were trying to integrate into their host country's predominant culture. Some, while abandoning daily religious practice, continued to observe the traditional holidays. Others, such as Herzl and Freud, forsook Judaism as a religion or even converted to Catholicism or Protestantism, although they did not deny their origins. Still others denied their past and their identity, demonstrating fierce hostility towards anything that might remind them of their origin. All, or nearly all, then found themselves facing another form of anti-Semitism: "social" anti-Semitism. Within the Jewish community, assimilationists suffered the vindictiveness of religious traditionalists. Many Jews viewed assimilation as a terrible epidemic.

Like many immigrants of the Second Aliyah, Aryeh Feigenbaum had a variety of mentors, including Maimonides, Spinoza, Goethe, Schiller, Shakespeare, Darwin, Ehrlich, Talmudists, Einstein, and. . . Freud. He saw the father of psychoanalysis as "a true representative of the ancient Hebrew, for his moral courage, and a perfect Hellene, for his intellectual courage, an embodiment of the Talmudic ideal. . . the most beautiful of Hellas in the tents of [the Semites]"[47] – in other words, as one of the great Talmudic masters whose wisdom combined biblical teachings with the highest form of rational thought.

Aryeh Feigenbaum also shared in the hopes of many Central and East European Zionists who sought to revive the Hebrew language: these immigrants enthusiastically joined the effort to translate and produce texts in modern Hebrew. Let us recall in this context that Eliezer Ben-Yehuda, the great revivalist of the Hebrew language, was active in Palestine during the late nineteenth century, while Chaim Nachman Bialik and his disciples in Odessa were concurrently producing works in Hebrew. Ancient Hebrew was transformed into a modern language in every sense – an unprecedented feat in human history.

Feigenbaum, like many other students of his day, pursued his studies at a variety of universities across Europe: after Kiel and Munich, it was in Vienna that, in 1911, he completed the medical studies he had originally begun in his hometown. Upon receiving his medical license, he returned to Germany and founded the Association of Jewish Physicians and Researchers in the Natural Sciences for the Promotion of Medicine and Biology in Palestine,[48] along with other colleagues who wanted to bring Palestine out of its state of backwardness. Earlier, in 1910, when he had decided to stay a few more years in Western Europe to finish his medical studies, he heard the call of the World Zionist Organization, urging the Jewish people to return to their homeland and take part in resurrecting the Hebrew language and culture in

Eretz Israel. After having played a key part in the grand "campaign against trachoma" launched in 1911 under the auspices of the WZO, he joined the pioneers of the Second Aliyah in 1913. He left for Palestine in the company of ophthalmologist Abraham Ticho and his wife Anna, who settled in Jerusalem, and Anna Smeliansky, who – with Max Eitingon, Moshe Wulff, and Ilja Schalit – founded the Psychoanalytic Society of Palestine two decades later.

As early as 1914, Aryeh Feigenbaum found himself immersed in a grueling wartime odyssey. Suspected of collaborating with the British, he was imprisoned and tormented by the Ottomans, then deported to Damascus with a convoy of prisoners. When the war ended he met David Eder, who at the time was Weizmann's right-hand man for political affairs and construction of the Jewish homeland. Their meeting turned out to be crucial, both in terms of the reorganization of the Yishuv's medical services and for the future of psychoanalysis in Palestine and, later, Israel. Both men had been strongly influenced by the personality and teachings of Freud. Long after Eder left Palestine in 1923, Aryeh Feigenbaum continued to promote psychoanalysis and Freudianism in Palestine and in Israel, with the unconditional and vital support of Henrietta Szold.

Aryeh Feigenbaum was not only an outstanding clinician. He also demonstrated exceptional organizational skills in a variety of institutions: from 1922 he served as director of the Ophthalmology Department at the Nathan Strauss Medical Center in Jerusalem; he served as president of the Medical Society of Jerusalem during 1925-1927; and in 1939 he founded and became director of the program for pre-medical studies at the Hebrew University. He had to wait many more years, however, before he could undertake the analysis he had long sought: during the 1920s, the only practicing analyst in Palestine was his own brother, Dorian Feigenbaum, as Eder was preoccupied with his own political and administrative responsibilities. Aryeh considered going to Berlin in 1927 for analysis, but he was too busy promoting healthcare in Palestine. Only in 1934, after Eitingon settled in Jerusalem, was he finally able to lay his head on a Freudian couch. Until then he engaged in a self-analysis of sorts so as to better explore his dreams, and towards this end he asked his psychoanalyst brother to fill the role that Freud had assigned to Wilhelm Fliess.[49]

Although Aryeh Feigenbaum was not a psychoanalyst, his involvement in all aspects of psychoanalysis in Palestine – his "great interests in this discipline" in his words – soon became widely known. This tireless pioneer of psychoanalysis in Palestine lived until February 20, 1980, when he died in a retirement home for former physicians in Haifa.

Siegfried Zadock van Vriesland: A Committed Freudian

Siegfried Zadock van Vriesland joined the Freudian circle thanks to Eder. Like Eder, he was a close associate of Chaim Weizmann in the WZO, and the two met in 1919 though the Zionist Commission for Palestine.

Van Vriesland was born in Rotterdam in 1886 into an assimilated Dutch family. As a young lawyer, he joined the Zionist movement in 1913. The following year, he was appointed secretary of the Dutch Zionist Federation, and when the war ended he accepted Chaim Weizmann's request to join the Zionist Commission.[50] He arrived in Jerusalem in June 1919. From 1927, van Vriesland served as the Dutch delegate, and in 1933 he was appointed as First Consul General of the Netherlands in Palestine. He held a large number of political, diplomatic, and administrative posts: treasurer of the Zionist Commission and, later, of the Zionist Executive (1919-1930), director general of Palestine Potash Limited (for the exploitation of Dead Sea minerals), general manager of the Tel Aviv port, philanthropist, and treasurer of the Palestine Orphans Committee, an organization devoted to assisting war orphans.[51]

For twenty years, he participated in the major enterprises that revolutionized the Yishuv and the entire country, including the recognition and development of psychoanalysis.[52] Van Vriesland was an elegant, highly educated, and exceptional figure, who unquestionably remained one of the most prominent and fascinating personalities of Yishuv throughout his life. His interest in psychoanalysis and psychiatry was presumably linked to the recurring manic attacks and depressive episodes from which he suffered. Indeed, he experienced only one extensive period of respite, thanks to the analysis he underwent in 1926 with Johan van Ophuijsen, a pioneer of psychoanalysis in the Netherlands.

Unsurprisingly, therefore, he was deeply involved in all projects related to psychoanalysis: fundraising for the opening of a private psychiatric clinic, where Aryeh Feigenbaum planned to have his brother appointed as director; support for the creation of a chair of psychoanalysis at the Hebrew University;

and the appointment of Max Eitingon to this post in accordance with Freud's wishes. Freud proposed that van Vriesland use *Imago*, one of the most important journals of the international psychoanalytic movement, to publish a text he had written during the course of his treatment, addressing the relationship between the Hebrew language and psychoanalysis.[53]

Siegfried Zadock van Vriesland committed suicide on December 4, 1939.[54] Naming him among David Eder and Dorian Feigenbaum, Max Eitingon eulogized van Vriesland: "He was not a member of the association, but one of its very few honoured guests. Twenty years ago he was one of the trio – all of them now departed – who were the first to discuss and propagate psychoanalysis in this country."[55] With Shmuel Horowitz, Judah Magnes, Edwin Samuel, and Rafael Pollack, Eitingon created a foundation in his name, to promote exchanges between artists and architects from the Netherlands and Palestine – the van Vriesland Foundation.[56] His wife Jeannette (Simcha) Hoofyen, whom he had married in 1927, died in an Arab ambush in October 1947 near Latrun, while accompanying a United Nations convoy.

Grete Obernik-Reiner: Spokesperson for Siegfried Bernfeld

This chapter on the pioneers of psychoanalysis in Mandatory Palestine would be incomplete if we did not mention the complex figure of Grete Obernik, the "first lady" of Freudianism in the country, and give her the credit she justly deserves. Grete Obernik-Reiner, who arrived in Palestine in 1920, was one of the first members of the Psychoanalytic Society of Palestine, whose founding is discussed in the next chapter. Her name – as the first woman in Palestine who was passionate about psychoanalysis and committed to its practice, promotion, and dissemination in the country – is one of the great forgotten names in the official historiography of psychoanalysis in Mandatory Palestine and in Israel.[57]

She was born in 1893 in Brno (Brünn),[58] the capital of Moravia at the time and now a major city in Slovakia. Her father Adolf, who worked in heavy metallurgy in the city, died before WWII. During the Nazi invasion in March 1939, one of her sisters committed suicide and another disappeared. Her bother was able to flee and found asylum in Ireland. Other details about her life can be extracted from her correspondence with her friend Hugo Bergmann, a Czech Zionist pedagogue and philosopher, whom she met in Prague in 1915.[59] Bergmann introduced her to a group of young Zionist intellectuals in France, which included Robert Weltsch, Franz Kafka, and Max Brod. Her granddaughter Rony Reiner, who spoke with one of Kafka's biographers, related that Grete Obernik had had a love affair with the famous writer.[60] After fleeing to Vienna during WWI, and given her long-time interest in pedagogy, psychology, and the teaching methods of Maria Montessori, she cultivated a strong interest in working with children in Palestine. In the meantime she enriched her professional experience while in Vienna: she worked at an institution that took in refugee Jewish children escaping from Central and Eastern Europe, and she later taught Hebrew, initially at a girls' school run by Alfred Krauss, and later – in what became a formative experience – at the Jewish seminary Jüdische Pädagogikum, opened by Siegfried Bernfeld in 1917.

At this institution she worked in administration and the organization of activities, becoming Bernfeld's right-hand woman. In 1918, like many other young Zionists who came from Eastern Europe to work at the seminary, she joined a group named Jerubbaal (another name for the biblical figure Gideon, son of Joash), which gathered around Bernfeld. In a journal of the same name, she called on Jewish youth in Europe to "leave their families and find the charismatic leader who would lead them to Palestine,"[61] – in other words, to join Bernfeld. She ventured with him to the orphans' school he founded in 1919, Kinderheim Baumgarten, but decided to suspend her activities in Vienna and travel to Palestine to participate in an aid program for abandoned children.

In early 1920 she set sail for Palestine with Hugo Bergmann.[62] At first she stayed in Haifa. In a long letter she sent that autumn to Bernfeld, she thanked him for always helping and encouraging her in her work at the Jewish seminary, her career as a pedagogue, and her personal life, and for introducing her to the works of the German pedagogue Gustav Wyneken and of Freud.[63] She also complained about her deplorable living conditions and inability to find work in Haifa unless she was willing to work "like an animal" as well as the education council (Va'ad HaKhinukh) – that is, the very conservative pedagogues of the teacher's union in Palestine (Histadrut HaMorim BeEretz Israel). She found all of it discouraging. She advised that he wait a few more year before emigrating, and that he not make a final decision until he had lived in Palestine for some time.[64] After overcoming many financial, administrative, and personal difficulties, she eventually found work at the Reali School in Haifa. Informing Bernfeld of her new occupation, she expressed satisfaction at having employment and working with Jewish and Arab children, but voiced regret that she was unable to find any local material relevant to Maria Montessori's teaching methods, and that her work colleagues were not particularly interested in these methods.[65] More letters followed: she described Palestine and marveled about her visits to Jerusalem, where she had again met Hugo Bergmann. He occupied a key post in the movement HaShomer HaTza'ir, in which she was also deeply involved, and after being appointed as director of the National Library, he quickly became one of the most prominent intellectual figures in the Yishuv. She also informed Bernfeld of initiatives she had taken to disseminate his writings and support his projects: she told him about the article she had published in *HaPo'el HaTza'ir*[66] recounting the experiences of Kinderheim Baumgarten, in which she presented herself as his spokesperson, described the original teaching methods conceived and applied in this institution, and suggested that this experiment could be applied elsewhere as well.

In 1922 Grete Obernik left Haifa for Jerusalem, where she started working with Russian pedagogue Yichiel Heilperin to develop educational projects as well as writing for his magazine *HaGina*.[67] She created experimental discussion groups for mothers in the Old City, where they could talk about their children regardless of age, the problems that teachers were unable to handle, and the day-to-day issues they encountered. She wrote that she was surprised by the success of these meetings, where women of all ethnicities, who spoke a mix of languages, came together. Simultaneously she worked with Deborah Kallen, who ran the aforementioned liberal school,[68] and with Mordechai Brachyahu, whom Henrietta Szold had recently appointed as director of school health services on behalf of Hadassah.[69] Yet she strongly resented the fact that all educational institutions, even those run by the Zionist left, were governed by the Histadrut: "Everything is framed, everything has to comply with very rigorous and restrictive political programs." In 1923 she returned to Vienna, which is presumably where she met and married Markus Reiner.[70] They had two children: Efraim, with whom I met and spoke about her, was born in Jerusalem in 1924 (and passed away in 2009), and his sister Hannah was born in Vienna in 1926.

Psychoanalytic Training in Vienna:
Grete Obernik, Anna Freud, and August Aichhorn

In a letter to Bernfeld in May 1925, Grete Obernik-Reiner informed him that she would be in Vienna from August to November[71] in order to implement "psychoanalytic training for pedagogues" in the Vienna Psychoanalytic Society. On October 22, 1925, Anna Freud wrote to Max Eitingon that one of her patients,[72] a teacher from Palestine, was attending the Vienna Psychoanalytic Institute and participating in a seminar run by her "colleague" August Aichhorn.

Aichhorn (whose academic training was in pedagogy) was at the time the only psychoanalyst to have formulated a theory on the problem of young adolescents regarded as marginal. He also proposed a new clinic based on psychoanalysis. He was particularly interested in young people whom the Austrian government overlooked: delinquents and criminals left to their own devices. Rather than condemning them or trying to rehabilitate them, he decided to "listen" to them. When Grete Obernik registered for his seminar, his book about his experience and theories, with a preface by Freud, had just been published. The book, *Verwarhloste Jugend* (Neglected Youth), met with great success.[73]

Very little information is available regarding her years of training, between 1925 and 1935. Only one thing is known for certain: she was active in the field of psychoanalysis. In a 1930 issue of the journal *Internationale Zeitschrift für Psychoanalytische Pädagogik* we find an article by "G. Reiner, Haifa" that uses psychoanalysis to interpret the phantasms and symptomatic behavior that a little girl suddenly exhibited upon the birth of her brother.[74]

Grete Obernik returned to Vienna in 1933 for the last time. She delivered her first lecture at the Psychoanalytic Consultation Seminar for Educators (Erziehungs-Beratungs-Seminar), which Aichhorn had inaugurated on May 8 at the Vienna Psychoanalytic Society. Her presentation described the case of a delinquent adolescent treated by the analytical method[75] at the specialized clinic opened by Aichhorn the previous year.

After serving as Bernfeld's spokesperson, she worked on disseminating Aichhorn's teachings in Palestine during the 1930s. David Idelsohn, who produced the first Hebrew translation of Aichhorn's book (originally published as an article in 1948)[76] followed a similar course. During the early 1940s, Jerusalem saw a steady succession of spokespersons: from Mordechai Brachyahu to Shmuel Nagler to Fanny Lowtzky, all of whom implemented Aichhorn's teachings and led seminars to train analysts and pedagogues to conduct research in the field towards which he had paved the way.

Grete Obernik's Tel Aviv Practice

In March 1933 Moshe Wulff settled in Tel Aviv, where he met Grete Obernik. In a letter to Max Eitingon, who was staying in Berlin at the time, Wulff informed him of his plans to establish a new stronghold of Freudianism in Palestine along with Obernik and other local pedagogues, and to begin training in psychoanalysis.[77] Eitingon arrived in Jerusalem in April 1934, a few days before the official opening of the Palestine Psychoanalytic Society, scheduled for May 5.

After several trips to Vienna and back (while her children resided in the children's village founded in Ben Shemen by a former member of Jerubbaal),[78] Grete Obernik eventually settled in Palestine in February 1934 and sought a meeting with Eitingon.[79] On June 1 she sent him a more detailed letter:[80] She informed him that she was living in Ben Shemen with her children and that, contrary to her expectations, she was unable to find work there; she told him of her plans to create a psychoanalytic seminar for teachers, as Aichhorn had done in Vienna, where cases would be presented and discussed; and towards this end she sought his support, noting that although she had already participated in "test cases" with Aichhorn and Anna Freud, she would be more confident if she could proceed under the supervision of an experienced psychoanalyst such as him.

Did Eitingon reply? That remains unclear. But in any event, after giving some thought to settling in Jerusalem, she decided to join Yichiel Heilperin. He hired her on July 1, 1934, to work at Dugma, a model school for young children in the heart of Tel Aviv, with the prospect that in the future she could implement cutting-edge teaching methods. She found a home nearby and settled with her children at 24 Melchett Street, in one of the classic Tel Aviv Bauhaus-style neighborhoods, not far from Moshe Wulff and Martin Pappenheim.

Grete Obernik, who had been treated by Anna Freud and trained with Bernfeld and Aichhorn before entering Supervision with Anna Smeliansky (another analyst in whom Eitingon had full confidence), was thus the "first Freudian lady" of Palestine. But despite her professional skills and commitment to analysis, she was a teacher, not a doctor, and it was unlikely that the psychoanalytic establishment would recognize her as a "fully qualified analyst." Indeed, the CPEI only accepted analysts trained according to very strict guidelines or analysts who had been members of the Vienna Psychoanalytic Society before immigrating to Palestine. One such example was Lilli Peller-Roubiczeck, a student and assistant of Maria Montessori in Austria.

During its early years, the CPEI would not grant Grete Obernik the status and privileges she had enjoyed under the auspices of the Vienna Psychoanalytic Society but, rather, recognized her as a "permanent guest" (*ständiget Gast*) who was permitted to attend all its meetings.[81] Was her name excluded from the list of candidates because she was not a physician? This is not inconceivable: analysis by non-physicians (*Laienanalyse*) was a delicate matter at the time, as Eitingon himself, chairman of the nascent CPEI, noted during a lively debate on the question at a psychoanalytic congress in Lucerne.[82] But Obernik's exclusion was not permanent. In response to a request she made on February 20, 1935, Obernik granted her the right to continue the work she had begun in Vienna: she could resume analytic Supervision twice monthly, this time under Smeliansky, Eitingon's former assistant at the Berlin Psychoanalytic Institute and a founding partner of the CPEI.[83] Although her name never appeared on the CPEI's membership list, Eitingon regarded her, alongside Aryeh Feigenbaum and Siegfried van Vriesland, as one of the original witnesses of this ground-breaking group created by Dorian Feigenbaum and Montague David Eder during 1921-1922 in Jerusalem.[84]

Beginning in 1934 she regularly took part in the activities of the Psychoanalytic Institute of Jerusalem.[85] She was one of the first to deliver a lecture at the Institute, in 1935, in which she explored educational issues in light of psychoanalytic theory.[86] In 1936 she again approached Eitingon, seeking admission to the CPEI as an "external member" (*Außerordentliches Mitglied*). Her candidacy was accepted[87] in March 1936.[88] She was among the signatories to a letter of solidarity that Eitingon sent Freud on behalf of the CPEI immediately after Nazi troops invaded Vienna in March 1938.[89] That same year she delivered another lecture, on the sexuality of Palestine's children, before the Psychoanalytic Society.

Grete Obernik continued to treat children in Tel Aviv, offering psychotherapy or diagnostic services. They were referred to her by David Idelsohn, an important figure in the field of special education and psychoanalysis in Tel Aviv, or by the neuropsychiatrist Martin Pappenheim, a Viennese member of the Palestine Psychoanalytic Society, who sent his first patients to her. Nevertheless, according to her son, Grete Obernik "developed a genuine paranoia towards psychoanalysts, who did not recognize her as one of their own."

Tragic Figure of the Psychoanalytical World: Grete Obernik – Her Madness and Death

In early 1936, Anna Freud wrote to Max Eitingon, after having learned that her student was going through a difficult time.[90] She requested that he inquire further and keep her informed. Grete's husband, Markus Reiner, was planning to return to Palestine around this time. In July 1936 Eitingon received another letter, from Dorian Feigenbaum, voicing concern about the future of the couple's children. Feigenbaum added that he had become well acquainted with Grete Obernik during his time in Palestine from 1921-1924, and that although she was undeniably an "excellent person," she was also "very neurotic."[91] In 1936 she was institutionalized in a private clinic in Haifa run by Dr. Kurt Blumenthal and began to receive electroshock therapy. Her son Efraim, who regularly visited her with his sister and occasionally with his father, described these memories as very painful. We do not know when or under what circumstances Grete Obernik returned to Tel Aviv. In 1946 she ended her own life, at the age of 53. Her contribution to the acceptance of Freudian doctrine in Palestine, and later Israel, is due less to her publications, which were few in number, and more to her conviction: she never stopped believing that pedagogy and education could only progress if they incorporated the lessons of psychoanalysis. As a devoted member, alongside Aryeh Feigenbaum and Siegfried van Vriesland, in the Psychoanalytic Study Group[92] founded in 1922 by Dorian Feigenbaum and Eder, she was, from the 1920s, the creative force behind the introduction and success of this discipline among the city's progressive pedagogues. The "passion for psychoanalysis" personified by her tragic figure cannot be denied.

"The Psychology of the Depths in the Rocky Soil of Jerusalem"

The Psychoanalytic Study Group of Jerusalem, founded by Dorian Feigenbaum and David Eder was, without a doubt, the "cornerstone" – in Eitingon's words[93] – of the Freudian movement in Palestine. Dorian confirmed this in his eulogy for David Eder.

In 1953, more than three decades after this group was founded, Aryeh Feigenbaum wrote to Milton Rosenbaum, who was planning to inaugurate a Department of Psychiatry at the Hebrew University Medical School with a lecture on psychoanalysis:

> It is deeply regrettable that some people are no longer here to see that the academic recognition of psychoanalysis in Jerusalem has become a reality – not my beloved brother Dorian, who. . . did everything during 1920-1923 to sow the first seeds of the psychology of the depths in the rocky soil of Jerusalem, nor the admirable pioneer Max Eitingon, (who for the second time in his life founded a psychoanalytic institute – this time [1933] in Jerusalem), nor, last but not least, Freud.[94]

Nevertheless, as we shall see, the university did not prove to be fertile ground for the development of psychoanalysis. Institutional efforts and failures are of great importance in assessing the resistance to psychoanalysis during its early days. But first let us explore how, twelve years after the emergence of the Psychoanalytic Study Group in Jerusalem, the Palestine Psychoanalytic Society was born.

CHAPTER 3

The Institutionalization of Psychoanalysis: The Palestine Psychoanalytic Society (1934)

From the 1930s, Mandatory Palestine had a coherent system of legislation, a reasonably functional system of administration, and a network of democratic institutions under the auspices of the British authorities or the Jewish Yishuv and Jewish National Council (Va'ad Leumi, the national executive body of the Yishuv). The diminishing influence of religious institutions, rapid economic growth of 1933-1935, and political calm of the early 1930s combined to create fertile ground for the acceptance and dissemination of Freudian ideas. With the arrival of thousands of new immigrants from Germany, the demand for psychoanalytic treatment grew exponentially: at that time, psychoanalysis was quite popular in Germany, and new arrivals soon turned to psychoanalysis to alleviate their psychological suffering after having been brutally uprooted from the culture, language, and country they had known. The psychoanalysts, many of whom had also just arrived, performed extraordinary and unparalleled work among adults and children alike.

Even before the arrival of the Fifth Aliyah, Freud's work found a prominent place in modern Hebrew culture. From 1933, recently arrived psychoanalysts began to enjoy a degree of public support that had never been available to Dorian Feigenbaum. The great pioneers, the true "pillars" of the Freudian movement in Palestine, welcomed the new arrivals enthusiastically. These pioneers included colleagues such as Aryeh Feigenbaum, Siegfried van Vriesland, Andor Fodor, and Mordechai Brachyahu, as well as the pedagogues – to whom we shall return – Grete Obernik, David Idelsohn, Shmuel Golan and Zvi Sohar, among others. It was this meeting between psychoanalysts from Germany and Austria, on the one hand, and the pioneers of Freudianism in Palestine, on the other, that gave rise to the golden age of Freud's teachings during the Mandate era and early statehood.

Max Eitingon and the Berlin Model in Jerusalem

Eitingon was born in 1881 in Orsha, near Mogilev, Belarus, which at the time served as the Jewish seat of the Russian Empire. His religiously observant family supported the Zionist movement even before Herzl. Thus, he grew up in an atmosphere steeped in both religious tradition and Zionist ideology. The family resided for a while in Moscow, where Eitingon's father, Chaim, worked as a fur merchant and did quite well for a brief period. The onset of anti-Semitic persecution following the murder of Tsar Alexander II in 1881, and the subsequent laws prohibiting Jews from living in Russia's major cities, put an end to his trade and forced him to leave the city. At the time Jews were being expelled en masse from Moscow and forbidden from residing there. This sad chapter in the history of Russian Jewry is known as the "Moscow Exile." Chaim Eitingon left Russia for good and settled in Leipzig, where he earned his fortune, becoming one of the city's wealthiest residents as well as a noted philanthropist of the Jewish community and the city itself. Among other activities, he founded an Orthodox synagogue and a large modern hospital, while also supporting Zionist enterprises and purchasing land in Palestine.

After completing his studies at the Realschule in Leipzig, Max Eitingon enrolled at the University of Halle in 1900, where he attended courses taught by the great philosophers of the time: Hans Vahinger, Edmund Husserl, Theodore Conrad, and many others. In 1909 he completed his medical studies at the University of Zurich, where his dissertation advisor was the renowned psychiatrist Eugen Bleuler, director of the psychiatric clinic at Burghölzli.[95] During the early twentieth century, Burghölzli served as an important center of psychiatry, where many foreign students came for training. These included the German Jew Karl Abraham, who later became a disciple of Freud and founder of the German Society for Psychoanalysis. Eitingon maintained strong ties and cooperated closely with Abraham until the latter's sudden death in 1925. Both were involved in the development of psychoanalysis in Germany. At Burghölzli Eitingon met Carl Jung, who – like Bleuler, his assistant – was interested in Freud's discoveries. It was Jung who introduced Eitingon to the works of Freud. On December 6, 1906, Burgholzli's new trainee began to correspond with the father of psychoanalysis. He traveled to Vienna in 1907 to meet Freud, becoming the first foreigner to rescue the latter from his Viennese isolation.[96] Nonetheless, if we are to believe one of his patients in Jerusalem, Eitingon remained loyal to Freud yet always spoke of Jung with a certain degree of nostalgia.[97]

In 1909 Freud invited Eitingon to return to Vienna, where his disciple underwent analysis so as to advance his training. Eitingon thus became the first analyst to benefit from *Kontrolleanalyse* ("control analysis" – termed "Supervision" in English),[98] a form of psychoanalytic therapy intended to prepare a candidate for work as a psychoanalyst. Freud also invited Eitingon to participate in the famous "Wednesday meetings" – that is, the initial gatherings of what would become the Vienna Psychoanalytic Society.[99] This marked the start of a firm friendship that lasted three decades.

In 1910 Eitingon and his friend Albert Nacht settled in Berlin. That same year, Eitingon, who had always maintained close ties with the culture of his native Russia and a fascination with Russian literature, brought Freud a literary study on Leonardo da Vinci and gave him a complete fifteen-volume set of the works of Dostoyevsky. He also introduced Freud to the works of his friend, the Russian philosopher Leon Chestov, which he himself had translated into German. Eitingon knew Chestov through his sister, Fanny Lowtzky, who, after studying philosophy like her brother, became a psychoanalyst and practiced in Moscow, Berlin, Paris, and eventually Jerusalem. After Eitingon invited her to work alongside him at the Jerusalem Psychoanalytic Institute in 1939, she went on to become one of the prominent figures in the Freudian movement of Mandatory Palestine and the State of Israel.

When Eitingon responded to the call of the World Zionist Organization and came to Palestine in 1910, he discovered conditions that were unsuitable for the development of psychoanalysis. He therefore returned to Germany, where he contributed to the further development of this discipline, but he kept a close watch on the situation within the Yishuv until he left Germany for good in 1933.

Berlin, a New Capital of Psychoanalysis

When the First World War broke out, Max Eitingon served as a military doctor in the Austro-Hungarian army: as a surgeon and as a neuropsychiatrist in Kassa from August 1915, then later in Igloo, and finally as a chief medical officer in Miskolc, where he mainly addressed what would soon become known as the war neurosis.[100] From time to time he would receive leave to visit Freud in Vienna or his wife Mirra and parents in Leipzig. He also traveled to the Fifth International Psychoanalytic Congress, which took place in Budapest on September 28-29, 1918, and where the lectures and discussion focused primarily on the problem of war neurosis. Freud, believing that the analytical method offered an appropriate treatment for these diseases, proposed a new idea: he argued that men, women, and children should be treated at designated clinics free of charge. Eitingon took this proposal seriously and by 1919, with Ernst Simmel, he launched a project to establish a psychoanalytic polyclinic in Berlin, with ties to the German Psychoanalytic Society.[101] This coincided with Freud's decision to integrate his student into his famous "secret committee," established in 1912 at the initiative of Ernest Jones with the aim of preserving psychoanalytic doctrine in the face of any deviation, perversion, or misinterpretation on the part of Freud's disciples (as occurred with Adler, Steckel, and Jung). The committee included Freud's most loyal disciples: Karl Abraham, Hans Sachs, Otto Rank, Sandor Ferenczi, Ernest Jones, and Anton von Freund.

In 1920, committee member von Freund, one of Freud's dearest friends, passed away. Freud asked Eitingon to take his place and, through his daughter Anna, sent his disciple the traditional ring granted to members as a sign of loyalty to him and to the principles of psychoanalysis. Henceforth the Freud family viewed Eitingon as one of its own, and Eitingon himself remained a loyal disciple of Freud and cultivated close ties with Anna Freud throughout his life.

The Berlin polyclinic opened its doors on February 14, 1920. Eitingon provided most of the funding, with smaller contributions from Ernst Simmel and Anna Smeliansky. Thus, following Vienna, Berlin became a new capital of psychoanalysis, until the Nazi rise to power.

Eitingon devoted considerable time to administrative work, both at the clinic in Berlin and within the international psychoanalytic movement. Among other duties, he was responsible for overseeing the training of psychoanalysts. He also became a senior official in the International Psychoanalytic Association. In April 1925, he was appointed as secretary of the Association and, upon the death of Karl Abraham, who had served as president of the Association, he fulfilled the latter's duties until the next Congress took place, in Bad Homburg in 1927. At the recommendation of Freud and with the support of Jones, he was then appointed as president of the Association.

Debacle in Berlin: The Dissolution of the Berlin Psychoanalytic Institute and the Aliyah of Max Eitingon to Palestine

In 1931, despite having lost none of the prestige it had acquired during its first eleven years of activity, the Berlin Psychoanalytic Institute encountered a new set of problems: a severe economic crisis befell Germany, while Max Eitingon, the Institute's main shareholder, whose family assets were invested mainly in the United States, had been badly hit by the 1929 crash of the New York Stock Exchange.[102] Freud himself intervened in order to raise funds and prevent the Institute's closure. At the same time, other prominent German psychoanalysts, members of the Berlin Institute, were invited to join institutes abroad and left the country. After the Nazi party achieved victory in the elections in March 1933, psychoanalysts departed Germany in droves, mainly to the United States. On March 19, 1933, on the eve of Hitler's election, Eitingon shared his concerns with Freud and sought his advice regarding the Institute's future and its operations.[103] After Hitler's rise to power, on March 23, despite Freud's advice yet in line with other Jewish colleagues, Eitingon concluded that he could no longer remain in Germany. In April the German government decreed that Jews could no longer serve on the board of directors of scientific organizations, and like Ernst Simmel and Otto Fenichel, Eitingon too was forced to resign from the German Psychoanalytic Society.[104] He was also forced to resign from his position as director of the Psychoanalytic Institute and cede all responsibilities to Felix Boehm, a true "Aryan."[105] Eitingon provided considerable assistance to his Jewish colleagues who encountered obstacles while seeking to leave Nazi Germany, which had become particularly dangerous. In a certain sense, he served as an "emigration bureau" for the psychoanalytic movement, and with the cooperation of Anna Freud and Ernest Jones, he enabled many Jewish intellectuals to find asylum in other countries.

In May 1933 Eitingon corresponded with Moshe Wulff, a pioneer of psychoanalysis in Russia who had settled in Palestine in March and committed himself to establishing a Palestinian psychoanalytic movement. Eitingon also received a warm letter of recommendation from Montague David Eder, addressed to his old friend Aryeh Feigenbaum. Eder reminded the renowned ophthalmologist that Eitingon was a "long-time Zionist" who held senior positions in the international psychoanalytic movement. On June 14, in a eulogy honoring Sandor Ferenczi, Eitingon publicly announced that he was leaving Germany for good, without specifying his destination. He was fully aware that, in light of the new National-Socialist decree prohibiting Jews from practicing their trade in public institutions, large numbers of German Jewish physicians were arriving in Palestine and encountering great difficulty obtaining permission to practice medicine from the local authorities.

Palestine, Autumn 1933

Max Eitingon soon decided to establish a psychoanalytic institute. On November 2, 1933, he wrote to Freud that "my decision to open a psychoanalytic institute after becoming permanently settled here has created a strong impression. A new institute, the fruit of the labor of an important, world-renowned Jew definitely has a place here! And without being asked for anything in return."[106] He was reunited with old colleagues from Berlin: Moshe Wulff, Ilja Schalit,[107] Anna Smeliansky, and Walter Kluge.[108] In late September 1933, they gathered at Wulff's home in Tel Aviv and decided collectively[109] to found the Palestinian Psychoanalytic Society.[110] Eitingon assumed the position of chairman, Wulff was appointed as his deputy, and Ilja Schalit as secretary and treasurer. On October 28, 1933, on stationery bearing the letterhead of the King David Hotel, Eitingon drafted the founding document of the future society.[111]

Of the five signatories, all of whom had worked in Germany (and four of whom – Eitingon, Wulff, Smeliansky, and Schalit – had been born in Russia, as Alexander Etkind rightly observes[112]), only Walter Kluge, who resided for a while in Jerusalem, left Palestine and eventually settled in the United States.

In that same letter of November 2, 1933, Eitingon informed Freud of the establishment of the new society, adding that its five founders would announce the new organization in the local press and, with Jones's mediation, in the *International Journal of Psycho-Analysis*.[113] He also informed Freud that other contacts, including kibbutz members Shmuel Golan and Zvi Sohar, were interested in psychoanalysis. Regarding the opening of a psychoanalytic institute in Jerusalem, Eitingon knew that implementation of the project would entail overcoming problems that were related, in his words, to the residents' poverty, the absence of a library, and so forth. Nonetheless, he was determined to persevere, adding that he would gladly address the difficulties he was to encounter. On the eve of his departure to Berlin, he wrote that although Palestine was not the anti-Semitic and persecutory Germany of 1933, it was not a land of peace and tranquility. His departure was delayed, however, because on November 2, the anniversary of the Balfour Declaration, the Arab community of Palestine staged a protest strike, accompanied by rioting. He wrote that Arab opposition in Palestine was growing stronger.[114] His remarks were not far from the truth: in early 1936 Arab nationalists sparked violent riots that plunged the entire country into the chaos of civil war – the "Troubles" or Arab Revolt – which lasted until the spring of 1939. On December 31, 1933, Max and Mirra Eitingon left Germany for good, traveling via Saint-Jean-Cap-Ferrat on the French Riviera, where they took an extended vacation before leaving for Palestine in April 1934. While there, Eitingon received a letter from Schalit informing him that Freud had proposed not Eitingon himself, but rather Wulff, as a candidate to run the psychoanalytic chairmanship at the Hebrew University.[115] Whatever Freud's reasons,[116] this was a bitter revelation. It is reasonable to assume that he began to feel jealousy and mistrust towards Wulff. Notably, Wulff himself evidently said nothing during his stay in Palestine in autumn 1933. This affair is presumably related to the deterioration of relations between the two after October 1934. We will return to this matter.

The Founding of the Palestine Psychoanalytic Society (Chevra Psychoanalytit BeEretz Israel)

The bylaws of the Palestine Psychoanalytic Society, the twelfth Psychoanalytic Society to be recognized by the International Psychoanalytic Association, were written in German by Max Eitingon during his final days in Berlin, before leaving Germany for good in late December 1933.

On January 11, 1934, after Moshe Wulff accepted the bylaws (which Eitingon had sent him by mail), Eitingon presented them to the local authorities in two versions: one in Hebrew, apparently translated from German by David Idelsohn, and a second edition in English. To these documents Eitingon attached an initial action plan for the new organization. He also sought Wulff's opinion about the appointment of Freud, his daughter Anna, and Montague David Eder as honorary members of the Society, and Wulff naturally concurred.

The founders and honorary guests participated in the opening ceremony and first official gathering of the Society on May 5, 1934, one day before Freud's birthday. Eitingon opened the ceremony with some "Freudiana" – that is, a lecture praising Freud personally as well as his work. The first members of the Society were then presented: active members, permanent members, and guest members – Siegfried van Vriesland, Arnold Zweig, Martin Pappenheim – as well as honorary members – Sigmund Freud, Anna Freud, and Montague David Eder. Agenda items included membership dues, the dues that the society had to pay to the International Psychoanalytic Association, the objectives of their work, the Society's schedule of future activities, questions related to the International Training Commission (ITC), relations with other psychoanalytic societies abroad, and the training of analysts. Thus began a new chapter in the history of psychoanalysis. The psychoanalysts who arrived from Germany, the new expatriates, were the ones who laid the foundation for the institutionalization of psychoanalysis in Palestine. Moshe Wulff, who had arrived in March 1933, and began to consolidate a group of people interested in psychoanalysis, particularly among pedagogic circles in Tel Aviv. We will return to this figure in the second half of the book.

As noted, Max Eitingon, who had settled in Palestine a year earlier, sought to create a second "bastion" of psychoanalysis in Jerusalem. Given his prestige as a senior and skilled official within the German psychoanalytic movement and the International Psychoanalytic Association, as well as the funds at his disposal for financing new posts in a future psychoanalytic institute, he sought to reproduce the legendary Berlin experiment in Jerusalem. Towards this end, he relied on the presence and assistance of a number of young intellectuals who had arrived from Germany, where they had already undergone some training under the auspices of the German Psychoanalytic Society (Deutsche Psychoanalytische Gesellschaft). The news of Eitingon's having settled in Jerusalem and of the founding of a psychoanalytic society in Palestine spread quickly among the psychoanalytic communities of Europe and drew the attention of German Jewish psychoanalysts who had not yet managed to leave Germany or find temporary asylum in other European countries. The presence of such a prominent figure from the international psychoanalytic movement attracted many Freudians: analysts, candidates at various stages of training, patients, and supporters of the Freudian movement all sought to make contact with Eitingon so as to explore the possibility of continuing their professional activities, their training, or their therapy in Palestine. Non-Jewish physicians and psychoanalysts in Germany referred their Jewish patients, who were forced to leave their country, to Eitingon. Physicians residing in other European countries, such as France, England, and the Netherlands, referred family members or longtime patients to him, whether for treatment on his own couch in Jerusalem, or in order that he provide them with the names of analysts receiving patients in other cities in Palestine. Eitingon's personal archives, which I was fortunate enough to peruse, contain a vast number of letters expressing such requests.

Shortly after settling in Jerusalem, Eitingon instituted a seminar on psychoanalytic technique at his home in the neighborhood of Talbieh. The gatherings took place every Wednesday, in accordance with the tradition Freud had initiated in Vienna in the early days of psychoanalysis.[117] We know from Gumbel's records that Eitingon advised his students to intervene during the course of a session, rather than wait until the end to offer patients their interpretations and observations. Gumbel, who was influenced by Eitingon, wrote, "I have come to realize that it is not necessary to avoid deviating from the technique, as long as the analyst is aware of the purpose of his intervention for the patient at any given moment, and that more can be achieved with greater intervention. The sense of intervention is not a deviation from the correct path, nor is it a sign of unwanted counter-transference."[118] He further added, "The essential tasks for him [Eitingon] were: to validate psychoanalysis in its entirety, to help disseminate it, and to educate the next generation."[119]

The First Wave of Psychoanalytic Immigrants: Itinerant Immigration

The migration of psychoanalysis was a crucial issue throughout the history of the discipline, and it is at the heart of the history of psychoanalysis in Palestine. To cite only one noteworthy example, before 1933 psychoanalysis had no official practitioners in Palestine. Whatever attention and implementation psychoanalysis enjoyed during the 1920s was, as we saw, thanks only to the "pioneers" and "foreign workforce." Contrary to Eitingon's expectations, which stemmed from his experience in Berlin, very few psychoanalysts were able to complete their training quickly at the Psychoanalytic Institute in Jerusalem.

From 1933 psychoanalysts began migrating to Palestine, mainly from Germany. At the same time, some members of the Vienna Psychoanalytic Society did arrive from Austria: Martin Pappenheim in 1933 and Lili Peller-Roubiczek in 1934. Other Austrian psychoanalysts began arriving in large numbers after 1938, when the Nazi army invaded Vienna and declared the Anschluss (annexing Austria to Germany) (see Chapter 4).

The reasons why certain German psychoanalysts decided, after March 1933, to emigrate to Palestine rather than Britain or the United States are complex and difficult to identify. Evidently there was no ideological, financial, familial, professional, or other motive that provided a common denominator for this migratory influx of psychoanalysts except, perhaps, for the presence of Eitingon and the news of a new "bastion" of psychoanalysis in Jerusalem. In any event, these immigrants were following their own singular destinies, which often intersected when it came to fundamental issues (such as Zionism or the relation of training to psychoanalysis).

There is another decisive factor that allows us to better describe the conditions surrounding psychoanalytic practice in the early 1930s. A letter from Wulff to Gumbel reveals the following information, of particular value for our study: Wulff wrote that the only individuals permitted to practice psychoanalysis privately were those with the necessary title (a medical degree) as well as permission from government authorities.[120] I was unable to discover who enacted this peculiar law, given that before 1933 psychoanalysts were not employed in medical facilities in Palestine, and this law prohibited anyone who is not a physician from practicing psychoanalysis. Nor is it clear to me why neither Wulff himself, who reported on these regulations, nor Eitingon implemented these provisions even though, as leaders of the Palestine Psychoanalytic Society, they must have been involved in this issue. Moreover, during the years 1933-1953,[121] psychoanalytic training was not reserved solely for physicians; on the contrary, arguably it was the psychoanalytic training of pedagogues – without any medical skills – that justified the existence of two institutes, in Jerusalem and Tel Aviv.

Only in 1943, after Eitingon's death in July of that year – and regardless of any government or legal regulation – did Gershon Barag, Wulff's main rival within the Palestine Psychoanalytic Society, fiercely advocate that psychoanalysis be reserved for physicians only. Likewise, as president of the

Israel Psychoanalytic Society, in 1953 Erich Gumbel insisted, in opposition to Eitingon (who had managed to sustain a status quo of sorts that allowed European psychoanalysts recognized by the Palestine Psychoanalytic Society to practice), that only physicians be permitted to practice psychoanalysis. His stance led to direct confrontations with Wulff and other Society members who lacked medical training.

The Early Years of the Palestine Psychoanalytic Society and the Psychoanalytic Institute in Jerusalem

The minutes from the meetings of the Palestine Psychoanalytic Society, as published in the *International Journal of Psycho-Analysis*, offer a fairly precise picture of the Society's activity. After its founding, in May 1934, Eitingon initiated its first activities. On July 7, 1934, Killian Bluhm launched a series of lectures, starting with a presentation involving a case of depression, followed by discussion among members.[122]

On July 21, 1934, replying to a letter Freud had written in May,[123] Eitingon wrote that he was confirming his attendance at the upcoming Congress in Lucerne, and he provided an initial survey of the state of affairs of psychoanalysis in Palestine. He related that he was "generally satisfied with my overall situation in Palestine," adding, "My work is not going badly, and I already have a few patients. I am slowly preparing the Institute [in Jerusalem]. Given that these issues have received no recognition here, there are no clear legal norms or, indeed, any norms whatsoever. I must proceed with extreme caution so that no obstacle suddenly emerges in my path from behind some bush."

The following month Eitingon traveled to Lucerne to attend the XIIIth Psychoanalytic Congress (August 26-31), as both the chairman of the International Training Commission (ITC) and the president of the newly founded Palestine Psychoanalytic Society.

The Congress in Lucerne was of paramount importance because it constituted the first gathering of exiled German Jewish psychoanalysts since the Nazi rise to power. It was also important to Eitingon himself because his attendance reaffirmed his place in the upper echelons of the International Psychoanalytic Association, where he had served as president until 1932. He was also the only representative of the Palestine Psychoanalytic Association,[124] and thus, for the second time in the history of psychoanalysis, an analyst from Jerusalem was representing Palestine at the International Psychoanalytic Congress.[125]

Participation by members of the Palestine Psychoanalytic Society in the meetings of the International Psychoanalytic Association had long been quite limited, for several reasons: political instability; the difficulty of leaving and returning to Palestine freely because of British entry restrictions after the closure of borders during World War II and the outbreak of the War of Independence in 1948; the limited number of analysts who formed the Palestine Psychoanalytic Society; their need to reorganize their personal and professional lives in a new and difficult country; the lack of sufficient personal resources; and the economic difficulties facing the country. The Lucerne Congress marked an important milestone: on the one hand, the Palestine Psychoanalytic Society was accepted into the International Psychoanalytic Association; on the other, Eitingon also managed to have the guidelines of the International Training Commission, which regulated the training of psychoanalysts, officially adopted. Henceforth, any psychoanalytic institute that sought official recognition from the Association needed first to obtain approval from the ITC. Furthermore, analysts who were members of a psychoanalytic institute recognized by the Association were prohibited from participating in the formation of another institute or in the activities of an institute not recognized by the ITC. The ITC did not, however, object to having recognized analysts engage in teaching activities in educational institutions, such as schools, universities, academies, and the like. During that year, 1934, the ITC only granted permission to engage in psychoanalytic training to nine psychoanalytic institutes, including the Berlin and Jerusalem institutes.

The rules promulgated at the time by the ITC regarding the training of analysts are particularly interesting, as all the psychoanalysts of the Palestine Psychoanalytic Society had to obey them: although each psychoanalytic institute could choose its own faculty, it had to abide by the training guidelines of the ITC. The criteria for admission to an analytical training program, which applied to all institutes recognized by the Association, including the Palestine Psychoanalytic Society, stipulated that the candidate must demonstrate maturity, a heightened sense of responsibility, and skills and knowledge in the field of psychology. Thus, the Jerusalem Institute accepted candidates who had undergone medical training, as well as non-physicians who had acquired an advanced academic education and were able to demonstrate knowledge of biology, physiology, psychopathology, and medical pedagogy.[126] Applicants with severe neurotic disorders were rejected. Moreover, the accreditation of a candidate required not only treatment or Supervision with a selected and officially authorized analyst; it also required individual training within the institution.

The Inauguration of the Jerusalem Psychoanalytic Institute, October 1934

In concluding his speech at the Congress of Lucerne, Max Eitingon invited his colleagues to consider the issue he had raised and urged them to initiate discussions regarding the legislation in force in each of their countries, with respect to both the training and the engagement of pedagogues in psychoanalysis.[127] In 1934 he published a report in the newsletter of the International Psychoanalytic Association on the state of psychoanalysis in Palestine, which included the following passage: "The living conditions in this small country are very difficult. It is much smaller than many of you imagine, but the demands on us are great. We have to be very careful, because some of the demands directed at us are superficial in nature, while others, such as the issue of educating children, are so important and pressing that it is not easy to assume responsibility for them."[128] On October 13 he opened the gates of the Institute in Jerusalem, which was intended to follow the Berlin model. On the following day, the local press reported on the event, and he personally wrote about it to Freud.[129] The Institute offered a wide range of activities aimed at meeting the needs of educational, social, or medical institutions and organizations that dealt with children, especially immigrants. These children and adolescents presented educators, social workers, and physicians with serious problems.[130] According to Eitingon,

> The Jerusalem Psychoanalytic Institute[131] opened in the autumn of 1934. We announced its existence, under this name, to the authorities, and until then we had not encountered any resistance. The public sees it as an institute for work after school, and this

> is for the best. So far, there have been no problems with the Ministry of Education and we hope that there will not be any in the future. Using due caution, I would say that we should be able to train teachers in therapeutic educational work, including analysis of children. Another matter, the question of non-physician analysts, is so sensitive here,[132] that we are forced to ask [those concerned] to trust our judgment for the time being. I hope that within two years I will be able to provide a detailed report on some of the achievements.[133]

Indeed, psychoanalysis in Palestine developed within the field of education. It followed this course because in Tel Aviv, as well as Jerusalem and Haifa, members of the Psychoanalytic Society allowed non-physicians, and especially pedagogues, to receive psychoanalytic training and become "analytical pedagogues."

The offices of the Psychoanalytic Institute in Jerusalem, which became the headquarters of the Palestine Psychoanalytic Society, were located at 138 Abyssinian Street, a beautiful stone house situated on one of the city's main arteries at the time. A path lined with flowers led to the entrance. The house itself consisted of a large hall with tall ceilings and shelves laden with books (acquired from the library of the Berlin Psychoanalytic Institute, which Eitingon owned) as well as three additional rooms where analysts could see patients.[134] The Society held its first meeting at the Institute's offices, where Eitingon delivered the opening speech as well as a summary report on the Lucerne Congress. This was followed by the appointments of Martin Pappenheim and Killian Bluhm as members of the Society (although each also remained an associate member of the psychoanalytic societies of Vienna and Germany, respectively).

A review of the relevant archives further informs us that the Palestine Psychoanalytic Society launched the publication of a psychoanalytic glossary in Hebrew. Indeed, in 1935, Eitingon was invited, as director of the Jerusalem Psychoanalytic Institute, to join the prestigious Hebrew Language Committee. Nevertheless – and despite the concerted efforts of the Yishuv's intellectuals to turn Hebrew into a modern language capable of representing all fields of science, art, literature, and psychoanalysis – German remained the official language of the Institute for many years.

The Training of Analysts and Reception of Patients at the Psychoanalytic Polyclinic

The teaching and training activities of the Psychoanalytic Institute of Jerusalem[135] appear to have been rather limited initially, with Eitingon carrying the lion's share of the burden (and, as noted, hosting a seminar for candidate analysts at his home every Wednesday). At the time, the Institute's activities focused mainly on psychotherapy – indeed, from the outset it accepted large numbers of patients of all ages – rather than psychoanalytic training or research.[136] It became a true center for instruction and training only in 1941, with the arrival of Fanny Lowtzky. At this stage, psychoanalysis in general and the Institute in particular began to gain popularity within the Yishuv, particularly given that until its opening in 1934, there had been no psychiatric or psychological facility that could offer local residents real psychotherapeutic treatment. For quite some time the Palestine Psychoanalytic Society remained the only facility to offer psychoanalytic training as well as psychotherapy (within the framework of the Institute) conducted in accordance with Freudian doctrine. It also long remained the only Institute to promote research on the psyche as it relates to other fields of study, such as social research, medicine, pedagogy, literature, and art. Its members – in particular Eitingon, Wulff, Pappenheim, and Friedjung – gained reputations as exceptional therapists or counselors, and were often solicited by public and private institutions of the Yishuv, including educational and social institutions and organizations.[137]

Two documents published in the *International Journal of Psycho-Analysis* (both of which are well known among historians of psychoanalysis in Israel), in conjunction with the autobiography of Erich Gumbel and reports of the Palestine Psychoanalytic Society, help us shed light on the psychotherapeutic activities and preventive measures taken by the Institute. The first document, a compilation prepared by Ilja Schalit and Margareth Brandt, contains several speeches and lectures that took place in June 1941 at the Institute, on the occasion of Eitingon's sixtieth birthday. It includes two lectures that describe the Institute's activities in detail, as presented by Schalit and Brandt.[138] The second document is an article authored by Margareth Brandt, supplementing the lecture she delivered in 1941, which commemorates the Institute's first ten years of operation (it appears in another collection, published in 1950 in Eitingon's memory).[139]

Many of the patients were new immigrants from Germany and, later, other Nazi-occupied countries: children and adults who were forced to leave their home, often under very difficult circumstances, abandon their language, and endure extreme distress.

The population group comprising German immigrants to Palestine during those years is relatively well defined sociologically and culturally. Regarding the psychological difficulties that characterize it, we have at our disposal detailed information that deserves a brief review. Official Yishuv reports on the health of the immigrants indicate that ties they severed in Europe and their emigration to a foreign country were the main causes of the psychological disorders that afflicted immigrants from Germany in the 1930s. According to studies conducted by Heinz Herrmann, director of Ezrat Nashim, the German immigrants to Palestine suffered primarily from bipolar disorder, neurotic depression, and suicidal ideation. He further notes that a number of severely ill patients had to be repatriated to Germany.[140]

Presumably, a certain number of immigrants from Germany – patients, physicians, healthcare workers, social workers, and the like – knew that the former director of the Berlin Psychoanalytic Institute and Polyclinic had founded a new Institute in Jerusalem in accordance with the Berlin model. According to Schalit, a number of patients who had had to interrupt their treatment abroad were, therefore, able to continue their therapy in Palestine.[141] The analysts, however, also offered therapy in languages other than German[142] and did not only treat secular and assimilated Jews from Germany. There were many patients from other countries in Central and Eastern Europe, including Poland, Russia, Hungarian, and Yugoslavia, and their treatment took place in Yiddish, their native tongue. Immigrants who did not speak German, as well as the psychoanalysts themselves, had to deal with a complex linguistic reality and the inherent difficulties of the Hebrew language. Indeed, Brandt argued that it took at least three years of schooling to become fluent.

Much to the surprise of Brandt and her colleagues, long-time ultra-Orthodox Jewish residents of Palestine also turned to the Institute for psychotherapy. According to Brandt's report, the analysts saw the symbolism offered by religion as a tool of enormous importance in treating these patients, both as a means of explaining the significance of analysis and as a means of conducting therapy. The vast importance that religion attributes to dreams, myths, and even to the myth of the *dybbuk* (possession) is not too far removed from the inherent symbolism of psychoanalysis.

Very few patients were able to meet the financial burden of treatment. Like the Berlin Institute, the Jerusalem Institute also treated patients who were in the midst of analysis free of charge. Some patients, whose financial situation was particularly difficult and who suffered from severe neurosis, even received material assistance: after debating among themselves, the psychoanalysts would decide to intervene and offer funds collected among their colleagues. If we are to believe Gumbel, Eitingon held that just as one must not refuse analysis to patients who were unable to pay for it, so too "analysis cannot be conducted on an empty stomach." Other patients were referred by the Histadrut health management organization to the Psychoanalytic Institute or to members of the Psychoanalytic Society. According to Brandt, the Institute signed an agreement with the Health Fund, under which the latter subsidized treatment for its patients, who were then responsible only for a portion of the cost.

The psychoanalysts of Palestine played a major role in providing psychotherapy to children, preventing psychological disorders among children, and training educators and social workers to work with children who needed mental healthcare. In Jerusalem, children who suffered from psychological disorders were referred directly to the Institute by the staff of those institutions where they studied. Eitingon himself took responsibility for the most serious cases. Even when he was ill – and against the advice of his personal physician – or in the midst of a stifling heatwave, he never failed to make a daily appearance at 128 Abyssinian Street in order to see the largest possible number of patients and to guide, advise, and train young educators. During the first ten years of the Institute's operation, a total of two hundred and thirty people – children and adults – received treatment at the Institute. Most were referred by former patients of the Institute itself, with a smaller number referred by their attending physician. A few were referred for psychoanalytic treatment by their physician abroad.

Max Eitingon's Final Years

Shortly after the opening of the Psychoanalytic Institute in Jerusalem, disagreements arose between the two bastions of the psychoanalytic movement in Palestine – Tel Aviv and Jerusalem. Beyond the rivalries and personal ambitions that led Moshe Wulff to distance himself from Eitingon and his supporters, there also emerged profound differences of opinion regarding the very conception of psychoanalysis, its modes of transmission, and the organization of the psychoanalytic establishment. Because of these disagreements, Wulff began to seek his own autonomous sphere of activity, where he could implement a policy that would perhaps be less "elitist" than that of Eitingon in Berlin or Jerusalem. Wulff preferred a form of psychoanalysis that was more open to dialogue and exchange with representatives of other, non-medical professionals, especially the pedagogues who were interested in Freud's teachings.

A sad affair that took place in 1938 disrupted the course of Eitingon's life: a Parisian judge suspected him of serving as an accomplice to the Russian singer Nadezhda Plevitskaia, who worked for Stalin's secret service alongside her husband, General Skoblin, and participated in the assassination of a Soviet dissident who had escaped to France. The trial concluded on December 14, 1938.[143] The singer and her husband received a life sentence, while Eitingon – with the assistance of Princess Marie Bonaparte and René Laforgue, the second leader of the Freudian movement in France – was acquitted for lack of evidence.[144] There remain more than a few mysteries and question marks surrounding the life and personality of Eitingon, but there is at present no basis to assume that he collaborated directly or indirectly with the Soviet secret service. At the same time, it is worth noting that his stepson, Yuli Khariton (1904-1996), was one of the architects of the Soviet nuclear program and is regarded as "the father of the Soviet atom bomb." The Soviet secret service monitored Max and Mirra Eitingon closely, but this does not mean that they themselves served in the Soviet secret service (NKVD).[145]

After 1938 Eitingon did not leave Palestine ever again, and a dark cloud settled over his life as a result of several factors: Austria's annexation to Germany (the Anschluss) and the consequent threat to Freud in the psychoanalytic community of Vienna; the dispute with Wulff; the state of health of his loyal friend Arnold Zweig,[146] who was injured in a car accident; the dire news from Germany regarding the situation of Jews there; the confiscation of the hospital his father had founded in Leipzig and the arrest of its Jewish physicians; and the burning down of the Etz Chaim synagogue in Leipzig, also founded by his father, in 1922, in memory of his deceased wife. All these were compounded by severe financial hardship and his deteriorating health.[147]

The year 1939 brought Eitingon more bad news: the passing of Freud in September, the outbreak of World War II, and the suicide of his dear friend Siegfried van Vriesland, all of which affected him deeply.

Max Eitingon during the War: League V

On June 22, 1941, four million German soldiers and their allies invaded the Soviet Union. Faced with the rapid advance of the German army into Soviet territory, Stalin called on Western Allies and the entire world to help the Soviet Union stop this "fascist monster" that managed to reach the outskirts of Moscow within four months. The assault on Moscow failed. But in July 1942 the German army launched a major offensive against the city of Stalingrad, and before long German forces were able to capture four-fifths of the city.

Stalingrad became a symbol of resistance to fascism. Military experts predicted that the Red Army would soon crumble in the face of the powerful German military and its allies. But in 1943 Soviet forces were able to repel the Nazi offensive and turn the tables. The German forces in Stalingrad surrendered, and the city's heroic stance made a great impression on the entire free world. The Jewish community in Palestine mobilized to assist the Red Army, and political figures as well as intellectuals, including psychoanalysts, were very proactive in enlisting support for the Soviet war effort.

In response to Stalin's call of August 1941, the actor and director of the Yiddish Theater in Moscow, Solomon Mikhoels,[148] established the Jewish Anti-Fascist Committee in October 1941 with the aim of mobilizing world Jewry in support of the Red Army.[149] He found a receptive ear within Palestine's intellectual community. Two organizations were founded that year to assist the Soviet Union: the Public Committee to Aid the Soviet Union in Its War against Fascism, in Tel Aviv,[150] and the League for the Soviet Union (known as League V, for "victory"), in Haifa. The legalization of the

Palestinian Communist Party (Palästiner kommunistisch Partei, or PKP), which brought it out of the underground,[151] the March 1942 agreement signed between Britain and the Soviet Union to seize Iranian territory,[152] and the active participation of many members of the political left, (especially the PKP and what was then termed its "periphery," which included leftist intellectuals such as Hugo Bergmann), all contributed to the great success of these two organizations among Palestine's Jewish population. Other initiatives deserve mention as well: the Arab communists of Palestine, for example, also mobilized in support of the Red Army, initially in cooperation with Jewish communists, and later on an independent basis. Moshe Wulff, too, was very active in the Public Committee to Aid the Soviet Union throughout as well as after the war.[153] This committee was more political than League V and included mainly activists from the PKP, MAPAI, and HaShomer HaTza'ir.[154]

League V included two additional analysts: Eitingon[155] and Friedjung. Its first chairman was Arnold Zweig, who had been trying, since the outbreak of civil war in Spain, to form an organization in Palestine to combat fascism.[156] Many other public figures joined as well, taking an active part in various propaganda activities, fundraising, and solicitation of other material support in aid of the Red Army. The members of League V included Martin Buber and Hugo Bergmann, as noted, as well as Henrietta Szold, Judah Magnes, Max Brod, Mordechai Avi Shaul, Alexander Penn, Hanna Rubinah, and David Schorr. According to one of the documents I found in the course of my research, Eitingon was appointed chair of the League in 1943, shortly before his death.[157]

Eitingon, alongside Arnold Zweig's friend Max Brod, was responsible for the League's public relations. He organized a number of artistic and literary meetings with famous artists and writers in order to attract public attention and sympathy, enlist support for the Red Army, and raise the funds necessary to purchase vehicles, medical equipment, and the like.

The League's efforts met with success. Even Aryeh Feigenbaum, to whom we could hardly ascribe any affinity with the Soviet regime, pledged his support: he called on physicians to help create a *cordon sanitaire* ("sanitary corridor" for the safe transfer of goods) between Palestine and the Soviet Union. Thus, by way of Tehran, medicine, medical equipment and staff, funds, and three ambulances (which reached Tehran on April 28, 1943, where they were delivered to the Soviet embassy) were donated in aid of the Red Army.[158]

At the initiative of Zweig, and in collaboration with the German Jewish journalist Wolfgang Yourgrau and several members of League V, an independent German-language weekly, *Orient*, was founded in Haifa in 1942. It focused on the Middle East, covering social, cultural, economic, and political issues,[159] with the aim of becoming the intellectual avant-garde journal of Palestine's German-speaking public. During the few months of its existence, psychology and psychoanalysis held a place of honor among its pages. For example, Harry Obermayer, one of its writers, published an article on "the psychology of the masses" discussing left-wing political perspectives and the theories of Marxist psychoanalyst Wilhelm Reich regarding youth sexuality.[160] Max Marcuse, too, authored articles on sexuality.[161] Much attention was also devoted to the events taking place in Stalingrad. From the outset the editorial board, led by Zweig, made clear its pro-Soviet and anti-colonialist position and fiercely attacked nationalist circles in Yishuv. Adopting a tone that was often provocative or even aggressive, the weekly lashed out at Zionist leaders and Yishuv authorities who demanded that Hebrew be made the compulsory language of youth education in the Yishuv, although many of these immigrants spoke German. It encouraged German-speaking youth to resist the dominance of Hebrew in the education system and cultural life of the Yishuv, sparking the ire of public opinion. *Orient* ceased publication in April 1943. When the war ended, League V continue to support the Soviet Union, and on January 17, 1946, its name changed to the League for the Promotion of Friendship with the USSR.[162]

Max Eitingon and the Egyptian Freudians (1943)

The reputations of Eitingon, the Palestine Psychoanalytic Society, and the Jerusalem Institute spread beyond Palestine, reaching Cairo and Alexandria, where there resided two individuals who were particularly fascinated with the works of Freud, psychoanalysis, and the activities of the Palestine Society.

In April 1943, jurist Dr. Hamdy Abdel Hamid, vice president of the Egyptian Court of Appeals, who was well versed in Freud's work, sought to establish contact with Eitingon through Josef Friedjung. In a letter to Friedjung,[163] Abdel

Hamid stated that he had read nearly all of Freud's works[164] and requested that Eitingon be informed of his interest in participating in the activities of the Palestine Psychoanalytic Society. Friedjung took this task upon himself and invited the Egyptian jurist to Jerusalem to participate in a meeting of the Society scheduled for May 8, 1943.

By the spring of 1943, however, Eitingon was in a poor state of health and no longer engaged in the affairs of the Psychoanalytic Society.[165] On July 13, 1943, he wrote to Friedjung, asking that he reply affirmatively to the request of "Professor Abdel Hamid from the University of Alexandria."[166] Eitingon had actually confused the jurist from Cairo with another Egyptian was also enthusiastic about psychoanalysis, Dr. Moustapha Ziwar, a psychiatrist trained in Paris and Lyon. Ziwar, who was teaching in Alexandria at the time, was a pioneer of psychoanalysis in Egypt.[167] On May 27, 1943, unaware that Eitingon was in Palestine, Ziwar wrote for the first time to the president of the Palestine Psychoanalytic Society,[168] requesting information about the Society's activities and how he might join. His letter remained unanswered, but in the meantime Ziwar learned that the Society's president was none other than the famous Eitingon.

Max Eitingon passed away on July 30, 1943. Ziwar was unaware of his death, and sent him the following letter on August 23,[169] as translated from the French:

> I was pleased to learn that you are the chairman of the Psychoanalytic Institute in Jerusalem. Anyone familiar with the history of the psychoanalytic movement knows how much you invested as director of the polyclinic in Berlin, as well as the tireless work you undertook, in collaboration with K. Abraham, in the development of Berlin's psychoanalytical society. I am grateful therefore, for the opportunity to correspond with a renowned pioneer of psychoanalysis. Personally, I work as a psychotherapist and oversee instruction in psychology at Farouk University and in Alexandria. Although I was never admitted into psychoanalytic circles during my time in Europe, I make extensive use of Freudian doctrine, both in my classes and in the treatment of my patients. I would be sincerely grateful if you would permit me to participate in the Institute's activities and

if you would indicate, if necessary, what the conditions are for joining the Institute as a member by correspondence.

Yours respectfully,
Dr. M. Ziwar

P.S. I would be grateful to learn whether the Institute has a library that contains the works of Freud, Abraham, Ferenczi, and yourself, as well as journals.

Ilja Schalit responded to the letter,[170] providing a range of information about the activities of the Psychoanalytic Society – its members, the Institute in Jerusalem, the library and its collections – adding that he was pleased to learn that there was someone in Egypt so interested in the activities of the Palestine Psychoanalytic Society.

The Death of a Major Figure of the Yishuv

The death of Max Eitingon marked the end of the first decade of a highly successful era in the history of psychoanalysis in Palestine and Israel. The institutionalization process that was now underway, especially in Jerusalem, undoubtedly contributed to the introduction and development of the discipline in the country.[171]

Like his father before him, Eitingon became a prominent figure in the annals of Zionism and a major philanthropist in the history of the Yishuv. Symbolically, he was known in Palestine both for his directorship of the Psychoanalytic Institute in Jerusalem and for his activities on behalf of the Bezalel School of Arts, where he served as administrative director. With his passing, Moshe Wulff indisputably became the leading authority on psychoanalysis in Palestine.

Martin Pappenheim and Freudianism
in Neuropsychiatry in Palestine

The members of the psychoanalytic Society had a vital role in the development of psychiatry in Mandatory Palestine and during the first three decades following independence. Writing about the history of psychoanalysis in Palestine, Heinrich Zvi Winnik observes, quite accurately, that "it was not until 1935 that a neuropsychiatric society was established, following the model of Central Europe, and several of its members received analytical training. . . . Psychoanalysis thus encountered much less resistance then in Europe, where traditional psychiatry – that is, "school psychiatry" (*Schulpsychiatrie*) dominated.[172]

In 1933 Martin Pappenheim settled in Tel Aviv, and his presence had a profound impact on the history of psychiatry in Palestine and Israel. His contribution to the dissemination of psychoanalysis within this discipline was decisive. While he presided over the Palestine Society for Mental Hygiene (Chevra Eretz-Israelit LeHygiena Ruhanit), psychiatrists and mental health specialists were receptive to psychoanalysis and psychoanalysts. The importance he attributed to Freud and Freud's work, as well as his activities as a member of the Vienna Psychoanalytic Society and later in Palestine, played a very important part in paving the way towards fruitful cooperation between the neuropsychiatric community and the psychoanalytic community during 1930-1940. Nonetheless, this cooperative endeavor met with quite a few political obstacles, which deserve our attention.

Before 1934 Palestine had only two facilities for psychiatric patients: Ezrat Nashim, in Jerusalem, and the Government Psychiatric Hospital in Bethlehem, which the British government inaugurated in 1922 and oversaw. Tel Aviv, the largest Jewish city, had no psychiatric facility capable of treating people with mental health issues, despite the large number of immigrants, particularly from Poland, who settled in and around the city beginning in 1924 (with the start of the Fourth Aliyah).

In 1925 Meir Dizengoff, the mayor of Tel Aviv, entered into negotiations with the Mandatory government in the hopes of launching a project for the construction of a psychiatric hospital in the immediate vicinity of the city. The plan was presented to Montague David Eder (who visited Palestine for the last time that year, to attend the inauguration of the Hebrew University). Eder then undertook to raise the funds necessary for this project upon returning to London.[173]

In 1927, Dizengoff, along with Dr. Leibowich, entered into negotiations towards this end with the local British authorities.[174] In a letter to the district governor, Leibowich described the situation as "catastrophic": the city, which numbered 50,000 residents at the time, had no facility that could accommodate or treat people suffering from mental illness, and even if some of the mentally ill could stay with their families or a "foster family," many others were left to roam the streets of the city.[175] But these efforts did not bear fruit.

Dizengoff needed the support of the Commission for the Mentally Ill, a group that had originated as an informal alliance and developed over time into an association,[176] in order to secure permission from the British authorities for the construction of the psychiatric hospital in Bnei Brak. The Institute opened in 1934, with 110 beds: 60 for women, 40 for men, and 10 for children.[177]

In a letter dated July 23, 1933, Dizengoff turned to the newly formed association to advise them of the imminent arrival of the "renowned and highly experienced" Viennese neuropsychiatrist, Professor Martin Pappenheim: he was due to visit Tel Aviv, with the aim of settling in Palestine and working as a psychiatrist at hospitals and as a physician in the city. Dizengoff added that Pappenheim thought a psychiatric hospital should be opened in Tel Aviv and a psychiatric ward established in the general hospital.[178] A few days later, from Haifa, Pappenheim sent Israel Rokach, the deputy mayor of Tel Aviv, a plan for the establishment of a psychiatric hospital with 40 beds (a figure regarded as sufficient for a population of 100,000), which would be capable of accommodating dangerous patients. He enclosed a brief curriculum vitae attesting to his extensive professional experience in Austria and other countries, noting his membership in the World Organization for Mental Hygiene, among other qualifications. Dizengoff planned to meet him again to discuss the project and to request that he establish a consultancy in Tel Aviv. But the members of the Commission for the Mentally Ill insisted that under no circumstances should Dizengoff hire him. While in Vienna, according to the Commission members, Pappenheim had drifted away from Judaism and aligned himself with Russian communists – indeed, he had originally considered settling in Soviet Russia. Johan Kremensky, a long-standing Zionist leader in Vienna and close associate of Herzl, warned his friends in Palestine of the "disturbing" situation regarding Pappenheim, at the same time as Shoshana Persitz, a Tel Aviv city councilor and director of the municipal education department, was planning to hire him. Kremensky, alerted by the rumor spreading through Vienna, urged that his candidacy be rejected and another physician hired.

Around this time the Viennese Jewish newspaper *Neue Welt* published a short article titled "Strange Emigration to Palestine" fiercely denouncing the plans to appoint Pappenheim as a consultant psychiatrist for the Tel Aviv

Municipality and granting him oversight over the establishment of a psychiatric hospital in the city. The anonymous author demanded that a psychiatrist "of the Mosaic faith" be appointed, adding that it was inconceivable that a Jewish expert in this field could not be found. Dizengoff and Rokach thanked their informant and promised the association's members that they would sever all ties with Pappenheim. Rokach wrote to Robert Stricker, editor-in-chief of *Neue Welt*, that "our institution does not employ traitors."[179]

Opposition to Pappenheim came from other sources in Palestine as well: the Mizrahi movement requested that the Tel Aviv Municipality "not allow such a thing in the country's first Jewish city." Nonetheless, a committee in support of Pappenheim's appointment, led by Yichiel Heilperin, formed in Tel Aviv. Moreover, the poet Chaim Nachman Bialik, as well as the prominent Rabbi Kook and other figures from the rabbinic world, mobilized in support of his candidacy and requested that the Association work with the distinguished Viennese professor. The Municipality of Tel Aviv eventually conceded to the pressure, appointing Pappenheim as consultant to the psychiatric hospital in Bnei Brak, whose construction was completed in 1934. Pappenheim served as director from 1936 to 1938.

Martin Pappenheim and the Society for Mental Hygiene in Palestine

On March 10, 1936, Pappenheim founded the Society for Mental Hygiene in Palestine (which later became the Israel Psychiatric Association), in Tel Aviv, and served as its president until his death in 1943. His name is still associated with this institution. The Society's main objective was to provide treatment for the mentally ill, regardless of religion, and it operated within the framework of the World Organization for Mental Hygiene. In his opening remarks, Pappenheim praised the figure and genius of Freud, who "contributed to the advancement of science by identifying, during early childhood years, the psyche responsible for a person's normal or pathological mental health." The Society's first meeting included psychoanalysts, pedagogues, social workers, jurists, and members of the Jewish, Arab, and British communities of Palestine. A number of these participants were elected to the board of directors.

Over time, members of the Palestine Neuropsychiatric Society and neuropsychiatrists who had settled in Palestine during the 1930s joined the

Palestine Mental Hygiene Society. These included, in particular, Lippman Heilpern, who headed the Department of Neurology at Hadassah Hospital, Kurt Lowenstein, Otto Feldman, Arnold Kutschinski, Simon Fleischman, a Mr. Binyamin, and Dr. Moses, a child psychiatrist who adhered to the theories of Alfred Adler. Several members of the Palestine Psychoanalytic Society also participated in the activities of the Mental Hygiene Society: Pappenheim, naturally, as well as Daniel Dreyfuss, Shlomo Rothschild, Aaron Isserlin, Karl Gross, Abraham Weinberg, Abraham Schossberg, and Moshe Wulff, who, along with other figures from the psychoanalytic world, founded the Society for Child Psychiatry in 1941.

From 1934 until his death in November 1943, Martin Pappenheim was the most prominent figure in the world of psychiatry and mental health in Palestine. He was the main instigator of interaction between the world of psychiatry and the world of psychoanalysis, and throughout the years 1930-1940 he managed to sustain a level of virtually unparalleled partnership and collaboration between the two, while also honoring the uniqueness of each discipline.

CHAPTER 4

The Arrival of Austrian Psychoanalysts in Palestine (1938)

The year 1933 marked the beginning of German Jewish immigration to Palestine by the thousands. The new arrivals included psychoanalysts, members of the German Psychoanalytic Society (Deutsche Psychoanalytische Gesellschaft). In 1938, when Hitler's troops entered Vienna, new immigrants from Austria and Central Europe began arriving in Palestine as well: scientists, reputable professionals, academics, visionary intellectuals, and several members of the Vienna Psychoanalytic Society. The latter, although fewer in number than their German colleagues, would play a crucial role in the introduction and development of psychoanalysis in Palestine. Yet their contribution in the years following Israel's independence has largely been forgotten and remains overshadowed by traditional, exclusively "German" psychoanalysis – that of Eitingon and a number of his close followers, particularly Erich Gumbel.

Why has their presence been forgotten? Why has the invaluable contribution of former members of the Vienna Psychoanalytic Society been overlooked? The prevailing assumption is that Austrian psychoanalysts, in contrast to their German colleagues, were quite politicized, that they were more detached from Jewish tradition and Zionist ideals, and that to a certain extent they were also more detached from the psychoanalytic establishment itself. Rather than address this difficult question, however, let us examine the fate of some of these Austrian psychoanalysts, in particular Josef Karl Friedjung, undoubtedly the most representative of the analysts trained in the Viennese tradition, who arrived in Palestine in 1938.

The Anschluss and the Exile of Austrian Psychoanalysts

If Freud, unlike Eitingon, still believed in early 1933 that psychoanalysis could survive in Nazi Germany, and that Austria would be safe from the Nazi threat, he soon realized the seriousness of the situation facing those Jews who remained in Germany. In February 1938, tensions increased between Vienna and Berlin, and clashes between the local police and Nazi militants on the streets of Vienna intensified. Austrian sovereignty was in jeopardy.

Freud informed Eitingon, who was on the other side of the Mediterranean, of the serious situation in Austria, praising the Austrian government's courageous resistance to the Nazi regime. But on March 12, 1938, contrary to the hopes of Freud and many other citizens, the Wehrmacht crossed the border and prepared to enter the capital. The next day the Board of Directors of the Vienna Psychoanalytic Society met and decided that, "to the extent possible, everyone should flee the country and the headquarters of the Society should be relocated to the city where Freud settles." Freud, who attended this meeting, added the following interpretation as recorded by Jones: "After Titus destroyed the Temple in Jerusalem, Rabbi Yochanan Ben-Zakai sought permission to open a school for the study of Torah in Yavneh. We will do the same. We are, after all, accustomed to being persecuted, given our history, our traditions, and the personal experience of some of us."[180]

The Nazi presence in Vienna aroused a great deal of concern among Freud and his colleagues, within the psychoanalytic community generally, and within the psychoanalytic community in Palestine. It marked the beginning of long, agonizing weeks for Freud, his family, and his Jewish colleagues, who encountered many difficulties trying to leave Austria. Anna Freud, Dorothy Burlingham, Ernest Jones, Max Eitingon, and in particular Princess Marie Bonaparte made a concerted effort to help Freudian Jews and their families.

On March 26, Eitingon sent a brief letter to Freud, signed by himself, members of the Palestine Psychoanalytic Society, and several supporters:

Dear, very dear Professor,

We learned with great sorrow of the profanation of Vienna, of the destruction of our Viennese association, [our] mother and constantly rejuvenated source of knowledge and analytic activity. But we are glad that you and Anna are leaving the soil of these sacred ruins. Our ardent wishes accompany you and we hereby pledge to do everything in our power to defend you and pursue what you have created, which is also the substance of our lives.[181]

Freud as a Hostage of the Gestapo

Freud and his family did not, however, depart Austria as quickly as anticipated. Between March and June 1938, the psychoanalytic movement experienced one of the most dramatic episodes in its history: the Nazis destroyed the Vienna Psychoanalytic Society, and simultaneously Freud and his family, threatened by the Gestapo, were prevented from leaving the country.

Initially, during the troubled days of March 1938, Freud was able to maintain a state of relative calm and serenity. With his daughter Anna, he devoted some of his time to producing a German translation of a book by Marie Bonaparte dedicated to her dog, Topsy. Even when the Nazi police burst into his home and confiscated what little money he had, he remained impassive. He only realized how dangerous the situation facing himself and his family was during the last week of March, after Gestapo agents arrested his children, Martin and Anna, and interrogated them for several hours in the Gestapo's Vienna offices before releasing them. In late March Eitingon shared his concerns with his colleague Jones, namely, that Carl Müller Braunschweig and members of the German Psychoanalytic Society (Deutsche Psychoanalytische Gesellschaft) – that is, the management of the Göring Institute (named after Hermann Göring's cousin), which had appropriated the Berlin Psychoanalytic Institute in 1933 – would also appropriate the offices of the Vienna Psychoanalytic Society as well as the publishing house of the International Psychoanalytic Association, the Verlag. Subsequently, through his son Martin, Freud asked Eitingon to consider transferring the publishing house to the Netherlands or Palestine. Eitingon promised to give the matter serious attention along with the prominent editor and publisher Zalman Schocken, his neighbor in Jerusalem.

The Exile of Freud

Upon her return to Vienna on April 11, Marie Bonaparte entered into direct negotiations with the Nazis: she proposed settling the debts of the Verlag, and in exchange they would permit Freud and his family to leave Austria. She made it clear that she would not transfer any funds until Freud and his entire family had crossed the Austrian border. Three weeks later, on April 13,[182] Jones delivered the good news to Eitingon: Freud and his family had received passports and permits to leave Austria. They were scheduled to depart for London, by way of Paris, on May 22.

Then came a dramatic reversal: Gestapo agents in Vienna prevented Freud's departure from the country, holding him hostage and asserting that he was responsible for the debts of the Verlag and the International Psychoanalytic Association. The Gestapo refused to provide train tickets for Freud and his family unless the debt was immediately settled in German marks and transferred to a bank account in Germany.

Once again it was Marie Bonaparte who stepped in, enabling Freud and some of his family members to leave Austria. She intervened at the diplomatic level by involving William Bullit, the US ambassador in Vienna, and she personally paid the ransom demanded by the Nazis to release Freud. Along with some of his family,[183] he departed Vienna for London on June 3, accompanied by Marie Bonaparte. In order to receive his exit visa, he had to sign the following statement: "I, the undersigned, Professor Freud, hereby certify that after the Anschluss of Austria by the German Reich, I was treated by the German authorities, and the Gestapo in particular, with all due respect and consideration in light of my scientific reputation, that I was able to pursue my activities as I wished, that I was able to count on everyone's support, and that I have no cause to complain. I can cordially recommend the Gestapo to all."[184]

A few days after Freud's arrival in London, many prominent figures who held the father of psychoanalysis in high esteem paid him a visit. One of these was Chaim Weizmann, who expressed admiration and gratitude for his loyalty.

The Destruction of the Verlag

Although Freud and his family were able to escape the trap set by the Nazis, thanks to Marie Bonaparte's intervention, the fate of the Internazionaler psychoanalytischer Verlag – the publishing house of the International Psychoanalytic Association – was a different story. Through their consular representatives abroad, the Third Reich officials stationed in Vienna pursued the Verlag's debtors wherever they were, including Max Eitingon and Gershon Barag in Palestine. Salman Schocken was unable to purchase the publishing house because the Nazis destroyed it. This was a serious blow for Freud, as Jones underscored. Eventually the British publisher John Rodker, who met Freud shortly after the latter's arrival in London, founded the Imago Publishing

Company with the aim of publishing the journals of the International Psychoanalytic Association and the writings of Freud.

Preparation for Emigration

As early as March 1938, Anna Freud, in collaboration with Ernest Jones, Marie Bonaparte, Max Eitingon, and other figures from the international psychoanalytic movement in Europe and America, arranged for the exit of Jewish Austrian psychoanalysts,[185] including emigration to Palestine for some of them. As Jones reported to Eitingon at this time, seventy-eight members and eighteen candidate members of the Vienna Psychoanalytic Society were desperately seeking to leave Austria, and most were being denied entry visas to countries such as France, the Netherlands, Switzerland, and Sweden.

Jones then sought to contact Chaim Weizmann and seek his intervention on behalf of Austrian psychoanalysts, to enable their immigration to Palestine. Weizmann, however, was not in England at the time. Jones managed to meet with Professor Selig Brodetzky, Weizmann's deputy, who informed him on behalf of the World Zionist Organization that he could not intervene to facilitate the immigration of these psychoanalysts to Palestine, as such a procedure had to be arranged with the Mandate authorities. Any application for entry had to be submitted on an individual basis rather than in the name of an institution.

Jones turned to Eitingon to ask if he could advance the funds necessary for entry visas to Palestine for two of their Viennese colleagues. The fee for a "capitalist" or "category A" visa amounted to £ 1,000.[186] He added that Anna Freud would be extremely grateful if he would receive the analysts and candidate members of the Vienna Psychoanalytic Society.[187]

Following Jones's advice,[188] Eitingon turned to the British Commissioner for Migration and Statistics in Palestine, seeking his approval for entry visas for four or five Viennese psychoanalysts and ensuring that they would not be in competition with other healthcare professionals. On May 18, 1938, he wrote as follows to the High Commissioner:

> I have the honour to confirm our conversation of yesterday, in which
> I informed you that the International Psycho-Analytical Association
> through, its President, Dr. Ernest Jones of London, requested me

to appeal to you on behalf of a small number of psychoanalysts in Vienna who wish to settle in Palestine.

The distressing situation in Vienna is, I am sure, well known to you. Psychoanalytic circles have not been the least to suffer. The Psychoanalytic Society of Vienna, as well as its Training Institute, has been closed. The books, the journals, and all the other publications of the Psychoanalytischer Verlag have been confiscated and are about the be destroyed. The entire staff of the Society, the Institute, and the Verlag is without work or help of work. Individual Jewish analysts have been compelled to dismiss their patients. Jews are not permitted to transfer any capital, and if they leave Austria they must do so penniless.

A plan has been drawn up by the International Psycho-Analytical Association for the absorption of the seventy Jewish psycho–analysts in Vienna, in addition to the twenty Jewish students in the graduating class of the Institute, in the various countries of the world. Four or five of them have been assigned to Palestine. The Palestine Psychoanalytic Society, of which I have the honour to be the Chairman, will assume responsibility for them and will guarantee that they will not become a public burden. In their capacity as analysts, they offer no competition to other physicians in the country.

Our appeal to you is to grant four or five psychoanalysts in Vienna special certificates – as explained above, they cannot enter as capitalists – in order that they may come to Palestine at the earliest possible moment.

We are confident that we may count on your understanding and assistance in the tragic position in which our Austrian colleagues find themselves.[189]

In May 1938, a few days before departing Vienna for London via Paris, while she and her family were still under threat, Anna Freud was pleased to learn from Jones that Eitingon was preparing to receive five Viennese psychoanalysts in Palestine: a child analyst in Jerusalem, "who would have to spend six months learning Hebrew," two analysts in Tel Aviv, and two in Haifa.[190] These members of the Vienna Psychoanalytic Society, now destroyed by the Nazis, were especially grateful to Eitingon and Anna Freud for their invaluable support. It is presumably for this reason that Palestine's psychoanalytic community tended largely towards the "Anna Freudian" approach, particularly during the 1940s, after Eitingon's death.

The Austrian Heritage of Psychoanalysis in Haifa and Jerusalem

The First Arrivals

Most of the founders of the Palestine Psychoanalytic Society were Germans who already belonged to a psychoanalytic society or association in their country of origin. As we know, they essentially arrived together, in 1933. This was not the case with the Austrian immigrants. While Martin Pappenheim and Lili Peller-Roubiczeck, members of the Vienna Psychoanalytic Society, settled in Palestine in 1933 and 1934, respectively, and Grete Obernik returned in 1934, most of the analysts in Vienna reached Palestine only in 1938, after the Anschluss.

Among these, Josef Karl Friedjung and Berta Grünspan were probably the most representative of those trained in the Viennese tradition. Yet other analysts, members of the Vienna Psychoanalytic Society, candidates in training, and education and healthcare professionals with close ties to Freud also reached the Haifa port after the Anschluss: Karl Gross and Shmuel Nagler in 1938; Heinrich Zvi (Heinz) Winnik in 1940, and Lizzi Rosenberg in 1941.[191] The contribution of these Austrian psychoanalysts to the development of psychoanalysis in Palestine was invaluable, especially in the field of child psychoanalysis and the "applications"[192] of psychoanalysis in the field of education. Some underwent training with Anna Freud. Moreover, after World War II psychoanalysts from Palestine completed their training with her in London, where she had resided since 1938. These analysts, trained in Austria and later in London, alongside Moshe Wulff as president of the Palestine Psychoanalytic Society during 1943-1953, represented and defended the spirit of "lay analysis" – that is, the doctrine that anyone trained in this discipline, not only physicians, can practice psychoanalysis.

Psychoanalysts on Mount Carmel: The Haifa Group

Anna Freud, along with Max Eitingon, intervened to enable Josef Karl Friedjung and Berta Grünspan, both fervent social democrats and members of the Vienna Psychoanalytic Society, to leave Austria for Palestine. After receiving their entry visas, thanks to direct intervention by Eitingon,[193] they joined Ilja Schalit in Haifa to form a small but very influential stronghold of Freudianism in this northern port city.

Before immigrating to Palestine in the summer of 1938, neither of them was a Zionist. After World War II, however, Friedjung came to regard Palestine as the only place in the world where Jews could live in peace, while Grünspan, formerly an anti-Zionist, became a fervent Zionist after immigrating to Palestine.

Max Eitingon officially announced the arrival of these two Viennese analysts on October 19, 1938,[194] in a statement issued to members of the Palestine Psychoanalytic Society. The statement noted that "Privat Dozent" (PhD Lecturer) Josef Karl Friedjung and Dr. Berta Grünspan would settle in Haifa, and that as analysts recognized by the Vienna Psychoanalytic Society, they would be accepted de facto as members of the Palestine Psychoanalytic Society. Eitingon added that Friedjung, temporarily residing at Kibbutz Mishmar HaEmek, was planning to institute the traditional seminar on child psychoanalysis for teachers (which he had conducted in Vienna) in Haifa. With Friedjung's presence in Haifa and Grünspan's support, a new chapter in the history of the Freudian movement in Palestine began.

Josef Karl Friedjung: The Journey of a Freudian Social Democrat

Friedjung arrived in Palestine in August 1938. He had three causes to which he was committed and which he would defend to his dying breath: socialism, Freudianism, and children. His physical appearance, refined manners, and accent, as well as his love of music and militant and combative character, made him the quintessential personification of Austria and the Viennese spirit in Palestine. Admired or even revered by some, disliked or detested by others, this former Social-Democratic member of the Austrian Parliament and former health official in the Municipality of Vienna succeeded, despite many obstacles, in greatly advancing the psychoanalytic cause in Palestine during his final years. His sworn enemies – religious and right-wing nationalist Jews – sought time and time again to challenge the integrity and destroy the career of this Viennese gentleman, but they failed.

Before coming to Palestine, Friedjung had made extraordinary contributions to the spread of psychoanalysis in the fields of pediatrics and pedagogy in Austria. In Palestine he became one of the great advocates of the analytic cause in the field of education, particularly in the area of care for immigrant children in distress. Nonetheless, historians of the Freudian movement in Austria and Palestine are not well acquainted with the story of his life.[195]

Bittersweet Memories of Vienna

Born in 1871 in Nedwieditz, Czechoslovakia, Josef Karl Friedjung was the third of eight siblings.[196] His father, a tradesman, died prematurely, which left the family without a regular source of income, subsisting from hand to mouth. The young Josef was the only one of the children who managed to leave, departing for Vienna in 1895 to study medicine.[197] During 1897-1904 he completed his medical training as an assistant physician in the children's ward at the General Polyclinic in Vienna. His entire medical career was in the field of pediatrics, and he was one of the first of Freud's disciples to apply psychoanalytic doctrine in this area.[198]

In 1899, under the influence of the socialist leader Victor Adler, he joined the Viennese socialist movement. Friedjung was the first psychoanalyst to participate actively in a political movement.[199] He fought for the cause of "socialist education," believing that it was the only way to achieve the socialist ideal and, accordingly, complete human self-actualization.[200] In 1905, this assimilated Jew, a devoted lover of music without attachment to religious Jewish tradition, married the singer Johanna Neumann, daughter of the famous Austrian operetta composer Alexander Neumann.[201] On his marriage license he described himself as "atheist."[202]

Unsurprisingly, therefore, when Friedjung arrived in Palestine, he was able to identify to some extent with the educational perspective of HaShomer HaTza'ir,[203] although he harshly criticized the movement's intentions of transmitting its ideology and worldview to the children and adolescents of the kibbutzim through the pedagogical and educational methods they had developed.[204]

In 1908, Friedjung, a classmate of psychoanalysts Paul Federn and Eduard Hitschmann,[205] attended the First Psychoanalytic Congress, in Salzburg. Henceforth he also participated in Freud's "Wednesday Psychological Society" and became a new Freudian disciple.[206] He was the first to introduce the new psychoanalytic concept of infantile sexuality into pediatrics. He produced a vast number of publications,[207] in which he dealt with questions of psychoanalytic clinical practice and the application of psychoanalysis in the fields of pediatrics and pedagogy – particularly with regard to sex education – as well as politics. Friedjung was a supporter of Alfred Adler, but he adopted a moderate position in the controversy between Freud and Adler that shook the psychoanalytic community during the years 1910 and 1911: without denouncing Adler, he opted to side with Freud.[208] In 1919 he was elected to the National Council (lower house) of the Austrian parliament, and from 1923 to 1934 he served as one of the assistants of the famous pathologist Julius Tandler, director of health services at the Municipality of Vienna.[209] After the attempted coup of February 12, 1934, which ended in failure, Friedjung was accused of having organized the health services of the Republican resistance and, along with many other social democrats, was arrested.[210] According to the warrant issued by the Vienna police, he was imprisoned at the Wöllersdorf Prison in April 1934 and was not released until June.[211] Although he had the opportunity to emigrate to America,[212] he preferred to go to Palestine and join his eldest son, who was already living there. He left Vienna and pre-war "Old Europe" for good in August 1938.

Eitingon introduced Friedjung to Henrietta Szold, a longtime friend of psychoanalysts. Szold and Friedjung made common cause, both for the welfare of immigrant children and for the sake of peace between the Arab and Jewish peoples and against fascism in Europe.[213] They remained firm friends until Szold's death in 1945. She enlisted him to work with the children of Aliyat HaNo'ar, asking that he train the organization's young counsellors (*madrikhim*), aged 16-22, in child psychology and sex education.

Szold, Friedjung, and the Analytic Training of the Madrikhim of Aliyat HaNo'ar

Aliyat HaNo'ar, an aid organization for immigrant Jewish children and adolescents, is associated to this day with Henrietta Szold. It was founded in Berlin in February 1932 by a Jewish pedagogue, Recha Freier. At the time it dealt with troubled Jewish teenagers who had been orphaned or abandoned by their parents. When the situation in Germany began to deteriorate dramatically, she decided to send these youths to Palestine, where they might find a better future. Towards this end she approached Enzo Sereni, a Zionist leader of Italian origin, who put her in touch with Szold.[214] The scope of Szold's concerns and the work of her organization went far beyond the mission of helping refugee children flee Nazism in Europe.[215]

Beginning in 1933, Aliyat HaNo'ar brought Jewish children, mainly from Germany, to Palestine. But after the Nazi threat spread to other European countries, thousands of Jewish children began to arrive from other countries as well, including Austria, Czechoslovakia, Poland, Hungary, Romania, and the Balkans. They were transported legally as well as clandestinely, sometimes directly and sometimes after a compulsory wait of several months or even years, to one of the settlements in Palestine or to a refugee camp funded and administered by Aliyat HaNo'ar, which dispatched special teams of nurses, physicians, educators, and *madrikhim* to provide assistance.[216] By the end of World War II, Aliyat HaNo'ar had brought 15,000 children and adolescents to Palestine.

Some of those who came from Germany were taken in by the children's village of Siegfried Lehmann in Ben Shemen, and others by kibbutzim, particularly those of HaShomer HaTza'ir, which gladly lent a hand to Szold and her organization. Several children's institutions were transferred en masse from Germany to Palestine, thanks to Szold's efforts. The famous Berlin orphanage Ahavah ("love" in Hebrew), along with all its young boarders and entire staff, relocated to Neve Sha'anan, Haifa. In late December 1938 this institution welcomed a prestigious delegation: the psychoanalyst and princess Marie Bonaparte, accompanied by Szold and Eitingon, paid a visit and decided to provide financial support.[217]

Friedjung produced invaluable testimonies describing his five years of intensive work with the children, adolescents, and *madrikhim* of Aliyat

HaNo'ar. These are available in the collection of documents published in 1950 in memory of Eitingon.[218]

What was the role of a *madrikh* (singular of *madrikhim*) in HaShomer HaTza'ir with regard to the education and personal development of adolescents on the kibbutz? The *madrikhim* were tasked with training, instructing, and guiding these youths through the difficult stage of adolescence; they were supposed to help adolescents achieve "self-fulfillment" as social beings, as human beings, and no less important, as Jews who had returned to their ancestral homeland. For the children, the *madrikh* had to serve simultaneously as an educator, a role model, and a confidant with whom the child could freely and openly discuss any question, including the most intimate. To assume this heavy educational responsibility, the *madrikh* had to receive appropriate training, which only a specialist in child and adolescent psychology could provide. Friedjung provided instruction for the *madrikhim* of Aliyat HaNo'ar as well as those of HaShomer HaTza'ir (whose kibbutzim received young immigrants) and offered them training in sex education.

Between 1940 and 1945, throughout the cold, wet winters and the blistering summers, Friedjung, despite his age, tirelessly traveled to dozens of kibbutzim and centers for children and adolescents across northern Palestine to train *madrikhim* and lend an ear to immigrant children in psychological distress.[219] According to a summary report he provided for Aliyat HaNo'ar, he conducted 423 interventions in kibbutzim or at various facilities across the country; 8,265 male and 5,584 female *madrikhim* were trained in accordance with his approach; 400 to 500 *madrikhim* benefited from his personal supervision; and he treated 2,291 children,[220] usually in a tent rather than a clinic and on an orange crate rather than a psychoanalyst's couch.[221]

Friedjung further described his meetings with *madrikhim* and teachers aged twenty to fifty from very diverse socioeconomic backgrounds, and with varying degrees of religious identification. Many *madrikhim* showed great enthusiasm for their role as educators, while others strongly disliked their work. He also reported meeting *madrikhim* who suffered from severe neurosis or schizophrenia.[222]

He underscored that the expectations among *madrikhim* were disproportionate to what he could provide, and that his work had been a source of disappointment, especially for *madrikhim* trained at kibbutzim or by religious Zionist organizations. Some openly and rather arrogantly questioned whether the training he offered actually had any relevance: "What can this new immigrant, with no experience in this country, possibly offer us?"[223] The *madrikhim* of religious Zionist organizations objected far more than the others to psychoanalytic teachings in the area of sex education generally and with respect to their young pupils specifically. Friedjung's activities, unique personality, and thinking sparked a great deal of protest among many *madrikhim*, and Aliyat HaNo'ar officials seriously considered putting an end to his educational endeavor. The *madrikhim*'s organizing committee of the German Jewish settlements in Palestine (an aid organization for German immigrants), for example, tried to have his work terminated, arguing on the one hand that he did not speak Hebrew – although some of the *madrikhim* did not speak German – and on the other hand that he had only approached kibbutz *madrikhim* while ignoring the religious *madrikhim* who attended his sex education seminar. In any event, as there was no suitably qualified replacement, it was decided not to suspend Friedjung's work. Shmuel Golan, whose opinion was sought in this regard, intervened on behalf of Friedjung and evidently tipped the balance in favor of continuing the latter's activities.[224]

Like Martin Pappenheim and others before him, Friedjung did not lack enemies who sought to destroy his career. He was attacked for having renounced the Jewish religion and for being a freemason (as evidenced by the correspondence that his grandson was kind enough to share). Although misunderstood by those around him,[225] he never renounced his views on sex education for youths or his transmission of those views to *madrikhim*. He bravely and patiently confronted the criticism he encountered and the resistance among *madrikhim* whose ideology differed from his own perspective and doctrine.

Nevertheless, Friedjung recounted that many *madrikhim* benefited from his supervision and were thus able not only to overcome the difficulties they encountered with their young mentors and address problems related to sexuality, but also to find answers to their own questions, which were otherwise ignored or addressed dogmatically.[226] He noted that there was a great deal of discomfort among *madrikhim* regarding youth sexuality, adding that even within the "progressive" and "avant-garde" kibbutz community, *madrikhim* had superficial conceptions shaped by an ideology that camouflaged their individual neuroses.[227] The educational "methods" advocated by kibbutz ideology (whose transmission by *madrikhim* Friedjung criticized) were nothing but the resistance of a "pseudo-revolutionary conservatism." In his view, these methods were intended to preserve the individual narcissism of the *madrikh* and prevent children and adolescents – who continue to flounder with their own questions about sexuality, dependent on the private neurosis of the *madrikh* – from speaking freely with the *madrikh*.[228] These *madrikhim*, he continued, were such prisoners of their own feelings of guilt and anxiety that they could not freely address their young pupils' questions relating to sexuality. Friedjung also helped the *madrikhim* prepare and organize their work, providing them with material on issues related to sexuality and other topics and offering seminars followed by debates, the theme of which could be chosen by the *madrikhim* themselves. One of these lectures – "We and our drives" – introduced the *madrikhim* to Freudian terminology sought to familiarize them with psychoanalytic theory.[229]

Friedjung also received adolescents for counseling.[230] He reportedly adopted a more pedagogical and less psychoanalytic approach with them. Thus, for example, during their meetings he initially sought to assuage their feelings of guilt and anxiety surrounding masturbation, explaining that this was a universal phenomenon. He added the following interpretation: "It must not be overlooked that whatever tranquilisation follows a private talk does not last long, the castration fear linked with masturbation being too deeply rooted to yield to a brief clarification. The fear is ever returning and its infantile roots must always be extirpated afresh."[231]

In his psycho-educational prescriptions, Friedjung adopted a somewhat medical approach to human sexuality. In his view, only through a sexual education that thoroughly explores questions of one's own sexuality, and satisfies personal curiosity, could a child embark on a path that would lead to a fulfilling sex life and a "love ethic" throughout adulthood.[232]

Friedjung's Commitments: Psychoanalysis, Education, and the Struggle against Fascism

In Palestine, Josef Friedjung joined a group of intellectuals of the pacifist left that included Arnold Zweig, Martin Buber, Henrietta Szold, and

Hugo Bergmann, among others. He published articles in the German-language newspaper *Orient*, edited by Zweig. Drawing on the teachings of psychoanalysis, he criticized the education system in Palestine and attacked the pedagogues of the Zionist left and the nationalist right alike.

In his view, education should not be the sole purview of parents and traditional pedagogy, nor can it be seen as unrelated to "psychic hygiene, whose prophylactic value in the psychological development of both the child and adolescent Freud, the great son of the Jewish people, has demonstrated."[233] Education, he believed, had to adopt a "scientific" approach based on the role played by drives and their various manifestations.[234] "Education must not be a private matter, that is to say entirely in the hands of parents, as in the *moshavim* [autonomous agricultural cooperatives], nor should it be subject to political dogmatism, as seen in kibbutzim."[235]

In another article Friedjung asserted that education "must also take into account the foundations of the 'new ethics of sexuality' that Freud identified some forty years ago, a sexual ethic that, alongside the drive, creates the foundation for human morality, education, and serious mental illness."[236]

Thanks to Friedjung, as well as Max Eitingon, Henrietta Szold, and Shmuel Golan, thousands of children were able to find a measure of happiness and well-being in their new home in Palestine, having been saved by Aliyat HaNo'ar from the crimes and horrors taking place in Europe, while their parents and other family members along with millions of their fellow Jews, were being slaughtered in Europe.

Very little information is available regarding Friedjung's psychoanalytic activities Haifa and within the Palestine Psychoanalytic Society. We do not know exactly what activities were carried out by the Haifa group he founded along with Ilja Schalit and Berta Grünspan. However, one of his former patients, Abraham Ben-David, who had survived the concentration camps as a teenager and managed to reach Palestine towards the end of World War II, confirmed that in addition to the training, supervision, and consultation that Friedjung conducted in the Jezreel Valley and northern Palestine, he had a large private clientele whom he saw at his office on Mount Carmel in Haifa.

Josef Karl Friedjung passed away on February 20, 1946, only a few months after the death of his wife. An important figure among the Austrian psychoanalysts who immigrated to Palestine during 1938-1946, he promoted psychoanalysis in the field of pedagogy and education through his works and deeds. His contribution is among the most important in the history of psychoanalysis in the country.

Berta "Betty" Grünspan, a Viennese in the Jezreel Valley

Like Josef Friedjung, Martin Pappenheim, Lili Peller-Roubiczek, and Heinrich Zvi Winnik, Berta Grünspan too was a member of the legendary Vienna Psychoanalytic Society.[237] A discreet woman who left no written works, she was a member of the Palestine Psychoanalytic Society from the time of her arrival in the country, in September 1938, until her death in 1975. She introduced many analysts, educators, social workers, and health professionals to Freudianism. Along with Ilja Schalit and Josef Friedjung, she was part of the "Freudian trio" of Haifa, which brought psychoanalysis to the northern part of the country.

Berta Grünspan was born in 1890 in Niedzybrodie, near Bielytz, Galicia, to a poor family steeply immersed in the values of Judaism. She attended a German-language primary school, but circumstances compelled her to seek employment at the age of fourteen. To help her family finance her own studies, she worked as a teacher for the children of a Jewish family in a neighboring town.[238] With the modest savings she accumulated, she left for Vienna at the age of seventeen to train as a nurse. While working at the surgery department of the Rothschild Hospital in Vienna, her skills were soon recognized and she was offered an important position in the department.[239] When World War I broke out, she volunteered as a surgical nurse on the Serbian front, under extremely difficult conditions.

After returning to Vienna and passing the exams required for high school matriculation, Grünspan embarked on a medical career. She received her medical degree in 1924 and went on to specialize in surgery. Vienna of the 1920s exposed her to the socialist worldview, and she joined the popular Austrian Social Democratic Party. She was an advocate for human rights and the emancipation of women, and she followed the customary feminist practice at the time of wearing her hair short. For a while she was also active on behalf of Zionism, until her Zionist convictions came into conflict with the Viennese principles of social democracy. Later, as anti-Semitism became rampant in

Vienna and shortly before she emigrated to Palestine, she re-examined her views on Zionism.[240] The lively cultural scene and fascinating intellectual debates of Vienna during the 1920s diverted her from her medical vocation. She became passionate about Freud's teachings,[241] and in the late 1920s she joined the Vienna Psychoanalytic Society. According to her niece Tamar Naveh, Grünspan would have undergone analysis with Anna Freud towards the end of the 1920s, while working alongside her at the Vienna ambulatory clinic.[242] In 1932 she was appointed a guest member (*Gast*) of the Vienna Psychoanalytic Society and in 1937 she became an external member (*Außerordentliches Mitglied*) of the Society.[243] Starting in 1935, with the rise of anti-Semitism in Austria, she began to think about leaving the country and decided to accept Anna Freud's proposal to move to Palestine.

Betty Grünspan in Haifa

Following a stopover in Venice, Berta Grünspan and her niece Trude sailed to Palestine on board the *Galilea*, disembarking at the port of Haifa on September 26, 1938. Ilja Schalit offered her guidance during her early days in the country.[244] Berta (henceforth known as Betty) Grünspan settled in Haifa and began to study Hebrew intensively. According to Shmuel Nagler, it took her only two years to master the language and become one of the few immigrants of the Fifth Aliyah who was soon able to read books in Hebrew.[245] In November she visited Max and Mirra Eitingon in Jerusalem.[246] Following this visit Eitingon confided to Schalit that Grünspan's presence in Haifa would undoubtedly contribute greatly to the Palestine Psychoanalytic Society specifically and to the Freudian movement in Palestine generally.

Betty Grünspan devoted most of her time to seeing her many patients and, along with Schalit and Friedjung, organizing the activities of the Psychoanalytic Society in Haifa. According to Tamar Naveh, her aunt worked up to twelve hours a day, seeing patients in her new office, which she had furnished as elegantly as the one in Vienna.

Upon her arrival in Palestine, Grünspan, as a former member of the Vienna Psychoanalytic Society, was recognized by the Palestine Psychoanalytic Society as a didactic psychoanalyst. Thus she began receiving psychoanalysts in training, referred to her for analysis by Eitingon and Schalit. Some of the better known among them had already begun psychoanalysis or were under the care of other psychoanalysts who belonged to the Society: Shmuel Nagler, Alice Weiss-Stadthagen, Victoria (Vicky) Bental, Reuben Kritz, and Siegfried Flügelmann. She also trained the psychiatrist Victor Magal, one of the first Zionist (and Freudian) immigrants from Argentina.

Grünspan traveled abroad as needed to participate in international psychoanalytic congresses, and she assumed the presidency of the Israel Psychoanalytic Society.[247] She played an increasingly important role in the psychoanalytic movement in northern Palestine after the death of Josef Friedjung in 1946, and more so after the premature death of Ilja Schalit. She was the only representative in Haifa of "old guard" in the Palestine Psychoanalytic Society who was authorized to train analysts, and she was far more involved in the world of psychoanalysis in Mandatory Palestine and Israel than heretofore thought. In 1946 she replaced Friedjung and began hosting the psychoanalytic seminars for educators at her home, in parallel to the seminars run by Moshe Wulff, David Idelsohn, and Lizzi Rosenberg in Tel Aviv and – successfully, as we shall see – by Fanny Lowtzky (with Nagler's help) in Jerusalem.[248] Betty Grünspan regularly traveled to Mishmar HaEmek to teach psychoanalysis to instructors from the Kibbutz Artzi movement.[249] She also conducted analysis or Supervision for many *madrikhim* from Aliyat HaNo'ar and educators undergoing training, whom Shmuel Golan referred directly to her.[250] These included Rachel Manor, Menachem Gerzson, Menachem Ayalon, and Nehama Levy.[251]

In 1954 she left Haifa to live with her niece Hanna on Kibbutz Yif'at in the Jezreel Valley. At Yif'at she received large numbers of educators from various kibbutzim in the region. She continued to provide Supervision, on an individual or group basis, and organized reading groups around the foundational texts of Freud. She supported Shmuel Nagler in his important work with Kibbutz Artzi pedagogues undergoing training at the Oranim Seminar in Kiryat Tiv'on. She was responsible for completing the psychoanalytic training of pedagogues who had begun training at the Psychoanalytic Institute in Jerusalem but had to suspend their studies when the War of Independence broke out, in order to return to their kibbutzim and participate in the defense of the new state.[252]

She stopped receiving patients for analysis in 1959, and devoted herself almost exclusively to the training of analysts, educators, and health professionals. Nevertheless, according to Nagler, though relatively tolerant of kibbutz society and its education system, Grünspan, like other analysts, was very critical of their conceptions regarding sex education and communal sleeping quarters and showers for children and teenagers of both sexes. On this matter, Nagler added, Grünspan held lively discussions with Golan, who was always willing to revisit his conceptions and educational methods in light of her observations and critiques.[253] She also provided psychoanalytic training for physicians and nurses. While living on Kibbutz Yif'at, she regularly visited the hospital in nearby Afula to supervise the staff of the psychiatric department.[254]

In October 1973, during the early days of the Yom Kippur War, most of the hospital's doctors served on the frontline. Grünspan, 82 years old at the time, traveled two or three times a week to the hospital to care for patients and provide moral support for the staff.[255] On May 21, 1975, she died of cancer at the age of 85.[256]

Shmuel Nagler: From Vienna to Jerusalem

The son of Jewish, social-democratic activist parents who had immigrated from Eastern Europe, Shmuel Nagler was born in Vienna in 1914. He studied philosophy and, later, psychology, primarily with Karl Bühler at Psychological Institute of Vienna. At the time he was already a participant in psychoanalytic study groups and was giving serious thought to embarking on the Freudian path. Immediately following the Nazi invasion of Austria in 1938, he emigrated to Palestine and settled in Jerusalem. Upon his arrival, he contacted Max Eitingon, who intervened personally on his behalf by approaching Judah Magnes to request a scholarship from the Hebrew University.[257]

Nagler, a defender of lay analysis, was among the most creative analysts trained at the Psychoanalytic Institute of Jerusalem, where he delivered two lectures in 1941 dealing with child psychoanalysis in relation to pedagogy.[258] In 1946, after undergoing analysis with Fanny Lowtzky and with her encouragement, he left for London to complete his training with Kate Friedlander and Sylvia Paynes.[259]

Shmuel Nagler in Haifa and the Problem of Abandoned Adolescents

Upon returning to Palestine, Nagler settled in Kiryat Tiv'on, near Haifa, where alongside his compatriots Betty Grünspan and Lizzi Rosenberg, he actively participated in the psychoanalytic training of teachers working on kibbutzim – particularly within the framework of the new Oranim Seminar.[260] In an article published in the journal *Ofakim* in 1948, he provided a detailed picture of the circumstances behind the creation, and the activities, of what was known as "the psychoanalytic seminary for pedagogues,"[261] to which we will return. According to him, a group of students from Vienna, who had studied the concepts of psychoanalysis, decided to initiate regular discussion groups in Jerusalem to further explore the field.[262] The group was guided by Eitingon, who tasked Daniel Dreyfuss with coordinating its activities, and the latter proposed reading texts by Freud.[263] Nagler, however, proposed waiting for Fanny Lowtzky, the psychoanalyst who came from Paris in late 1919, to set up a true psychoanalytic seminar for pedagogues under the auspices of the Psychoanalytic Institute of Jerusalem.[264] The aim was to train educators in psychoanalysis, that is, to prepare them for work with the "problem" children and adolescents they were likely to encounter at their various workplaces, whose cases had to be approached from a psychoanalytic angle. With Lowtzky, the pedagogues in training read each chapter of Freud's *Three Essays on the Theory of Sexuality*.[265] Working alongside Mordechai Brachyahu at Hadassah Hospital, Nagler treated a large number of abandoned children and adolescents who would regularly gather near the hospital under police supervision.[266] He joined the teaching staff of the Psychoanalytic Institute of Jerusalem[267] and – as David Idelsohn had done in Tel Aviv – founded a psychoanalytic seminar in Jerusalem devoted to the problem of abandoned adolescents[268] and operating in accordance with the principles of August Aichhorn.

The efforts of these analyst pedagogues on behalf of immigrant and abandoned children not only facilitated the acceptance of psychoanalysis in the Yishuv, they also contributed significantly to the Zionist cause, as Nagler solemnly expressed: "Eretz Israel will be the refuge for thousands of children and adolescents from the Diaspora. Among the hundreds who have come to us in recent years from the forests of Europe or the concentration camps, and among the thousands who will arrive in the future, many suffer from psychological imbalance. The Yishuv will face educational tasks of a magnitude and entailing a responsibility on our [analyst pedagogues] part that cannot be overstated."[269]

Nagler, who never shied away from pointing out the failings of Palestine's education system, argued that it must be adapted to actual needs and the reality on the ground. The country, he added, was not prepared to address the difficulties encountered by immigrant children from Europe any more than it was able to do so for children from Eastern countries or those born in Palestine.[270] He estimated that more than a hundred children, suffering from severe difficulties in adjustment and psychological disturbances, required psychotherapy with an analyst, and that a large number of parents and institutions would benefit from the advice of psychoanalytically trained pedagogues, as only the latter could help them overcome their difficulties. He concluded that, regretfully, the country was badly lacking in analyst pedagogues who could help the children, parents, and educators, noting that "all our efforts must henceforth concentrate on the psychoanalytic training of educators."[271]

Shmuel Nagler was not mistaken: psychoanalytic training for educators was a crucial issue in the introduction and development of psychoanalysis in Palestine. The following chapters will address this topic. Indeed, despite two decades of unremitting effort by Mordechai Brachyahu and Henrietta Szold on behalf of children in need, the country was unable to solve the problem of abandoned children. During the 1940s, concerns regarding the situation of children and adolescents wandering the streets resurfaced. According to Nagler, no institution or kibbutz could accommodate these immigrant children, while a growing number of children who had survived Europe's concentration camps were arriving in Palestine through Aliyat HaNo'ar.[272]

PART II

Psychoanalysis and Pedagogy

CHAPTER 5

Children of the Kibbutz: Pedagogy and Psychoanalysis

Alongside the formation of the first group of psychoanalytic studies in Jerusalem, a second path to psychoanalysis opened in the 1920s, paved by leftist circles and the socialist Zionist youth movement immigrants of the Third Aliyah – HaShomer HaTza'ir (the Young Guard).

The thought devoted to pedagogy on the kibbutz and to the education of kibbutz children is a crucial element of the history of psychoanalysis in Palestine and, to some extent, the history of psychoanalysis itself.

History of HaShomer HaTza'ir: From Galicia to Palestine

HaShomer HaTza'ir was founded in 1913 in Eastern Galicia by a group of young Jewish men and women, at a time when Zionism was flourishing in Central Europe. Within a few years the movement spread to hundreds of new branches throughout Poland and from there to other countries. On the eve of the Holocaust the movement had 70,000 members across the world. Members of the movement began arriving in Palestine with the start of the Third Aliyah, in 1919. The movement gradually assumed a political character, until it became a political party and the third largest force within the Israeli left. Its members were among the architects of a new model of social, economic, and ideological organization based on shared values – namely, the kibbutz.

During World War I these young Galician intellectuals developed an ideology based not on political values but rather on educational, moral, intellectual, and spiritual values. They differ from the followers of official Zionism represented by the WZO or those of the Socialist International and official Marxism. Their basic assumption was that the transformation of humankind and society would occur not through a "dictatorship of the proletariat" but through a profound alteration of human subjectivity, and Jewish subjectivity in particular. In 1925, when like other movements it rallied around Marxism, it did not abandon its original beliefs or plan: to bring forth a new people in Palestine, modeled after the new ideal, workers who would simultaneously be erudite and hard-working, free and free-spirited, in a word – revolutionary.

The activists of HaShomer HaTza'ir sought above all to produce this subjective transformation in themselves, within their own organization. In order to forge their "typology," borrowing a term attributed to Elkana Margalit and Matityahu Mintz, they drew inspiration from a number of intellectuals, including Martin Buber, Gustav Wyneken, Hans Blüher, Siegfried Bernfeld, Gustav Landauer, and Aaron David Gordon, as well as Nietzsche, Marx, and Freud. Freud's writings provided the foundation for the new structure created by the leaders of HaShomer HaTza'ir. As Walter Laqueur points out,

> The romantic enthusiasm that had gripped the younger generation throughout Europe did not spare the young Jews of the Eastern European bourgeoisie. Their early writings are filled with allusions to the religious rites and symbols of youth movements: the "confessions," the campfires, the redemption of the soul. Their meals would have been acts of communion. In the early days the atmosphere on the kibbutzim of HaShomer HaTza'ir differed only slightly from that of holiday camps in Poland. The work on the roads was exhausting, the environment was unusual, but there was compensation: the long nights, the dancing, the endless conversations, the lectures on subjects such as "Eros and Our Society."[273]

The innumerable documents that remain to be explored in the archives of HaShomer HaTza'ir at the Yad Yaari Research and Documentation Center in Giv'at Haviva, and at other kibbutzim associated with the movement, would shed further light on the relationship between HaShomer HaTza'ir and psychoanalysis. Still, there can be no doubt that the movement provided psychoanalysis with an important platform for its development and spread in Palestine.

The Origins of HaShomer HaTza'ir in Galicia

To understand the movement's enthusiasm for psychoanalysis and the extraordinary contribution it made to the development of psychoanalysis in Palestine, we must return to its origins. From the late nineteenth century until the outbreak of World War I, Jews from Poland, the Ukraine, Bohemia,

Hungary, and Romania, infused enthusiasm for Herzl's new ideas, formed large numbers of Zionist youth movements in Austro-Hungarian Galicia.

In 1867, after the Habsburg Empire granted Jews the right to engage in commerce, attend universities, and participate in public life, they began moving in large numbers from the Austro-Hungarian countryside to the major cities of Galicia.[274] The Imperial decree did not, however, put an end to anti-Semitism, which was far more intense in this part of the Empire than in other districts, towns, or the seat of the Empire itself. During the early twenty-first century, therefore, there emerged various organizations determined to fight anti-Semitism, including, notably, one by the name of Tze'irei Tzion ("Youths of Zion").

As early as 1911, under the leadership of Zvi Steiner, high school teenagers in Galicia began adopting the principles of the Polish Scouts movement, itself inspired by the English scouting movement that was very popular in Europe at the time. Through this framework they engaged in intellectual and physical activities consistent with the ideals of fraternity and solidarity, while maintaining strict observance of the rules and principles that, like their penchant for emblems, they had borrowed from the Scouts. In 1912, this small group decided to call itself HaShomer ("The Guard")[275] after the self-defense association then based in Palestine whose members vowed to defend Jewish institutions against Arab attacks, and thus offered these youths a role model. HaShomer published and disseminated a booklet titled *Yizkor* ("Remember"), in memory of fallen defenders of the Yishuv. Like the militants of the Tze'irei Tzion movement, they would meet to discuss the future of the Jewish people in Palestine, but unlike their elders, they held their meetings in the wilderness, outside of the city and away from traditional educational institutions and overly intellectual groups. They also denounced the hypocrisy of their parents' generation, accusing them of ignoring the growing and increasingly extremist anti-Semitism in Polish Galicia.

Their language was neither the German of the liberal bourgeoisie living in major urban centers, nor the Yiddish of Orthodox Jews from their own country and the Ukrainian shtetls. Although those languages formed part of their rich linguistic background, their mother tongue was Polish, and most felt deeply attached to Polish culture, to the events that shaped its history, and to its national literature. Despite feeling consistently excluded from this society and lacking any hope of escaping Polish anti-Semitism, they passionately read the works of exiled Polish writers such as Adam Mickiewicz, Juliusz Slowacki, and Zygmunt Krasinski, whose novels extol the values of their country and celebrate emotion, mysticism, heroism, and nostalgia with an almost ecstatic love for the homeland. These high school students could conceive of no future other than immigrating to Palestine and participating in the revival of their ancient homeland, and thus actualizing the ideals of Tze'irei Tzion. They devoted themselves to studying the history and geography of Eretz Israel, promoting the values of the new Hebrew culture, and deepening their knowledge of Hebrew, which indeed they soon mastered.

In September 1914, Tsarist troops crossed the mountains of eastern Galicia, occupied "Little Russia" (present-day Ukraine), and advanced to Krakow, conquering a large part of the province of Galicia as well as several towns and small villages in Bukovina. Only in July 1917, repulsed by Austrian and German armed forces, did they retreat. Fleeing the Russian invasion, 400,000 Jews from eastern Galicia began arriving in Moravia, Bohemia, and the Austrian capital in particular. The leaders of Tze'irei Tzion and HaShomer were among these refugees. Members of HaShomer, known as Shomrim (guards), organized themselves hierarchically into *gdudim* (brigades), *kvutzot* (groups), and *kenim* (cells) headed by *madrikhim* (movement leaders) – a framework that drew much inspiration from the British and Polish Scouts movements, reformulated in terms of Zionist values. When World War I broke out, this small group of elitist, auto-didactic youngsters, still members of Tze'irei Tzion, argued that the only way to achieve the emergence of the "New Jew" was through youth education.

It was during their exile in Vienna that division took place. At the 1918 Tarnawa Wyżna congress in Poland, the rupture of HaShomer with Tze'irei Tzion was ratified. By the time of the Tarnow congress in 1919, the movement had become completely independent of Tze'irei Tzion and adopted a new name: HaShomer HaTza'ir. It expanded very rapidly, eventually turning into one of the most important political bodies of the left in Palestine and, later, Israel.

Their forced exile in Vienna gave them a platform for meeting leaders of other – Austrian and German – Jewish youth movements and sparked hopes of future action: Gustav Wyneken, Martin Buber, and Siegfried Bernfeld were a major source of inspiration for the young Shomrim. At the same time, they had also become familiar with the socialist theories of Aaron David Gordon, the leading ideologue of Hapo'el HaTza'ir (The Young Worker); Gustav Landauer, a prominent German Jewish socialist leader; and Karl Marx. But imbued with biblical spiritualism and mysticism, even though they were not religious, they rejected "historical materialism" because they believed that genuine revolution must take place through individual revolution, by way of youth education, rather than through militancy, political proselytizing, and the subjugation of the masses. Once they arrived in Palestine, they developed new codes based on other foundations, translating into Jewish culture the concepts they had borrowed from European youth movements. They had their own unique dialect – Hebrew mixed with their original vernacular – which they had already cultivated by 1911 while still in Galicia. The primacy they ascribed to contemplation, introspection, and spontaneity fostered their own sense of self-criticism, to the extent that it became something of a sacred calling.

The Establishment of HaShomer HaTza'ir in Palestine (1920)

The Shomrim were not indifferent to the October Revolution or the Balfour Declaration. These events inspired much hope within the movement but did not convince its leaders to give the signal for a massive exodus to Palestine.

With the retreat of the Tsarist troops in July 1917 and the end of the war, most Shomrim returned to their hometowns; former participants in the exciting developments in Vienna now multiplied the cells of HaShomer, creating new strongholds. The new ideas they brought with them inspired much enthusiasm among young Galician Jews, especially those from Poland, who were eager to attain independence. The massacres perpetrated in Poland and the Ukraine, after the proclamation of an independent Polish republic and the fall of the Ukrainian republic, convinced them of the necessity and urgency of establishing a homeland for the Jewish people in Eretz Israel. They decided to immigrate to Palestine without delay, settling in the Galilee.

It was at the congress of April 1920, in Lvov that the leadership of HaShomer HaTza'ir, headed by Meir Ya'ari, exhorted members of the movement to move to Palestine, join those who were already there, and participate in founding the Shomrim Settlement (Moshava Shomrit) in Palestine. Between 1920 and 1923, several hundred members of HaShomer HaTza'ir immigrated to Palestine, constituting the largest group within the Third Aliyah. These enthusiastic young activists, most of whom were not even twenty years old, arrived firmly convinced that they would be able to actualize the program formulated by Meir Ya'ari, who himself was not much older than any of them. But they encountered opposition on the part of Second Aliyah pioneers who had arrived much earlier and become active in other Zionist leftist groups, and who accounted for a sizable portion of Palestine's Jewish population at the time. The latter accused the Shomrim of engaging in "misguided romanticism" as well as "mysterious and obscurantist practices." Socialist leader Berl Katznelson labeled them fighters in the "Army of the Messiah" while Russian members of the parties Ahdut HaAvodah (Unity of Labor) and Po'alei Tzion (Workers of Zion) wanted to rid them of the concepts of "Nietzsche, Buber, and all this Galician intellectualization."

The Intellectual Foundations of HaShomer HaTza'ir

It was Gustav Wyneken who first inspired HaShomer HaTza'ir's ideologues and leaders in the field of education, especially in the area of "collective kibbutz education": to lend substance to their theories, HaShomer HaTza'ir members adopted his concept of "free autonomous school communities" (*Freie Schulgemeinden*). His program, devised in the framework of youth rebellion against parental authority, bourgeois social values, and the narrow-minded family system, advocated free expression, freedom of spontaneity, and free education for young people.

Wyneken was among the early twentieth-century leaders of German youth movements who argued that adolescence was not merely a period of "preparation for later life and adulthood"; rather, it should be ascribed the utmost importance: during adolescence an individual achieves a "spiritual awakening" and a sense of self-worth. At Wikersdorf, the free school founded in 1906, Gustav Wyneken fought fiercely against the authoritarianism of the official education system, a legacy of Bismarckian rule. His program had no standard curriculum or teachers. Lessons were taught by professionals, craftsmen, and engineers from various trades, and only the students decided which subjects they would pursue.[276] Their "spiritual awakening" (devoid of religious connotations) would take place through a primary relationship with an adult: the child, the adolescent, needs to identify with a leader he admires, whose student and loyal follower he seeks to be. Such a relationship between an adolescent and a leader constituted "the highest form of education a person can achieve."[277] This approach served many reformist pedagogues in the formation of youth groups in Germany and Austria.

As it happens, however, Wyneken's positions were quite close to those of other German youth movement ideologues, such as Hans Blüher, leader of the youth movement Wandervogel ("Migratory Bird"), another source of inspiration for HaShomer HaTza'ir – but only briefly so: founded in 1898, Wandervogel, a movement of young German bourgeoisie, could be considered one of the forerunners of the Hitler Youth in Germany. Very popular and very powerful in Germany as well as German-speaking countries, the Wandervogel comprised leagues (Bünde) similar to those of the Scouts. They promoted camaraderie and gatherings in the countryside, far from the city and the traditional school system. The movement's ideologues were inspired by Wyneken's theories about the importance of a privileged relationship between a teenager and a "leader," but they gave a particular twist to the notion of the leader: a "Führer" – chosen by each nation-state as its representative and granted absolute, unlimited power. Teenagers would blindly obey and unconditionally submit to this idealized figure. Initially Wandervogel's leaders exalted the emancipation of German-speaking European youth, but gradually the movement came to affirm the superiority of man over woman, then the superiority of the German people over all other peoples, and eventually that of the Aryan race over all others. Jews – regarded as too romantic, too prone to intellectualization, and too effeminate – were, like women, excluded from Wandervogel.

The Jewish youth groups founded in Europe during the years 1910 to 1913 adopted the image promoted by Wyneken at the time: a charismatic leader able to win over the hearts of followers by cultivating self-criticism and free discourse.[278] Meir Ya'ari and HaShomer HaTza'ir formulated their theories about youth and education on the basis of this very perspective. Other Zionist youth movements – such as Gordonia in Galicia and Poland, or Blau und Weiss (Blue and White) in Germany – did not have a Führer, that is a *manhig* (leader), but a *madrikh* – a guide, escort, and mentor.[279] In any event, as early as 1918, at the Tarnawa Wyżna congress in Poland, HaShomer HaTza'ir leaders decided to break with Wyneken, who seemed to them "too imbued with German romanticism, too meditative, too prone to sentimentalism and passivity, and also too experimental" as well as "sickly" and "solipsist." In other words, he personified quite the opposite of the heroism and idealism embodied in their vision.

At this stage Siegfried Bernfeld entered the picture. During World War I, he was one of the few assimilationist Jews to take an interest in the fate of youth movement activists from Galicia (of which he was also a native) and of the exiled political party activists in Vienna; he even participated in their assemblies. They, in turn, consistently demonstrated great respect towards both Bernfeld himself and his theories, never forgetting that this great leader, this eminent intellectual, always addressed them, these young Galicians, as equals.

Siegfried Bernfeld: Revolutionary Pedagogue, Zionist Leader, Socialist, and Freudian

Bernfeld (1892 to 1953) was a complex figure: a revolutionary pedagogue, socialist Zionist leader, and prominent Freudian. Never having set foot in Palestine, he exemplifies the complex sources of inspiration that drove the Zionist movement, leftist pedagogues, and in time, proponents of psychoanalysis in Palestine. Many of the latter, while still in Europe, began treatment and training in psychoanalysis under his care at the Berlin Psychoanalytic Institute (which Freud invited him to join in 1925)[280] or that of his colleagues in Berlin or Vienna. By disseminating Freudian theories based on Bernfeld's revolutionary formulations, his disciples – including Grete Obernik, David Idelsohn, and the pedagogues of HaShomer HaTza'ir – managed to introduce psychoanalysis and give it a grounding in Palestine.

He was born in 1892 in Lvov, Galicia, to a family of textile merchants who later relocated to a suburb of Vienna. He attended the University of Vienna , where he studied pedagogy, psychology, and mathematics.[281] His first mentor was the German pedagogue Gustav Wyneken, whose teachings, as noted, played a crucial role in the early ideology of HaShomer HaTza'ir.

Bernfeld's Efforts to Reform Education in Austria: *Anfang* (The Beginning)

In his struggle to promote reform of the Austrian education system, Bernfeld drew much inspiration from Wyneken. In 1913 he founded the Academic Commission for School Reform (Das Akademisches Komitee für Schulreform), through which he tried to promote the ideal of "youth culture"[282] among high schoolers and students in Vienna. Taking into account the unique nature of adolescence, this ideal aimed at establishing an educational program that cultivates self-management, without authoritarian adult intervention. That same year, alongside Georges Barbizon (Georg Gretor) and Walter Benjamin, Siegfried Bernfeld founded *Anfang* (The Beginning), a journal focused on matters related to education, the economy, and politics. They aimed to spread their ideas throughout Austria and Germany and to influence public opinion and the course of events in these two countries.

Jewish high school students then began promoting youth culture and organizing as groups to rebel against parental authority and adult control over education. An elite following of secondary school students formed around *Anfang* and Bernfeld. The journal's popularity grew steadily, as did its founders' enthusiasm, and soon there emerged a youth movement under the same name. Before long, however, the German government accused Anfang and its leaders of propagandizing against religion and against Christian schooling and sexual morality, claiming that they were engaging in revolutionary activities and undermining public order. The journal published its final issue in July 1914.

The Seal of Freud

This brief experience provided Bernfeld with the essential foundations for his "Zionist utopia": the nationalism and romanticism of young Zionist Galatian exiles in Vienna during the war, the adventures of Anfang, new and innovative pedagogical concepts, and engagement with Freud's writings. In 1915 he first attended a session of the Vienna Psychoanalytic Society, and with Freud's encouragement became a member in 1919. Having discovered Freud's theory of the unconscious, he left academic psychology for good. Besides forming an interest in psychoanalysis, while in Vienna he also encountered two wings of the Zionist left: leftist Zionist leaders expelled from Palestine by the Ottoman regime, and young Zionist leaders from Austro-Hungarian Galicia who had fled the Tsarist invasion. His renowned book, *The People and the Youth* (*Das jüdische Volk und seine Jugend*), published in 1919,[283] became a primary reference for the ideologues and pedagogues of HaShomer HaTza'ir who participated in the formation of kibbutz society. He soon came to be known as an ideologue and leader among Jewish and Zionist youth in German-speaking Europe.

1917: the Jewish Pedagogic Seminary (Jüdische Pädadogikum)

With his experience in youth movements, and having identified with Zionism since World War I, in late 1917 Bernfeld founded a Jewish seminary in Vienna to train Jewish pedagogues, building on the new values of Jewish culture, Zionism, and socialism. The students were to apply his pedagogic concepts in Palestine, adapted to the needs of the national Jewish home, which he foresaw as socialist. Bernfeld believed that the seminary would provide Jewish youth with a foundation to embark on *shlihut halutzit* (a pioneering mission):[284] through education, to fundamentally change the religious and bourgeois diaspora youth into bold young revolutionaries who would participate in building a socialist Eretz Israel. This was indisputably one of the most daring and original programs in modern pedagogy. It gained ground in the aftermath of the Balfour Declaration, as it resonated among Zionist youth who had fled to Vienna and with Zionist intellectuals from Central and Eastern Europe, who were prepared to leave for Palestine and take part in the establishment of a national Jewish movement.

Bernfeld believed that Jewish children should receive an education based on the values of Jewish culture and socialism, and the first necessary step was to provide appropriate training to the educators. He personally taught classes in child and adolescent psychology at the seminar. Theodore Reik, another disciple of Freud, gave a series of lectures under the heading "Erziehung bei den Natürvolkern" – which translates as "Learning from the Primitive Peoples."[285] Grete Obernik, his principal assistant,[286] was responsible for teaching Hebrew.[287] Zionist intellectuals across the spectrum also participated in the educational program: Professor Edmond Jerusalem, son of the prominent psychologist Wilhelm Jerusalem, Martin Buber, Richard Beer-Hoffman, Robert Weltsch, Abraham Schwadron (Sharon), Georges Halpern, Markus Reiner, and others close to HaPo'el HaTza'ir gave lectures or seminars.[288]

With the Balfour Declaration and the October Revolution, and the promise of social, economic, political, cultural, and educational reform they brought, the time had come: "Jewish youth must prepare to leave for Palestine. In Zion. . . a cooperative society will emerge," asserted Bernfeld.[289] But the British arrival in Palestine, in late 1917, did not produce the results that Bernfeld and leftist Zionists had hoped to see.

1919: *The People and the Youth* - The Utopia of a New Socialist Society in the Land of Israel

In this book, written during the war and published in 1919, Bernfeld presented, for the first time, a comprehensive description of his "Zionist utopia" and his views on a new educational system in Palestine, which would be Jewish, socialist, and based on collective values. Exiled Zionist activists in Vienna assimilated his theories on youth and free education (which became increasingly Freudian), adapting them to their own ideological apparatus. They saw him as their mentor and a guide towards an enlightened Zionism, more spiritual, more intellectual, and closer to Buber's cultural Zionism than to the bourgeois political Zionism of the WZO.

The People and the Youth, which proposes a comprehensive program beginning even before birth, served as a major reference for HaShomer HaTza'ir pedagogues in developing their own educational curriculum. Every midsized city would have rest homes available for women who wish to reside there, beginning with their fifth month of pregnancy until after giving birth. From the outset children would grow up within an "autonomous society," in a rural environment, surrounded by greenery, gardens, fruit trees, and flowers, as well as animals. They would have playgrounds, event halls, a music conservatory, and a library. Children and adults would enjoy a "free education" that allowed them to choose which subjects to study and how much time to devote to each subject. A range of options would be available to them: history, geography, folklore, mineralogy, biology, Jewish culture, and the like. To design suitable programs, educational research institutes would be established, based of course on the concept of free and independent education, and managed by "pedologists," that is, experts on "pedology" – pedagogy and child psychology. Boys and girls under the age of twenty sentenced by a court would be entrusted to professional education services.

Psychoanalysis would enable them to achieve the goals of collective education. Bernfeld believed that "my method has matured over time. It embodies love and humanity, and pedagogy therefore views it as of the highest value. Psychoanalysis makes it possible to diagnose specific disturbances of the mind, so every educator working with children must be familiar with this method and know how to use it well: thanks to it, the child will receive proper psychological treatment."[290] This was the path that Grete Obernik, David Idelsohn, Yehuda Ron-Polani, Shmuel Golan, and Zvi Sohar followed.

Bernfeld never reached Palestine, although he attempted to do so three times. In 1918, after the Balfour declaration, he was denied an entry permit.[291] Then, in 1920, he considered opening an institute for research on youth at the Hebrew University, to be located in the pedagogy department and directed by him. But disciples who were already in Palestine, including Grete Obernik, dissuaded him, saying that the country was not yet ready for his revolutionary ideas. The third instance was a year later, when Meir Ya'ari, leader of HaShomer HaTza'ir in Palestine, wrote from his home in Beitania Illit to his Vienna-based colleagues in HaShomer HaTza'ir, urging that they not act prematurely in seeking to implement Bernfeld's program: "We are waiting until we settle into the kibbutz and establish ourselves here. We do not want to trouble [Bernfeld] when there is nothing to do."[292]

1919: The Kinderheim Baumgarten and the Psychology of War Orphans

Shortly after the publication of *The People and the Youth*, Bernfeld began to implement his views on collective education at the orphanage Kinderheim Baumgarten, which opened its doors in 1919. The institution, which received orphaned children in Vienna, was the first experimental undertaking in collective education based on the principles of psychoanalysis. It is the model that HaShomer HaTza'ir pedagogues used in developing a curriculum for their "Children's Society" at Kibbutz Beta Alpha.

In 1916 Bernfeld published an article titled "War Orphans" in the prestigious Jewish newspaper *Der Jude*,[293] drawing the attention of assimilated Jewish communities in Germany, Austria, and Poland to the plight of thousands of orphans left to their own fate and wandering the war-torn cities of Galicia. Most of these children, from Bukovina, Moravia, Ukraine, or southern Austro-Hungarian Poland, came from poor Jewish families in the countryside or shtetls – that is, from the Jewish proletariat, in Bernfeld's eyes.[294] Their parents had been killed during the war or the pogroms in Poland and the Ukraine, or had abandoned them because they could not meet their most basic needs. Thus by the end of the war, more than 20,000 Jewish children were wandering the streets of Galicia in desperate need of food, clothing, and education – children who knew no life other than one of poverty, crime, exploitation, and humiliation.

Bernfeld began to mobilize wealthy assimilated Jews: businessman, teachers, artisans, and others. Representatives in Vienna of the Jewish American Joint Distribution Committee (the Joint), an aid organization for war refugees, provided Bernfeld with essential funding for the implementation of his program, and the City of Vienna offered him the abandoned barracks of the former military hospital in the Baumgarten district as a premises. In August 1919 the barracks became available for his use, and on October 15 the facility received 240 Jewish orphans, aged 3 to 16, most of whom suffered from severe psychological disorders. Two months later only one hundred and fifty children remained at Baumgarten; the rest had been transferred to adoptive families in Denmark or the Netherlands. The educational staff working alongside Bernfeld at Baumgarten comprised mostly teachers trained at the Jüdische Padagogikum. In particular, Grete Obernik worked there briefly before emigrating to Palestine. Other participants in this experiment included HaShomer HaTza'ir members such as Willi Hoffer, a veterinary student and former activist in the liberal Jewish youth movement Blau und Weiss in Czechoslovakia. Hoffer, one of Bernfeld's key collaborators, was as interested in establishing a new education system in Palestine as he was in psychoanalysis. He later went on to found a Hebrew-language pedagogical journal with David Idelsohn and Yehuda Ron-Polani, and in time became a major figure in the international psychoanalytical world.

Initially Bernfeld questioned whether it might not be best to return these children to their home villages, rather than integrate them into makeshift orphanages or Orthodox foster families, thereby relegating them to the unproductive religious life of the village or the ghetto. He considered the possibility that they might be better off if adopted by proletariat Jewish families from the poor suburbs of Vienna such as Leopoldstadt, or even Frankfurt or Brooklyn. Eventually he rejected this alternative, deciding the children should receive a secular education based on the values of a new Judaism – that is, Jewish culture and socialism – to prepare them for work in the agricultural communities of Palestine and include them in the construction of the new Jewish socialist homeland. "Eretz Israel will be socialist, or it will not be,"[295] declared Bernfeld, raising eyebrows among advocates of liberal Zionism in the WZO, such as Albert Einstein, and Jewish philanthropists who supported the more traditional curricula of Histadrut HaMorim, the Jewish teachers union in Palestine.

Accordingly, Bernfeld ordered the installation of children's dormitories in the orphanage, as well as a kitchen and a number of auditoriums: one for meals and others for reading, sports, and debates ("the politics hall").[296] In keeping with Wyneken's ideas, and inspired by Wikersdorf's "Free School," Bernfeld aimed to ensure that the children gain a measure of autonomy. He suggested that even the youngest participate in designing their own curriculum, choosing the subjects they would study and organizing the institution's activities and daily chores: kitchen duty, cleaning the auditoriums, finances, leisure activities, and the like.

During day-to-day and school activities, whether at the institution or elsewhere, the children were always accompanied by properly trained pedagogues intended to serve as role models for the children, rather than figures of authority who had to be obeyed unconditionally. In contrast to the mystical Führer of Wandervogel, the leader, or *manhig*, of the orphanage played the role of a mediator between the child and reality, with complete respect for the child's freedom of choice. The *manhig* was expected to accompany the children in mastering their own autonomy in all spheres of life so they could emancipate themselves from adult tutelage.[297] Most of the leaders had been trained at the Jewish Seminary, and Bernfeld himself won the hearts of the suffering children and teenagers. Some even went on to study at the Seminary.

Language was as crucial a question as it was complicated, and Bernfeld gave it special attention.[298] The Polish children, for example, refused to speak Polish, which they viewed as the language of pogrom perpetrators, though they did speak Yiddish, their parents' language.[299] However, Bernfeld and the Zionist activists of the left, especially HaShomer HaTza'ir members, regarded

Yiddish as the language of the ghetto, from which children must be protected. For Bernfeld and most *halutzim*, Yiddish was the language of the submissive, humiliated, and unproductive religious diaspora Jew – representing everything the Zionist activists were determined to fight. All the children therefore had to learn the language of the Yishuv, and Hebrew was made the official language of the orphanage: mentors spoke Hebrew with the children, and Hebrew lessons formed an important part of the instruction and daily life at the orphanage. Likewise, the children celebrated the Jewish holidays, in a warm festive atmosphere with a strong spirit of nationalism. Discussions often centered on Eretz Israel, its geography, its history, and the ancient days in which the Jewish people still resided on this land. The children were instilled with a love for emblems, which Bernfeld had brought with him from HaShomer HaTza'ir. In short, the lives and futures of these young residents were directed towards one objective: Eretz Israel. Bernfeld also borrowed certain terms from the pioneers: children of all ages were organized into *kvutzot* (groups), with teenagers usually taking care of the younger ones; a group of children aged 10 to 14, known as *Histadrut HaShotrim* (the Police Association), was responsible for maintaining order and discipline at the institution; *sikhot* (conversations) were discussions the children conducted completely freely, with the attentive presence of the leader; *asefot* were the gatherings during which even the youngest could discuss all the important questions, such as relations among themselves or daily life at the orphanage.[300]

Having experienced war, pogroms, and complete devastation before arriving at the orphanage, most of these children suffered from severe psychological disorders and difficulties adapting to social life. Bernfeld, aware of this, sought to remedy the problem by drawing on the educational works of Gustav Wyneken, Maria Montessori, and the German pedagogue Berthold Otto, in addition to psychoanalytic theory. He did not focus at the orphanage on child education in the traditional sense, or in making the children "normal," but rather on understanding the unconscious processes that determine their pathological and antisocial behavior. He wanted to offer them a path that would let them become part of society. The portrait he presented of these children was a sad one: intelligent but selfish, antisocial, filled with spite for all others and the entire world, unable to cultivate camaraderie, suspicious, stubborn, and provocative. In particular, they lacked parental figures who would enable them to "transform their narcissistic libido into an object libido" – that is, to invest in people and objects from the outside world. In his view, the orphanage community had to fill the role of the imaginary, missing parent. "The fixed pathology," he explained, "will be released and transferred to the leader, to comrades, to Histadrut HaShotrim, and to the orphanage as a whole." The child would transfer his "narcissistic and pathological libido" onto these "entities" in the orphanage and be able to invest in objects from the outside world in the broad sense – not necessarily material objects, but ideas, culture, the other, creation – and in this way to sublimate his aggressive impulses. Then he will be able to understand the rules of fellowship and integrate into them, learn to respect hierarchy, and have a greater desire to learn. To account for the dynamics of the unconscious processes involved in the psyche and behavior of the children, Bernfeld infused his account of the experimental developments at Kinderheim with numerous psychoanalytic references.

This text, which time has forgotten, has long been one of the main references in the field of psychology and pedagogy of orphaned children. The revolutionary attempt to use psychoanalytic theory to explain an experiment in collective education provided a basis for the educational programs of leftist pedagogues in Palestine, particularly on the kibbutzim of HaShomer HaTza'ir, where children were separated from their parents while growing up. No educator familiar with Bernfeld's pedagogical ideas and his thesis on Kinderheim Baumgarten can ignore the contribution of psychoanalysis to the field of education.[301]

How many children from the orphanage made Aliyah? How many achieved the goals Bernfeld had set for them? We do not know for certain. What we do know is that the young idealists of HaShomer HaTza'ir, who left for Palestine beginning in 1919, carried with them the works of Bernfeld as well as essays by Freud.

Siegfried Bernfeld and the Pedagogy of the Kibbutzim

With the publication in 1925 of *Sysiphos oder die Grenzen der Erziehung* (Sisyphus or the Limits of Education),[302] Bernfeld distanced himself from some of the leading pedagogues of HaShomer HaTza'ir: he discarded his youthful illusions regarding education and his belief in the power of a specific education to bring about a new being. His views were unacceptable to HaShomer HaTza'ir members, especially as youth education was the spearhead of their ideological apparatus, which was already leaning towards Marxism by the mid-1920s. Meir Ya'ari accused Bernfeld of sharing Freud's pessimism regarding the possibility of change. Others, such as Zvi Sohar and Shmuel Golan, defended him within the movement and continued to draw inspiration from him in developing its ideological foundation. Bernfeld's works, translated into Hebrew (alongside those of Freud, Paul Federn, Heinrich Meng, Moshe Wulff, Otto Fenichel, and other psychoanalysts of the left) long continued to form part of the body of texts studied by the movement's pedagogues. For his part, Bernfeld, who did not adhere to the official Marxist doctrine of HaShomer HaTza'ir's pedagogues, opposed the authority and rigidity of the new education system that the movement's pedagogues were implementing on their kibbutzim.[303]

Nonetheless, the psychoanalytic seminars for pedagogic training that Bernfeld organized in 1930 at the Berlin Psychoanalytical Institute were intended for educators who would then help implement collective education on the kibbutzim. Despite the differences that emerged between Bernfeld and HaShomer HaTza'ir pedagogues, he remained a major authority for socialist educators in Palestine generally, and in HaShomer HaTza'ir specifically.

The Cooperative Erotic Society of Upper Beitania (1920-1921)

In April 1920, a small group of friends arrived from Vienna: twenty-one boys and four girls. Among them were Shmuel Golan, Eliyahu Rappaport, David Horowitz, Aryeh Elwil, and other former members of the HaShomer HaTza'ir cell (*ken*) in Vienna. They were to become important figures in the local movement. David Yermanowitz, who had bought land on behalf of the Jewish Colonization Association (ICA) on the hill of Beitania, southwest of the Sea of Galilee, welcomed them. He helped them set up a tent camp, and members of the group helped pave roads in the area surrounding Tiberius and helped dig holes for olive groves.[304] In April 1921, after construction (in which they were supposed to participate) was halted on an electricity plant in Naharayim, and after the roadworks in the area were completed, they were let go. Forced to disperse, most relocated with the Shomriya battalion (in Ramat Yishai today), which was involved in paving the Haifa-Jeddah road.

Amidst this atmosphere of romanticism and metaphysical, even mystical sentiment, Meir Ya' ari founded the Cooperative Erotic Society in Beitania Illit. In a lengthy 1921 circular to HaShomer HaTza'ir members abroad, Ya'ari listed the main points of his concept:

> In our supra-governmental community, where everyone can, as they wish, both release and connect their thoughts, forming a band of brothers, in which boys will declare their love to girls, and girls to boys, inventing their own economic system, their own services, their own education. . . erotic relationships will create a fluidity that will generate a sense of belonging and intimacy. Thus the work becomes an orgy and sublimation of desire. It is the very expression, the imperative from which cosmic love reveals itself, the act of creation. . . . We will allow the eroticism of the community to emerge in our consciousness by being careful and smart, but also by giving ourselves over to such pleasure as we have never known.

These words, which exalt to the point of ecstasy the spiritual and irrational values concealed in man – in this particular case, the heroic Jew – could be attributed to a Hassidic rabbi. Ya'ari's proposed path was not that of Hassidism, however, but a bold invitation to study Freud: "I would like you to become acquainted, accurately, with Freud's works, with his school of thought. I do not know how many of you are able to fully grasp his theory, but I hope that it will purify our charged atmosphere."[305]

Meir Ya'ari

Before denying any Freudian influences (in the late 1920s, having joined the Marxist camp following the failure of the first "community" experiment at Beitania Illit), Meir Ya'ari described how enthusiastically HaShomer HaTza'ir members in Vienna had responded to Freud's works. He himself had attended Freud's classes.

Ya'ari was born on April 24, 1987, in the town of Kanchuga (Polish Galicia at the time) to a Jewish family of Hasidic heritage. On his sixth birthday, his parents moved to the nearby town of Rzeszów (known as Raysha among Jews), which many sources cite as his birthplace.[306] Family tradition was important: the Hasidic movement, founded in the Ukraine around 1750, defied the intellectual and elitist traditions of Talmudic study, seeking to restore the spontaneous and joyful piety of the ordinary Jew and placing all believers on equal footing. Hasidism spread rapidly throughout the Ukraine, Galicia, and Eastern Europe, reaching as far as New York. It enthusiastically, even ecstatically, called for *mitzvot* (commandments) to be performed with joy, sanctifying every manifestation of vitality, even the most banal: dancing and singing, even if not ritualistic, were ascribed great importance.

With the outbreak of World War I, his family moved to Vienna. At age 17, Ya'ari volunteered for the Austrian army, then fought on the Russian front and in the Balkans, serving as an officer until the war ended. Discharged in 1917, he returned to Vienna, where he was appointed leader of the "Nesher" cell, to which two other high-ranking members of the movement already belonged: David Horowitz and Zvi Sohar. Ya'ari began studying agriculture at the university and working at the Wöllersdorf weapons factory about fifty kilometers outside the city. His experience there and what he regarded as the degenerate lifestyle of the young workers enraged him: "There I tasted the proletarian life. I was put to work next to a machine, sweating hard for meager wages, by girls whose sexual mores were quite loose! This was the first time I saw what is described as laxity in relations between men and women. As a *shomer* [member of the Shomrim] I did not let myself be taken in.[307]

These were strange remarks coming from the leader of HaShomer HaTza'ir: far from the typical *shomer* approach advocating sexual revolution, Ya'ari came across as someone with a strict moral code. He made sexual abstinence one of the rules of the movement, whose observance was expected to make it easier for teenagers to approach this "*shomer* typus," comparable to Nietzsche's super-man or the "heroic man" (*Männerheld*) of Wandervogel. As to his last name, in keeping with a fashionable Zionist practice at the time – shedding another facet of the "old" identity and its negative connotations, to be reborn in the new culture of the Jewish people – he Hebraized his name: Meir Wald became Meir Ya'ari.

Ya'ari wrote about himself that he "drank in the fountain of psychoanalysis."[308] But his references to psychoanalysis were always by way of Bernfeld, whom he knew personally from the Jewish intelligentsia circles in Vienna with which he had become fascinated towards the end of the war.

Regarding psychoanalysis, he rejected "its deeply rooted pessimism about the power of education to change human nature, just as Freud's book *Civilization and Its Discontents* expresses deep pessimism over progress and the power of culture to change human nature. In contrast, the philosophical approach of Marxism is optimistic and hopeful about the social and spiritual progress of human beings in society, if only they are provided with the necessary elements sexually, economically, and educationally." [309]

With an ironic reversal of Freudian thought, he then stated, "When I became a Marxist, I decided to refrain from efforts to integrate the concept of psychoanalysis as a philosophy or as a worldview."[310] In addition, "although I myself participated in reading psychoanalytic texts, I was not taken in by Freudian theory because as a socialist I reject his pessimistic conclusions about human progress."[311]

It was Blüher's formulations in particular, and paradoxically his glorification of paganism, that seemed to Ya'ari most appropriate for combatting the image of both the Orthodox Jew and the bourgeois, assimilated Jew. In 1919 he wrote, "We Jews have destroyed culture in the most barbaric way; we have imposed on the world a faith and principles. Let us not stop here to count them, let us not try to sum up the universe. One day another Jew will enter the world, in Eretz Israel: the pagan Jew."[312] Was he trying to prove that Jews, like Aryans, have the capacity for revival among themselves – with the Chosen Jew from the time of Prophets and Judges – a uniquely Jewish Eros?

Even before setting out for Beitania Illit, Ya'ari formulated a clear plan: to forge an ideal "*shomer* typus, with a unique Jewish Eros"[313] – in contrast to the "heroic man" Männerhelden of Wandervogel – that is, a People with a destiny, a People of *cohanim* (heroic leaders). In a letter to the leadership of HaShomer HaTza'ir in Lvov in the autumn of 1919,[314] he stated that he had set as his main goal to bring out "the erotic spontaneity unique to Jews" (*haspontaniyut haerotit hameyiukhedet*), a legacy of biblical times, of the Song of Songs and the days of Prophets and Judges, which every *shomer* can rediscover within himself.

Through Ya'ari's pen, psychoanalysis was diverted into a practice of purification aimed at catalyzing the subjective revolution he sought: in the group, among its members, and first and foremost in oneself.[315] He attributed to psychoanalysis the capacity to break the "psychic armor" that prevents drives from emerging. This "internal revolution" requires a "wild self-analysis" – that is, internal introspection to the point of extremism, because that is the only way to reach the depths of the psyche, to release the drive from the bonds holding it and pave the way to discovery of one's internal Eros, to autonomy, and to fulfillment. At the same time he argued that, "impulses are chains. I hate the use of force, but I aim with all the power of my intellect to enter into the world of my unconscious and expose myself. I feel this is the only route to independence, that only in this way can life flourish and the eyes see. I am speaking in Freud's language."[316]

This rather naïve way of imagining "self-analysis" is more suggestive of Buber, but Ya'ari focused on Freud's 1912 comparison between the art of psychoanalysis and the art of surgery:

> By analyzing and cutting off my own thoughts, like a surgeon working with the cold blade of his scalpel, I make an account of my thoughts, an inventory that psychoanalysis proves able to explore [by delving into] the depths of the soul and clarifying these thoughts, only so as to intensify the mystery, and finally to be swept away at the final barrier. Without a spark of creativity, without completely unconditional madness, without an overwhelming act of will, you will not pierce the shell, you will not experience and you will not create.[317]

The Freudian unconscious has nothing along the lines of the "deposits" that Ya'ari thought to unearth, decrypt, and cut up. Nonetheless, as distorted as this presentation of psychoanalysis (or the Freudian revolution) was, it resonated well among the Shomrim and served as a source of inspiration for their concept of the individual, the community, the collective, and later, education.

Beitania Illit and the Cooperative Erotic Society

Beitania Illit embodied the fulfillment of Ya'ari's dream. After tedious days toiling in the fields, on construction sites or road crews, the young Shomrim would gather around a campfire and share a meal under the starry sky of the Lower Galilee, in the bosom of the "cooperative erotic community." As the ideal communal organization, this was to be "one big family" with the love of all for all – Eros in the broadest sense, in the language of the times – creating the atmosphere, the "fluidity" in which the group was to live.[318] This framework was expected to produce the "*shomer* typus."

With an intense sense of community and mystical elation, the young pioneers held nighttime group discussions: all members of the community had to reveal their innermost thoughts "spontaneously" and without inhibitions. Certain moments left an imprint. Walter Laqueur, for example, cites an entry from a personal diary describing events that took place in 1922:[319]

> Suddenly at midnight, when everyone was asleep, the group members were summoned to an urgent meeting. They rushed to the tent where meetings were held. One of the "kibbutz" members solemnly announced, stressing his words (like a high priest of the Temple), with downcast eyes, "I called this meeting because I. . . I wanted to say that we, Comrade A and I, have just now started a family." A long discussion then followed, as people recall it, one of the most beautiful ever.

As he had argued before arriving in Palestine, Ya'ari was convinced that "only through the fusion of 'spontaneity' with the land can we achieve salvation and erotic self-fulfillment."[320] In their tents, members of the commune would read Freud's works. In the local newsletter, *BeKehilatenu* (In Our Community), one of the community's six women described the passionate interest in Freud, with no small measure of irony: "Dror[321] was reading *Totem and Taboo*. . . And I wanted to find objective arguments to justify the nausea that psychoanalytic philosophy provoked in me, with its argument that ultimately whole world is an erogenous zone of God."

The Myth of Beitania Illit

But the community of Beitania Illit was destined to abandon its hilltop. Most of its members joined the nearby Shomriya battalion,[322] which had formed that year: 120 young men and women who were admitted to HaPo'el HaTza'ir upon their arrival in Palestine and had established an autonomous Labor battalion in accordance with the principles of HaShomer HaTza'ir. Indeed, according to Dorian Feigenbaum,[323] "these enthusiastic new immigrants" often used a "superficially understood and fashionably adopted" psychoanalysis, and "there was danger of harm from some of this kind of activity." Psychoanalysis is diluted, even distorted, once it is used to serve the ideals of an ideological, political, religious, or other movement; its aim is not to issue or validate promises of a brighter future, whatever these ideals, whether individual or collective. One cannot deny, however, that even if HaShomer HaTza'ir members had a naïve understanding of Freud's work, they gave it a place of honor during the early years of their movement as they consolidated their ideological apparatus.

This first community experiment lasted less than a year (from August 1922 to April 1921), but the experience enabled HaShomer HaTza'ir to mature, solidify its program, and make its communal values more democratic and realistic, and therefore better attuned to the economic, social, and cultural realities of Palestine. Working with members of Shomriya and other Shomrim from Galicia and Poland, as well as Shomrim born in Palestine, the pioneers of Beitania Illit founded Kibbutz Beta Alpha on November 4, 1922, a prototype for many other kibbutzim established both before and after the founding of the state.[324] And despite its failure, the experience of Beitania Illit turned into a myth about new beginnings that would long remain alive: fifty years later, the Israeli playwright Yehoshua Sobol would write a now-famous play about this episode, *Leil HaEsrim* (The Night of the Twentieth).[325]

Freud and HaShomer HaTza'ir

Freud's critique of any and all ideologies did not cease to preoccupy the activists of HaShomer HaTza'ir, HaPo'el HaTza'ir, and other leftist groups in Palestine. Thus for example, in a chapter of *New Introductory Lessons on Psychoanalysis* (1933), Freud attacked "worldviews" and Marxism in particular. The text, translated a year later into Hebrew by renowned HaPo'el HaTza'ir intellectual Israel Cohen, was a source of constant debate.[326]

Psychoanalysis remained deeply rooted in the discourse of HaShomer HaTza'ir members and, generally speaking, in that of kibbutz members associated with the movement. Though excluded from the movement's "ideological paradigms," it has always remained an authoritative reference in the eyes of cultured members of HaShomer HaTza'ir and the pedagogues of HaKibbutz HaArtzi. Until the early 1950s – when the demands of Marxist critique reduced it to a product of bourgeois capitalist thought – psychoanalysis suited these groups as a discipline to help them design a new education system. Educators, especially Zvi Sohar and Shmuel Golan as the originators of collective education, were aware of the contributions by psychoanalysis to education and to understanding the psyche of the child, and therefore of the adult. They sought to develop a pedagogical system different from any to date – combining the established, traditional bourgeois education system with the "free education" system sweeping across Europe and the United States at the time – a "revolutionary" system that would, in the kibbutz setting, produce the New Jew, the new human being.[327]

The works of Freud, which informed the thinking of HaShomer HaTza'ir members while exiled in Vienna, provided the substantive content that later drove their discourse and shaped their practices in Beitania Illit.

CHAPTER 6

David Idelsohn and Unprecedented Experiments in New Education

David Idelsohn, a Central Figure in New Education

David Idelsohn, who arrived in Palestine from the Ukraine in 1910, became one of the main agents of psychoanalysis in the country. Like Grete Obernik, he had arrived at the discipline through Bernfeld's works, and the two had actually met and become friends. He soon attained prominence in leftist Zionist educational circles and was able to implement in Palestine avant-garde pedagogical methods that were prevalent at the time in Western Europe and Soviet Russia, as well as the principles of psychoanalysis. With the participation and support of Bernfeld and Hoffer, Idelsohn and his colleague Yehuda Ron-Polani carried out a number of revolutionary projects. As early as the 1920s, alongside other pedagogues identified with the Zionist left who also viewed Bernfeld as a mentor, he made psychoanalysis the definitive psychology in the area of "New Education" – the education of pioneers' children – and granted it a status it had never had before as a pedagogic program.

Like Grete Obernik, he had developed an interest in Viennese psychoanalyst August Aichhorn's innovative theories and practices for the treatment of juvenile delinquents. He managed to introduce and replicate them in Tel Aviv, and the municipality assigned him responsibility for the care and education of delinquent children roaming the streets. He translated and disseminated Aichhorn's writings while simultaneously completing this project, alongside Moshe Wulff and Martin Pappenheim, during 1930-1940.

Historians of education recognize Idelsohn as a pioneer of New Education and modern pedagogy who contributed greatly to the dissemination and implementation of psychoanalytic principles in the areas of pedagogy, education, and social work. He was influenced by his encounter with three renowned psychoanalysts: Siegfried Bernfeld, who introduced him to psychoanalysis in the 1920s, Moshe Wulff, with whom he founded the psychoanalytic movement in Tel Aviv in the early 1930s, and August Aichhorn.

Idelsohn, the only son of an ultra-Orthodox (Lubavitcher) Jewish family, was born in 1892 in Nikolayev, a small town near Odessa. As a teenager he attended a lecture organized by Tze'irei Tzion for the local Jewish community and heard about the new ideas of Zionism. He registered for classes in the history of the People of Israel under the guidance of Chaim Fialkov, a local member of Tze'irei Tzion. And it is there that he met his future friend, loyal ally, and biographer, who too was spreading the theories of Bernfeld and Freud in Palestine: Yehuda Ron-Polani.

With the breakout of riots in 1905, anti-Semitic persecution swept across Russia and the Jewish community in his hometown organized to defend itself. The fourteen-year-old Idelsohn hid weapons in the garden of the family farm. His parents, learning of his underground activities and fearing his exposure to the tsarist police, granted him permission to immigrate to Palestine at age 15, and in 1910 he settled in Jerusalem. His five years of high school study in Russia allowed him to register at the Jerusalem teachers seminary of the Ezra Society (Hilfsverein der Deutschen Juden, a German philanthropy that provided assistance to Jews). The seminary, run by David Yellin, still employed traditional teaching methods to which Idelsohn objected. He had trouble accepting the impersonal approach, religious education, and system of threat and punishment practiced by the traditional establishment, and rebelled against the authoritarianism of the educators in charge of Jewish schools in Jerusalem. Eventually he and some of his friends were denied their diplomas after speaking out against foreign-language instruction at the seminary.

Idelsohn then left Jerusalem and, after passing the exams of Histadrut HaMorim, received a teaching certificate. During the years 1911 to 1912 he taught elementary school at the youth village Meir Shfeiya and attended teacher training classes. While at Shfeiya, he was joined by his old friend Ron-Polani, with whom he had immigrated to Palestine. Their experience at the youth village school inspired them to think about the future of education for Eretz Israel, and in particular the education of pioneering workers' children. In their search for the elements to create an educational curriculum for the children of socialist *halutzim* (pioneers), Idelsohn and Ron-Polani traveled to

Europe to complete their education in pedagogical methods that were in vogue there at the time.

Between 1912 and 1914, Idelsohn studied pedagogy, psychology, and visual arts at the University of Zurich and at the art school in Haystack Peine, a small town in northern Germany midway between Hanover and Braunschweig, in a school run by the Ezra Society. Upon returning to Palestine, he taught for four years at the elementary school in Hartuv, a colony of Bulgarian Jewish immigrants near Hebron. The settlement had attempted once previously to establish Palestine's first "free school," based on avant-garde principles and melding Jewish and socialist education.[328]

In 1918 Turkish authorities accused him of spying on behalf of the British and sent him to prison. He managed to escape and, with assistance from the *mukhtar* of Hartuv, he reconnected with Yehuda Ron-Polani in Jaffa. Having accumulated enough experience and knowledge in education, he spent five years working as a teacher at a girls' elementary school in Neve Tzedek, near Tel Aviv, and instructing young women at the teachers' seminary.

Idelsohn then left again for Europe, where he remained for six months, tirelessly visiting all the places where New Education flourished in Germany and Austria. In Vienna he finally met Bernfeld, and together they decided to publish a new Hebrew-language educational journal under the auspices of the Bernfeld Youth Research Institute, with David Idelsohn, Siegfried Bernfeld, Yehuda Ron-Polani, and Willi Hoffer as co-founders. The first issue of *HaKhinukh HaKhadash* (New Education) was published in Vienna in 1922, in Hebrew, with articles by the four co-founders and two articles that Bernfeld translated from German. Before long, however, this adventure came to an end for reasons that remain unclear.

New Education in Tel Aviv: The Work School (1921)

In September 1921 a new kindergarten and private school opened in Tel Aviv: "The Work School" ("Beit Sefer Omlani" in Hebrew, "Arbeitsschule" in German). An announcement about the school's opening stated that children of workers would be welcome from an early age, to be educated in accordance with the values of Jewish culture, Zionism, and socialism that had inspired the *halutzim* of the Second and Third Aliyah. The announcement also noted the architects of this New

Education – Idelsohn and Ron-Polani – whose aim was to build a secular, Jewish, and socialist homeland. In contrast to the two other approaches prevalent in the Yishuv at the time – those of Histadrut HaMorim and of the religious movement Zionist Mizrahi, both of which had integrated into the WZO in 1913 – the socialist educators of Palestine, headed by David Idelsohn, intended "to adapt educational methods to the specific needs of the child, not vice versa."[329]

After successfully experimenting with various pedagogical methods, Idelsohn and Ron-Polani gained prominence as educators, and the National Council of the Jewish Community of Palestine (Va'ad Leumi) decided to grant them the funds to establish a school in Tel Aviv that would provide children with an education suited to the realities of their lives.[330] Their aim was to design and apply original educational methods that would, to the extent possible, enable native-born children of workers and immigrant children to adapt to the pioneering life in Palestine. The education would be secular, strictly oral, and in Hebrew. Emphasis would be placed on listening to all the children and understanding what motivates or interests them, so as to provide them with the intellectual and manual training needed to cope with harsh reality.

The school's educational program drew inspiration from Wyneken and two of his disciples, Georg Kerschensteiner and Berthold Otto, but slightly altered the doctrine of the pioneer of modern education, incorporating the objectives and teaching methods of the *Arbeitsschulen* (the Work School). The program was based primarily on the concepts of German pedagogues who had begun to reform education in their own country, and of the American philosopher and pedagogue John Dewey, who believed that children should be educated on the basis of democratic principles and be able, for example, to participate in developing their own curriculum and choosing the teaching methods and subjects best suited to their personal abilities.

The role of the teachers was to "prepare children for life," satisfy their curiosity, and answer questions in the fields of science, society, or psychology, as well as questions about cultural life, artistic endeavor, daily tasks at school or at home, material management at workshops or factories, and activities in the vegetable garden or the henhouse.

The Work School of Tel Aviv initially sought to eradicate the coercive methods characteristic of traditional and formal education in Europe and

Palestine. The school's educators viewed that approach as based on educational curricula suited to "Sodom's bed" because it did not take into account the natural laws of child development, psychological maturation, or the child's pleasure or social life. The Work School, in contrast, sought from a very early age to foster the child's independence in all spheres and prepare each child for an independent life, with a heightened sense of responsibility towards society – that is, a workers' society founded on democratic values.[331]

Achieving these goals was not easy, however. Ron-Polani himself described the innumerable difficulties the staff encountered and the chaos at the beginning: "If there were other studies of this sort underway, we knew very little about them, and those about which we knew (Ernst Meumann[332]) were not of much use."[333] It took a person of Bernfeld's skill and stature to bring the school to life. Thanks to Grete Obernik's mediation, disoriented young pedagogues were able to benefit from the support of Siegfried Bernfeld, and they established an active correspondence with him even before Idelsohn met him in Vienna, in May 1922.

Bernfeld provided them with the authoritative theoretical references and the logistics they needed, introduced them to child psychology and modern pedagogy, and offered them advice on developing their project, evaluating their experience, and learning from it. Bernfeld confirmed what Idelsohn had believed from the outset – that school performance and the accumulation of knowledge were not the prime objective – and in particular he advised combining the children in one class, as at Baumgarten.

After a haphazard start with some empirical trial and error, the founders succeeded in establishing a structured program based on "studies in child psychology that can reveal much about the stages of social-institutional development" based primarily on the writings of Freud, Anna Freud, Piaget, Gesell, Eysiks, Bernfeld, and Charlotte Bühler."[334] Without these authoritative references, and without the initiative, energy, and persistence of Idelsohn, the school would not have achieved the objectives its staff set at the outset of the experiment.

To their great surprise, the two educators discovered an entirely new world, rich with the experiences and fantasies related to sexuality that the children began describing enthusiastically in conversations with their teachers. They spoke of their experiences at previous schools; experiences with pets; anecdotes related to their siblings and parents; the dugouts behind the synagogue where teenagers, boys and girls, would meet on Saturdays; the various myths and legends about how children are born. . . in short, the entire range of the imaginary products of "sexual theories" on childhood as Freud had observed, explored, and described them at the dawn of psychoanalysis, particularly in *Three Essays on the Theory of Sexuality*.

Throughout this experience, there arose many educational and psychological questions, and it was especially with regard to sexuality in the "autonomous community of children" that Bernfeld's work was illuminating for the young Tel Aviv educators. While Bernfeld and Idelsohn were refining the project in Vienna, Yehuda Ron-Polani finished reading Bernfeld's *Kinderheim Baumgarten*,[335] and through Bernfeld's many commentaries, discovered the works of Freud. This was an important moment. He wrote in his diary: "Sivan 15 [6-8 June 1922] – After reading Bernfeld's book, I have the feeling that Freud's theory can be of great help in answering our complicated questions concerning the sexuality of children, issues that are emerging daily and causing us unnecessary concern in our work. . . . Similarly, [Freud's theory] could help us develop a perspective and criteria concerning the affects, feelings, desires, and motivations of the child."[336] And thus, thanks to Bernfeld and his work, a minor revolution took place among leftist pedagogues in Palestine, with repercussions for their educational approaches. Henceforth it would not be possible to ignore the question of infantile sexuality in child education. It was no longer merely a phenomenon, to be observed like many others in any community of children; rather, it was an important factor with a direct impact on the child's psyche, on education in the broad sense, and on pedagogical approaches and teaching methods.

Unfortunately, the question of sexuality caused a scandal in Jerusalem, because of which Dorian Feigenbaum was forced to leave Palestine. It also sparked a controversy in the Work School, which in turn led to a dispute between Idelsohn and Ron-Polani over how best to address the problem. That dispute triggered yet another one, political in nature, which led to the closure of the Work School and the end of this educational experiment. In any event, Idelsohn soon found an opportunity to conduct educational experiments with even closer ties to psychoanalysis.

Conformist Halutzim versus Revolutionary Halutzim and the End of New Education in Tel Aviv (1923-1924)

In May 1923 the Histadrut held its first discussion on the need to establish its own school system in cities and villages. At one of the meetings of the newly formed education committee, Yehuda Ron-Polani proposed that the association take the private experimental school recently founded by David Idelsohn under its auspices. Although this proposal was rejected, the Committee on Culture and Education was prepared to entrust the two with the expansion of a school it had established, provided that the new institution not be perceived as an extension of their previous school.

Towards the end of the first year (1923-1924), deep differences of opinion emerged between the teachers – who advocated a pioneering type of education, freer, more open, and essentially anti-bourgeois – and the education committee responsible for monitoring their work. Most committee members rejected the school's form of instruction, and the teachers and principals resigned. Around this time Idelsohn was drawing closer to Gdud HaAvodah (the "Labor Battalion named after Joseph Trumpeldor), where his views met with greater acceptance. Gdud members devoted a great deal of attention to children's education and were genuinely interested in innovation. Fearing ostracism or boycott of the Gdud's activities, however, most of the other teachers,, including Ron-Polani, preferred to join mainstream schools. The dismissal of teaching methods and materials that Ron-Polani, Idelsohn, and their staff practiced during their pilot year amounted, in effect, to a categorical rejection of all educational perspectives implemented by the progressive wing of the labor movement, in terms of both pedagogy and its aims for the new society under construction. The conservative approach prevailed: "First experiment on your own children, then come to us," raged Shmuel Yavnieli, a Second Aliyah immigrant.[337]

Idelsohn argued that the school provided an education specifically designed to train pioneering workers. He accused Histadrut members of clinging to outdated bourgeois methods and of criticizing his program without understanding the basic elements of education a worker requires, but to no avail. In 1924 the Histadrut's Committee on Culture and Education (Merkaz HaTarbut VeHaKhinukh) changed it is name to the School for Children of Workers (Beit Khinukh LeYaldei Ovdim) and imposed its own program.[338]

David Idelsohn and Gdud HaAvodah (1924)

Convinced that this experience was just a step along the path leading to the establishment of a New Education in Palestine, David Idelsohn decided to continue his work among children of pioneering workers in the north. He set out towards the socialist stronghold in the Jezreel Valley and the Galilee, where he knew he would find Gdud HaAvodah workers who had devoted much thought to children's education and begun to implement original teaching methods. This in fact was the reason that Histadrut leaders (Ben-Gurion in particular) regarded them as a nuisance the left must bear and a revolutionary faction that had crossed the line.

Idelsohn immediately began cultivating ties with Shneur Zalman Pugachov, who had arrived that year at the children's village in Giv'at HaMoreh, near Afula, where he was applying the pedagogic system he had already tried in his native Russia. Pugachov gave the children considerable decision-making power and autonomy, both in designing their curriculum and in their social lives and other areas, and Idelsohn was deeply impressed by his work. Pugachov was well known in Jewish circles in Europe for having opened the first Jewish school in Warsaw. On returning to Russia in 1917, after the Bolshevik revolution, he applied the teaching methods of humanist educator Boris Shatzky, whom Idelsohn met during his visit in Soviet Russia in the early 1930s. Pugachov decided to leave the Soviet Union when the Jewish section of the Soviet Communist Party, Yevsektsiya, shut down the School for Culture (which he later founded in Moscow). After a brief imprisonment by the secret police in Moscow and two years in Berlin, Pugachov immigrated to Palestine in 1924. He founded Kfar HaYeladim (the Children's Village), an institution for orphaned children and World War I refugees, at Giv'at HaMoreh, where he tried to apply the teaching methods being applied in Soviet Russia. He placed emphasis on collective values and the work of the land, which he saw as fostering a new democratic society and fulfilling the aspirations of the New Jew. But his colleagues could not endorse an education based on children creating their own "autonomous societies." The evaluation report received by the Histadrut was unfavorable, and the latter soon shut down this experiment.

David Idelsohn in Degania

By the end of 1924, Idelsohn had settled in Kibbutz Degania. As soon as he arrived at this socialist stronghold, he began meeting with pedagogues and people associated with the left at Degania as well as Kfar Giladi, Ein Harod, Tel Yosef, Heftziba, Beit Alpha, and other settlements in the Jordan Valley, Jezreel Valley, and the Galilee. He tried to persuade those he met to help establish a network of schools based on the principles of New Education. The failure of the Work School and disputes with members of the Histadrut's Committee on Culture and Education did not discourage him. He continued trying to persuade Histadrut members of the validity of his approach and to enlist their support for the implementation of this new experiment, but unsuccessfully. The committee categorically rejected his ideas. Convinced that they were "conducting a war against him" (Shimon Reshef) – in other words, that they had no intention of educating the youth in accordance with revolutionary socialist values – he turned to members of the radical left, who were increasingly critical of the dictates and conformism of the Histadrut. Thus the Jezreel Valley became an ideological battlefield, with Gdud HaAvodah more determined than ever to spread the global revolution that had begun in Russia in 1917, and to transform the country into a socialist Zionist state. Idelsohn, along with Gdud HaAvodah and HaShomer HaTza'ir, would go on to implement his revolutionary plans for the children of the Jewish proletariat in Palestine.

Preferring the world of education over the toil of the land, while at Degania Idelsohn worked as a teacher at Tel Yosef, one of the strongholds of Gdud HaAvodah, whose views on education correlated closely with his own. Kibbutz Tel Yosef was established in November 1921 by members of Gdud HaAvodah, most of whom had been active in the movement HeHalutz in Germany or Czechoslovakia. HeHalutz aimed to provide young people with a socialist education and the manual skills necessary to settle and work in Palestine and to organize independent farming communities that could accommodate many more Jewish immigrants. Tel Yosef was named after Joseph Trumpeldor (1888-1920), among the first members of the movement in Russia and founder of the mule corps in Palestine, who fell in battle during World War I while defending Tel Hai.

Kibbutz Beit Alpha (1924)

In late 1924, Idelsohn met a strange figure at Kibbutz Beit Alpha: Eliyahu Rappaport. Ernst Eliyahu Rappaport was born in Slovakia in 1889, but grew up and studied philosophy and mathematics in Vienna. He was a brilliant student of two renowned scholars: Martin Buber in 1910, and later Siegfried Bernfeld (with whom he worked at the Jewish Pedagogic Seminary in Vienna). He had developed a strong interest in Freud's work long before immigrating to Palestine. With fellow HaShomer HaTza'ir members Meir Ya'ari, David Horowitz, Shmuel Golan, and others, he participated in founding Beitania Illit. After the settlement disbanded, like Ya'ari, he took part in paving the Jeddah-Haifa highway. But before long Rappaport sank into a state of loneliness and misery, to the extent that word of the situation reached Bernfeld in Vienna, who then asked Hugo Bergmann to intervene on behalf of "this overgrown child, who is wandering around barefoot, neglecting himself completely, and has not eaten or slept in several days."[339] It was in Haifa that they finally found him, teaching at the Reali School while training as a shoemaker. During his time at Beit Alpha he was able to put his various skills to use, dividing his time among kitchen duty, shoe repair, and the education of five children at his workshop, which he transformed into a classroom as well.

The year 1924 marks an important moment in the country's history: that year thousands of refugees, mostly fleeing the impact of anti-Semitic legislation in Poland, began arriving in Palestine. In contrast to prevailing opinion, they were not only members of the bourgeois class; the Fourth Aliyah (1924-1932) included laborers, merchants, craftsmen, and workers of various trades, many of whom settled in the north, especially in the Galilee and Jezreel Valley.[340] Some of these Jewish workers joined the Marxist members of Gdud HaAvodah and settled with their families in Tel Yosef and Heftzibah, among other places.

Eliyahu Rappaport decided to devote himself to educating the children of nearby workers by establishing a children's community at Beit Alpha for the twenty or so children in the vicinity. Shmuel Golan took a strong interest in the initiative and provided assistance. Idelsohn suggested that he implement the principles of New Education, drawing on Bernfeld's experience at Kinderheim Baumgarten. Rappaport, inspired by Idelsohn's enthusiasm, appeared to have adopted his program. The children's community of Beit Alpha began to take shape. When he saw that there were not enough children of workers to establish an autonomous community, Idelsohn – perhaps thinking of the Baumgarten orphanage – proposed that Jewish children from abroad be brought to the community. The JDC (Joint) responded to his request affirmatively and sent orphaned children and teenagers, mostly from Poland, to Beit Alpha.

When Bernfeld told Idelsohn that "there is no good pedagogue who has not undergone psychoanalytic training and has not also become a good analyst,"[341] his words had a powerful impact. They shook his beliefs and cast doubt on everything he was aspiring, with a deep sense of calling, to achieve in Palestine. Bernfeld himself had long been claiming that education and appropriate teaching methods can, by themselves, lead to the emergence of a New Man. If that were not enough, when Idelsohn arrived at Beit Alpha for the first time, in early September, he realized that Rapaport had suddenly decided to abandon everything despite their plans to organize this children's community together. After clashing with members of the movement who disagreed with his methods, Rappaport left the kibbutz and severed ties with HaShomer HaTza'ir.[342] Little is known about his activities in the years that followed, except that, after living in Jerusalem for a while, he moved to Tel Aviv and devoted himself to repairing violins until his final days. In any event, Idelsohn then turned to Shmuel Golan, with whom he had worked in the past, to continue the adventure he had begun with Rappaport.

Utopian Teaching Methods

The Children's Society at Beit Alpha was one of the most important efforts to implement the principles of New Education undertaken in Palestine. One may view it as an encounter between representatives of different streams in the Zionist left: the pedagogues of HaShomer HaTza'ir and David Idelsohn. Yet it also reflected and further deepened the divide between various socialist groups. In those days the educators of HaShomer HaTza'ir were engaged more than ever in developing the ideal educational curriculum, one that would give birth to the Ideal Man, the New Jew. Idelsohn[343] and Shmuel Golan provided accounts of the Children's Society around this time.[344] He and the educators of Gdud HaAvodah and HaShomer HaTza'ir had decided to make Beit Alpha a place where children would be educated along the principles of New Education, with the aim of fostering the creation of a society based on collective values rather than the individualistic principles of the classic family, of traditional education, and of bourgeois society generally. In his words, "Society as a whole must replace the individual."[345]

In early 1926 Idelsohn assumed responsibility for the education of thirty-six children, aged six to sixteen, who resided at the foot of Mount Gilboa in seven shacks made available by Beit Alpha members. A year later the number of children admitted to the Society had grown to fifty, including children from the kibbutzim Tel Yosef and Heftzibah, orphans from Europe, and former students from the Work School. The setting and arrangement of the classrooms seemed straight out of Bernfeld's vision, as described in his socialist Zionist utopia and achieved in Vienna.[346] The place included a dining room, a kitchen, a storage area, two classrooms, and a large auditorium for the children to meet and hold discussions, as at the Baumgarten orphanage. Four shacks were designated as sleeping quarters, and the facility contained a library, music conservatory, gardens and an orchard. In this beautiful rural setting, against the backdrop of Mount Gilboa, where every stone had Biblical significance, the long-awaited child of Zionism, the New Jew, the pioneer child, was to be born.

Freudian Psychology for the Children of Halutzim

Because these immigrant children came from different countries across Central and Eastern Europe, Idelsohn had to cope with problems of language as well as the need for different levels of instruction. Hebrew became the official language of the children's community, of course, and Bernfeld's work provided the modalities that Idelsohn needed to address disparities in the children's level of education. But there were other challenges: many of the children had been referred to Beit Alpha by the Joint, HaShomer HaTza'ir in Europe (particularly Poland), or Gdud HaAvodah because the institutions caring for them could no longer continue to do so. Idelsohn therefore tried to design a program capable of receiving these orphans and providing appropriate care. The psychology of the orphaned child particularly drew his interest, as evidenced by a report he wrote on the topic.[347] Here we see once again how Bernfeld's experience provided the vital elements for his program's success. What he had tried unsuccessfully to accomplish in Tel Aviv with Ron-Polani and Hoffer now became a reality at the foothills of Mount Gilboa. It is to Idelsohn's credit that the lessons of psychoanalysis made their way into the framework and guidelines of New Education in Eretz Israel.

For those interested in the education and psychology of immigrant children, orphans, or "problem" children, Beit Alpha would have offered fertile ground for experimentation. And the challenge was daunting: their aim was to help children regarded as difficult, not suited for communal life, or even lost, to overcome their problems and become model *halutzim*. Idelsohn also claimed that he was the only one treating children considered "unsuitable," "aggressive," or "too submissive," who had exhibited "deviant sexual behavior" – the only one who aimed to instill a prophylactic element in the children's community. The goal he set for himself, in line with his mission on behalf of HaShomer HaTza'ir and Gdud HaAvodah, was to enable these children to adapt to their new reality, the socialist Eretz Israel, and integrate into it professionally. He was convinced that the education they had received abroad completely distorted their view of reality and adaptability, and he therefore organized the children's and teenagers' lives along two main axes: early confrontation with the realities of work, and their initiation into "the work of preparing for the socialist national enterprise." Basing himself on Freudian theory, he asserted that only the prohibitions imposed by parents or educators on the immediate satisfaction of children's demands or impulses can enable them to access the real world and culture, and to prepare themselves to become members of society. His colleagues in the community attacked his ideas: they believed that denying immediate satisfaction of an impulse conflicts with the principles of New Education. In countering their criticism, he explained the role of the educator:

> For the child to be able to conquer reality, it is therefore necessary that the educator impose certain prohibitions and restrictions, as in reality, thus denying him immediate satisfaction. This seemingly contradicts the New Education principle of freedom for children. [But] it would be a mistake to confuse the objective of education (educating the free man) with the means of education. It is not possible to educate by granting children absolute freedom to do and act as they wish. . . . We have to carry out all the restrictions and prohibitions even if the child objects, because in our view we are doing it for the good of the child. .

. . Although it is the educator's role to ease prohibitions for the child, and the younger the child the fewer prohibitions and limitations there should be, but at the same time the educator knows he is not educating because he is not creating the impulses the child needs to overcome desires. There is no denying that freedom is necessary, for only through freedom of action within clear boundaries will the child be able to forge a stable and balanced "ego" capable of regulating his relationships with his surroundings and with society. The demands that the educator makes of the children and which set limits on the child's desires have value only if the child recognizes and tends to agree with these demands.[348]

It was always by referring to psychoanalytic theory that Idelsohn sought to overcome the obstacles he encountered in educating the immigrant "problem child." But he was unable to persuade his colleagues, or to convince them of the need to take the Freudian concept of the *incest taboo* into account in order to allow the child to access the symbolic order, the legal order, and thus to engage with reality, the dimension of the other, of civilization, and of culture.

Sexuality in the Adolescents' Group

At Beit Alpha, where alongside Golan and Sohar, Idelsohn treated children and adolescents aged 12 to 17, the approach to questions related to sexuality became a crucial one. New Education, according to Idelsohn, should distance itself from traditional education, which contradicted "the natural sexual maturation of the child." He interviewed these adolescents immediately upon arriving, which reinforced his views. Relying once again on *An Introduction to Psychoanalysis*, he explained in "Freudian" terms:

A group of youngsters who had grown close to me during the first year, and with whom I spoke a great deal, was in a perpetual state of inner conflict between their sexual impulses and those of the "ego.". . . Repressed sexual impulses, excluded from the realm of consciousness, will as we know explode later in various hidden ways, disrupting the psychic balance of children and that of the Society [of children] as a whole.[349]

The children at Beit Alpha, whose education abroad had ruled out any consideration of sexuality or ways of approaching the issue, found this embarrassing, all the more so because, unlike their previous schools, the Children's Society at Beit Alpha was a mixed community of boys and girls. Idelsohn saw it as his duty to help them overcome their unconscious conflicts and "inhibitions": he did his best to listen to them and encourage them to tell him about their desires.

He accused HaShomer HaTza'ir pedagogues of "sabotaging his work"; the resistance he encountered came not from girls but from other educators who "opposed my method of work, creating a split between boys and girls."[350] His commentaries on the Children's Society always granted girls and women an important role in the future socialist society of Eretz Israel, where women would be equal to men. He was convinced that pedagogy, no matter how revolutionary, was not enough by itself. Regarding manifestations of hysteria among adolescent girls, for example, he claimed that "it is possible to achieve positive results through psychoanalysis, more than by pedagogical means."[351] In any event, he was enthralled with psychoanalysis even at that time, and in the midst of the Beit Alpha experiment he left for Berlin with the aim of finally completing his training in this discipline.

The role ascribed to family and parents was another point of contention among the pedagogues of the Children's Society. In contrast to the other socialist and Marxist groups in Palestine, the ideologues of HaShomer HaTza'ir called for the abolition of the "bourgeois family": in their ideal society, parents would have no role in the education of their children; the community of adults – that is, kibbutz society – would take this responsibility upon itself. Idelsohn, however, believed that even if children should be raised in an autonomous community, apart from adult society, there was no reason to condemn the traditional family: "In a regular society, there is great value to the family, to its traditional lifestyle, to relations between the father or mother and the children, to the education of children and their adaptation to future life as part of society. The father is the most important factor in the child's transition from the individualistic egoism of early life to a social life with others."[352] The socialist workers' children at Tel Yosef and Heftzibah did indeed live apart from their parents, but in his view this was no reason to reject occasional family visits. The topic proved a source of aggravation for HaShomer HaTza'ir educators, who claimed that the parents who visited, especially those from nearby Kibbutz Heftzibah, were rudely interfering in their children's education.

The leaders of HaShomer HaTza'ir realized a little too late that the specialist on whom they had counted did not belong to their movement, and that the education system he intended to create did not accord with the movement's overall ideology or any of its specific aspirations.[353] As the political and ideological divisions that split the left in Palestine at the time intensified, so too did the tension between Idelsohn and HaShomer HaTza'ir pedagogues. The state of co-existence achieved by various political movements – HaShomer HaTza'ir, Gdud HaAvodah, Ahdut HaAvodah, Po'alei Tzion, Po'alei Tzion Smol, to name but a few – was shaken to the core. A few of the parties officially recognized by the British government concealed prohibited factions. Activists of the Palestinian Communist Party (PCP), for example, who took their orders from Moscow and often engaged in violence (and were being pursued by the British secret service) sometimes operated under the guise of Gdud HaAvodah or the left wing of Po'alei Tzion.[354]

The year 1926 saw the first attempts to establish the Kibbutz Artzi Federation of kibbutzim. With its actual founding in 1927,[355] the new organization shifted away from other streams in the Zionist left, even more sharply than Ahdut HaAvodah and HaPo'el HaTza'ir. The pedagogues of HaKibbutz HaArtzi decided henceforth to rely only on their own resources. Although they did not turn their backs on Beit Alpha immediately, they put all their efforts into creating their own education system, which prioritized native-born children, who certainly would have conformed to their ideal of the New Man more than orphaned refugees or the children of other political movements.

The Beit Alpha Children's Society continued to operate until 1929. After the Arab riots that year and the attack on Beit Alpha, the children were transferred to Kibbutz Geva, and the children's group fell apart at the end of that school year. Many view this unprecedented educational enterprise, initiated by the leftist movements of Palestine, as the first historical step towards true collective education. The educational system established by HaShomer HaTza'ir pedagogues on their kibbutzim also served in those days as a model for many kibbutzim from other movements.

Golan, Sohar, and Idelsohn met again a few years later, when psychoanalysis drew them together around a new mentor – Moshe Wulff. Idelsohn, after leaving Beit Alpha, had returned to Tel Aviv, where he worked at the Dugma School (Model School), founded and run during 1931-1932 by Yichiel Heilperin. He apparently divided his time between working at the school and temporarily residing abroad, where he devoted some of his time to exploring new educational and teaching methods in Western Europe. In the early 1930s he visited the Soviet Union, where he took an interest in important educational experiments then underway. With the assistance of Lenin's widow, Nadezhda Konstantinovna Krupskaya, Commissioner for Education Affairs at the time, he was able to stay four months and visit a number of institutions for abandoned children and juvenile delinquents. One of these was Professor Stanislaw Shatzky's pedagogical experiments facility, where labor-based teaching methods were being used, with the aim of enabling marginalized children to reintegrate into society. Idelsohn's report on his stay in the Soviet Union and observations from the visits he conducted while there appeared in early issues of *Ofakim*, the journal on education and culture of HaShomer HaTza'ir.[356]

During 1932 Idelsohn stayed in Berlin, where he completed his studies in psychoanalytic pedagogy and was accredited to treat neurotic and abandoned youth by the Berlin Psychoanalytic Institute. The Nazi rise to power forced many foreign Jews residing in Germany to leave, and Idelsohn returned to Palestine in March 1933. In 1934 he began working in the childcare department of the Tel Aviv Municipality, where he was responsible for the education of delinquent children roaming the streets of the city. Towards this end, in 1934 he founded the "Club for Delinquent Children," the "Club for Working Children," and other institutions in the same spirit. Over time he came to occupy various senior positions in the Tel Aviv Municipality . He also served as August Aichhorn's spokesman in Palestine, and was the first to translate his work into Hebrew. Having been Bernfeld's disciple in the 1920s, Idelsohn eventually became a disciple of Wulff, the great patron of psychoanalysis in Tel Aviv and an expert in child psychoanalysis. From the time Wulff arrived in Palestine until Idelsohn's death in 1956, they joined efforts to create a psychoanalytic movement in the country.

PHOTO ALBUM

Fig. 1: The Board of Ezrat Nashim, founded in 1894
© Herzog Hospital (formerly Ezrat Nashim) Library, Jerusalem

Fig. 2: Ezrat Nashim – the facility and its residents
© Yosef Y. Rivlin. Yosef Y. Rivlin Collection, *75 Shana LeEzrat Nashim*, 1895-1970 [Ezrat Nashim at 75 Years, 1895-1970] (Jerusalem: Ezrat Nashim Mental Health Association, 1970), p. 28

Fig. 3: Simon Frankel (1809-1880)
© Nissim Levy, *Prakim BeToldot HaRefua BeEretz Israel 1799-1978* [Chapters in the History of Medicine in Eretz Israel, 1799-1978] (Tel Aviv and Haifa: Hakibbutz Hameuchad Publishing House and the Bruce Rappaport Faculty of Medicine, Technion, 1998)

Fig. 4: Front row, center: Chaya Tzippa Pines (1895-1919),
founder and first director of Ezrat Nashim, surrounded by her daughters
© Herzog Hospital (formerly Ezrat Nashim) Library, Jerusalem

Fig. 5: Ezrat Nashim – the facility, staff (on the balcony), residents
© Yosef Y. Rivlin. Yosef Y. Rivlin Collection *Ezrat Nashim at 75 Years, 1895-1970*
(Jerusalem: Ezrat Nashim Mental Health Association, 1970), p. 30

Fig. 6: The staff of Ezrat Nashim, circa 1925. Center row, right to left: neuropsychiatrists Heinz Hermann (with hands clasped), Dorian Feigenbaum's successor at Ezrat Nashim and founder of the Palestine Neuropsychiatry Society (1936), alongside Abraham Rabinowitz (in glasses)
© Yosef Y. Rivlin. Yosef Y. Rivlin Collection *Ezrat Nashim at 75 Years, 1895-1970*
(Jerusalem: Ezrat Nashim Mental Health Association, 1970), p. 2

(LEFT) Fig. 7: Ita Yellin, director of Ezrat Nashim, 1919-1943
© Yosef Y. Rivlin. Yosef Y. Rivlin Collection *Ezrat Nashim at 75 Years, 1895-1970*
(Jerusalem: Ezrat Nashim Mental Health Association, 1970), p. 2

(RIGHT) Fig. 8: Montague David Eder, psychoanalyst, Zionist leader, and British socialist
© Dorian Feigenbaum, "Obituary: Montague David Eder, M. D. (1866-1936)" *The Psychoanalytic Quarterly*, vol. V, 1936, p. 444

Fig. 9: Chaim Weizmann (in white suit) with Montague David Eder behind him (circa 1918-1920), surrounded by other prominent Yishuv figures and representatives of the British Military Administration in Palestine © Israel State Archives, *Chaim Weizmann: The First President – Selected Letters and Speeches*, Commemorative Series: The Presidents and Prime Ministers of Israel. Series editor: Yemima Rosenthal. Editor: Louise Fischer (Jerusalem: Israel State Archives, 1994)

Fig. 10: Zionist leaders and close associates of Chaim Weizmann, at the Zionist Congress in Basel, 1927. Front row, left to right: Henrietta Szold, Chaim Weizmann, Montague David Eder. Back row, left to right: Harry Zacher, Siegfried van Vriesland, Frederick Kisch
© http://jwa.org/media/henrietta-szold-with-zionist-leaders-at-basel-zionist-congress-1927

(LEFT) Fig. 11: Henrietta Szold, American Zionist leader, founder of Hadassah Women's Zionist Organization of America and Hadassah Medical Organization © Private archive, all rights reserved

(RIGHT) Fig. 12: Henrietta Szold in the 1940s © Private archive, all rights reserved

Fig. 13: Henrietta Szold surrounded by the first class of nurse trainees (1921)
© Private archive, all rights reserved

Fig. 14: Mordechai Brachyahu, founder of child psychiatry in Palestine, member of Hadassah Medical Organization, and Freud's Hebrew-language translator © Archives of Jewish Education in Israel and the Diaspora, Tel Aviv University

(LEFT) Fig. 15: Siegfried van Vriesland, circa 1920 © Siegfried van Vriesland. May 2nd, 1886 - December 4th, 1939, Collected Documents (Jerusalem, National Library of Israel: 1941), p. 22

(RIGHT) Fig. 16: Siegfried van Vriesland, Tel Aviv, May 1939 © Siegfried van Vriesland. May 2nd, 1886 - December 4th, 1939, Collected Documents (Jerusalem: National Library of Israel, 1941), p. 7

Fig. 17: Dorian Feigenbaum with his violin, circa 1924 © Private archives of Lou Seinfeld, New York

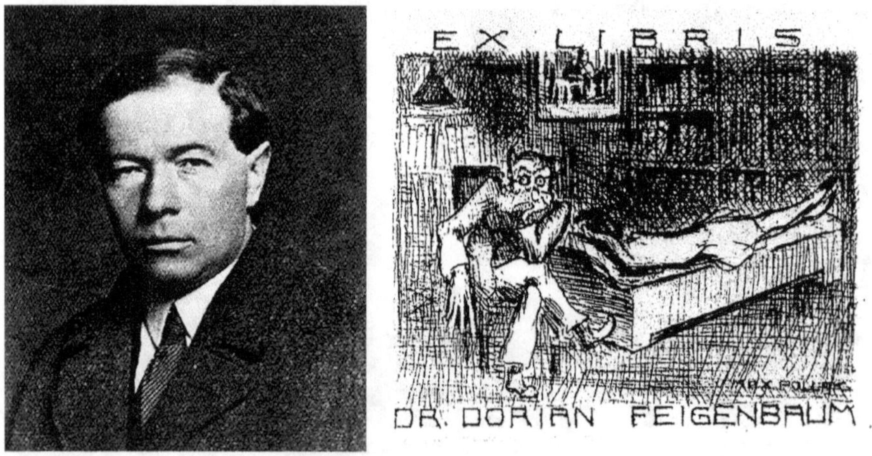

(LEFT) Fig. 18: Dorian Feigenbaum (1887-1937) © Private archives of Lou Seinfeld, New York

(RIGHT) Fig. 19: Dorian Feigenbaum at his clinic in New York, caricature by his friend, artist Max Pollak © Private archives of Lou Seinfeld, New York

(LEFT) Fig. 20: Caricature of Dorian Feigenbaum, Salzburg Psychoanalytic Conference, 1924 © Olga Szekely-Kovacs and Robert Bereny, *Karikaturen vom Achten Internationalen, Psychoanalytischen Kongress Salzburg Ostern 1924* Leipzig-Vienna-Zurich: Internationaler Psychoanalytischer Verlag, 1924)

(RIGHT) Fig. 21: Aryeh Feigenbaum, who defended Freud at the Hebrew University and spoke out against religious authoritarianism © Private archive of Naomi Belsitzmann, Tel Aviv

Fig. 22: Aryeh Feigenbaum, the most Freudian physician in the Near and Middle East
© Private archive of Naomi Belsitzmann, Tel Aviv

Fig. 23: Grete Obernik, a teacher in Jerusalem, circa 1920-1921
© Private archive of Efraim Reiner

Fig. 24; Grete Obernik-Reiner in Vienna, 1926, with her son Efraim and daughter Hannah
© Private archive of Efraim Reiner

Fig. 25: Shmuel Hugo Bergmann, first director of the National Library in Jerusalem
© Private archive, all rights reserved

Fig. 26: Yichiel Heilperin, pioneer of modern pedagogy and ally of psychoanalysts © David Tidhar,
Encyclopedia LeHalutzei HaYishuv U-Vonav [Encyclopedia of the Yishuv Pioneers and Builders]
(Tel Aviv: Hotza'at HaRishonim, 1947-1971), p. 256

Fig. 27: Siegfried Bernfeld, circa 1914
© Karl Fallend, Johasnnes Reichmayr (eds.), *Siegfried Bernfeld oder die Grenzen der Psychoanalyse.*
Materialien zu Leben und Werk (Basel-Frankfurt: Nexus/Stroemfeld, 1992), p. 52

Fig. 28: Caricature of Siegfried Bernfeld, Marxist, Zionist, Freudian, and defender of lay analysis ©
Olga Szekely-Kovacs and Robert Bereny, *Karikaturen vom Achten Internationalen, Psychoanalytischen*
Kongress Salzburg Ostern 1924 Leipzig-Vienna-Zurich: Internationaler Psychoanalytischer Verlag, 1924)

Fig. 29: Siegfried Bernfeld with Martin Buber

© Karl Fallend, Johasnnes Reichmayr (eds.), *Siegfried Bernfeld oder die Grenzen der Psychoanalyse. Materialien zu Leben und Werk* (Basel-Frankfurt: Nexus/Stroemfeld, 1992), p. 77

Fig. 30: Siegfried Bernfeld in San Francisco, circa 1950

© Karl Fallend, Johasnnes Reichmayr (eds.), *Siegfried Bernfeld oder die Grenzen der Psychoanalyse. Materialien zu Leben und Werk* (Basel-Frankfurt: Nexus/Stroemfeld, 1992), p. 316

*Fig. 30: Meir Ya'ari, Meir (standing) and Yaakov Hazan (to his left, pouring water)
during the Fourth World Congress of HaShomer HaTza'ir in Czechoslovakia in 1935.*
© Aviva Halamish, *Biographia Kibbutzit. Hamishim HaShanim HaRishonot 1897-1947*
[Kibbutz Biography: The First Fifty Years, 1897-1947] (Tel Aviv: Am Oved, 2009)

Fig. 31: Meir Ya'ari © http://wikipedia.org.wiki/Meir_Ya'ari

Fig. 32: The children's society at Beit Alpha, circa 1928
Back row, center (bearded): Zvi Sohar; furthest right: Shmuel Golan, with the children of Tel Yosef and
Heftziba © Kibbutz Beit Alpha Archives

Fig. 33 Shmuel Golan in the late 1950s © Kibbutz Mishmar HaEmek Archives

Fig. 34: Zvi Sohar in a conversation © Yad Ya'ari, HaShomer HaTza'ir Archives, Giv'at Haviva

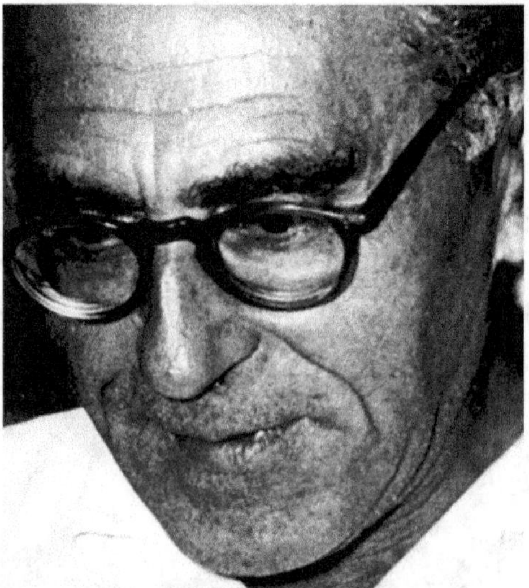

Fig. 35: Shmuel Golan, circa 1950-1955 © Kibbutz Mishmar HaEmek Archives

Fig. 36: David Idelsohn circa 1915
© Shimon Reshef, *Khinukh Hadash BeEretz Israel, 1915-1929*
[New Education in Eretz Israel, 1915-1929]
(Merhavia: Sifriat Poalim, 1985), p. 16

Fig. 37: David Idelsohn in 1930 at the Dugma School in Tel Aviv
© Archives of Jewish Education in Israel and the Diaspora,
Tel Aviv University, 5.202/5

Fig. 38: David Idelsohn at the Tel Aviv Girls School, 1921
© Archives of Jewish Education in Israel and the Diaspora, Tel Aviv University, 5.202/5

*Fig. 39: David Idelsohn with children from the Abandoned Youths Club in Tel Aviv,
planting trees on Tu Bishvat (Arbor Day)* © Archives of Jewish Education in Israel and the Diaspora,
Tel Aviv University, PIC-13-307

(LEFT) Fig. 40: David Idelsohn in the early 1950s © Tel Aviv Municipal Archives
(RIGHT) Fig. 41: Andor Fodor © Private archive, all rights reserved

(LEFT) Fig. 42: Immanuel Velikovsky, circa 1974 © Private archive, all rights reserved
(RIGHT) Fig. 43: Yohanan Tversky, first Hebrew-language translator of Freud
© David Tidhar, *Encyclopedia of Yishuv Pioneers and Builders*

Fig. 44: Chaim Weizmann © Private archive, all rights reserved

Fig. 45: Judah Leon Magnes © Private archive, all rights reserved

Fig. 46: Judah Leon Magnes in his later years © Private archive, all rights reserved

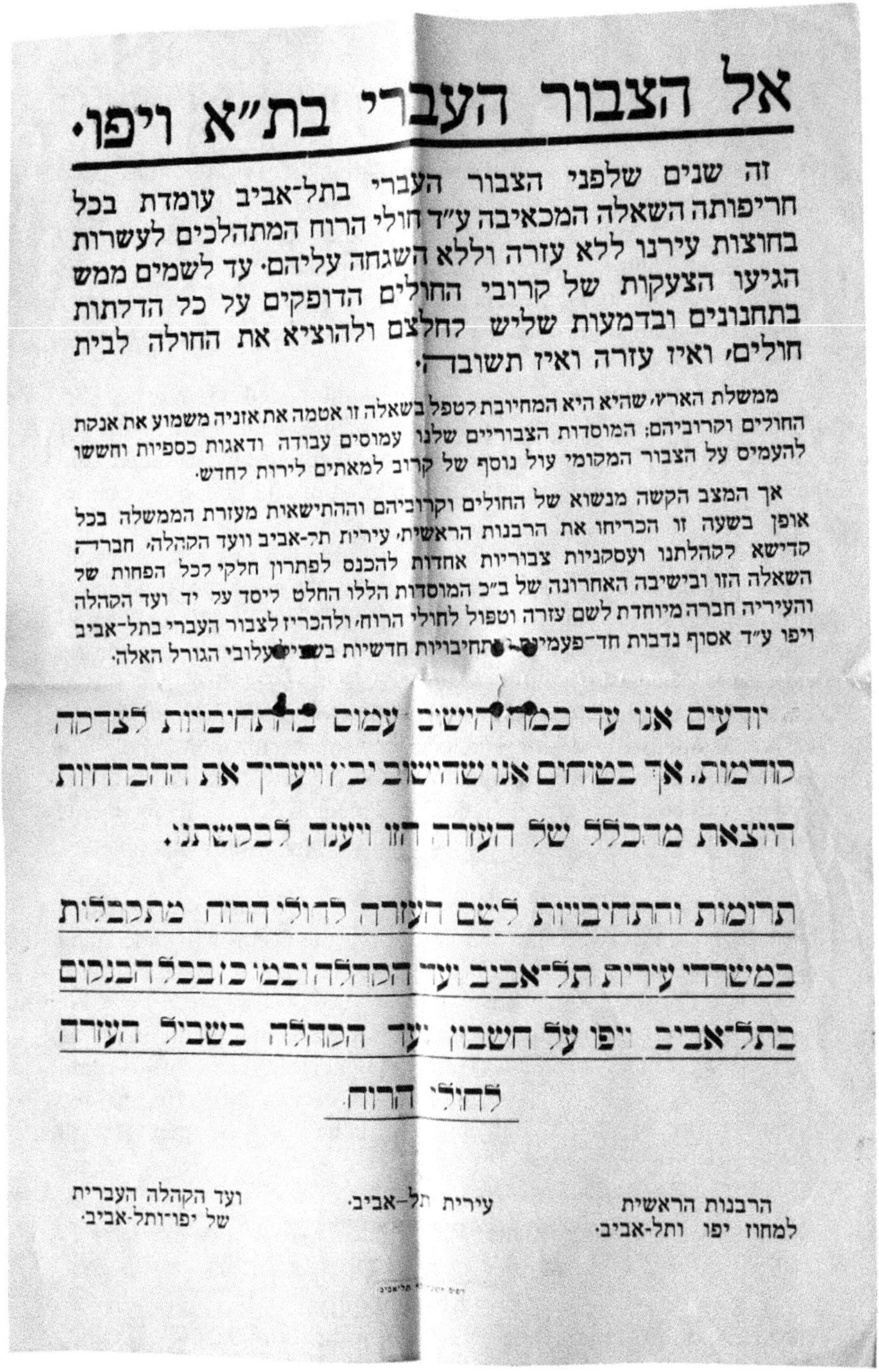

אל הצבור העברי בת״א ויפו.

זה שנים שלפני הצבור העברי בתל-אביב עומדת בכל חריפותה השאלה המכאיבה ע״ד חולי הרוח המתהלכים לעשרות בחוצות עירנו ללא עזרה וללא השגחה עליהם. עד לשמים ממש הגיעו הצעקות של קרובי החולים הדופקים על כל הדלתות בתחנונים ובדמעות שליש לחלצם ולהוציא את החולה לבית חולים, ואין עזרה ואין תשובה.

ממשלת הארץ, שהיא היא המחויבת לטפל בשאלה זו אטמה את אזניה משמוע את אנקת החולים וקרוביהם: המוסדות הצבוריים שלנו עמוסים עבודה ודאגות כספיות וחששו להעמיס על הצבור המקומי עול נוסף של קרוב למאתים לירות לחדש.

אך המצב הקשה מנשוא של החולים וקרוביהם וההתישאות מעזרת הממשלה בכל אופן בשעה זו הכריחו את הרבנות הראשית, עיריות תל-אביב וועד הקהלה, חברה קדישא לקהלתנו ועסקניות צבוריות אחדות להכנס לפתרון חלקי לכל הפחות של השאלה הזו ובישיבה האחרונה של ב״כ המוסדות הללו החלט ליסד על יד ועד הקהלה והעיריה חברה מיוחדת לשם עזרה וטפול לחולי הרוח, ולהכריז לצבור העברי בתל-אביב ויפו ע״ד אסוף נדבות חד-פעמיות ותחיבויות חדשיות בשביל עלובי הגורל האלה.

יודעים אנו עד כמה חשוב עמוס בהתחיבויות לצדקה
קודמות, אך בטוחים אנו שהישוב יבין ויעריך את ההכרחיות
הוצאת מדכלל של העזרה הזו ויענה לבקשתנו.

תרומות והתחיבויות לשם העזרה לחולי הרוח מתקבלות
במשרדי עירית תל-אביב יעד הקהלה וכמו כן בכל הבנקים
בתל-אביב יפו על חשבון יעד הקהלה בשביל העזרה
לחולי הרוח

<table>
<tr><td>הרבנות הראשית
למחוז יפו ותל-אביב.</td><td>עירית תל-אביב.</td><td>ועד הקהלה העברית
של יפו ותל-אביב.</td></tr>
</table>

Fig. 47: Poster from 1929 on behalf of the Association for the Mentally Ill in Tel Aviv
© Tel Aviv Municipal Archives (Translation on page 184)

To the Jewish Residents of Tel Aviv-Jaffa

For many years now, the Jewish population of Tel Aviv has been facing a problem of utmost severity, the painful problem of mentally ill roaming the streets of our city by the dozen, unassisted and unsupervised. Their family members cry and plead to the heavens above, as they knock on doors, weeping and begging to rescue the mentally ill and place them in hospitals. They receive no help and no response.

The Government of the Land, which is obligated to address this question, has closed its ears to the cries of the mentally ill and their families; our public institutions are overworked and underfunded, and they do not wish to place an additional burden of 200 lira on the public.

Yet the unbearable situation of the mentally ill and their families, with no hope of receiving government aid in any form at this time, have compelled the Chief Rabbinate, Tel Aviv Municipality, and the Central Committee of the Jewish Community as well as other public enterprises to seek at least a partial solution to this problem, and at their most recent assembly these institutions decided that the Central Committee and the Tel Aviv Municipality would establish a special organization to help and care for the mentally ill, and to announce to the Jewish residents of Tel Aviv and Jaffa that one-time donations and pledges of monthly payments are being solicited on behalf of these destitute and unfortunate persons.

We know what a burden the Yishuv is carrying because of preexisting charitable commitments, but we are certain that the Yishuv will understand and appreciate this exceptional need for assistance and will hear our plea.

Donations and pledges on behalf of the mentally ill may be made at the offices of the Tel Aviv Municipality and the Central Committee as well as all banks in Tel Aviv and Jaffa, to the account name of Va'ad HaKehila on behalf of the mentally ill

[Signed]
Chief Rabbinate
Jaffa and Tel Aviv District
Tel Aviv Municipality
Central Committee of the Jewish Community of Jaffa-Tel Aviv

*Fig. 48: **Martin Pappenheim*** © National Library in Jerusalem, Pappenheim Files

*Fig. 49: **Back row, left to right: Moshe Wulff and Ernst Simmel. Front row, left to right: Anna Freud, Sigmund Freud, and Assia Wulff, at the Schloss Tegel Psychoanalytic Clinic in Berlin, 1927*** © The Israel Annals of Psychiatry and Related Disciplines, vol. 16, no. 1-4, 1978, p. 83*

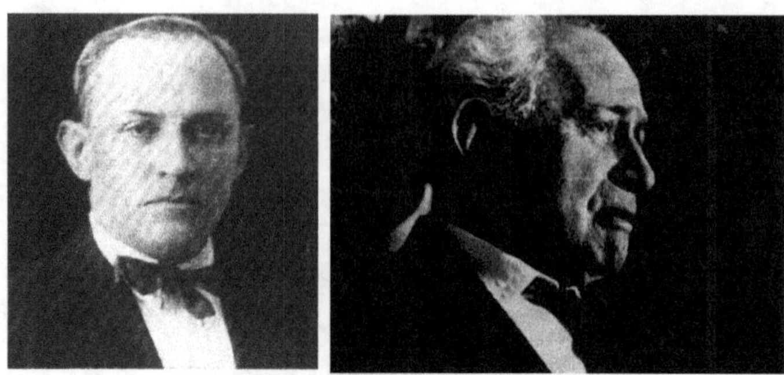

*(LEFT) Fig. 50: Moshe Wulff © Mosche Wulff, Zur Geschichte der Psychoanalyse
in Russland und Israel* (Tubingen: Diskord, 2002)
(RIGHT) Fig. 51: Moshe Wulff, circa 1968 © Mosche Wulff, *Zur Geschichte der Psychoanalyse in
Russland und Israel* (Tubingen: Diskord, 2002)

Fig. 52: Max Eitingon in the late 1930s © Israel State Archives, Max Eitingon Collection, 2973/6
Fig. 53: Max Eitingon © Israel State Archives, Max Eitingon Collection, 2973/6

(LEFT) Fig. 54: Caricature of Max Eitingon © Olga Szekely-Kovacs and Robert Bereny, *Karikaturen
vom Achten Internationalen, Psychoanalytischen Kongress Salzburg Ostern 1924* Leipzig-Vienna-Zurich:
Internationaler Psychoanalytischer Verlag, 1924)
(RIGHT) Fig. 55: Max Eitingon in Jerusalem, 1934 © Max Eitingon
*(founder and director of the Psychoanalytic Institute of Jerusalem, opened in October 1934.
In Memoriam*, Israel Psychoanalytic Society, Jerusalem, 1950

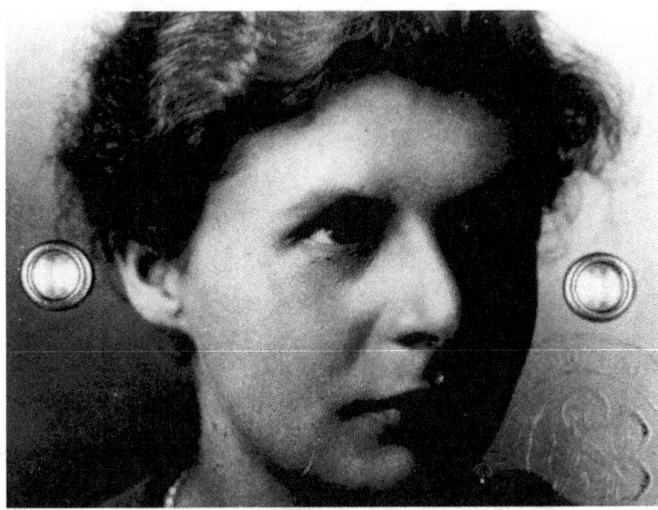

Fig. 56: Berta Grünspan in the 1920s
© Private archive of Hanna Adar, Kibbut Yif'at

Fig. 57: Left to right: Vicky Bental, unidentified woman, Siegfried Flügelmann's wife, Siegfried Flügelmann, and Betty Grünspan in the late 1960s © Private archive of Hanna Adar, Kibbut Yif'at

(LEFT) Fig. 58: Shmuel Nagler © Oranim Seminar Archives, Kiryat Tiv'on
(RIGHT) Fig. 59: Josef Karl Friedjung © http://www.psyalpha.net/biografien/wiener-psychoanalytische-vereinigung-bis-1938/josef-karl-friedjung-1871-1946

Fig. 60: Erich Gumbel © Erich Gumbel, *Al Hayai Im HaPsychoanalyza* [My Life with Psychoanalysis] (Jerusalem: Gefen, 1995)

ד"ר פאניה לובצקי הגי׳

מאת ד"ר מ. ברכיהו

בשישי בינואר חגגו תלמידיה וידידיה של האנאליטיקאית ד"ר פאניה לובצקי את יום הולדתה תשפונגים. רבים בארץ מכירים את ל. כססיכותירא׳סבסית מצויל־נת, כמחנכת של מדריכי נוער, מורים ועובדים סוציאליים בשדק הפסיכוהיגיי־נה. אולם מעטים מ־ כירים אותה כמחברת בשדה המדע הפסי־ כואנאליטי וביחוד כי־

דרך ארוכה לעיבורה של העיה, שהילדים העוזבים והעברייניים חזו מה־ סים לבילוי זמן בשיחות ומשחקים הלת תלמידיה שעברו אצלי במחלקת גיינה של בתי הספר מטעם הרסה. ל. אינה שומעת עברית ולא יכלה ל עם הילדים; אבל חשוב הזה לה תכל בהתנהגות העוזבים, כדי להיי בטיבם לא רק מד"רח ורשומות על

Fig. 61: Fanny Lowtzky in 1953, clipping from an article by Mordechai Brachyahu, "Dr. Fania [Fanny] Lowtzky Hegi'a LiGvurot" [Dr. Fania [Fanny] Reached Great Heights] © Kibbutz Mishmar HaEmek Archives, Rachel Manor Collection

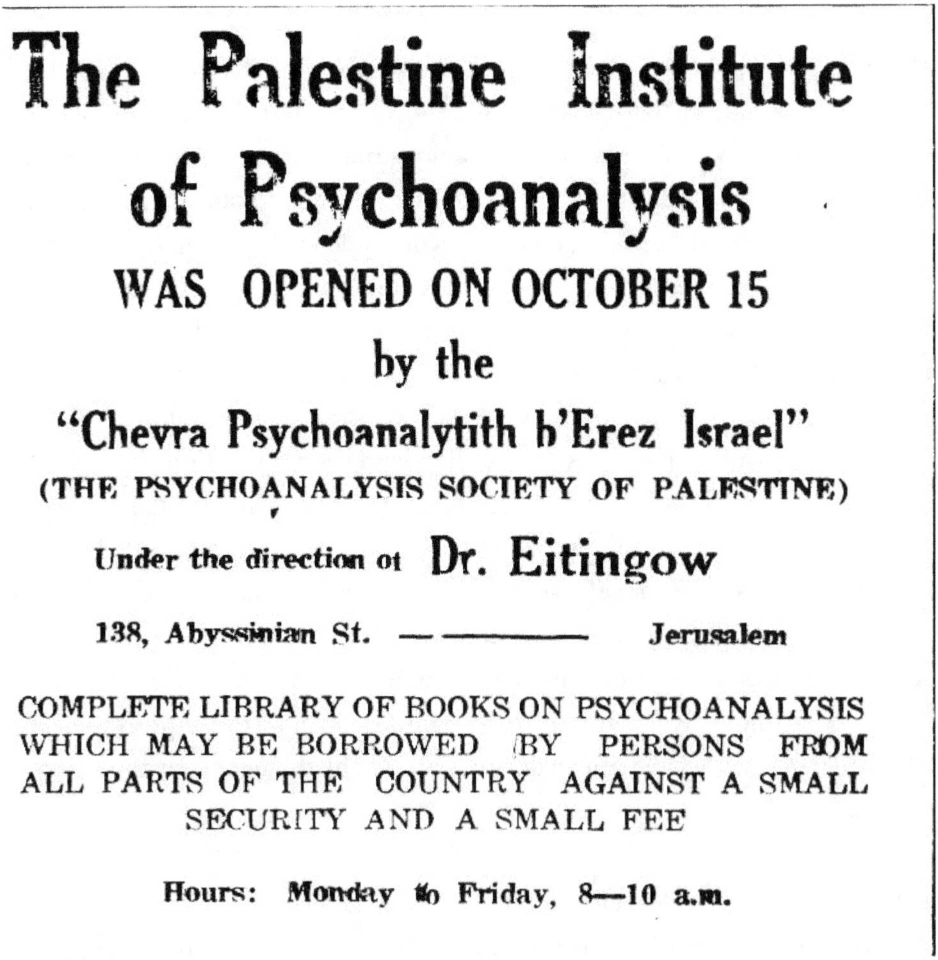

The Palestine Institute of Psychoanalysis

WAS OPENED ON OCTOBER 15

by the

"Chevra Psychoanalytith b'Erez Israel"

(THE PSYCHOANALYSIS SOCIETY OF PALESTINE)

Under the direction of **Dr. Eitingow**

138, Abyssinian St. ——————— Jerusalem

COMPLETE LIBRARY OF BOOKS ON PSYCHOANALYSIS
WHICH MAY BE BORROWED BY PERSONS FROM
ALL PARTS OF THE COUNTRY AGAINST A SMALL
SECURITY AND A SMALL FEE

Hours: Monday to Friday, 8—10 a.m.

Fig. 62: The Palestine Post, Friday, October 26, 1934; Page: 9,

CHAPTER 7

Moshe Wulff and Child Psychoanalysis in Tel Aviv of the 1930s

The Fifth Aliyah (1930-1939) brought large numbers of children and youth to Palestine. Institutions for Jewish children were transferred from Germany in their entirety. In 1935, for example, the famous Berlin-based orphanage Ahavah ("Love" in Hebrew) relocated to Palestine, where it first established temporary premises in Haifa before taking up permanent residence later that year in Kiryat Bialik. As a consequence of this unique combination of circumstances, the demand for psychoanalysis in the field of childcare grew considerably.

By the 1940s, the Freudian movement in Mandatory Palestine (and later, Israel) already had many psychoanalysts working in the major cities and kibbutzim, as well as a professional society and training institute recognized by the international psychoanalytic community. Though lacking the academic accreditation that would come later, the Freudian movement still had the advantages of official local government recognition and a great deal of support among pedagogues and educators. Moreover, HaShomer HaTza'ir's pedagogues, through *Ofakim*, and later Brachyahu, through *Mental Hygiene*, provided psychoanalysts with a platform in the form of prestigious journals that would play a decisive role in the ultimate establishment of psychoanalysis in Israel.

Tel Aviv and Child Psychoanalysis (1933-1943)

With the arrival of Moshe Wulff in March 1933, Tel Aviv became a bastion of psychoanalytic therapy for children and remained so until the early 1940s. In addition to being one of the best clinicians in the country, Wulff was a prolific theorist who worked tirelessly for the Freudian cause and defended one of the most cherished goals of Freud and his daughter Anna – namely, lay analysis. He served as president of the Palestine (later Israel) Psychoanalytic Society from 1943 to 1952 and in time as honorary president of the Israel Psychoanalytic Society, until his death in 1971. Wulff also enjoyed the immediate and important support of David Idelsohn in Tel Aviv, and of Shmuel Golan in the Kibbutz Artzi movement, which helped him introduce the teachings of psychoanalysis into the life of the Yishuv in Palestine.

The close cooperation between Wulff and two of his faithful disciples helped psychoanalysis gain momentum in Palestine and Israel between 1933 and 1953, and to achieve great success among pedagogues working in the country's educational and social institutions.

Moshe Wulff, Freud's Russian Translator

Moshe Wulff, the son of a merchant family, was born in Odessa on May 10, 1878.[357] After graduating from high school, like many other Jews barred from university studies by the Russian Empire's *numerus clausus* system, he left for Central Europe to continue his studies.

He enrolled in the Faculty of Medicine at Friedrich-Wilhelm University in Berlin in 1900 and graduated in 1905.[358] In 1907 he first encountered psychoanalysis: while completing his internship in psychiatry at Dr. Mendel's clinic, he discovered the discipline through *Studies on Hysteria* by Freud and Breuer and *The Psychopathology of Everyday Life* by Freud. Shortly thereafter, while still in Berlin and working at Otto Juliusburger's psychiatric clinic, he met Karl Abraham in what turned out to be a decisive encounter, and he soon became one of the latter's closest disciples.

In 1909 he returned to Odessa and began a correspondence with both Freud and the Hungarian psychoanalyst Sandor Ferenczi. In an article in *Psychotherapija*, which he had recently founded with Nicolai Vyrubov, he offered Russian readers a comprehensive review of the German-language psychoanalytic literature published that year, the first article of its kind to appear in Tsarist Russia. In 1911 he worked in Odessa as a psychiatrist and became a member of the Viennese Psychoanalytic Society. Before long, Freud came to describe him as "a writer who has studied the neuroses of childhood with great understanding – Dr. M. Wulff, of Odessa."[359] As a pivotal member of the psychoanalytic study group in Odessa, where "there seems to be a local epidemic of Psychoanalysis,"[360] Wulff began translating Freud's works into Russian.

Wulff belonged to that generation of pioneering psychoanalysts who had no personal experience of "the couch" themselves. In 1912 he left for

Moscow and, during World War I, served as a military doctor on the front and worked at various psychiatric institutes in the city. As a supporter of the 1917 October Revolution, he was invited to participate in various medical and educational programs. In 1920 he began working at the psychiatric ward of Moscow's military hospital. He married a non-Jewish Russian artist, Assia, who continued her work as a painter in Palestine and later Israel, remaining by his side until his final days.

In Russia, as in most countries before World War I, the official medical establishment remained hostile to psychoanalysis. In 1922, however, the Psycho-Neurological Institute of Moscow opened a laboratory for psychoanalysis, and it called on Wulff to join. In March 1921, with Professor Ivan Dimitrievich Ermakov, director of the Institute, and Dr. Otto Schmidt,[361] he had founded the Psychoanalytic Association for Research on Artistic Works, the first Freudian society in the Soviet Union.[362] In September 1922,[363] seven prominent members of the Society, including Ivan Ermakov, Vera Schmidt,[364] and Wulff himself founded the Russian Psychoanalytic Society.[365]

From the outset – as early as the 1920s – the Soviet regime viewed psychoanalysis as a discipline that conflicted with the aims of communism.[366] Wulff tried to disprove this claim, arguing that the discipline benefited workers as well as the regime,[367] but in 1930 the authorities prohibited the practice and teaching of psychoanalysis. Wulff himself had left for Berlin in 1927. In 1931, through Eitingon's mediation, he met with representatives of HaShomer HaTza'ir from Palestine at the Berlin Psychoanalytic Institute, while they were on a mission in Europe. After seeking Freud's support for his candidacy as Chair of Psychoanalysis in 1932, he left Germany and immigrated to Palestine in early 1933. Moshe and Assia Wulff settled in Tel Aviv in March, where they remained until their passing (1971 and 1976, respectively).

With the immediate and invaluable support of David Idelsohn, Wulff approached pedagogic circles in Palestine and began promoting the basic principles of psychoanalysis. Admittedly by 1931, two years before his arrival, local Jewish educators had already discovered the Hebrew translation of Anna Freud's *Introduction to the Theory of Psychoanalysis*, which was intended for educators.[368] But it was Wulff who provided them with a range of psychoanalytic texts in Hebrew specifically adapted to their daily work and training needs.

He was indisputably responsible for establishing a body of psychoanalytic literature in Hebrew – the first in the history of Palestine. Between 1932 and 1933, a small number of articles on the principles of psychoanalysis, authored by Shmuel Golan and David Idelsohn, had been published in Hebrew in pedagogical journals.[369] In 1935, however, these journals began publishing articles by members of the Palestine Psychoanalytic Society. That same year the Kibbutz Artzi movement also published a series of articles on the problems of early childhood education authored by Golan, Idelsohn, and Wulff, among others.[370]

In 1933, with Idelsohn and Pappenheim, Wulff began opening new treatment centers in Tel Aviv for marginalized children and adolescents. These institutions, founded on the principles and rules of psychoanalysis, also drew on August Aichhorn's recommendations for the treatment of delinquent adolescents. Thus psychoanalysis became one of the main sources of reference for Tel Aviv's social services during the 1930s and early 1940s. In 1934 in Jerusalem, Eitingon founded the first psychoanalytic Institute in Palestine. In 1937 Wulff established a psychoanalytic institute in Tel Aviv devoted to child psychoanalysis and the provision of psychoanalytic training for professionals working with children and adolescents in the fields of healthcare, education, and social work. Wulff served as director of the institute, named after Montague David Eder, who had passed away a few months earlier. It operated in accordance with the principles of lay analysis, of which Wulff was a major advocate.

With their extensive experience in the field of pedagogy, Wulff and Idelsohn embarked on new socio-educational enterprises in Tel Aviv, enhancing the prestige of psychoanalysis among the public in the city and among Yishuv institutions generally. Shmuel Golan invited Wulff to participate in the training of Kibbutz Artzi *metaplot* (women caregivers),[371] and the latter soon earned a reputation among pedagogic circles in Palestine. As a psychoanalyst and instructor at Merkaz HaGananot (the Center for Preschool Teachers affiliated with Histadrut HaMorim), he published a series of texts devoted to the psychological problems of infants and children, and to the applications of psychoanalysis in the field of education.[372] His name became ubiquitous in the pedagogic literature of Palestine during the 1930s and 1940s.

The Cause of Abandoned Youth in Tel Aviv

Shoshana Persitz (born in 1893 in Kiev in the southern Russian Empire, today the capital of the Ukraine), who oversaw children's educational and social services at the Tel Aviv Municipality, entrusted the responsibility for arranging care for Tel Aviv's neglected teenagers in Idelsohn's capable hands. As we know, while in Berlin Idelsohn had undergone training in medical pedagogy, which aimed to prepare healthcare and educational professionals for work in what is known today as child and adolescent psychiatry. Because of his interest in the new experiments on the social rehabilitation of young offenders that were then underway in the Soviet Union, he traveled there, as we recall, in 1930. Let us recall, too, that he had also received psychoanalytic training in Berlin. And when Persitz approached him, he had just begun to take a special interest in the psychoanalytic approaches of Aichhorn and Fenichel to the treatment of abandoned adolescents: following Obernik, David Idelsohn too became one of Aichhorn's successors in Palestine.

In his capacity as manager of the program, Idelsohn surrounded himself with a team of professionals: a counselor, a lawyer by the name of Weisel, and the psychiatrist Abraham Schossberg. Moshe Wulff, for his part, took responsibility for educational matters.[373] In 1933, upon assuming his new post, Idelsohn prepared a comprehensive and very detailed preliminary report for his superiors, in which he painted a dire picture.

These neglected youth, according to Idelsohn, had no future:[374] They came from extremely disadvantaged families, most lacked any schooling, and they engaged in delinquency – often quite severe – on a daily basis, at times exhibiting shocking tendencies towards violence and cruelty. The few who had enrolled in religious schools were too hungry to focus on their studies: rather than attend classes, they would run off to search for food or steal minimal basic supplies for their parents. They were "condemned by a society that rejects and punishes them for no reason," according to Idelsohn, who proposed the creation of "street clubs" – the first step to be taken in Tel Aviv to treat these marginalized youth. Shoshana Persitz then took it upon herself to persuade Tel Aviv's Deputy Mayor Israel Rokach, Yishuv leaders, and the local British authorities to allocate a special budget for the creation of these clubs, where dozens of teenagers, who would otherwise roam the streets and engage in delinquency, could spend their afternoons.[375]

In the same report, Idelsohn also proposed that as a first step, the educational institutions receiving these children provide them with free lunch and dinner, as well as toys and far more flexible classroom hours than those of other children. He added that it would be necessary to provide support for the teachers, so that they could best help these teenagers bridge their monumental learning gap and foster their personal development. The adolescents, aged 12 to 14, could spend their afternoons at a street club, where they would be able to learn a profession at one of the workshops designed for this purpose, watch plays, engage in sports or artistic or cultural activities, or participate in discussion groups. At the same time Idelsohn was also considering establishing a school specifically for repeat offenders with serious social integration difficulties. The school would serve about thirty children and adolescents, who would benefit from activities adapted to their abilities: classes would begin at 8 a.m. and continue until noon, and during the afternoons and evenings, until 8 p.m., they could – as in the street clubs – work, learn a trade, or participate in various leisure activities.

The Abandoned Youth Club

The first club for abandoned youth opened in Tel Aviv on March 15, 1934, and operated under Idelsohn's directorship until his death in 1956. Its first residents were five children who had been caught while committing theft and brought to the club by the police.[376] By August of that year the number of children attending the club – of their own free will, Idelsohn emphasized – had reached forty-six: six children of Ashkenazi origin (former residents of a religious institution who, abused or rejected after being labeled "retarded" or "troubled," had escaped), fifteen children from Georgia, seventeen children of Yemenite origin, and eight children from the Sephardic community. The group as a whole was quite diverse; it included orphaned children and teenagers, adopted children, children who had suffered physical violence, children with kleptomania, "pederast and gay adolescents," and a range of marginalized children and teenagers.[377]

In the course of his work, Idelsohn gave greater weight to what his psychoanalytic training had taught him than to modern or traditional teaching methods. He reported that the club operated "according to the psychoanalytic method."[378] Moreover, he proposed several measures the municipality could adopt to protect the city's abandoned children: a prohibition on child labor that would apply to children under age twelve, a prohibition on their employment as street or newspaper vendors, compulsory education for all children, and the opening of clubs for working adolescents.

He referred any teenager who had committed a crime to Wulff, "the best psychiatrist in Tel Aviv," for an expert opinion.[379] He spoke out openly against the use of psychological tests to diagnose marginalized youth because these tests were "not adapted to the reality faced by children in Palestine" and should not be applied indiscriminately to native-born children or immigrant children from completely different cultures.[380]

Likewise, he vehemently objected to the term "criminal child," which the social and legal services commonly used, believing instead that "neglected" or "abandoned" were more appropriate terms. He argued that he had not encountered a single "criminal child" among the 230 children referred to him for consultation by the Tel Aviv courts in 1935 and 1936, but only "children who had broken the law."[381] He stressed – in terms that reflect the spirit of psychoanalysis – that "there are children who are termed criminals yet only have a strong impulse to collect stamps, pictures, postcards, screws, and the like, simply for the sake of collecting" and that what causes their behavior – which teachers and parents narrowly view as "criminal" – is actually a powerful and uncontrollable desire to accumulate possessions.[382]

It took Moshe Wulff, David Idelsohn, and Martin Pappenheim less than a decade to earn psychoanalysis a prestigious reputation in Tel Aviv. The discipline enjoyed a great deal of acclaim across a variety of spheres: among pedagogues, social workers, and healthcare providers, and in municipal and governmental institutions. In the 1930s and 1940s it held a place of honor in the Yishuv, particularly in the country's most secular city. And thus, without losing any of its uniqueness, the discipline of psychoanalysis took hold in Palestine, developing through close cooperation with the country's psychiatric, pedagogic, municipal, and governmental institutions.

CHAPTER 8

Training the Pedagogues: The Education Department (HaMossad HaKhinukhi) of HaKibbutz HaArtzi

The leaders of HaShomer HaTza'ir, in their search to identify what role the youth would play in bringing about the "New Jew," had to expand their thinking and scope of action to actualize their vision of the pioneer. The kibbutzim would soon see the birth of dozens of children, destined to grow into courageous workers, intellectuals, and revolutionaries who were expected to change the face of the country.

How should these children and their mothers be educated, now that mothers, liberated from the role imposed on them in Old Europe, were to be trained by the *metaplot* (caregivers) and educators of the kibbutz, who themselves were learning the new teaching methods? The movement's ideologues and pedagogues had to decide whether children would be raised separately from adults, along the model of Beit Alpha, or near adult society, within the kibbutz. They decided on the latter.

Unlike other leaders of the Zionist left, the leaders of HaShomer HaTza'ir sought to abolish the traditional family and have the community, rather than the parents, educate children. This required them to address another question, which was both delicate in nature and decisive for the future of the movement: Who would be assigned responsibility for this education, and what would be its rules? They could not embark on this new adventure blindly, as doing so might give rise to irreversible psychological disorders among the children as well as their parents. Who should therefore assume responsibility in place of the parents for the care of infants and toddlers, to ensure their physical and psychological well-being? Who should be trained, and in what manner, to take on the heavy responsibility of educating children separately from their families and instilling in them the values of kibbutz life? During the years 1927-1929, the movement's pedagogues and leaders had to face a myriad of questions with no obvious answer. Furthermore, with the failure of Beitania Illit still a fresh memory, they did not want to risk embarking on new adventures without first acquiring a minimum of experience, or at least developing a firm pedagogic and psychological cultural foundation for their program, especially given that relations between David Idelsohn and the movement's members at Beit Alpha were deteriorating and another failure seemed inevitable.

Those two misadventures convinced the movement's leaders that they needed to formulate a collective education program specifically tailored to their kibbutzim and suited to their purpose. Towards this end they would no longer rely on pedagogic experts who did not belong to their movement; in fact they only approached psychoanalysts, and in particular Moshe Wulff.

The Education Department of HaKibbutz HaArtzi

In April 1927 representatives of the four kibbutzim of HaShomer HaTza'ir (Maabarot, Merhavia, Mishmar HaEmek, and Ein Shemer) gathered in Bat Galim and founded a national federation of kibbutzim – HaKibbutz HaArtzi. Many of the movement's members left Europe to join their comrades in Palestine and establish new kibbutzim. HaShomer HaTza'ir expanded rapidly, and the influence of this autonomous movement increased both in Palestine and abroad, soon becoming the third political force of the Zionist left. Because it never lost its spirit of exclusivity, it drew fierce criticism, particularly on the part of leaders of other leftist parties. In 1927 Chaim Arlozorov, a prominent leader of HaPo'el HaTza'ir at the time, denounced the "proletarian snobbery" and "psychological utopianism" of HaShomer HaTza'ir members.[383] His remarks are reminiscent of the mockery that the first activist immigrants had encountered some years earlier.

At its Fifth General Assembly one year later, in 1928, HaKibbutz HaArtzi decided to found its own independent Education Department (HaMossad HaKhinukhi Shel HaKibbutz HaArtzi),[384] with the mandate of developing a new collective education system for all the movement's kibbutzim. Its tasks included formulating new teaching methods, acquainting itself with progressive educational approaches abroad, gathering relevant facts and figures, and assembling pedagogic literature and material. Its aim was to train pedagogues, as quickly as possible, to be capable of raising and educating children separately from their parents and outside of the traditional school system, which the ideologues of HaShomer HaTza'ir had long ago rejected.[385]

A special commission of the movement's leading pedagogues was appointed in May for the purpose of founding HaShomer HaTza'ir's first school, to be directed and run exclusively by educators from the movement.[386] HaKibbutz HaArtzi's first "Educational Institute" (HaMossad HaKhinukhi, as the movement's schools were named) opened in 1931 on Kibbutz Mishmar HaEmek and began receiving the first generation of children born on the movement's kibbutzim. Mishmar HaEmek was also designated as the headquarters of the Education Department of HaKibbutz HaArtzi, whose members included Shmuel Golan, Yehuda Gothelf, Yaakov Hazan, Mordechai Shenhavi, Yaakov ("Poli") Padan (Polisiuk), and Meir Ya'ari, who had rejoined the movement in 1924.[387] The responsibility for developing a suitable educational program for the kibbutz children and ensuring its implementation was initially assigned to Shmuel Golan and Zvi Sohar, who was appointed the first director of the department. They dizzily but enthusiastically and determinedly immersed themselves in all the books available at the time that dealt with the physiological or psychological and emotional development of infants and toddlers, as well as books on psychology in general.[388] According to Golan, these works constituted the entire scope of their training in those areas.

Like pilgrims, Golan and Sohar, now linked by a common cause, perhaps a shared destiny even, untiringly disseminated their knowledge and spread their enthusiasm among kibbutz movement members across the country. They traveled far and wide, through rain and mud, carting two suitcases filled to the brim with educational material and obsolete supplies, offering lectures and lessons for the young pedagogues charged with educating kibbutz-born children. The educational revolution of HaShomer HaTza'ir, under Golan and Sohar's "collective education," was underway by 1931 and in full swing by 1933 on Kibbutz Mishmar HaEmek, with Golan its main theorist.

Zvi Sohar, Ambassador for Psychoanalysis in HaKibbutz HaArtzi

Zvi Sohar (Sonnenschein) was the ambassador and advocate for psychoanalysis in HaKibbutz HaArtzi, essentially serving as mediator between the European psychoanalytic movement and HaShomer HaTza'ir. His position was challenged at times, for he did not always adhere strictly to HaShomer HaTza'ir principles, but he remained a prominent figure in the movement, possibly more than any other leader, by virtue of his strong personality, expansive sense of culture, and diplomatic skills. These assets and his cumulative experience in the field of pedagogy allowed him to promote psychoanalysis as "the psychology best suited to the educational concerns" of the movement.

Zvi Sohar was born in 1899 in Rozdol, in the Polish part of Galicia, and attended high school in Brauhtein. During World War I he left for Vienna, where he completed studies in the natural sciences and agriculture. While a university student, he served as a counselor in the local chapter of HaShomer HaTza'ir.[389] When his comrades left for Palestine to found Beitania Illit, he stayed to complete his studies, earning a doctoral degree in biology from the University of Vienna. In 1920 he returned to Poland, working as a teacher first in the village of Mezritch and then in Lodz, where he also headed the local chapter of HaShomer HaTza'ir. In 1926 he immigrated to Palestine and began working as a teacher at the Children's Village in Giv'at HaMoreh and later at the Beit Alpha Children's Society. Sohar shared Golan's conviction – which was not devoid of "the unique romanticism of HaShomer HaTza'ir" – that "if the kibbutzim fail to develop their own education system, they will have no future."[390] A sober realist and exceptional administrator and mediator, he remained throughout his life one of the greatest advocates of psychoanalysis in the movement.

Sohar spent the years 1929-1934 in Poland as supervisor of the schools and youth division of Keren Kayemet LeIsrael – the Jewish National Fund (in 1939 the division was transferred to Palestine and Sohar was appointed director of its educational services). He also served as head of the education department of the Zionist educational network Tarbut (Culture), whose activities had been banned in the Soviet Union but continued in Poland, and as supervisor of Jewish schools in Poland. During his stay in Europe he formed close ties with the psychoanalytic movement in Vienna and Berlin, which he used to support the movement's educational projects and forge a pact between it and HaShomer HaTza'ir. Sohar took a strong interest in developments taking place among progressive educational circles in Germany, and was especially impressed by the experimental initiatives underway at the renowned Wickersdorf School founded by Wyneken. Upon his return to Palestine in 1934, he joined Shmuel Golan at Mishmar HaEmek to lay the foundation for collective education, refine its first programs, and develop new ones. His unwavering guiding principle was the concept that "man must be an inseparable part of the culture – in the broad sense of the term – as the creative forces of the kibbutz movement are galvanized by culture." Culture, according to Sohar, is essential for the formation of a human being, from the moment of birth, and it is transmitted first and foremost through education.

Although Sohar never abandoned the world of education, he gradually withdrew from the management of collective education, leaving it in the hands of Golan, and assumed responsibility for the cultural affairs and publications of HaKibbutz HaArtzi. In 1943 he participated in founding the movement's publishing house, Sifriat Poalim, and was appointed its editor-in-chief. In addition to authoring many articles, books, and pamphlets on art, culture, education, and of course psychology and psychoanalysis, he instituted a seminar for the training of *shlikhim* (envoys on behalf of the movement), which he ran until his death on February 16, 1975. Throughout his travels across Europe and North America, he promoted the training of teachers in the Zionist spirit.

As a theorist, Sohar believed that it was important to integrate the various pedagogic theories in order to define the educational goals of HaShomer HaTza'ir institutions. He argued that these could not be based solely on free education (which he regarded as quite vague), because in seeking to create the ideal human being, one cannot neglect the psychology of the child. And psychoanalysis was in his view the only discipline capable of addressing the ideological, educational, and cultural aspirations of movement. This was a very difficult position to defend, as many other leaders of the movement were strongly opposed to Freud (who in their view was overly pessimistic about the possibility of changing the individual and society). They believed that education should be based solely on the movement's ideology, while relying – if necessary – on so-called "scientific" psychology, which Sohar, like Bernfeld before him, rejected, believing that it served capitalism and contributed to the exploitation of workers. The debates that raged within the movement during the late 1920s and early 1930s between supporters of psychoanalysis and proponents of experimental psychology became even more animated after the movement officially aligned itself with Marxism and again around the time of Israel's independence, in light of Stalin's support for the creation of a Jewish state.

In 1927 the main opponent of the positions advocated by Sohar and Golan in the Education Department of HaKibbutz HaArtzi and the movement as a whole was Meir Ya'ari. He was a fierce proponent of Marxist views, with a strong hostility toward psychoanalysis and the theories of Bernfeld and Freud, and he believed that education must always have a political dimension. But his arguments were at odds with the fundamental principles of the movement, and Sohar, Golan, and other pedagogues loyal to Bernfeld succeeded over time in establishing an education system that was both consistent with the ideology of HaShomer HaTza'ir and devoid of any political dimension.

Although Ya'ari's views on psychoanalysis changed over time, he continued to support Blüher's notions on the "eroticism of the young." In a 1927 article in *HaKhinukh HaShomri*, the new Hebrew-language journal published by HaShomer HaTza'ir in Warsaw, he outlined the movement's mandate as he saw it:

1. HaShomer HaTza'ir strives to unite the inner emotional being, scientific ideology, and concrete political action.

2. HaShomer HaTza'ir encompasses all stages of a person's life, from the moment of birth, and it applies to the three phases of life in the form of (1) an educational organization, (2) a pioneering and youth movement, and (3) the sociopolitical and kibbutz movement in Palestine.

3. HaShomer HaTza'ir opposes the mechanical segregation of dynamic social action (politics), individual and collective self-actualization, and the influence of education, and it strives for the unification of these three functions in its work.[391]

The concept of free education propounded by Bernfeld (drawing on Wyneken) appeared to Ya'ari as one more myth among many: it was inevitably political, as it served the interests of the ruling power no less than the other approaches.

Yehuda Gothelf, another member of the Education Department, strongly criticized Ya'ari's statements and denounced "these trends in the movement against freedom of education and in support of of partisan and absolutist education" – that is, against the movement's own ideological principles: against "romanticism," against "play," and against "spontaneity."[392] He did not mince words, accusing Ya'ari of "tendentious psychosis" and "political opportunism," which run counter to "youth culture" and to the principles and values on which HaShomer HaTza'ir was founded, and even stunt the growth of the movement.

In 1929, shortly before joining Shmuel Golan in Romania, where the two represented the movement, Zvi Sohar stated that it is absurd to expect the teenagers of HaShomer HaTza'ir not to consider leaving the kibbutz after completing their studies. He strongly criticized the "idyllic" vision of Degania's members, who relied on "the mutual love that binds children and parents" as a means of ensuring their community's endurance. Sohar was referring here to socialist pioneers (*halutzim*) of the Second Aliyah who had founded the first agricultural community (*kvutza*) on the shores of the Sea of Galilee – the prototype and first experiment in establishing a kibbutz of any sort; Degania's members, although they had abolished private property, continued to abide by traditional family values that HaShomer HaTza'ir rejected as a matter of ideology.[393] In his view one must not confuse leaving the kibbutz for a while, in order to explore the world, with abandoning the kibbutz. Sohar argued that the most difficult task would be to convince young people to adopt the path of their elders. After all, he pointed out, the kibbutzim of HaShomer HaTza'ir do not exist in a vacuum within Palestine, and the kibbutz children are fully aware of their surroundings. It would be truly naïve, he added, to believe that these children would not, in time, oppose their parents and reject kibbutz life. Such resistance and tension are characteristic of adolescents everywhere and at all times, Sohar asserted, citing the theories of Adler and Freud.

Golan and Sohar believed that only psychoanalysis offered a foundation for collective education, and that only psychoanalysis could support their pedagogues in creating the new society of their vision and imparting it to future generations. Despite the strength of their convictions, however, debates within HaKibbutz HaArtzi and among the ranks of HaShomer HaTza'ir continued long after psychoanalysis was chosen over experimental psychology or the individual psychology of Adler.

Articles on Freud, Bernfeld, and psychoanalysis in general appeared often in the journals of HaShomer HaTza'ir: *HaKhinukh HaShomri* (Shomerian Education), *HaKhinukh HaMeshutaf* (Collective Education), and from 1932, *Ofakim* (Horizons), an educational and cultural journal founded by Sohar, which gave prominence to psychoanalysis and psychoanalysts during 1930-1940. These writings attest to the importance that HaShomer HaTza'ir members in Palestine and abroad, particularly in Poland, ascribed to psychoanalysis.

Nevertheless, Adler's theories continued to occupy an important place in the outlook of some of the movement's pedagogues and leaders. Were an in-depth study to be conducted on the correlation between the thinking of HaShomer HaTza'ir pedagogues and the individual psychology propounded by Adler, it would probably help us understand why the movement's activists were drawn to the theories of this socialist, whose views on humanity and the power of education were "less pessimistic" than those of Freud or Bernfeld. Indeed, Adler's followers never completely gave up; at the time of Golan's death, their resentment towards him for having imposed "theoretical patriarchalism" on the movement was still palpable. But in any event, the arrival of Freudians in Palestine beginning in 1933 fostered encounters, alliances, and cooperation between the international psychoanalytic movement and the pedagogues of HaShomer HaTza'ir. And with Adler's death in 1937, individual psychology lost both its appeal and its influence.

During one of the particularly passionate debates that animated the general assembly gatherings of HaKibbutz HaArtzi between 1929 and 1931 (and resounded throughout pedagogic circles abroad), Sohar – responding from Vienna in 1931 – told the adherents of experimental psychology that in order to consolidate an educational program for the movement, "we will have to rely on the progress made by modern psychology and pedagogy; this does not mean that we must adopt each and every new method or apply it in a fetishist manner." Borrowing the terminology of Meir Sharar, he added that the use of phrases such as *free education, life plans*, and *freedom at any cost* amounted to no more than "pedagogic phraseology" that contributes nothing to defining the methods and identifying the limitations of collective education.[394] He recalled Bernfeld's achievements[395] and criticized experimental psychology for describing itself as "pure psychology" – an absurd term, he noted, because whatever its pretensions, the officially accepted psychology would always serve the worldview (Weltanschauung) of the existing regime.[396]

Zvi Sohar was also accused of attempting to turn Kibbutz Mishmar HaEmek into an experimental laboratory, with its new system of collective education to be instituted in 1931. He did not dispute this, but did offer clarification: in order to identify new methods suitable to the children of workers living under the new conditions of the kibbutz, "whether we like it or not, this is certainly an experimental situation. And experimental means that the pedagogue believes in his method no less than in its limitations." Refusing to divide children into separate classes by age, as advocated by experimental psychology and encouraged by Meir Sharar, he added,

> It will be hard for the members of HaKibbutz HaArtzi to find someone who believes in experimental psychology, which still dictates rigid laws establishing curricula by age, division, and classroom. I would like to see Meir [Sharar] explore the possibility of implementing a permanent curriculum for the entire year in a society of children under the current regime, and then we shall see the extent to which he is building on illusory foundations. But this is not the question. The question is a psychological one, a question of genuine rationalization based on the exploitation of all the power of the workers.[397]

Psychoanalysis, however, was a different matter altogether: "Psychoanalysis, which opposes the official psychology, the modern psychology, has declared war on repression and silence. It calls on us to unveil the paradoxes of the soul and uncover the animalistic aspects of man that reside in the unconscious: it was Freud's research that revealed to us the existence of the laws of the unconscious, laws that govern our lives and our existence – for which the laws of the biological world do not provide an adequate explanation."[398]

The aim was to paint a psychological portrait of the "New Jew" – the pioneer, the *halutz* – and specifically the kibbutz member of HaShomer HaTza'ir, the Jew who over the years and over the course of his wanderings had undergone an "instinctual change" that no school of psychology had yet troubled to understand or explain. Only Freud's "psychology of the depths" was capable of doing so and of enabling the Jewish People to overcome the inferiority complex it had developed because of the trauma, poverty, suffering, and oppression to which centuries of life in the Diaspora had subjected it. Sohar argued that only the psychoanalytic couch provided a remedy: it alone offered an opportunity to resolve the Jewish People's "inferiority complex" and release the aggression it had accumulated from repressing persecution and oppression over the years. In his words,

> Under the present circumstances, we must begin by gathering material and facts. We must admit that we have yet to assemble the psychological material, even partially. When one hears about the degree of superficiality in serious pedagogic and intellectual circles that seek to address "the Jewish youth of today". . . . it becomes evident that much work remains for researchers in assembling and analyzing this material. . . . For the psychology of a nation that has undergone excessive "repression," we believe that the one and only research tool is Sigmund Freud's psychology of the depths. . . . We the heirs of the Bible and the Talmud, who approach the task of describing man and exploring his impulses honestly, must dispel the inner dishonesty that results from having a multitude of conventions, and approach man and his soul with open, impartial eyes. After seeing him in his entirety, including his animal essence, we will know how to approach him so as to raise him to the level of a cultured person. . . through our prophylactic efforts as well as our attitude towards his purpose and towards that which is inherent in his character.[399]

It took a good deal of effort on Sohar's part to persuade the members of HaKibbutz HaArtzi that psychoanalysis was the most appropriate and best adapted psychology for the pedagogic approach of collective education. This meant prevailing over both experimental psychology and individual psychology: he denounced Adler's "closed" character and his narrow conceptions of the human being, as well as his ideological prejudices regarding the function of the psyche.

For a few years no one but Freud enjoyed such acceptance – the same Freud who "cautiously concluded that. . . everything here is still in a state of genesis, relatively undeveloped, for the most part only beginnings and assumptions."[400] One of Sohar's tasks was to establish contact with members of the Vienna Psychoanalytic Society to solicit their support in the psychoanalytic training of educators at HaShomer HaTza'ir's kibbutzim. His meeting in 1929 with Paul Federn, among the most renowned psychoanalysts of the Vienna Psychoanalytic Society, combined with the support of the psychoanalytic movement (thanks to Federn's mediation) in implementing HaShomer HaTza'ir's plans in the areas of education and publications, had a decisive impact on future developments. In Sohar's words,

> The psychoanalytic circles of Vienna include Dr. Paul Federn. . . . We managed to establish contact with the management of the Berlin Psychoanalytic Institute – with Max Eitingon and a few others. One of the practical outcomes of this encounter was the Institute's willingness to accept our educators for training. Among these educators was Shmuel Golan. And Dr. Wulff, who was in Berlin at the time and was already known within the movement as a defender of lay analysis (Laienanalyse) – the practice of analysis by trained non-physicians – agreed to receive Golan for didactic analysis. There is no doubt that by virtue of this analysis, Dr. Wulff became familiar with our thoughts on education and – through his "patient" – developed an association with collective education at its inception. . . especially given that much of the preparatory work for the establishment of the Education Department at Mishmar HaEmek at the time was concentrated in Berlin. It is reasonable to assume that as a consequence Dr. Wulff's mind was opened to education in general."[401]

It was Paul Federn who responded favorably on behalf of the Vienna Psychoanalytic Society to Sohar's request for support. This affirmation was important because at the time HaShomer HaTza'ir's intellectuals were drawing harsh criticism from their colleagues in the Histadrut, particularly from HaPo'el HaTza'ir members, who opposed the official Marxism that HaShomer HaTza'ir now adopted even in the areas of culture and publications.

While in Poland, as part of the movement's educational and cultural programs that he had formulated and coordinated in 1930-1932, and to increase the effectiveness of HaShomer HaTza'ir's ambitious plans, Sohar founded *Ofakim*, the movement's highly instrumental journal on cultural and educational issues – and the preferred platform for psychoanalysis in Palestine. The new journal drew simultaneously on the plans formulated in Warsaw, in Berlin, and in Vienna.

1929, Difficulties with the International Psychoanalytic Movement

"At any rate, you should meet with Fritz Wittels [a member of the Vienna Psychoanalytic Society]. My meeting with him never took place because he indicated [in a phone conversation] that because of the riots in Palestine no one would want to donate to the publication of books related to Eretz Israel. Today however, he will not be able to use this excuse."[402] For some time after the outbreak of rioting in Hebron on August 24, 1929, the atmosphere across the country remained one of tension and deep disappointment. A number of assimilated Jewish psychoanalysts in Europe, and Freud in particular, were profoundly upset. Wittels, who before these events had promised to help HaShomer HaTza'ir members, changed his mind. He voiced strong reservations about the likelihood of success of the Zionist enterprises in Palestine, and retracted his offer of support for the movement's publication projects. Federn, in contrast, continued his efforts to help HaShomer HaTza'ir educators, as did Eitingon, Wulff, and Bernfeld.

In a letter dated September 17, 1930, Sohar reminded Federn that the movement was facing financial hardship and needed funds to realize its plans, namely, the publication of Hebrew-language books on psychoanalysis and pedagogy, the creation of a journal, and the establishment of a library dedicated to psychoanalysis in the Education Department of Mishmar HaEmek. After some twenty libraries for kibbutz pedagogues opened simultaneously, the movement's members began to take a strong interest in psychoanalysis. Sohar explained why they were keen to translate and publish these works in Hebrew: in *The Future of an Illusion*, he wrote to Federn, what spoke to them was Freud's perception of life in general, the world of the psyche, and religious phenomena; the book would be very instructive for educators, as it provided an excellent introduction to psychoanalytic thought. Wittels's book, for its part, "is perfectly suited for the practical work of our pedagogues" and had been very well received among preschool teachers. Sohar further proposed that they consider Federn and Meng's *Volksbuch*, noting that he was thinking about compiling a collective volume of psychoanalytic essays that address practical questions. Finally, Sohar, as a member of HaShomer HaTza'ir, argued that in contrast to what the movement's pure Marxists believed, Bernfeld's *Sysiphos* was "of great importance for our movement because it addresses both the socialist experience and the psychoanalytic experience."[403]

Having explained the need to translate and publish a Hebrew-language series of books on psychoanalysis, Sohar then confirmed that the movement's journal was soon to be published in the Diaspora, in Warsaw specifically. It would be free of scientific or academic pretensions, and "intended for the youth movement, addressing topical issues of interest primarily to young people, including questions related to sexuality and sex education." In addition, it would provide bibliographic references on psychoanalysis, with the aim of assisting the movement's counselors in their work. Finally, Sohar invited Federn to author a column devoted to psychoanalysis, informing Hebrew-language readers in Palestine and elsewhere of the psychoanalytic movement's activities. The publishers of *Ofakim* kept their promise and gave psychoanalysis a good deal of coverage in their journal and other publications.

Ofakim: A Platform for Psychoanalysis

As it turned out, Berlin showed more interest than Vienna in providing HaShomer HaTza'ir pedagogues with the psychoanalytic training they needed to promote the discipline in Palestine. Was this perhaps because Bernfeld and Eitingon – who were strongly sympathetic to the Zionist movement and the efforts of their co-religionists in Palestine – resided there?

The first issue of *Ofakim* was published in Warsaw in 1932, edited by Zvi Sohar. It became the first cultural and educational periodical of the international HaShomer HaTza'ir movement.[404] Thus Sohar won his first major battle within the movement, and specifically against its hardline Marxists. In doing so he had to fight along two fronts: On the cultural front, through *Ofakim*, he managed to provide his movement, both locally and abroad, with a genuine cultural platform that granted it a new form of prestige in addition to that which it had acquired by founding kibbutzim and becoming an important bloc within the left in Palestine. On the pedagogic front, having struggled on behalf of psychoanalysis as the psychological discipline best suited for achieving the movement's educational goals, he then successfully implemented other plans of HaShomer HaTza'ir – in the area of publications, among others – with the support (perhaps financial as well) of members of the psychoanalytic communities in Vienna and Berlin.

Sohar attained a position of considerable influence within HaKibbutz HaArtzi, which allowed him, if not to impose psychoanalysis on movement, at least to ensure that during 1930-1940 (and even thereafter) it held the privileged status that he and Golan sought. This marked yet another victory over the supporters of experimental psychology.

During the early 1930s, the trend among official pedagogic circles in Palestine as well as many of Jerusalem's academics, particularly at the Hebrew University, was the complete reverse: in contrast to HaShomer HaTza'ir educators and other pedagogues identified with the left, they turned to experimental psychology. It is significant, therefore, that beginning in 1932, with the founding of *Ofakim* and thanks to the efforts of Sohar, psychoanalysis gained ground in Hebrew-language professional literature.

Ofakim: A Spotlight on Psychoanalysis

As a periodical on cultural and educational affairs, *Ofakim* strove to be progressive, openly declaring its opposition to "bourgeois culture" and seeking to reach a wide audience, well beyond the scope of the movement. Although most of its articles dealt with problems related to culture and education, debates and polemics were not absent from its pages.

The theorists of HaShomer HaTza'ir naturally presented the readers of *Ofakim* with the works and thinking of those authors who had inspired them at the time of their movement's inception. The journal translated and published the founding texts of Gustav Wyneken, and discussed the influence of the Wandervogel movement on the pedagogic concepts of HaShomer HaTza'ir. It also explored the new psycho-pedagogical methods developed by the Belgian educator and psychologist Ovide Decroly, examined the Soviet Union's pedagogic experiments with juvenile delinquents in light of the theories of Aichhorn and Bernfeld, and described the experiments conducted at Bernfeld's orphanage. Golan translated an article by the psychoanalyst Otto Fenichel, whom he had befriended during his psychoanalytic training in Berlin, in which the author described an experiment conducted in the Soviet Union, at Bolshevo, a community that received juvenile delinquents. The journal also addressed the psychology of adolescent offenders: it translated an article by Aichhorn that the psychoanalytic movement regarded as groundbreaking and authoritative on the psychology of "dissocial" children and adolescents.[405] Ronia Sohar authored an article reviewing various theories of play – including those of Spencer, Lazarus, Wundt, Bühler, Hall, Gross, and Stern, among others – with special attention to psychoanalytic theories of play. In another article she explored the psychology of the adolescent, relying heavily on psychoanalytic theory and concepts and explaining such notions as the latency period, the libidinal object, the incest taboo, and the like, in terms that the Hebrew reader could understand; at the time, these concepts received barely any mention in official publications such as *HaKikhnukh* and *Hed HaKhinukh*. The psychoanalyst Heinrich Meng published a well-researched and highly informative article titled "Nervous Diseases of Childhood," marking the first publication in Palestine of an article specifically devoted to childhood psychopathological problems such as somnambulism (sleepwalking), obsessional neurosis, pavor nocturnos (sleep terror), kleptomania, enuresis (bedwetting), and so on.

Through *Ofakim*, Hebrew-language readers also learned about psychoanalytic publications on education and advances in modern psychology, to the extent that these correlated with the worldview of HaShomer HaTza'ir. In addition to articles by foreign psychoanalysts, the journal published pieces by immigrant psychoanalysts who had fled the Nazis. It featured many essays on psychoanalysis by Sohar, Golan, and their colleagues in the Palestine Psychoanalytic Society, most of which addressed questions relating to child psychology and psychoanalytic perspectives on education.

The number of psychoanalytic texts published in *Ofakim* throughout the 1940s and early 1950s attest to the privileged relationship HaShomer HaTza'ir had with the Freudian movement in Palestine – especially during the years in which Moshe Wulff presided over the Palestine Psychoanalytic Society, that is, between 1943 and 1953. In addition to Hebrew translations of Freud's writings (to which we will return), *Ofakim* featured articles authored by other foreign psychoanalysts, such as "Childhood Anxieties" by Anna Freud (examining the anxieties of children during the London Blitz of World War II); "Anti-Semitism in Light of Psychoanalysis" by Otto Fenichel; and "The Scholastic Failure" by the Swiss psychoanalyst Hans Zulliger.

Between 1941 and 1948, *Ofakim* published a large number of articles penned by Wulff, some of which were reprinted in 1949 in the second volume of his book *Nefesh HaYeled* (The Psyche of the Child), which gained much popularity among the general public. Other essays were included in another of his books, *HaYeled HaKatan* (The Young Child), which his biographers have overlooked. After 1953, however, the attention devoted to psychoanalysis in the pages of *Ofakim* – and in the ranks of HaShomer HaTza'ir more generally – steadily diminished in response to growing Marxist criticism of psychoanalysis within the movement, according to descriptions by Shlomo Yitzhaki, a witness to these developments.

1943: The Founding of Sifriat Poalim

The publishing house of HaShomer HaTza'ir, Sifriat Poalim (The Workers' Library), founded in 1943 and directed by Zvi Sohar, published many psychoanalytic texts translated into Hebrew by HaShomer HaTza'ir intellectuals. One of the first books of Freud printed by Sifriat Poalim was *Selbstdarstellung*[406] (An Autobiographical Study), initially published in 1925. The platform provided by the movement to psychoanalysis during 1931-1953 undoubtedly constituted one of the major developments in the history of psychoanalysis in Palestine, not to mention the evolution of modern Hebrew. The translation of writings by Freud and other psychoanalysts, as well as the status that HaShomer HaTza'ir granted psychoanalysts in Palestine through its periodicals and training centers, made the movement one of the most important channels for the transmission of psychoanalytic teachings in Mandatory Palestine and the State of Israel.

Shmuel Golan: Leader and Pedagogue, a Shomer and a Freudian

Once in Berlin, Golan became fascinated with the strange, complex, enigmatic, and vibrant life of the German capital just before Hitler's rise to power, but even more so with psychoanalysis. He developed an enthusiasm for Freud's ideas and psychoanalysis in general, and after arriving in Palestine he transmitted this enthusiasm to the many students he trained in pedagogy at various venues of HaKibbutz HaArtzi. While HaShomer HaTza'ir is arguably indebted to Zvi Sohar for the prestigious alliance he forged with the psychoanalytic movement, which benefited both parties, after 1933 it was Golan who personified the pact between HaShomer HaTza'ir and the psychoanalytic movement in Palestine. The psychoanalysts who immigrated to Palestine from 1933 onwards (especially Eitingon, Wulff, and Friedjung) saw Golan as one of the most loyal allies of the Freudian movement in Palestine, and as one of their closest collaborators.

Shmuel ("Milek") Stanislaw Goldschein was born on April 22, 1901, in the village of Pidvolochysk, near Lvov, to a secular Jewish Galician family who spoke Polish and German. His father, Pesach Goldschein, an Austrian government official, served as stationmaster for the town's railway. Apart from Shmuel and one of his nieces, the entire Goldschein family was killed during the Holocaust.

Like other Jewish families from Eastern Galicia who fled the invasion of tsarist troops in 1914, the Goldschein family took refuge in Vienna, returning to Lvov after the war. Shmuel joined HaShomer HaTza'ir around 1917,[407] serving as leader of the group in Vienna and later heading the chapter in Lvov. In April 1920 he was elected to the leadership of the movement, and in June of that year he immigrated to Palestine, where he joined HaShomer HaTza'ir's commune, which Meir Ya'ari had helped found, at Beitania Illit. When this experiment failed and the group dispersed, he turned to agricultural labor and roadworks before joining Kibbutz Beit Alpha and participating in the creation of the Children's Society.

In 1928, after clashing with Idelsohn, Golan left the Children's Society. He was convinced that this experiment – which continued for another year – would never achieve its aims. In 1929 he left Palestine to represent the movement in Romania, delegating to his friend Zvi Sohar the responsibility for implementing the new pedagogical principles that would form the basis of collective education, as adapted to kibbutz life, within HaKibbutz HaArtzi.

From the outset of their collaboration on behalf of the Education Department at Mishmar HaEmek, and despite their very different personalities, the two became inseparable. Vacillating between hope and fear of failure, they tirelessly supervised the children's and infants' homes to ensure the smooth running of this experiment in collective education, which was in full swing. They were so close to each other that kibbutz members called them "Zvilek" – a fusion of the names Zvi and Milek. In 1929 Golan was sent to study psychoanalysis in Berlin and undergo analysis with Moshe Wulff. Some months after his arrival, he sent a letter describing the political unrest in the city and his impression that the fate of the world was at stake.[408] Towards the end of 1932 he attended his first meeting of members of the Berlin Psychoanalytic Institute, the mecca of psychoanalysis. In the meantime the Education Department at Mishmar HaEmek, which opened its doors in 1931, awaited his return to launch its revolution in collective education. In late 1932 or early 1933,[409] he received two books that he read with special attention. In the first, *Introductory Lectures on Psychoanalysis*, it was the final chapter, devoted to the problem of Weltanschauung (worldview), on which he focused. Golan translated this chapter into Hebrew, and the text became a topic of conversation throughout leftist circles in Palestine. The second book was *De Vriendt Kehrt Heim* (De Vriendt Goes Home) by Arnold Zweig,[410] which had just been published in German. Golan's commentary confirms that this book sparked a scandal among Zionist circles in Germany.[411]

Golan also took a special interest in a book by the British anthropologist Bronislaw Malinowski, which dealt with the sexual life of the indigenous peoples of Oceania.[412] He saw this work as an essential text for training the movement's pedagogues to work with adolescents, and believed that it would inspire thinking about the sexual life of kibbutz children and teenagers raised according to the principles of collective education. Indeed, Golan found Malinowski's conclusions on the sexual life of indigenous adolescents so thought-provoking that he launched an experiment in "communal showers" among adolescent boys and girls.[413]

In March 1933, with chaos and violence rampant in Germany, he left the country for good and returned to Palestine. For quite some time, until the early 1940s, he remained the only educator in HaShomer HaTza'ir who had benefited from proper psychoanalytic training. Although this was not sufficient in the eyes of the psychoanalytic authorities in Berlin or Jerusalem to qualify him as a practicing psychoanalyst, it provided him with the knowledge that enabled him to develop, test, and implement the new kibbutz education system of which he was the principal architect.

In April 1933, as expected, he was appointed director of the Education Department at Mishmar HaEmek, where he coordinated the activities of children in accordance with the principles of collective education and oversaw the pedagogic training of the *metaplot* and preschool teachers who would assume the sensitive task of educating kibbutz children from the moment of their birth. Wulff, his former analyst and mentor, who had settled in Tel Aviv in March 1933, was already working to chart the course of the future psychoanalytic movement in Palestine, in advance of Eitingon's arrival. Golan was indebted to the latter for securing his acceptance into the Berlin Psychoanalytic Institute and thus facilitating his psychoanalytic training.

The psychoanalysts who arrived from Germany in 1933 had no special commitment to the leaders of HaShomer HaTza'ir. Indeed, they were anxious to find new partners in Palestine in order to promote Freudianism in academic and medical as well as literary and pedagogic circles, not necessarily restricted to the framework of HaShomer HaTza'ir. This was a source of concern for Golan, all the more so because Wulff was committed to establishing a base for psychoanalytic training that would serve Tel Aviv educators. Towards this end, Wulff would be working with Idelsohn and other figures from pedagogic circles – including members of the Histadrut, the leading rival of HaShomer HaTza'ir. In October 1933 Golan warned Zvi Sohar, who was still in Warsaw, about the contacts that Wulff was establishing, through David Idelsohn, with Histadrut representatives. According to Golan, Idelsohn had the ear of Shmuel Yavnieli, the senior supervisor of the Pedagogic Commission of the Histadrut's Central Education Administration, which was lending its support to the creation of an institute for the training of "psychoanalytic educators."[414] Although Golan welcomed the arrival of psychoanalysts in Palestine, he also voiced the concern that it was absolutely essential to establish new contacts among them. He informed Sohar that, thanks to Eitingon, he had known since July that they were planning to establish a new psychoanalytic society, and that he was weighing the possibility of a partnership between it and HaShomer HaTza'ir. He told Sohar that, with the cooperation of colleagues who had just arrived from Germany, he intended to establish a psychoanalytic group at

Mishmar HaEmek. Evidently he believed that as soon as his friend returned from Warsaw, they would implement this plan. He added that the presence of "Rorschach expert" Ilja Schalit in Haifa, only twenty kilometers from Mishmar HaEmek, would be of great assistance to the kibbutz pedagogues. Finally, he informed Sohar that Wulff was receiving patients in Tel Aviv, as well as teaching, lecturing, and conducting seminars for pedagogues, and that these seminars were apparently very popular among teachers.

Faced with this situation, and "so as not to miss the opportunity to establish contact with these people" in his words, he adopted a political rather than ideological stance. (Let us recall that he had clashed with Idelsohn and Histadrut pedagogues over educational issues at the Beta Alpha Children's Society.) He proposed that Sohar reestablish contact with Idelsohn: "This would be a good opportunity for HaShomer HaTza'ir to renew its relationship with the pedagogues of New Education." If Golan's hopes were indeed realized and a certain rapprochement did take place between him and Idelsohn, it would primarily have been thanks to Wulff, who had been their analyst and a mentor to both of them in Berlin, and became their collaborator and friend once he arrived in Palestine.

Beginning in 1933, Wulff served as the leading authority on psychoanalysis for the pedagogues of HaShomer HaTza'ir. In April 1934 Golan wrote to Sohar that Wulff's psychoanalytic seminars for teachers in Tel Aviv were evidently "excellent." He added that the psychoanalysts were thinking of inviting Anna Freud to Palestine around Passover to present a series of lectures.

A year after his return, Golan was still anxious. He feared that psychoanalysts were organizing themselves without taking into account the projects of HaShomer HaTza'ir. At the same time, he found it somewhat reassuring that Freudians did not hesitate to approach him, and that without *Ofakim*, "the psychoanalysts have no means of expression." He regarded it as prudent to make the journal available to them, and many of their articles began to appear on its pages when it reopened in Palestine in 1943.

The members of HaShomer HaTza'ir, for their part, had no cause for concern. On the contrary, not only had Golan and Sohar been accepted as members of the Palestine Psychoanalytic Society, and not only had a number of HaShomer HaTza'ir pedagogues received psychoanalytic training at the Psychoanalytic Institute of Jerusalem, but they also benefited from the lessons, advice, guidance, and critiques that psychoanalysts provided them in developing and implementing collective education on the kibbutz. Relations between HaKibbutz HaArtzi educators, on the one hand, and psychoanalysis and the psychoanalytic movement, on the other, continued to solidify and improve during the 1930s and 1940s, despite growing criticism on the part of those activists in the movement who adhered to the principles of Marxism.

Golan and Sohar maintained close ties with Wulff, while also cultivating professional and amicable relations with analysts who arrived in Palestine later, including Ilja Schalit, Josef Friedjung, Betty Grünspan, Lizzi Rosenberg, Shmuel Nagler, and Alice Weiss, among others. In 1937 Sohar resigned from the Education Department of HaKibbutz HaArtzi to focus on the movement's cultural affairs, and Golan assumed responsibility for the organization and coordination of HaKibbutz HaArtzi's educational and pedagogic activities, until his death in 1960. In summation, whether in the field of pedagogy and education or culture generally, Zvi Sohar and Shmuel Golan went on to become the main facilitators of psychoanalysis in Palestine, and in HaShomer HaTza'ir in particular.

CHAPTER 9

The Founding of the Eder Institute in Tel Aviv (1937)

Max Eitingon's aspirations of bringing the experience he had accumulated in Berlin to Palestine led to the founding of the Jerusalem Psychoanalytic Institute as a place of training for new analysts. The Eder Institute, in contrast, had its roots in collaborative efforts between the Freudians of Tel Aviv and the city's pedagogic and welfare circles, which led to David Idelsohn, Martin Pappenheim, and Moshe Wulff founding the Eder Psychoanalytic Institute in Tel Aviv in 1937. The history of psychoanalysis overlooks the fact that Tel Aviv, too, had a psychoanalytic institute, and as we have managed to reconstruct the history of this institute, the time has come to present it.

The new institute aimed to enable psychoanalysts to meet the demands of pedagogy and social pedagogy in Palestine. The idea of establishing a second psychoanalytic institute emerged first among the medical and educational staff of the Abandoned Youth Club in Tel Aviv and members of the Society for Mental Hygiene. As David Idelsohn reported, "The Abandoned Youth Club was already operating along the principles of psychoanalysis. In cooperation with the Department of Medical Pedagogy of the Society for Mental Hygiene in Palestine, we decided in 1937 to establish the Eder Psychoanalytic Institute in Tel Aviv."[415] The Institute's founders recruited its first members from the staff of the Abandoned Youth Club; indeed, Idelsohn and all the nursing and educational staff working under his direction at the Club participated in the Institute's activities.[416] The pedagogues, *metaplot*, and preschool teachers who gathered around Moshe Wulff also hoped to acquire psychoanalytic training.

The Institute's lecturers and counselors were "specialist" physicians and pedagogues: Aaron Isserlin, Gershon Barag, Moshe Wulff, Martin Pappenheim, David Idelsohn, Dr. Yichielevich, Dora Strauss-Weigart, Dr. Dov Pollack and Dr. Nathalia Pollack.[417] The first series of seminars took place between January and July of 1938, with meetings held two or, when necessary, three evenings a week.[418] To be accepted for training, candidates had to provide a signed certificate from a physician of their choice affirming that they intend to engage in psychotherapy only with children.[419] We can infer from this requirement that in 1937 the Mandate authorities still prohibited anyone not trained as a physician from practicing psychoanalysis with adults. Candidates had to be at least twenty-five and no more than thirty-five years old, and they had to produce a "Certificate of Good Mental Health," preferably accompanied by the results of a Rorschach test[420] administered at the same time, as well as a formal certificate attesting to experience with infants or children under the age of five, preferably in an institutional setting.[421] The Institute's training included at least six months of individual analysis at the candidate's expense, as well as lessons in "medical pedagogy" in Hebrew and classes in basic German, because according to the Institute's bylaws, Hebrew still lacked the "appropriate scientific terminology" – that is, a specifically psychoanalytic vocabulary. The core courses were divided into four main sections. The first, for which Wulff was responsible, included lessons in the psychology and psychopathology of the child and the adolescent; the second, under Pappenheim's guidance, included the psychiatry and neuropsychiatry of the child as well as training in the diagnostic methods of cerebral pathologies; the third, also directed by Pappenheim, covered the anatomy and physiology of the brain and the nervous system; and the fourth section, directed by Idelsohn, included classes and seminars in "medical pedagogy."[422]

The candidates had to supplement their theoretical training with fieldwork at a clinic or any place that provided counseling (psychological, educational, or "mental hygiene") that would allow the candidate to study children's cases in light of developmental theories (according to age) while taking into account the social conditions in which the child was growing up. During their second or third year of studies, candidates who wanted to practice child psychology had to engage in psychotherapy with children under the supervision of a qualified Institute member.

In 1939 Eitingon, Wulff, and Anna Smeliansky established a local Training Committee to incorporate the teaching and instruction guidelines of the International Psychoanalytic Commission.[423] Henceforth, Wulff and Eitingon would work together to defend the position of psychoanalysis in Palestine – at the Hebrew University for example, alongside Aryeh Feigenbaum, Andor

Fodor, and Martin Pappenheim. During 1941 the Eder Psychoanalytic Institute continued to operate successfully,[424] and that same year in Tel Aviv, in cooperation with the Institute's staff, Moshe Wulff established the first Society for Child Psychiatry in Palestine.

Idelsohn reported that in 1943, in accordance with a decision of the Va'ad Leumi (Jewish National Council), the Abandoned Youth Club was transferred to a rural setting, after which it "operated under entirely different educational principles"[425] – which may be translated as "no longer relied on psychoanalysis." Furthermore, within a few short months the psychoanalytic community lost two of its leading figures, with Eitingon passing away in July 1943 and Pappenheim in November of that year. Widespread changes began to take place in the institutional landscape of psychoanalysis after Wulff succeeded Eitingon as president of the Palestine Psychoanalytic Society, if only because Jerusalem and Tel Aviv then joined efforts to enhance the presence and foundation of psychoanalytic training for educators and social workers.

CHAPTER 10

The Seminar for Pedagogues
in Jerusalem (1943)

The issue of abandoned immigrant children posed difficult problems for educators and social workers, leading to questions about the provision of psychoanalytic training for pedagogues. Thanks to the efforts of Max Eitingon's longtime friend Fanny Lowtzky,[426] who had arrived from Paris in late 1939, and those of her student Shmuel Nagler, in 1943, after two years of coordination and preparation, the Jerusalem Psychoanalytic Institute finally began offering comprehensive psychoanalytic training specifically designed for pedagogues. The training was also available to educators, social workers, and the medical staff of Hadassah Hospital.

Immediately upon her arrival in Palestine, Fanny Lowtzky, an experienced analyst and didactician recognized by the International Psychoanalytic Association, assumed responsibility for the training of candidate psychoanalysts. Under her directorship, the Jerusalem Psychoanalytic Institute opened the Psychoanalytic Seminar for Pedagogues, with the participation of some of Eitingon's students: Daniel Karl Dreyfuss, Margareth Brandt, Erich Gumbel, and in particular Shmuel Nagler, who, even before he began participating in the psychoanalytic training of HaShomer HaTza'ir pedagogues, had been one of the main actors in, and a first-hand witness to, the history of this seminar for "pedagogue-analysts."[427]

In an article published in *Ofakim* in 1948, Nagler provided a detailed description of the Seminar's founding and activities. The impression that emerges from his account is that the center of gravity for lay analysis shifted from Tel Aviv to Jerusalem during this period.

Fanny Lowtzky had become aware of the harsh reality of abandoned adolescents in Palestine. She also learned that Nagler, who worked with child psychiatrist Mordechai Brachyahu at Hadassah Hospital, was providing care for a considerable number of abandoned children and adolescents who would regularly gather around the hospital under the close supervision of the local police. In 1942, therefore, after the Seminar's reorganization, she invited Nagler to join the teaching staff of the Jerusalem Psychoanalytic Institute, and following his advice, she founded a seminar for psychoanalysis in Jerusalem – as Idelsohn had done in Tel Aviv – specially dedicated to the problems of abandoned adolescents and operating in accordance with the principles of August Aichhorn.

Born in Kiev on December 24, 1873, Fanny Lowtzky was the daughter of a prominent local Jewish philanthropist, one of the first Zionist activists in Russia. She evidently first underwent analysis with Sabine Spielrien in Geneva and gradually became one of the latter's disciples. After settling in Berlin in 1922, she met Max Eitingon and began "didactic" analysis with him. During the 1920s she published her first psychoanalytic writings, completed her training, and, in 1928, was accepted as a full member of the German Psychoanalytic Society (DPG). With the Nazi rise to power in 1933, she left Berlin for Paris, where like other exiled members of the Russian intelligentsia, including her brother Léon Chestov, she settled in the sixteenth arrondissement (district). She soon joined the Paris Psychoanalytic Society, whose president at the time was Marie Bonaparte, and became an active member as well as the first foreign analyst to be admitted to the organization. Alongside Marie Bonaparte, Rene Laforgue, Charles Odier, and Rudolph Lowenstein, she participated in the training of candidate psychoanalysts and ran seminars on psychoanalytic techniques. She also received the renowned writer Raymond Queneau for analysis; it was probably through Boris Schloezer, a member of the intellectual circles that gathered around Chestov, that Queneau had met the Russian psychoanalyst. She left Paris for Palestine at the end of 1939, after accepting Max Eitingon's invitation to join him in Jerusalem and participate in the training of candidate analysts.

The seminar facilitated by Nagler met with great success, and a Hadassah commission decided to fund classes specially designed for street children, and to support training for the educators who worked with these children in the framework of the Psychoanalytic Seminar for Pedagogues. The Jewish National Council joined the efforts of Hadassah, and thanks to their collaboration a number of pedagogue-analysts received training in Jerusalem before being recruited by public agencies to work with abandoned children and adolescents.

Nevertheless, in an article on the topic, Nagler expressed deep regret that none of these institutions deemed it necessary to contribute financially to their training. Notably, the pedagogues who received this psychoanalytic training were not authorized to treat adults, and could only treat children and adolescents under the supervision of a physician.

Aside from Shmuel Nagler, there were two women who worked with Brachyahu at Hadassah Hospital in the so-called Clinic for Nervous Children (*yeladim atzbani'im*): Naomi Glickson, a psychoanalyst and member of the Palestine Psychoanalytic Society, and Luzzi Panhaes, an educator trained in psychoanalysis. In 1946, presumably at the initiative of Brachyahu's staff, the hospital established Hadassah Pathway, an association in support of pediatric psychiatry. Its mission included fundraising for the psychological, social, and therapeutic monitoring of abandoned children (along psychoanalytic principles) and encouraging the pedagogue-analysts trained in Jerusalem to work with these children.

The pedagogues of HaKibbutz HaArtzi were sent to Jerusalem for psychoanalytic training, which would take about one year. The movement helped educators who lacked their own resources to find work and accommodation in Jerusalem. But the outbreak of Israel's War of Independence in 1948 forced most of the teachers to abandon their training and return to their kibbutzim. A few, stranded in Jerusalem, went on to complete their studies. Among the renowned HaShomer HaTza'ir pedagogues who trained under Fanny Lowtzky in Jerusalem and played an important part in training successive generations of the movement's educators, Rachel Manor-Katzenstein deserves special mention. One of Shmuel Nagler's collaborators at the Education Department of Mishmar HaEmek, she also became one of Fanny Lowtzky's preeminent students in Jerusalem.

Seven years after opening, the Psychoanalytic Seminar for Pedagogues in Jerusalem, operating in coordination with similar seminars in Tel Aviv and Haifa, had forty candidates in various stages of training. By 1948, twenty educators trained in psychoanalysis were working throughout the country. Some held important positions in the public institutions of the Yishuv and planned to establish a national organization of "educators and pedagogue-analysts" to bring together professionals from across the country "in order to consider and discuss their daily work on a rigorous scientific basis" – that is, in accordance with the teachings of psychoanalysis.

Nagler, who never failed to point out the shortcomings of the Yishuv's education system, argued that it must be adapted to reality in order to meet basic needs, adding that the Yishuv was not adequately prepared to address the problems of immigrant children from Europe or the East, nor those of children born in Palestine. In his view, children who had severe difficulties adapting, or who suffered from psychological disorders, required psychotherapy at the hands of a psychoanalyst, and a great many parents and teachers would benefit from consultation with psychoanalytically trained pedagogues, who in fact were the only ones who could help them overcome their problems. He noted, regretfully, that Palestine was seriously lacking in pedagogue-analysts who could help these children, parents, and educators, concluding that "all our work efforts must now focus on the psychoanalytic training of educators."[428]

Hygiena Ruhanit: **A New Platform for Psychoanalytic Publications**

One of the most important contributions that Mordechai Brachyahu made to the psychoanalytic movement in Palestine was the dissemination of large numbers of psychoanalytic texts through the journal *Hygiena Ruhanit* (Mental Hygiene), which he founded in 1943 to address questions of mental hygiene, psychology, pedagogy, and children's education in general.[429] Like *Ofakim* (which in 1943 began once again to devote extensive space to psychoanalysts and their discipline), perhaps even more so, *Hygiena Ruhanit* offered a privileged platform for articles by psychoanalysts from Palestine and abroad. It also published reports about congresses and debates in which members of the Palestine Psychoanalytic Society participated, as well as comprehensive information about the local and international activities of the psychoanalytic movement. Through this journal Brachyahu, a pioneer and fervent supporter of psychological literature in Hebrew, participated actively in promoting psychoanalytic works in the Hebrew language.

It should be noted that by the time *Hygiena Ruhanit* first appeared, in 1943, articles on psychoanalysis and references to the discipline itself had disappeared from the pages of *HaKhikunkh* and *Hed HaKhikunk*, which were mainly devoted to the major psychologists of the Yishuv, faithful adherents of academic psychology: Moshe Brill, Fishel Schneeurson, Enzo Buonaventura, and Sarah Fayans-Glück, to name some of the more prominent ones. *Hygiena Ruhanit* published many articles on pedagogy and education but continued to devote special attention to psychoanalytic texts.

A number of the authors are already familiar to us: Mordechai Brachyahu of course, as well as Moshe Wulff, Erwin Hirsch, Fanny Lowtzky, Shmuel Nagler, Alice Weiss, Aaron Isserlin, David Idelsohn, and Naomi Glickson. We should also mention contributions by Reuben Krik, Julius Zellermayer, and Gottfried Bloch, representatives of the new generation of analysts who had received training in the framework of the Palestine Psychoanalytic Society under the presidency of Moshe Wulff.

Most of the articles on psychoanalysis were written in clear, basic Hebrew and accessible to the lay reader. In the second issue, published in 1944, Erwin Hirsch addressed the eating habits of the capricious child, drawing on a clinical case, and Nagler reported on his experience with abandoned adolescents roaming the streets of the Jerusalem neighborhood of Bucharim.[430] Wulff published an article on the problems of delinquent teenagers – "Parents Who Are Difficult to Educate" – arguing that behind every child with learning difficulties there were "difficult parents." He further argued that by simply listening to parents and understanding them, it was possible to modify their conception of education so that they stopped causing harm to their child's psychological balance. In other words, attentive listening by a professional could lead to a dramatic improvement in the child's psychological state. Wulff added that "punishing the parents" was no more effective than punishing the children, and that educators and professionals must make parents understand that teaching methods based on their own personal conceptions, even if seemingly grounded in common sense, not only create an impasse for the child but even exacerbate mental problems. "Specialists in psychological work" must, according to Wulff, help parents understand that through the teaching methods they spontaneously applied, their own psyche – which itself was shaped by unconscious factors – had a direct impact on their child; sorrow on their part, for example, or fatigue, irritation, or a formative experience of their own could all have a decisive influence on their children's psychological disorders.

As part of a lengthy series of articles on psychological problems in the field of education, Erwin Hirsch addressed the pathological behavior and learning problems of children that stem from "misguided educational practices" in their learning environment.[431] In 1948, Brachyahu, a strong supporter of psychological testing, devoted an article to the Rorschach test, and in a later article he addressed the psychology of the immigrant. Alice Weiss, a pioneer of group psychotherapy in Israel, offered the readers of *Hygiena Ruhanit* a survey of the various techniques of this discipline.

Hygiena Ruhanit published many other works dealing with educational problems, such as the psychology of orphans and of children victimized by war or the Holocaust. The journal's editors also translated a large number of texts from foreign languages. Among the well-known authors in the issues accessible to us, we found the names of August Aichhorn, Anna Freud, Hans Zulliger, Wilhelm Stekel, John Bowlby, and Karl Menninger.

Part III

Freud in the Yishuv: Reception and Resistance

CHAPTER 11

Psychoanalysis Fails to Take Hold at the Hebrew University (1925-1948)

A Brief History of the Hebrew University

Supported by most of the world's Jewish communities, the concept of establishing a Jewish university arose at a time when emancipation had become a reality for a majority of West European Jews but not for the Jews of Central and Eastern Europe.

Under the rule of Tsar Alexander II, Russia's Jews had enjoyed relative tolerance; the restrictions imposed earlier had been substantially eased. With the assassination of the tsar in 1881, however, this golden age came to an end and one of the most dramatic periods in the history of Russian Jewry ensued – a period of pogroms and bloodshed that lasted until 1884. During 1903-1906, after two decades of relative calm, the violence and attacks against Russian Jews resumed: the infamous Kishinev pogrom, in which forty-five Jews were slaughtered, and the massacre of eight hundred and ten Jews within two weeks in Gomel and Jitomir in October 1905 are two examples. Thousands of Jews left Russia around this time, some making their way to Palestine as part of the First or Second Aliyah. Many of those barred from entering Russian universities continued their studies in the major cities of Western Europe – Berlin, Frankfurt, Hamburg, Zürich, Bern, Basel, Geneva, and Vienna. They formed small but highly influential groups of Russian Jewish students who, over time, joined the international Zionist movement.

In response to the pogroms and new restrictions imposed on Jews in Russia and Romania, a mathematician from Heidelberg University named Herman Shapira published a series of articles in the periodical *HaMelitz* between 1882 and 1884 calling, for the first time, for a Jewish university to be established in Palestine. Jewish public opinion around the world welcomed his proposals, and the First Zionist Congress, which took place in Basel in August 1897, addressed the issue, although it did not act on it. The writer and philosopher Ahad Ha'am, however, and a group of Jewish students who had gathered around him in Geneva did adopt these proposals. They began promoting the concept of a Jewish center of learning that would provide a foundation for the cultural and spiritual revival of the Jewish People as a "light unto the nations." In December 1901 during the Fifth Zionist Congress, again in Basel, Chaim Weizmann – then president of a Zionist student organization – declared an urgent need to establish a Jewish center for higher education in Palestine.

Embracing this project with enthusiasm, Theodore Herzl then approached the Turkish Sultan Hamid II to solicit his support: although the founders of the future university would be members of the World Zionist Organization, it would be open to students throughout the Ottoman Empire. The Sultan, however, was not interested. A year later, in 1903, Chaim Weizmann, Martin Buber, and Berthold Feiwel – all members of a student group named "The Democratic Fraction" – published a pamphlet titled *A School of Higher Education for Jewish Studies* (*Eine jüdische Hochschule*) with the aim of drawing public attention to the plan. Yet it was only adopted at the Eleventh Zionist Congress in Vienna in 1913. Chaim Weizmann (who in the meantime had become a senior official in the World Zionist Organization) declared that the establishment of a Jewish university in Jerusalem was one of the main objectives of Zionism. He had the support of Russian Zionist organizations and as well as the financial backing of the renowned German Jewish physician Paul Ehrlich, the well-known German Jewish botanist Otto Warburg,[432] and Baron Edmond de Rothschild. The German sociologist and statistician Arthur Ruppin, who had settled in Jaffa in 1907 and began serving as a WZO delegate in 1908, assumed responsibility for negotiating the purchase of land on Mount Scopus in northeastern Jerusalem – Sir John Grey Hill, named after its owner. The deal was signed in 1916.

But the outbreak of World War I thwarted these plans. In 1917, drawing on the authority of the Balfour Declaration, Chaim Weizmann assembled a group of experts to prepare the foundation for a national Jewish homeland in Palestine and complete preparations for the establishment of the University. On July 24, 1918, only four months after the Committee of Delegates had arrived in Palestine, Weizmann – with the authorization of the British military government[433] and alongside Eder, another principal architect – laid the cornerstone for the University on Mount Scopus.[434] Also present were General Allenby, Commander of the British forces in Palestine, other senior British military officials, and representatives of the Jewish and Christian communities in Palestine. The announcement sparked much enthusiasm among Jewish communities worldwide, mobilizing them to participate in the ambitious project. American Zionists, seeking to be more active in international Zionist affairs, donated generously towards the founding of the University. The alliances and deals Weizmann had to make and the compromises he was compelled to accept in order to implement the project threatened to undermine his hegemony in the international Zionist movement, as well as the lofty scientific character he envisioned for this institution.

A stormy political confrontation ensued between the secular European Zionists, who wanted to establish a "Prussian" University that would serve first and foremost as a place of research and progress, and the traditional American Zionists, who sought to prioritize the study of Jewish culture and philosophy, the Hebrew language, and the history of the Jewish People. In the midst of the crossfire, Freud and Eder were nominated as candidates to the University's Board of Governors, and Chaim Weizmann ensured their election. Although Freud was never a supporter of political or cultural Zionism,[435] in practical terms he played a part in the Zionist ambitions of Chaim Weizmann and the WZO. The opening ceremony for the Hebrew University took place on April 1, 1925. Among the speakers were Lord Balfour, Chaim Weizmann, the British High Commissioner Herbert Samuel, and the "national Jewish poet" Chaim Nachman Bialik, Israel's future poet laureate.

The first struggle over the introduction of psychoanalysis into the Hebrew University took place during 1925-1926. Five days before the opening ceremony of the University, Freud published an announcement titled "To the Opening of the Hebrew University" in the March 27, 1925, issue of the British Jewish newspaper *The New Judea*:[436]

> Historians have told us that our small nation withstood the destruction of its independence as a State only because it began to transfer in its estimation of values the highest rank to its spiritual possessions, to its religion and its literature.

> We are now living in a time when this people has a prospect of again winning the land of its fathers with the help of a Power that

dominates the world, and it celebrates the occasion by the foundation of a University in its ancient capital city.

A University is a place in which knowledge is taught above all differences of religions and of nations, where investigation is carried on, which is to show mankind how far they understand the world around them and how far they can control it.

Such an undertaking is a noble witness to the development to which our people has forced its way in two thousand years of unhappy fortune.

I find it painful that my ill health prevents me from being present at the opening festivities of the Jewish University in Jerusalem.

Thus it appears that Freud and psychoanalysis were very much a part of Weizmann's plans in the founding of the Hebrew University.

A Chair of Psychoanalysis at the Hebrew University

Although Bernfeld had already put forward the idea of integrating psychoanalysis into the University's curriculum in 1922, his proposal related only to the Department of Education. In 1925, Montague David Eder invited Eitingon to the opening ceremony on April 1 of that year. In 1926 the psychoanalyst Leo Kaplan, a follower of the traditional German academic camp, proposed establishing a chair of psychoanalysis at the University.

Psychoanalysis was not included in the curriculum of the new University, but two of its representatives became members of the prestigious Board of Governors. Freud, who was elected during the second general assembly in Munich in September 1925, joined Albert Einstein, Edmund Landau, Arthur Ruppin, Montague David Eder, Nahum Sokolow, Chaim Nachman Bialik, Martin Buber, Rudolph Ehrmann, Leonard Orenstein, Norman Bentwich, and Hirsch (Zvi) Perez Chajes (Tzvi-Peretz Hayot), the chief rabbi of Vienna. Yet Freud's position was purely honorary: for reasons of health, he did not participate in the Board's meetings, and he declined every invitation to Palestine to see the actual achievements of the Jewish People, including the University. Although he apparently received continuous updates about the University, he took an interest only from afar. Yet he never hesitated to summon his authority as a Board member in supporting the appointment of a psychoanalyst to the faculty: first Bernfeld in 1925, and later Wulff in 1932 and Eitingon in 1933.

Religious Resistance to Freud: Opposition to *The Future of an Illusion*

In November 1927 Freud published *The Future of an Illusion*,[437] a direct attack on the illusions and idealism of various ideological systems, and religion in particular. The book reasserted some of the concepts he had presented in a 1907 article comparing religious ritual with obsessive behavior.[438] He also recalled some of the themes he had developed in *Totem and Taboo* regarding the origins of the psyche, social organization, and belief.

In *The Future of an Illusion* Freud takes a further step towards understanding the origin and function of religious representation, specifically questioning what religious concepts and emotions might represent from a psychological perspective. He concludes that religious symbols are in fact illusions, and more specifically the manifestation of – or a substitute for – repressed primal desires. He bluntly denounces the deceptive nature of illusions perpetuated by religion for misleading people through false hopes of an afterlife or the coming of a messiah. In fact, having earlier compared religious texts to obsessive acts, Freud now compares the religious illusions perpetuated by religion to psychotic delusions. *The Future of an Illusion* dealt a harsh blow to religion but was not intended as a declaration of war. The book had a political aim: to defend the sovereignty of psychoanalysis. Indeed, if his book on lay analysis[439] can be described as a defense of psychoanalysis against its appropriation by physicians, then *The Future of an Illusion* may be described as a defense against priests and against the rabbis and adherents of Jewish mysticism gathered around Martin Buber.

The publication of *The Future of an Illusion* embarrassed the Catholic Church and shocked members of the Orthodox Jewish community in Palestine and elsewhere. With religious academics at the forefront, they sought to prevent the introduction of psychoanalysis into the Hebrew University. Martin Buber, whose reputation as a sociologist of religion already preceded him, was one of the fiercest opponents, as Eitingon wrote to Freud after meeting Buber in 1938 in Jerusalem. Moshe Wulff, the leading advocate of psychoanalysis in Palestine and later in Israel, then joined the struggle against the discipline's detractors.

Opposition to Freud was a multi-headed monster; it was not restricted to the "moderate" religious and intellectual circles surrounding Buber. One of the staunchest opponents was undoubtedly Fishel Schneeurson, a rabbi of Lithuanian origin as well as a psychologist and expert in child psychiatry, who had immigrated from the United States in 1932 and settled in Tel Aviv. Since 1925 he had been a regular contributor to the pedagogic periodical *HaKhinukh*,[440] which had earned him a reputation among conservative pedagogues in the Yishuv and traditional Jews in Europe and the United States.

Against this open opposition on the part of religious academics and in the context of continuing clashes between European and American academics at the University, in late 1933 Freud and Judah Magnes, Chancellor of the Hebrew University, began discussing the possibility of creating a chair in psychoanalysis. As mentioned, Freud had been invited by Eder and Weizmann to take part in founding the Hebrew University in Jerusalem. He gladly and proudly accepted the invitation, agreeing to join the Board of Governors. At that point – as early as the 1920s – Freud had already begun weighing the question of introducing psychoanalysis into the Hebrew University.

Freud and the Candidacy of Moshe Wulff

During 1927-1932 Freud appeared to be indifferent to the activities of the Hebrew University. Was this because the plans to introduce psychoanalysis into the curriculum, which had initially sparked his interest, were not realized, or was it perhaps due to the religious opposition? Maybe the reasons have nothing to do with developments at the University itself: Might it be possible that the deteriorating political situation in Palestine and the severe crisis that befell the Zionist movement after the riots of 1929 were a deciding factor in Freud's disengagement? In any event, the Hebrew University did not become a part of Freud's agenda again until 1932.

In late June of that year he responded favorably to a request from Wulff, who was planning to leave for Palestine and sought Freud's support in recommending him to the University authorities.[441] A recommendation from Freud would have carried much weight. The Hebrew University could not have found a better candidate to head a program in psychoanalysis, not only because Wulff was a superior clinician, an expert in child psychoanalysis, and a prolific writer deeply immersed in the world of publication, but also because he was an experienced instructor who had already established an impressive academic career in Russia and the Soviet Union before emigrating in 1927. Surprisingly, however, by 1933 Freud decided to back Eitingon (who planned to settle in Palestine) rather than Wulff for a chair in psychoanalysis at the Hebrew University.

Eitingon arrived in Jerusalem on October 5, 1933. He soon wrote to Freud (not knowing that his mentor had already expressed support for Wulff's candidacy), seeking a certificate attesting to his psychoanalytic career and a recommendation to Magnes supporting his appointment as chair of psychoanalysis.[442] In autumn of that year he tried to convince Magnes of the importance of establishing such a chair, while also seeking to enlist support among noted figures in the Yishuv. Unlike Wulff, Eitingon was by no means a psychoanalytic theoretician, and from the outset he lacked the skills required of a university instructor.[443] If in late 1933 Freud opted to back him rather than Wulff, it would almost certainly have been because of their long-standing friendship and the mutual loyalty they had developed over the years. Freud's decision certainly had an impact on the relations between Moshe Wulff and Max Eitingon, and the tension that formed between the two during the 1930s would determine the different orientations of psychoanalysis in Palestine and Israel.

In 1933 Eitingon met van Vriesland, who, as noted, had belonged to the psychoanalytic study group during the 1920s – alongside Eder, Feigenbaum, and Grete Obernik – and the two formed a friendship. In an effort to persuade Magnes that introducing psychoanalysis into the University would enhance its international prestige, van Vriesland also pointed out that the University's financial hardship would not pose a problem, as the creation of a chair of psychoanalysis did not require any special equipment. He explained,

> This new science can well be called a specific product of the Jewish
> mind, and as such it is suffering from the prosecution of all that is
> Jewish; it might even be said that it is banned from Germany where
> it was highly developed. It would, therefore, only be fitting to give

> it a place at the Jewish site of learning, the Hebrew University of
> Jerusalem. . . . I consider. . . the fact that Psychoanalysis should be
> taught in this country, of such paramount importance for the Hebrew
> University, for enriching the Yishuv in general, and for widening the
> educational outlook of our teachers, that I considered it my duty to
> recommend warmly – though with due modesty and reverence – the
> scheme put forward by Dr. Eitingon.[444]

But the Freudian camp hit a stone wall. Van Vriesland, enraged by this hostile reception, considered unleashing his fury in an article but, as he confided to Eitingon, decided to restrain himself. Eventually he did publish an article titled "Why Don't I Have Any Friends at the Hebrew University?" denouncing the disparaging attitude of the academics in an ironic tone.

Responding to Freud, Judah Magnes explained that given public opinion it would be premature to introduce psychoanalysis before a chair of psychology had been established.[445] Freud was quick to reply, writing on December 5, 1933, "My thoughts in this matter are as follows: Psychoanalysis, too, is psychology – that is, the science of *unconscious* emotional processes, while the subject which is taught as academic psychology is confined to a consideration of *conscious* phenomena. There need be no opposition between the two. Psychoanalysis could be taught as an introduction to psychology. Actually, however, the opposition results from the fact that the academicians do not want to know anything about psychoanalysis."[446]

Kurt Lewin's Candidacy and Andor Fodor's Second Battle

On February 14, 1934, the Hebrew University's Board of Governors convened to discuss the possibility of establishing a chair in psychoanalysis. The odds that it would actually accept such a proposal were slim to none. Magnes had already voiced his support for experimental psychology and, behind the scenes, was planning to raise the funds necessary to establish a pedagogy department and hire Kurt Lewin, a renowned German Jewish psychologist, to oversee instruction in psychology. Moreover, Buber, who continued to oppose Freud and psychoanalysis, was also a participant in the meeting.

In early 1934, one of the Hebrew University's founders and a professor of chemistry, Andor Fodor, joined a group of intellectuals that included

Siegfried van Vriesland and Aryeh Feigenbaum, among others, who were advocating the inclusion of psychoanalysis in the University's curriculum. Fodor, born in Budapest in 1884, had earned an engineering degree in 1907 and a doctorate in 1909 from the Technische Hochschule (Technological Institute) of Zürich, after which he worked in Switzerland and Sweden. In 1922 he was appointed a professor of biochemistry at the University of Halle in Germany. In 1923 he emigrated to Palestine and began preparations to establish a chemistry institute at the Hebrew University, where in 1925 he was appointed Professor of Biochemistry and Colloid Chemistry and Dean of the Faculty of Chemistry.[447]

Fodor, who enjoyed much prestige and influence among the Hebrew University staff, soon came to head the Freudian camp alongside Aryeh Feigenbaum in the University's hierarchy. Like the Italian psychologist Enzo Buonaventura, Fodor, an Orthodox Jew saw no conflict between Freudian theory and his religious conceptions.[448] On January 29, 1934, a meeting convened at his home to discuss the place of psychoanalysis at the University.[449] We do not know who, other than Feigenbaum, participated in the meeting or what they discussed. Apparently neither Freud nor Eitingon knew at the time that the future of psychoanalysis at the University attracted such interest and that the individual who intended to promote its cause was, surprisingly, Andor Fodor, an Orthodox Jew.

In a letter dated July 21, 1934,[450] Eitingon informed Freud of discussions regarding the introduction of psychoanalysis into the University, mentioning Fodor for the first time:

> I have heard that since the rejection of analysis by a previous commission, there has emerged a second commission, headed by a University chemist, a certain Professor Fodor, who is highly supportive of analysis. I have seen the report and I hope to be able to send it to you in the near future, but if not I will bring it. The chemist in question very much wants you to know that "there are among the University professors here some who are neither parasitologists nor Orthodox Hebraists, who know what the world owes you and especially what the Hebrew University owes you, and they want to support the cause of psychoanalysis." They say that further discussion of this issue has been postponed until autumn.

And indeed, discussions about introducing psychoanalysis into the University did continue.

Apparently, however, in 1934 Freud was more disengaged than ever from the Hebrew University: the Nazi rise to power in Germany, the growth of anti-Semitism in Austria, his illness, and his research and writing on Moses all drew his attention away from the clashes on Mount Scopus. Nonetheless, he continued to refer to the Hebrew University as "our University," not necessarily to underscore his membership in the Board of Governors but to reinforce his belonging to the Jewish People and express solidarity with the cultural and scientific enterprises of his People in Palestine. Reciprocally, in May 1936, on the occasion of Freud's eightieth birthday, various commemoration events in his honor took place in Jewish Palestine.

Aryeh Feigenbaum, the Most Freudian Physician in Palestine and Israel

In 1936 a meeting was held at the Hebrew University to discuss the possibility of opening a "University Hospital Center" in Jerusalem, as a first step towards creating a faculty of medicine.

On May 9, 1939, the Rothschild-Hadassah Hospital on Mount Scopus inaugurated a premedical training program, which in time became the Hebrew University's Faculty of Medicine. Aryeh Feigenbaum, one of the first ophthalmologists in the country and the main instigator of the program, was appointed as dean. But he would have to wait a long time, too long, before seeing the Jewish People establish a place of higher learning for medicine on its ancestral land. The foundation provided by this program only partially addressed the demands and ambitions of the Zionist physician. He regretted that the new center did not offer the students a full curriculum of studies but only a residency, and only after earning a medical degree abroad. It also troubled him that training in psychiatry and instruction in medical psychology were not included among the residencies available to students.[451] Moreover, in his opinion the Hebrew University specifically, and the Jewish medical world and Jews of Palestine more generally, still owed a "debt of honor to the creator of psychoanalysis," whom he viewed – alongside the prominent German Jewish physician Paul Ehrlich – as one of the "geniuses of the Jewish People."[452] He viewed the failure to include the works of Freud in the University's curriculum or the coursework of medical students as inconceivable, even scandalous. Until 1956, in his articles and public appearances, he never failed to denounce this injustice and express his hope that one day the Hebrew University would finally honor one of its most illustrious members.[453]

The creation of a medical faculty in Palestine posed difficult problems for religious representatives of the Yishuv, including physicians and academics, given that the study of medicine entails the study of anatomy and pathological anatomy – two disciplines that require students to conduct autopsies. The rabbinic authorities had categorically banned autopsies because the Halakha (Jewish Law) views dissection as desecration of the dead and necessitates immediate burial of the deceased (except on the Sabbath and Yom Kippur). Only in 1946 did Rabbi Herzog, the Chief Rabbi of Palestine, lift this prohibition, finally permitting the Hebrew University to institute a Faculty of Medicine.[454]

Aryeh Feigenbaum was consistently critical of what he regarded as religious intrusion into the sphere of science and of the barriers religion posed to Zionist ideals and to the realization of the Jewish enterprise in Palestine. He accused the religious authorities of confining medical practice to the terms and methods of the ghetto and blocking the road to progress.[455] Thus the Hebrew University effectively shunned the disciplines of medicine and psychoanalysis, barring entry to both: the former because it desecrates the physical human body, and the latter because it desecrates the human soul by exposing the "organs" of the psyche and the sexual substrate Freud attributes to them.

Psychoanalysis as Part of University Medical Training

In a 1942 article that appeared in a New York-based medical journal, Aryeh Feigenbaum, seeking to justify the inclusion of psychoanalysis in medical studies, cited the American psychoanalyst Gregory Zilboorg's description of psychoanalysis as an extension of the Renaissance in light of its contribution to the liberation of science, not to mention the liberation of medicine from theology and metaphysics.[456] Even more than he aspired to train doctors in the psychotherapeutic aspects of psychoanalysis, Feigenbaum wanted to offer students the means of acquiring a measure of psychological maturity, which he viewed as essential for engaging in their future profession. He firmly believed that anyone who sought to practice medicine should first undergo personal analysis.[457]

Although an optimist, he knew that it would be a difficult struggle to introduce psychoanalysis into the curriculum: he had to cope, on the one hand, with the demands of a group of physicians who wanted to prioritize a department of neuropsychiatry over a department of psychoanalysis, and on the other, with academics who sought, after negotiations with Kurt Lewin failed, to persuade the University administration to establish an autonomous psychology department, separate from the Department of Pedagogy. The latter efforts ran into stubborn opposition on the part of Werner Senator, Administrator of the University since 1937, who represented the Board of Governors. During that spring of 1942, accordingly, Aryeh Feigenbaum enlisted members of the Palestine Psychoanalytic Society in the struggle to persuade University officials to include instruction in psychoanalysis as part of the premedical training program.

This plan correlated with the ambitions – or, more precisely, the vision – he had had since 1924, when he tried to convince Israel Spanier Wechsler (a Polish-born neurologist and psychiatrist who had established a reputation in the United States) to create a department of neuropsychiatry at the University – to be run by his brother Dorian, who would introduce instruction in psychiatry into the curriculum. For the time being, he suggested inviting representatives of the Hebrew University's local governance to the Psychoanalytic Institute – Rector Leon Roth, Administrator Werner Senator, and all members of the premedical program's administrative committee – with the aim of persuading them of the advantages of psychoanalytic training for physicians. A year later, however, in 1943, the psychoanalytic movement in Palestine was dealt a harsh blow when two of its leaders passed away: Max Eitingon in July and Martin Pappenheim in November. Moshe Wulff then became the leader of the Freudian movement, accompanied henceforth by Feigenbaum, who continued to struggle unremittingly for the inclusion of psychoanalysis in the University curriculum.

During that year, 1943 the medical community in Palestine learned about the establishment of a medical faculty that would include a department of psychiatry. On October 7, Aryeh Feigenbaum and Lippman Heilpern, Director of the Neurology Laboratory at Hadassah's premedical program, decided to create a commission composed of professionals in the field of mental health to discuss preparations for the future training of psychiatry students.

On May 28, 1946, a second gathering took place to discuss a future psychiatry department. Participants included Aryeh Feigenbaum, Chaim Yassky, Lippman Heilpern, and the great Italian psychologist Enzo Buonaventura. Once again Feigenbaum proposed establishing a department of medical psychology based on "psychoanalytic science" to provide training for psychiatry students as well as medical students more generally because, in his view, medical students had to learn psychoanalytic theory just as they had to learn anatomy and physiology.

Heilpern and Buonaventura agreed with Feigenbaum on the importance of psychoanalysis in the teaching of medical psychology, but they believed that the training of mental health professionals should include other branches of psychology as well. At the same time, however, they did accept another of Feigenbaum's proposals, namely, the inclusion of a "specialist in psychoanalysis" in the commission to help lay the groundwork for instruction in medical psychology and psychiatry at the University.

Buonaventura proposed establishing a program of studies in medical psychology that would incorporate psychoanalysis.[458] And he was true to his word: in July 1946 he delivered a program of instruction in medical psychology to the other commission members, which included a focus on psychoanalysis. But during a meeting in September 1946, the discussion took a different course from the direction Feigenbaum had sought. His hopes were to establish a department of medical psychology, but the other members preferred to offer instruction in classical psychiatry.

In early 1947 Feigenbaum again mobilized the members of the Palestine Psychoanalytic Institute to persuade Jerusalem's academics and the essential American donors of the advantages of providing instruction in psychoanalysis at the Faculty of Medicine. As president of the Society, Moshe Wulff called on his colleagues to help promote psychoanalysis among medical circles in Palestine, as he himself was doing by offering classes on psychosomatic medicine for the physicians of Kupat Holim (the Yishuv's healthcare network for workers), while relying on the theories of Freud and lessons of psychoanalysis.

Within the framework of the Palestine Psychoanalytic Institute, another important psychiatrist and psychoanalyst already mentioned here, Heinrich Zvi Winnick, gave a presentation of his research on the relationship between the physician and psychoanalysis. Winnick, Wulff's great adversary in the Society, was among the first instructors eventually appointed to the future Department of Psychiatry at the Faculty of Medicine that was to open in 1954. In time he would become its director and a leader of the psychiatric movement in Israel.

Meanwhile, on August 29, 1947, discussions resumed at the Hebrew University on a future program of study in medical psychology or psychiatry. On April 9, 1948, however, during the capture of the Arab village of Deir Yassin near Jerusalem, members of two nationalist Jewish paramilitary groups, the Irgun (Irgun Tzva'i Leumi – National Military Organization) and Lehi (Lohamei Herut Israel – Fighters for the Freedom of Israel), committed one of the vilest acts in the history of the State of Israel by indiscriminately massacring more than a hundred villagers. A few days later, under the indifferent watch of British soldiers stationed in northeastern Jerusalem, Arab rioters attacked an armed convoy transporting medical staff of Hadassah Hospital and employees of the Hebrew University while the convoy was passing through the neighborhood of Sheikh Jarrah. Seventy-eight passengers on the convoy – physicians, nurses, professors, University instructors, and students, including two supporters of psychoanalysis, Chaim Yassky and Enzo Buonaventura – were slaughtered in cold blood.

CHAPTER 12

Translating Freud into Hebrew

"It is with particular joy that I hold in my hands
a copy of my *Group Psychology and the Analysis of the Ego*,
translated into our sacred language."

— Sigmund Freud to the members of Histadrut HaMorim, 1928

After World War I, at the impetus of eager young immigrants who arrived with the Third Aliyah, Yishuv intellectuals set out to launch a genuine cultural revolution. The news about the founding of a university in Jerusalem also sparked fresh enthusiasm among the intelligentsia of Palestine. This renewed social and cultural fervor created fertile ground for the reception of Freudian theory in Palestine, even if it did not generate the conditions necessary for psychoanalysis and psychoanalytic practice to take root definitively.

Freud in Hebrew: Language of Reception, Language of Exile

From a sociological and demographic perspective, the Yishuv in Palestine was quite heterogeneous. Nonetheless, most of the immigrants agreed on one point: the absolute necessity of making modern Hebrew the official language of the Yishuv. A process of Hebraization therefore began, with the aim of promoting a new Hebrew culture based on the works of Jewish writers and intellectuals, primarily from Eastern Europe, including Ahad Ha'am, Chaim Nachman Bialik, and their followers.[459] Zionist intellectuals were aware that language forms the realm of culture, and that Hebrew must become one of the fundamental pillars of the new national identity they sought to forge and of the intergenerational transmission of that identity. According to their vision, the Jewish People would be "reborn" not only by returning to its ancient homeland but also through the resurrection of its language.

These pioneers combined their struggle to establish Hebrew as the official language of the Yishuv with their struggle against the mentality of the Old

Yishuv, whose members supported the Khalukah. They promoted the literary, artistic, and philosophical works of Jewish culture, while also exploring the works of the great minds who had left their mark on history and contributed to the Enlightenment, including Aristotle, Plato, Tolstoy, Goethe, Schiller, Shakespeare, and William James, as well as Marx, Nietzsche, and Freud. Their works and many other texts were translated into Hebrew. Many of the translators were intellectuals of the Second and Third Aliyah, and their efforts to transmit and disseminate these universal works in modern Hebrew were not limited to the Yishuv. The Hebrew language and modern Jewish culture, the "pure product of Jewish Palestine," were propagated throughout the entire Diaspora.

The year 1925 marked a turning point for the reception of Freud's work in Palestine. Until then Freud's texts had drawn attention only within small circles: HaShomer HaTza'ir members read and studied them, as did the psychoanalytic study group in Jerusalem and other intellectual circles that did not belong to a particular ideological or political movement or to a specific profession. From 1925, however, after Lord Balfour praised the founder of psychoanalysis,[460] and after the latter was appointed to the Hebrew University's Board of Governors (in September), the intellectuals of the Yishuv became fascinated with Freud's works. Scholars, intrigued by the social significance of psychoanalysis, translated his texts on the origins of peoples, civilization, morality, and religion into Hebrew.

From 1926 onward there was a growing interest in the early Hebrew translations of Freud's texts – the products of efforts by writers and scholars, often from the Zionist Left. The translation of Freud's writings into Hebrew naturally contributed to the dissemination of his work, while also shaping the development of modern Hebrew and transforming it into a living language. This endeavor greatly enriched the language, as the translators devised and refined new terms to express the concepts of psychoanalysis.

After Freud's appointment to the Hebrew University's Board of Governors, interest in psychoanalysis increased among intellectual circles, particularly among writers, pedagogues, and members of HaShomer HaTza'ir. They took it upon themselves to transmit the works of Freud and integrate them into the Yishuv, producing commentaries and critiques in both the specialized press and the general print media, thus disseminating the principles of Freudian thought among the public.

The Early Translations

Three of Freud's texts were translated into Hebrew during the late 1920s: "The Resistances to Psychoanalysis" by Yohanan Tversky in 1926, *Group Psychology and the Analysis of the Ego* by Judah Dwossis (Dvir) in 1928, and *The Future of an Illusion* by Shmuel Golan in 1929.

Until recently it was believed that 1928 marked the first appearance of a Hebrew translation of a text by Freud, but we have discovered an earlier translation. In 1926 the writer, historian, journalist, and psychologist Yohanan Tversky, a native of the Ukraine, produced a translation of "The Resistances to Psychoanalysis,"[461] which appeared in New York in *HaDo'ar*, the newspaper of the Histadrut Ivrit of America (Hebrew Federation of America). Tversky was one of the young "zealots of the Hebrew language" who had known Bialik in Odessa, and during the years that followed he made a substantial contribution to Jewish culture and the revival of the Hebrew language. Although his own views were close to those of Adler (who had converted to Protestantism at a young age), Tversky chose to translate a text by Freud rather than one by his dissident disciple.

The intellectuals of Palestine developed a growing interest in texts that addressed social and cultural issues, such as *Totem and Taboo* or *Group Psychology and the Analysis of the Ego*, rather than the more clinical texts. With the Yishuv struggling over the question of its future in Palestine, they believed that Freud could bolster the Zionist enterprise. In 1928 the first Hebrew version of Freud's major work, *Group Psychology and the Analysis of the Ego* (originally published in 1921), appeared in Jerusalem.[462] The translator was the pedagogue and writer Judah Dwossis (later Dvir), and the publisher was the new publishing house established by the editors of *Hed HaKhinukh*. A year earlier this journal – founded by members of Histadrut HaMorim BeEretz Israel, the Jewish Teachers' Union of Palestine[463] – had published a groundbreaking article addressing the applications of psychoanalysis to pedagogy and education, authored by Dorian Feigenbaum and translated into Hebrew by Mordechai Brachyahu (a prominent translator of Freud's works after the founding of Israel as well).[464]

In a letter of thanks to his translator, Freud wrote, "One of my associates, who has mastered our ancient – yet already rejuvenated – and sacred language sent me your letter and assured me that your translation of my *Group Psychology* was excellent. I can easily imagine the difficulties you had to overcome, and I thank you for your efforts in this regard."[465] Indeed, Dwossis encountered significant challenges while producing this first translation of a book on psychoanalysis, as evidenced by the appendix he found it necessary to include, listing the main psychoanalytical concepts in their original German alongside their Hebrew translation. In his appendix Dwossis noted that various Hebrew language experts, such as the writer and teacher Yitzhak Epstein, had contributed to his efforts to find Hebrew equivalents to the psychoanalytic concepts expressed in German.[466]

There were lively, unceasing debates among Freud's first translators regarding the translation of psychoanalytic terms into Hebrew. The search for Hebrew terminology to express psychoanalytic concepts greatly preoccupied immigrant Jewish intellectuals, "zealots of the Hebrew language and Jewish culture," who invested much effort in translating the works of Freud and other psychoanalysts into Hebrew.

The 1930s: Introductory Lectures on Psychoanalysis

Upon concluding his translation of *Group Psychology and the Analysis of the Ego*, Judah Dwossis received Freud's authorization to translate additional texts. He became Freud's official translator in Palestine, and the two maintained a warm correspondence until 1938.[467] In May 1936, on the occasion of Freud's eightieth birthday, Dwossis published an article in *Haaretz* on the translation of Freud's works into Hebrew.[468] He was not the only translator of Freud; during the 1930s and 1940s, as psychoanalysis was undergoing a tremendous boom in Mandatory Palestine, many other Yishuv intellectuals strove to translate the writings of the father of psychoanalysis. A letter from Freud to Dwossis reveals that the latter had evidently sought permission to translate *Totem and Taboo*.[469] Freud gave his approval in principle but added that the timing seemed premature to him. He voiced concerns that this book, which differed somewhat from his other works, would be misunderstood by readers in Palestine, who were not yet familiar with the fundamental principles of psychoanalysis. He suggested that Dwossis translate *Introductory Lectures on Psychoanalysis* instead, as this work could help readers understand "how psychoanalysis works" and spark their interest, while also helping them see the new horizons that the discipline could open up before them. Freud acknowledged that this was a more voluminous text, undoubtedly posing new challenges for the translator, but he insisted: without the prior translation and publication of *Introductory Lectures on Psychoanalysi*s, the translation and publication of *Totem and Taboo* would be in vain and Dwossis's efforts might end in utter failure. Freud believed that his *Introductory Lectures* – the first two parts of which were published in 1916 and the entire volume in 1917 – could enlighten readers as to the principles, objectives, assumptions, and applications of psychoanalysis at the clinical level as well as the social and cultural levels.[470] Dwossis followed Freud's advice, and a translation of the first volume of this work was published in 1934 by Stybel under the title *Kitvei Freud: Shi'urim BeMavo LePsychoanaliza* (The Writings of Freud: Introductory Lessons in Psychoanalysis). This marked the first translation and publication in Palestine of a book by Freud addressing all aspects of psychoanalysis. Before its appearance, on December 15, 1930, Freud sent Dwossis two prefaces intended respectively for the Hebrew versions of *Introductory Lectures on Psychoanalysis* and *Totem and Taboo*.[471] The first preface, according to Freud, was quite "cold and objective" whereas the second – written for *Totem and Taboo* – adopted a "warmer" tone. These two prefaces are well known to Freud's exegetes, especially to those who have studied Freud's relationship to Judaism and Zionism.

In his preface to the first Hebrew edition of *Introductory Lectures on Psychoanalysis*, Freud wrote, "Readers of Hebrew and especially young people eager for knowledge are presented in this volume with psychoanalysis clothed in the ancient language which has been awakened to a new life by the will of the Jewish people. The author can well picture the problem which this has set its translator. Nor need he suppress his doubt whether Moses and the Prophets would have found these Hebrew lectures intelligible."[472]

A review of Freud's correspondence with Dwossis leaves no room for doubt that Freud was fascinated by Hebrew. The language – or, more accurately, its revival – embodied something mysterious, strange, and perhaps also distressing for the father of psychoanalysis – something indefinable that seemed to oscillate between the intimate and the bizarre, between the familiar and the uncanny.[473] In his correspondence with Dwossis, Freud underscored his regret over not speaking Hebrew or having had the opportunity to learn it: "My father spoke the sacred language as well as, if not better than, German. He raised me to be completely ignorant of everything concerning Judaism. Only as an adult did I begin to resent him for this."[474]

In his preface to the Hebrew version of *Totem and Taboo*, Freud wrote,

> No reader [of the Hebrew version of] this book will find it easy to put himself in the emotional position of an author who is ignorant of the language of holy writ, who is completely estranged from the religion of his fathers – as well as from every other religion – and who cannot take a share in nationalist ideals, but who has yet never repudiated his people, who feels that he is in his essential nature a Jew and who has no desire to alter that nature. If the question were put to him: "Since you have abandoned all these common characteristics of your countrymen, what is there left to you that is Jewish?" he would reply: "A very great deal, and probably its very essence." He could not now express that essence clearly in words; but some day, no doubt, it will become accessible to the scientific mind.[475]

Freud returned to this issue 1936, in a letter to Barbara Low following the death of her cousin, Montague David Eder. In this letter (with which historians are quite familiar) he explained that he had been unable to expose the underpinnings of his unique and enigmatic Jewishness in a "scientific manner" – that is, through psychoanalytic inquiry.[476] In 1939, with the publication of his book *Moses and Monotheism*, he made one more, final, attempt to find an answer.

At the end of the preface cited above, Freud pointed out that his book *Totem and Taboo* "deals with the origin of religion and morality, though it adopts no Jewish standpoint and makes no exceptions in favour of Jewry." Thus, Freud continued, "It is an experience of a quite special kind for such an author when a book of his is translated into the Hebrew language and put into the hands of readers for whom that historic idiom is a living tongue: a book, moreover, which deals with the origin of religion and morality, though it adopts no Jewish standpoint and makes no exceptions in favour of Jewry. The author hopes, however, that he will be at one with his readers in the conviction that unprejudiced science cannot remain a stranger to the spirit of the new Jewry" – that is, to Hebrew culture. He insisted on separating himself from Judaism so that no one could infer any allusion to religion in his writing – indeed, Freud consistently maintained a distance from religion – and so that it would be clear that he did not share any nationalist ideals, namely Zionism, as the text itself attests.

The Hebrew edition of *Introductory Lectures on Psychoanalysis* included a lexicon of basic psychoanalytic concepts; each entry indicated the original term used by Freud, the Hebrew translation, and because Dwossis considered it appropriate and useful, the name of the translator as well. Most of the contributors to this lexicon were members of the Society of Jewish Writers in Palestine. Mordechai Brachyahu translated the terms *Verdrängung* (repression) as *hadkhakah* and *Projektion* (projection) as *tishlukh*; Israel Riklis translated *Fehlleistung* (parapraxis) as *ma'aseh-keshel*; Yitzhak Epstein contributed translations for the terms *Selbsterhaltungstreib* (self-preservation instinct) – *yetzer hitkaimut* – and *Innervation* (innervation)– *yitzvuv*; and Dov Stück (Sadan) proposed that *Anschein* (image) be translated as *tadmit*.

The Hebrew publication of *Introductory Lectures on Psychoanalysis* in 1934 and the founding of the Psychoanalytic Institute in Jerusalem that same year prompted the Hebrew Language Committee to convene a commission of specialists in language and psychoanalysis – with Max Eitingon representing psychoanalysis – with the aim of creating an official Hebrew glossary for the discipline. The Hebrew publication of Freud's book sparked a number of reactions. In an article in *Hed HaKhinukh*, for example, the pedagogue and writer Aryeh Alkalay praised the publishers' efforts and saluted Dwossis for having successfully "provided us, in elegant Hebrew. . . a science in which any inapt word could alter or distort the issues or their meaning."[477] Aware of the strong resistance that the publication in Hebrew of a text by Freud could nevertheless arouse in Palestine, Alkalay also praised the courage of the man who had taken on the difficult task of introducing the Yishuv to "psychoanalysis, [which] embodies so many innovations and secrets, including concepts that conflict with old, longstanding opinions and disrupt deeply rooted feelings, that it inevitably incites resistance." Seeking to encourage his readers to engage with Freud's work, however, he added that all these innovations have roots in ancient Jewish sources, and therefore "this theory is not so foreign to us." He concluded, "The translator, whose aim was apparently to present us with Freud in Hebrew, will undoubtedly continue to provide us with the works of Freud and thus help bring this treasure 'home'. Would that we were able to bring home all of the works of ancient Jewish culture."

CHAPTER 13

Freud in E.I. – Eretz Israel

During the 1930s, against the backdrop of rising anti-Semitic violence in Germany and a flourishing, vibrant Jewish society in Palestine, Freud's work made its way into the Hebrew culture of the Yishuv, where it left its mark. After the Nazis had stigmatized psychoanalysis as a "Jewish science" and "the product of degenerate Jewish thought," the discipline came to symbolize Jewish fate and the fate of Jews who, forced to flee Germany, had reached Palestine. Freud benefitted from the admiration of intellectuals who translated, interpreted, and published his works, thereby also enriching modern Hebrew with new terminology grounded in his theories. The aim of the translators was no longer merely to resuscitate the "sacred language" but to wrest it from religious power and make it the pillar of a new culture.

The spread of Nazism across Europe threatened the standing of Freud's writings in their original language: as early as the 1930s they were banished from both the German language and German culture, even though the two had formed the very cradle of psychoanalysis and given rise to these texts. Hence Hebrew, now revived, provided a "refuge" for psychoanalysis. Beginning in 1933 and throughout the 1940s, interest in psychoanalysis steadily grew, quite independently from the establishment of psychoanalysis as a discipline. Citations of Freud's texts and commentary on his theories increased correspondingly: the early translators and commentators in Hebrew were writers, followed by the pedagogues and intellectuals of various Zionist Leftist movements, in particular HaPo'el HaTza'ir and HaShomer HaTza'ir. The translation of some of Freud's texts into Hebrew by HaShomer HaTza'ir members also sparked very lively debates. Freud's work generated so much interest in the Yishuv that the Hebrew translations of his writings drew praise, commentary, and positive as well as negative critiques in both the general and the professional, specialized press. The scale and scope of translations of Freud's writings into Hebrew attest to the status psychoanalysis held in the Yishuv discourse throughout the 1930s and 1940s.

In early 1936 Freud wrote to Dwossis – who at the time was working on his translation of *Totem and Taboo* – to thank him for his efforts. He expressed immense satisfaction that his books had become accessible to Hebrew-speaking intellectuals in "Palästina (E.I.)" – that is, Eretz Israel. To the best of our knowledge, this marked the first instance in which Freud used this highly symbolic acronym,[478] which carried much significance for Zionists and the Jews of Palestine but was categorically rejected by assimilated anti-Zionist Jews. Experts in Freud cannot ignore the fact that he wrote the letters "E.I." (indicating Eretz Israel) to refer to Palestine. It should be noted, however, that Freud's correspondence with Yishuv intellectuals – far removed from any political debate – provide the only source by which we can assess the evolution of his views on Zionism.

Freud was devoid of any nationalist sentiment and remained reticent towards Zionism, particularly after 1929. How did it happen, therefore, that he embraced the Hebrew name of the Promised Land, even if only briefly? The term "Eretz Israel" refers not only to the geographic birthplace of the Jewish People; for thousands of Diaspora Jews the initials "E.I." represent a return the Land of Israel. The term "Palestine (E.I.)" appeared in Hebrew on official British Mandate documents, stamps, and currency. Should we interpret Freud's use of this term as a sign of appreciation and empathy for his official translator and the Hebrew-speaking intellectuals in Palestine with whom he briefly identified? Or should we see it as indicating a closer bond and stronger affinity with the Yishuv? The latter is a reasonable assumption, particularly given that Freud's writings at the time did not display the reticence, doubts, or hostility he had previously voiced with respect to the Zionist enterprise. The resurgence of anti-Semitism in Germany and Austria had probably led him to reassess his views towards the movement and grant it – or at least its cultural enterprises – more credit than previously, to begin to regard it less as "illusory." Presumably the fact that some of his disciples had fled Nazi Germany and settled in Palestine, where they succeeded in founding a new psychoanalytic society – while the edifice of psychoanalysis in Europe was collapsing in the face of barbaric totalitarianism – would also have influenced his thinking.

In a letter acknowledging receipt of the proofs for the translation of *Introductory Lectures on Psychoanalysis*, Freud told Dwossis that he saw no reason to change the preface he had prepared in December 1930, and as he could not read Hebrew, he was unable to review the translation for corrections. He added, with some measure of enthusiasm, that his book on Moses was due to be published, that he intended to grant Dwossis the right, in advance, to translate this text, and that he was jubilant at the thought of this book on Moses one day being translated into the "sacred tongue." He explained that the book is a direct continuation of *Totem and Taboo*, elaborating on his views regarding religion, which had begun to take shape in 1913. At the same time, he warned that his new thoughts on religion, applied specifically to Judaism, might offend some Jews even though the theories assert no scientific claims.

The Hebrew translation of *Totem and Taboo* was published in early 1939 with, as noted, a preface that Freud had prepared in 1930 and sent to Dwossis along with the preface to *Introductory Lectures on Psychoanalysis*.

Announcements in England and the Netherlands regarding the forthcoming publication in German and English of *Moses and Monotheism*, an extract of which was translated into Hebrew and published by *HaPo'el HaTza'ir* in December 1938, raised concerns for Eitingon.[479] Indeed, the lack of a reaction among commentators and critics in Palestine to the Hebrew publication of *Totem and Taboo* was undoubtedly related to the announcements about a forthcoming book on Moses and to the public outrage that followed.

The Psychopathology of Everyday Life, published in Hebrew in early 1942, is among the important works by Freud that were translated into Hebrew even before Israel attained statehood.[480] Of all his translations, it was for this book that Zvi Vislevsky – also a translator of Schopenhauer, Marx, Hermann Cohen, and Georges Simmel – received the Tel Aviv Municipality's Tchernichovsky Prize for Excellence in Translation in 1943.[481] The Hebrew translation also included a preface by Eitingon, one of the very few essays he authored under his own name.[482]

The editors of *HaPo'el HaTza'ir*, who ascribed much importance to Freud's work, also published a text he had written while in London – "A Word about Anti-Semitism" (1938) – his first since leaving Vienna, according to the newspaper.[483] Echoing the political sentiment of the time, Joseph Schechter's translation of the first chapter of *Thoughts for the Times on War and Death* – titled "The Disappointments of War" – appeared in *Gilyonot* in 1940.[484] Revised translations of this essay were published later that year in the newspaper *HaShomer HaTza'ir*[485] and in 1943 in the periodical *Ofakim*.[486] In 1942 HaShomer HaTza'ir members also published a Hebrew translation of an extract from Freud's autobiography – under the title "The Dream of a Young Jew" – without attributing the source of this Freudian text, which Theodor Reik had cited in his book *From Thirty Years with Freud*.[487] In 1947 Zvi Sohar and Shmuel Golan published a second passage from Freud's autobiography under the title "My Life and Work" ("Hayai VePo'alai"),[488] and in 1948 Sohar published yet another excerpt, "The Relationship of Psychoanalysis with

Literature, Art, and Science," in *Ofakim*.[489] To this list one might add the 1925 preface by Freud to Aichhorn's famous text on the problem of juvenile delinquency, translated by David Idelsohn and published in 1948 as part of a series of articles in the periodical *Hygiena Ruhanit* and in 1956 as a book.[490]

In 1953 *Ofakim* published a translation of the sixth chapter of Freud's *A Childhood Memory of Leonardo da Vinci* (1910) under the title "Why Is Mona Lisa Smiling?"[491] Two translations of *Three Essays on Sexual Theory* appeared consecutively in 1953 in 1954: the first, titled "Three Essays," was translated by Shmuel Golan and published by Sifriat Poalim,[492] while the second, translated by Menachem Ayalon, was published by Ever Publishers.[493] In 1959 Mordechai Brachyahu completed his translation of the first part of *The Interpretation of Dreams* (published by Yavneh).[494] Unfortunately, his death that same year interrupted this work.[495]

Finally, in 1967-1968 a collection of Freud's works appeared in Hebrew. This selection of writings, translated by Aryeh Bar and Chaim Izaak, was published in four volumes by Dvir – the publishing house that Judah Dwossis (now Dvir) had founded.[496] However, from the late 1960s until the early 1990s, very few texts by Freud were translated into Hebrew. Does this inactivity indicate a loss of interest on the part of Israel's psychoanalysts, intellectuals, and public in general?

Israelis of Central European descent, including psychoanalysts from the Jerusalem Psychoanalytic Institute, continued to read and research Freud's writings in German, even though much of the Israeli public regarded German as the language of the Holocaust. English was the preferred language of study and research among new generations of academics and students, who drew their inspiration from the English-speaking world – even at the Sigmund Freud Center that opened at the Hebrew University in Jerusalem in 1977 and whose first director, Joseph Sandler, was an English speaker. It was not until 1999, at the initiative of Emanuel Berman, that new Hebrew translations of Freud's works began to appear, and they continue to do so to this day.

The various Hebrew translations of Freud's works, and the many commentaries, critiques, and debates surrounding them that appeared during 1930-1940 in both the general and the specialized press, attest without a doubt to the influence of Freud's work and to the dissemination of his theories throughout the new Jewish society generally and Hebrew culture specifically.

CHAPTER 14

The Reception of *Moses and Monotheism* in the Yishuv

The publication of *Moses and Monotheism* in April 1939 sparked a great deal of controversy in the Yishuv, which continued even after Freud's death in September of that year.

In a letter dated September 30, 1934, to Arnold Zweig, Freud explained why, during his vacation, he had undertaken a new study on the figure of Moses: "You are quite familiar with the starting point for my work; it is the same as that of your *Bilanz* (Balance).[497] In light of the renewed persecutions, we seek to know how the Jew became what he is and why he draws this eternal hate. I will soon find the formula. Moses created the Jew, and my work has received the following title: *Moses the Man*, a historical novel (it is more a historical novel than your novel on Nietzsche)."[498]

Arnold Zweig, like Eitingon, responded enthusiastically to Freud's plan and was pleased to hear that his text would one day be translated into Hebrew and published in Jerusalem.[499] Yet unlike Eitingon, presumably because of the lukewarm reception his own book *De Vriendt* had received, Zweig agreed with Freud that publishing *Moses* might provoke a scandal, aggravate Pater (Father) Schmidt,[500] and create problems for the analytic community: "I am concerned about your assessment that there is a threat to analysis here. Eitingon, to whom I confidentially reported your remarks, claims that the risk is not great. He argues that if *Totem and Taboo* and *The Future of an Illusion* have not brought Pater Schmidt onto the scene, neither will the novel on Moses. But there is no recently published book like the one that has just come out. It might trigger a scandal, and therefore I must, with great regret, agree with you."[501]

At the same time Zweig, his curiosity piqued, also expressed irritation at the idea that Freud could consign his bold theories to the drawer; he disputed Freud's decision not to publish the manuscript and requested that a copy be sent to him in Palestine: "Could you not send a manuscript of *Moses* here? According to Eitingon's accounts, this is a bold and exciting manuscript; and what you yourself suggested makes me furious – that you would want to leave such a work in the drawer, like Grillparzer's *Libussa*."[502]

The responses in Palestine to *Moses and Monotheism* were not solely hostile, far from it. Indeed, Freud had more than enough local intellectuals who were conversant with biblical text, some of whom praised the book and some of whom offered substantive critiques (in contrast to attacks by Agudat Israel supporters), and he responded to everyone. Zweig, for his part, waited until 1941 to conduct a brief review of Freud's *Moses*, in which he retraced the various stages that led to the final draft and publication of the book, portraying Freud as a major Jewish figure comparable to the great Talmudists of the Babylonian exile.[503]

When I reviewed the many documents attesting to the fiery reaction that the publication of *Moses and Monotheism* provoked in Palestine, I posed the following question to myself: Did the publication of this book – which dealt a harsh blow to Judaism by severing its greatest prophet from the lineage of Abraham – damage Freud's image and the dissemination of his theories among intellectuals and the general public, or conversely, did it in fact promote the spread of his theories and writings pre-state Israel? The latter seems to me to be the case. Even though the Orthodox Jewish community of the Yishuv viewed the publication of *Moses* as highly scandalous, nonetheless, as with the publication of *The Future of an Illusion*, the book awakened the secular Jewish consciousness of many intellectuals who took it upon themselves to defend Freud in the local press. During 1939, the year of its publication, and throughout the following years, we find many expressions of sympathy for Freud, even if others were vehemently calling for the excommunication of this "senile old Jew" afflicted by the "disease of assimilation," this champion of secularism and rationalism.

Yishuv intellectuals were able to read a first extract from *Moses* in Hebrew in the December 9, 1938, edition of *HaPo'el HaTza'ir*[504] – the first of two that Freud published anonymously in 1937 in the journal *Imago* – and to learn that a complete version of the text, under the title *Der Mann Moses und die monotheistische Religion: Drei Abhandlungen*, was due to be published in April 1939.[505]

Freud, Eitingon, and Zweig – as their correspondence attests – waited attentively for the publication of *Moses* and informed one another of reactions, both in Palestine and in Europe, once the book appeared. In February 1939 Eitingon wrote to Freud,[506] telling him that the public in Palestine awaited the book with trepidation. He added that an article praising Freud had appeared in *Haaretz*, authored by Ya'akov Steinberg, a member of the Yiddish Scientific Institute in Vilnius (today the YIVO Institute for Jewish Research, located in New York City). Eitingon wrote, "When will *Moses* appear? Here in Palestine, the mere anticipation of your book arouses great interest among some, [while others] are quick to denounce it. Recently the liberal bourgeois daily *Haaretz* published an article based on the visit by two gentlemen from the Yiddish Institute in Vilnius who met with you, titled 'The Unbelieving Jew" and authored by a certain Y. Steinberg, who is full of admiration for you but is not particularly clever."[507]

Eitingon also informed Freud about his meetings with Martin Buber. The conversations remain friendly, he reported, but Buber (who had learned about the publication of *Moses* from his students) categorically rejected Freud's new theses, as he had rejected other Freudian ideas in the past. Still, Buber expressed a desire to know more. Eitingon was surprised, however, that Buber had not been intrigued by the question of totemism:

> He, a sociologist of religions, found very little with which to agree in *Totem and Taboo*, given that its assumptions had been refuted long ago, in his view. But [after all], totemism was of little importance to him. It is different now that the subject is Moses. He also told me that he disagrees with your *The Interpretation of Dreams*. One cannot, according to him, reduce the overflowing creativity of dreams to such simple, rigid, and few forms. He himself had long been working hard on his own dreams, and [holds that] one cannot reduce them to a few grand formal principles while at the same time respecting the mysteries of this creative process. I told him that with such an approach, we would never achieve more than the old academic psychology had already achieved. I think I conducted the discussion with dignity, but it is clear that we have a fierce critic of psychoanalysis at home.[508]

In his response Freud sought to reassure his friend, stating that he was not too concerned about criticism from the renowned Jewish scholar: "Martin Buber's pious words will do little harm to *The Interpretation of Dreams* . . . . *Moses* is much more vulnerable, and I am prepared for the Jewish assault on it." Eitingon, however, had understood Buber accurately: a few years later, in his own book on Moses, the philosopher harshly criticized Freud, expressing his "astonishment and regret at seeing that a scholar as eminent in his field as Sigmund Freud decided to publish a work so completely devoid of scientific value and based on such unfounded and inconsistent hypotheses as his book *Moses and Monotheism* (1939)."[509]

Max Eitingon received a copy of *Moses and Monotheism* from the publishers in Amsterdam on a date he considered "highly symbolic" as he wrote, not without emotion, to Freud:[510] Friday, April 10, 1939, "the day of the Passover Seder (meal), when Jews read the Haggadah, recounting and commemorating the Exodus from Egypt *beyad khazakah u-vizro'a netuyah* – that is, 'with a strong hand and an outstretched arm'," he added, echoing the words of God to Moses and, no doubt, thinking of the fate of the thousands of Jews trapped behind the borders of Nazi Germany. Shortly after the publication of *Moses and Monotheism*, the National Library at the Hebrew University in Jerusalem was enriched by the German and English versions, thanks to Max Eitingon, who had sent several copies to Professor Meir Weil, then curator of the National Library.

Aware of the narcissistic wounds that the publication of *Moses and Monotheism* would inflict on representatives of Jewish communities everywhere, Freud had, well before the publication, prepared to respond to critics and to anticipated attacks from around the world.

Among the first responses in Palestine to the publication of *Moses and Monotheism* was that of the writer and journalist Shalom Ben-Chorin. In an article in *Davar* on May 5, 1939,[511] Ben-Chorin first introduced himself as an admirer of Freud. After summarizing the main theses presented by Freud in his work and the circumstances from which the book had emerged, the writer then expressed regret that an intellectual of Freud's stature had decided to undertake a scientific study on Moses "with the freedom of a novelist." Freud, according to Ben-Chorin, relied on "popular" historical and literary references, whereas he could have based his research on a vast rabbinic literature that included works such as that of the renowned Micah Joseph Berdichevsky, or that of Gustav Delmachen, a Christian biblical scholar who had already posited similar hypotheses.[512] In all, however, this article was moderate in tone and cannot be seen as a personal assault on Freud; other critics were far more vehement.

A writer by the name of Lask, for example, published a much less delicate reaction in the English-language *Palestine Review* of June 30, 1939.[513] Lask accused Freud of having selected contemporary texts and documentation to support his argument and reconstruct the image of a figure who had lived more than 1400 years before the Common Era; he further reproached Freud for not having drawn on Jewish tradition, going so far as to label him *"am ha'aretz"* (an ignoramus). The author then presented a long series of (reductive) arguments to refute the book's theses. First Lask pointed out what he regarded as contradictions: Freud maintained, on the one hand, that Moses had tried to return his people to a religious tradition born in Egypt, and on the other, that his ultimate aim was to distance the People of Israel from the religious tradition of Egypt so as to prepare it to receive the Ten Commandments at Mount Sinai. In Lask's view, however, "The real problem in this book is not the correctness or otherwise of Freud's theory about Moses, but the real subconscious reasons which induced Freud to write the book at all. And these can, in the circumstances, best be approached by the use of Freudian methods."[514] Like other critics of Freud, Lask was convinced that this book had its origins in Freud's conflict with his own Jewishness, the same conflict that afflicted many assimilated Jews of his generation and produced what Jewish believers regarded as a new "psychopathological entity" and even an "epidemic" among the Jewish People. Its symptoms manifested as assimilation, and Freud was one of its many victims.

Lask's arguments and observations would lead one to conclude that, like many Jews of his generation,

> Freud is beginning to suffer from a long repressed racial memory or aspiration. . . embodied in the idea of the Messiah. However, his super-ego or conscience has developed in the rationalist liberal and humanitarian atmosphere of the late nineteenth century in Central Europe. Such a super-ego must of necessity have tried to repress this racial memory. It might have succeeded had there not occurred during the life of Freud and his generation a certain trauma, which has permitted this racial memory to force itself to the surface in one form or

> another despite Freud's super-ego. This trauma was the rise to power of
> Hitlerism. After that his racial memory had to create an outlet.[515]

Freud's work, which Lask inaccurately described as written between 1937 and 1938, thus constituted "the first step taken by the unconscious in dodging the attention of the super-ego" and accordingly, the "lapses in the present work. . . are due to a long conscious life that has led him to try to 'sublimate,' interpret and explain away the urges of his inmost Jewish self."[516]

There appeared many psychological theses reducing *Moses and Monotheism* to a symptom afflicting Freud, a "poor old Jew suffering from repressed Jewishness." Articles in this spirit abounded in the local press, even years after the book's publication and Freud's death.[517] In 1942, for example, the magazine *Maaznayim* published an article titled "Freud's Repressed Jewishness,"[518] which relied on Freud's own "theory of repression" to explain the motives that had led the psychoanalyst to write this book about Moses – a book that was no more than a "symptom" of Freud's "repressed Jewishness." If it is true, as Freud argues (according to the anonymous writer), that "culture and the human soul are the source of repressed infantile sexuality," then Freud's theories are the product of his repression of his own "sexual drives." It would seem that this anonymous author viewed sexuality only from a narrow moralistic perspective. He later argued that in Freud's theories sexuality takes the place of that "repressed Judaism. . . as happened with other theories developed by assimilationists of his generation" – an argument that raises further questions because, for believing Jews, it places Judaism in the position and role of the unconscious in the Freudian sense of the term. He concluded, "As a symptom of the tragedy that befell Western Jews, namely, the widespread assimilation among Western and Central European Jews, the text on Moses casts a shadow on its author and exposes, without his knowing, Freud's desire for revenge against the Prophet Moses as well as his own subjective wounds."[519]

As Arnold Zweig had written to Freud on 8 August 1939,[520] the religious commentators of Agudat Israel did not pass up this opportunity to attack *Moses* and its author in their press. In his article "Freud the Jew and Moses the . . . Egyptian,"[521] for example, the writer, literary critic, psychologist, and Yiddish and Hebrew publicist Aharon Zeitlin accused Freud of "giving dangerous weapons to the professional haters of Israel and its spirit (*son'ei Israel*)."[522] He wondered how it came to be that this "famous Jewish scholar" had tried to use his science to prove that Moses was not Jewish but Egyptian, at a time when the forces of evil were taking over the world and the Jewish People were experiencing one of the greatest tragedies of their history. He continued,

> This scholar is, as we know, a victim of the Nazis. Because of his Judaism he was forced to leave Austria, and fleeing did not come easily. He was miraculously able to escape captivity, thanks to his prominent reputation and the efforts of influential people abroad. And thus Freud was saved from the fate of the Jews trapped in the fires of hell. Now we hear the first theory that he, having been saved from the flames, voices to the world after his rescue. And the great revelation, the revelation of this man who was to be tortured, is that the Jews must renounce our Prophet Moses because he was Egyptian.[523]

This criticism did not come as a surprise: Freud himself, and the disciples who accompanied him during the *Moses* adventure, had anticipated it as early as 1934. Zeitlin then compared Freud to Austen Chamberlain, the British anti-Semitic and Germanophile politician who, in his book *The Foundations of the Twentieth Century,* argued that Jesus was of Aryan rather than Semitic descent, thus Germanizing Christianity in order to please the Prussian emperor, Wilhelm II. By claiming that Moses was Egyptian, Zeitlin observed ironically, Freud was delving into the absurd no less than Chamberlain had when he sought to make Jesus "a German from Galilee"; and now Freud was "wresting the figure of Moses from the hands" of the Jews and supposedly proving, like the others, that the Jews had contributed nothing to humanity, thereby also confiscating the Bible from the hands of the Jews. In other words, Zeitlin was accusing Freud of anti-Semitism: by hiding his true face behind the image of an intellectual, Freud was providing new weapons to Israel's enemies. Like other critics of Freud at the time, Zeitlin accused the father of psychoanalysis of having taken up the theses of the German Protestant historian Ernst Sellin, who had put forward the idea that Moses was murdered by his own people; Zeitlin described this thesis as a "cheap copy" of the ancient anti-Semitic blood libel attributing the murder of Christ to the Jews; he asserted that "the

German critic's intentions are so obvious and his arguments so outrageous, that there is no need to engage with this scientific anti-Semitic nonsense that denigrates the word of the Torah in order to cast a scientific blood libel on the Jews."[524] In short, seeking at all costs to demonstrate that behind the figure of the psychoanalyst hid an agent of modern anti-Semitism, Zeitlin discredited Freud and his book, concluding that the publication of this book "was a serious mistake, culturally and scientifically, on the part of the famous old man."[525]

A few days later, in the same newspaper, Aharon Kaminka revealed to all the diabolical intentions of "Freud the assimilationist."[526] He described Freud as a man who lacked any methodology and whose discourse was hollow and disorderly, as evidenced by this book. Once again, Freud found himself accused alongside assimilated Jews who, according to Kaminka, were seeking to fan the flames of hatred against the Jewish religion and anything Jewish, and who, while claiming to be Jews, were devoid of any "national sentiment"; in the eyes of other Jews, as well as the Gentiles, they remained foreigners.

Freud had stated, wrote Kaminka, that the reason for his failure to obtain a position at the University of Vienna, despite efforts over the course of many years, lay in the university's anti-Semitism; but no, argued the author, it was merely a product of the imagination of a man "obsessed with anti-Semitism and persecuted by his own shadow"; no anti-Semitism could be attributed to the university, according to Kaminka, given that Freud himself was teaching at this Christian institution at the very same time, and one of his co-religionists, D. H. Miller, held the post of a professor of philosophy at the same university. The cause was therefore to be sought elsewhere: "If there was no place for Freud at this university, it was not because he was Jewish," Kaminka concluded. Furthermore, he asserted, Freud "did not realize and did not want to recognize that his science was a source of shame and an abomination for intellectuals, and that the Hebrew University, which respects itself and the great spiritual strength that gave rise to everything exalted and sublime in Jewish culture, would not accept as a professor a man who from the outset dismisses all the positive and creative influence of the human spirit and denies the very foundation of belief and the divinity in human beings."[527]

Let us bring to a close this list of insults and slander that Kaminka hurled against, in his words, an old exhausted man suffering from psychological complexes inherent to his "nervous disorder" – like every other assimilationist Jew "impregnated with foreign culture and seeking to destroy all that is Jewish." As such, the critic argued, *Moses* was no more than a clumsy attempt by Freud to return to the path of Judaism. In lieu of a conclusion, Kaminka expressed hope that Freud would soon be "redeemed" from his "hate complexes towards the Jewish nation" and recognize that Moses and the Torah represent the truth.

Officials and intellectuals of the Yishuv were notably more eloquent in addressing Freud and challenging his hypotheses on Moses. Among the first was Raphael Da Costa, who hastened to write to Freud as soon as he had finished reading *Moses and Monotheism*.[528] He criticized Freud for doubting the truth of the biblical account without even considering that one might deduce truth from belief or religious fact.[529] Yet Da Costa also asked if he would have the honor of meeting Freud in Palestine and hearing him deliver a lecture as one of the chairs at the Hebrew University in Jerusalem. Da Costa was not the only one to make such a request of Freud, who had declined every invitation to Jerusalem since 1925 on the grounds of illness and fatigue. Freud did, however, respond to these objections swiftly and with some measure of astonishment, even irritation: "How can one conduct a biblical study that relies exclusively on a religion claiming to have a monopoly over the Bible?" he asked, adding that this is simply an instance of *ich glaube weil ich glaube* – "I believe because I believe."[530]

Another correspondent in Palestine, Siegfried Wolff of Haifa, while expressing great respect for Freud and his work, attempted to demonstrate, in a long letter to the psychoanalyst, that there exist non-biblical references that would provide equal support for either Freud's hypothesis about the Egyptian ancestry of Moses or the claims that the Prophet was of Hebrew ancestry.[531]

In July 1939, Nahum Perelmann, a leader of the Zionist religious party HaPo'el HaMizrahi, sent the *Palestine Post* and *Maaznayim* an article titled "Professor Freud and the National Product of the Land [Jewish Palestine]" (Professor Freud VeTozeret HaAretz), accompanied by an open letter to Freud.[532] In this brief article, Perelmann attacked not only Freud; he accused assimilated Jewish intellectuals in general of "pouring 4,000 years of Jewish spiritual heritage into the sea" and of leaving the door open for "foreign intellectual products that could jeopardize the existence of both the Yishuv and Judaism itself." In the accompanying open letter, he queried Freud about the necessity and purpose of what is termed "literary" biblical criticism by secular Jews:

> Surely you are aware, dear Professor, that many of our brothers in Eretz Israel consider critiques of the Bible to be a foundation of Jewish literature, without realizing that in fact they are cutting off the branch on which they sit – something that some would view as consistent, for as everyone knows, we Jews are *Luftmenschen* ["people of air" – see endnote].
>
> But not only do masses of readers welcome and promote this science; renowned Jewish thinkers and writers have also paved these paths, without considering that all the archaeological discoveries to date that have anything to do with the Torah of Israel confirm the words of the Bible and prove the folly of biblical criticism.
>
> My question is the following: Where does this come from? Who are these Jews who cultivate this science and consider it right?
>
> Surely you would agree, dear Professor, that we are dealing entirely with Jews who have, in one way or another, turned their back on traditional Judaism.
>
> Why must these Jews engage in critiques of the Bible?
>
> I am spelling out my question, to which I request an answer: Is not this commitment to criticism of the Bible by Jews aimed, knowingly or unknowingly, at justifying their own betrayal of the principles of the Jewish religion and laws of the Torah?
>
> I believe, dear Professor, that you are the person best suited to provide a complete answer to this question, and I believe that by answering this question you will earn the privilege of having contributed to the survival of Jewry far more than through your book *Moses*.[533]

It was Freud, of course, that Perelmann was challenging when he questioned the attitudes of assimilated Jews, and while claiming that Freud should respond, he put forward his own hypothesis, which understandably would disappoint a rationalist such as Freud. The virulent commentary and furious reactions of religious leaders in Palestine undoubtedly helped place Freud among the defenders of secular Jewish culture in the Yishuv.

We cannot close this chapter on the reception of *Moses and Monotheism* in Palestine without addressing the criticism by Israel Doryon,[534] a German sociologist who emigrated to Palestine and a Talmudist well known to scholars interested in Freud's relationship with Judaism. Doryon undertook a critical study of Freud's text, which was published for the first time in Hebrew in 1946.[535] He presented his work before the members of the Psychoanalytic Institute on May 15 of that year at an event commemorating Freud's ninetieth birthday. A French version of the study, under the title *Freud et le monothéisme hébreu*, was published in 1971 and included a long preface by one of the translators, Henri Baruk (to which we will return), as well as two letters sent by Freud to Doryon in October-November 1938, replying to the latter's remarks.[536]

In a letter he wrote to Freud on September 15, 1938, after the first anonymous publication of *Moses* in the journal *Imago* a year earlier,[537] Doryon initially asked him about the work of the Austrian Jewish philosopher Joseph Popper-Lynkeus: in his text Freud had quoted from a play about the story of Moses, *The Son of the Egyptian King* (*Der Sohn des Königs von Ägypten*),[538] and Doryon wondered whether another text by Lynkeus, *Fantasies of a Realist* (*Phantasien eines Realisten*), could also have influenced his thoughts on Moses. Doryon was very familiar with Lynkeus's work and at the time was preparing for the publication in Palestine and presumably abroad (in Hebrew and English) of his study on the work of the Viennese philosopher, with prefaces by Freud and Einstein.[539] Freud did not deny the possibility that Lynkeus's work had influenced the development of his hypotheses on Moses. He replied to Doryon that Lynkeus's work could very well have sparked his imagination and contributed to an atmosphere favorable for the formation of his conception of Moses, just as he was influenced by the works of other authors, including the great historian Eduard Meyer. "The idea that my hypothesis about the Egyptian origins of Moses has its source in the influence that Popper-Lynkeus was able to exert on me does not shock me at all," Freud replied to Doryon.[540] He added, however, that although *The Son of the King of Egypt* might have influenced him, he personally had no memory of *Fantasies of a Realist* by the same author.

But Doryon persisted: although initially he maintained that Freud had been strongly influenced by Popper Lynkeus's literary work, he later compared Freud's text to Lynkeus's *Fantasies of a Realist*, concluding that *Moses and Monotheism* was a pure product of the imagination, the fruit of Freud's "exceptional brain." Thus Doryon was reiterating the two main arguments of Orthodox Jews: on the one hand, the figure of Moses must correspond with that of the biblical account, which is indisputable historical truth; on the other hand, faith is the only possible way to draw close to the concept of God. Doryon shared the conviction of religious Jews that belief is a criterion for validating absolute truths (scientific or otherwise). Thus it goes without saying that no fruitful discussion could emerge between Freud and commentators of this sort, whether with respect to the hypotheses he posited in his book on Moses, or regarding psychoanalytic theory and concepts generally. When faith imposes itself as a prerequisite, any scientific discussion is doomed to fail or at least reach a dead end, which Freud refused to enter. Likewise, his aforementioned reply to Raphael Da Costa – "I believe because I believe" – thwarted any attempt at dialogue, as Da Costa's presupposition – that belief is a way to access the truth – was so "unscientific" that no reasonable discussion could be expected to ensue.

In the very first lines of his essay, Doryon declared that "Freud failed from the outset in his attempt to fit all of human history through the eye of a needle. . . because mortal man must never claim such a thing, nor expose before our eyes the heavy burden of human history with its powerful, brilliant, or disturbing activity, neither in general nor in a restrained manner. For after all, history is silent and cannot bear the roar of analysis, not even for the murmur of extremely delicate facts."[541]

In other words, Freud was no different from the historians or lay critics of the Bible, and could not claim the right to disrupt the "glory and beauty of history."

Doryon began by expressing admiration for Freud's intellectual courage, asserting, quite rightly, that Freud had never shied away from any question and certainly not questions about his Jewishness – whose mysteries he even sought to uncover through psychoanalysis – notwithstanding the resistance and hatred he drew both from his coreligionists and from Church leaders. After praising him, however, Doryon accused Freud of subordinating Judaism in *Moses and*

Monotheism to psychoanalysis. In his words, "in his last book, he went so far as to subjugate the father of the Prophets and his Torah to his style of psychoanalysis." But Doryon apparently wanted to salvage the image of "Freud the Jew" in his readers' eyes (after denigrating his "science"), and concluded by explaining that the publication of *Moses and Monotheism* "will not in any way diminish the moral greatness and brilliant power of Freud the Jew."[542]

Doryon's text probably constitutes one of the more reasoned critiques of Freud's *Moses,* if only because the author relied on solid biblical knowledge. Henri Baruk (an Orthodox Jewish French psychiatrist), in contrast, was far more critical of Freud in the preface he wrote to his translation of Doryon's book.[543] Baruk, whose preface is nearly as long as Doryon's text, attacked Freud with extreme virulence, describing his theories as nonsense and reproaching him for awakening "primitive and egotistical instincts," the "evil spirits" (*shedim*), and the "evil drive" (*yetzer hara*) of paganism, from which psychoanalysis draws its inspiration, rather than following "the paths of the science of the just" – that is, the path Baruk saw as the science of "justice" (*tzedek*) and of "reason." He accused Freud of wanting to use Jewish monotheism solely to exalt sexuality and initiate a return to matriarchy; because of his grounding in the Greek and Latin classics, "Freud divinizes sexual desire as the only God. This is why we regard Freud as the father of modern neo-paganism." He then described psychoanalysis as "imperialism that evades scientific discussion" and "a regression to primitivism," and Freud as the incarnation of the drama of assimilation.

Let us summarize the commentary that *Moses and Monotheism* received in Palestine. Its publication and the reactions that followed exposed the resistance to Freud and to psychoanalysis as well as the detractors themselves. Evidently it was only possible to challenge the arguments of these (mostly religious) detractors up to a certain point. The polemics to which the book gave rise in Palestine do, however, offer us another opportunity to appreciate the depth and persistence of the battles that raged ever since the emancipation of European Jews, whether openly or latently, between heirs of the Haskalah (Jewish Enlightenment) movement and followers of traditional Judaism, who saw belief and religious values as the essence of the Jewish People and preconditions for its survival.

And yet this new religious assault – far less discreet than that of the 1930s, when psychoanalysis was being introduced at the Hebrew University – failed. Neither

Freud nor his work were discredited as a result of the offensive. Nor was there damage to the "sciences" that embody the legacy of the Haskalah and rationalism, which inevitably clash with the dogmatic nature of religion and with any attempt to perpetuate a single truth that guarantees existence and survival.

Many leading figures, most of whom we have already mentioned, supported Freud: intellectuals working for a secular Hebrew culture as well as psychoanalysts who supported not Freud the "assimilationist" (as the Orthodox contemptuously labelled him) but Freud the rationalist, who did not hesitate to use his "science" to shatter religious "truths." These intellectuals believed that *Moses* served as both a tool and an illustration of Freud's investigation into the depths of the human soul in search of the myths, legends, and religious practices that shed light on the origins of all human beings and therefore of the Jewish People. In their view such a quest justified the desire of this People to forge a new identity that is neither religious nor assimilationist: an identity of a People who returned to the land of its ancestors to build a homeland and participate in the creation of a new Hebrew culture.

During those tragic and fateful days for the Jewish People, mainly in Europe but in Palestine as well, these polemics contributed to the prestige and importance of psychoanalysis as it gained ground in the Yishuv. The author of *Moses* drew much praise from those who saw him as one of the great guardians of secularism.

Freud died in London on September 23, 1939. The public in Palestine learned about his passing on the following day from a British radio broadcast out of London.[544] Many articles and tributes then appeared in Palestine's local press. Intellectuals across the spectrum – physicians, psychoanalysts, pedagogues, and religious scholars – paid tribute to the father of psychoanalysis, who remained in the eyes of all, for better or worse, a Jew. Even those who had violently denounced Freud's sacrilege of Moses a few months earlier paid homage to this "assimilationist" who despite everything, and unlike many others, had never renounced his Jewish identity.

Epilogue

Psychoanalysis in Israel after World War II: Ambiguity and Confusion

With the end of World War II, thousands of Nazi concentration camp survivors sought refuge in Palestine, often after an interim period in European refugee camps or British detention camps in Cyprus. Some received permits to enter the country legally, while others managed to reach the shores of Palestine clandestinely through the underground immigration operation conducted by the Yishuv. At the time, Palestine was embroiled in a bloody struggle against the British, which led to Britain renouncing its Mandate in 1947 and the UN adopting its Partition Plan, dividing Palestine into a Jewish state and an Arab state, on November 29 of that year, following which war broke out. The Arab military invasion, Israel's Declaration of Independence of May 14, 1948, and a War of Independence that lasted until 1949 depleted the young state of resources and took a heavy human toll. After several years of extreme shortage (1948-1952), known as *Tkufat HaTzena* (the Period of Austerity), Israel's economy continued to falter until 1956.

During this period, Jewish emigrants fled to Israel from warring Arab states (Iraq, Egypt) as well as non-warring Muslim states, including Yemen, Iran, Turkey, Tunisia, and Morocco. There also arrived many refugees from European detention camps and Romania. These new arrivals, most from disadvantaged socio-economic classes, resided initially in immigrant camps and later in makeshift "transit camps" often located on the outskirts of major cities. Some were sent to the new development towns under construction in the Negev Desert or northern Israel.

The year 1948 also marked the start of a new chapter in the history of psychoanalysis in the country, very different from that of the pioneering era. Henceforth, psychoanalysis developed along new political, conceptual, demographic, intellectual, scientific, and artistic tracks in the context of Israel's struggle with one armed conflict after another, for just as well as unjust causes, balancing hope and disarray. To this day, psychoanalysis in Israel is in a seemingly insurmountable state of crisis, despite the many forces that continue to sustain it; disconnected from its Freudian roots, it has difficulty finding its way. The history of psychoanalysis in Mandatory Palestine and later in the State of Israel is one of increasing bureaucratization of its training guidelines, particularly because of the medical training requirement. The situation in Israel is emblematic of the dangers of circumscribing psychoanalysis by subjecting it to the power of the state or another institution, and the medical establishment in particular.

The Future of Psychoanalysis in Israel: Debates over Lay Analysis

Lay analysis – that is, psychoanalysis by non-physicians – is one of the issues that has long divided the international psychoanalytic movement. The Freudian movement in Palestine and Israel is no exception; indeed, the question of who was qualified to practice gave rise to one of the most severe crises that plagued this movement. Opposition to Moshe Wulff and the supporters of lay analysis in Palestine surfaced as early as the 1940s in the Palestine Psychoanalytic Society. In the 1950s, after Wulff's term as president of the Society ended, there began two developments (led primarily by Gershon Barag and Erich Gumbel) that Freud in his day had consistently resisted: bureaucratization and medical psychoanalysis.[545] The first victim of this conflict was Fanny Lowtzky: in 1952 opponents of lay analysis forced the closure of her psychoanalytic seminar for pedagogues and expelled her from the Psychoanalytic Institute in Jerusalem.

To better understand the challenges facing psychoanalysis in Mandatory Palestine and the State of Israel, a brief historical observation is in order. As early as 1925, at the Ninth Psychoanalytic Congress in Bad Homburg, Max Eitingon sought to establish standardized guidelines for psychoanalytic training and for the practice itself, which would apply to all societies affiliated with the International Psychoanalytic Association (IPA). This standardization process, however, went hand-in-hand with the bureaucratization of the international psychoanalytic movement. Freud opposed this growing trend, which Eitingon and Jones, among others, supported. He reaffirmed the "natural" need for psychoanalysis to be "open" – not bound by rigid, restrictive rules that would curtail or preclude the analyst's freedom and creativity and would prevent those whose university or professional training was not medical from practicing. He believed that psychoanalysis must not become "merely a chapter on psychopathology in a *Manual of Psychiatry*."

The following year, at the 1927 Innsbruck Congress presided over by Eitingon, American psychoanalysts called for the practice of psychoanalysis to be reserved strictly for physicians. The Europeans hesitated. Freud strongly opposed this measure, as did his daughter Anna. Eitingon, who initially supported the American proposal, eventually adopted his mentor's position. The dispute remained unresolved and for many years continued to poison the air in the international psychoanalytic movement.

Freud wanted psychoanalysis to be self-governing, with its own criteria and modalities for practice, training, transmission, instruction, and research. He also believed that psychoanalysis could only exist, survive, and stay creative and inventive if it remained open to other disciplines – that is, if it were also taught as part of other fields of study and, reciprocally, welcomed representatives of those fields, including jurists, literary scholars, psychologists, physicians, philosophers, anthropologists, and theologians, among others. Such individuals, once they became analysts, could prove to be good clinicians, contributing through their diversity to the advancement of psychoanalysis and to human progress generally. In his view, just as psychoanalysis is fueled by other disciplines and borrows from them, any other discipline could also benefit from the new information revealed by the unconscious and its modes of operation. Freud consistently maintained that psychoanalysis must not be subordinated to any other discipline or entity such as psychology, philosophy, medicine, the state, or the church; it must not seal itself off within its own institutions by imposing guidelines for training and practice on its members; and it must not adhere to uniform conceptions. Yet Eitingon, both in Berlin and in Jerusalem, attributed great and perhaps excessive importance to the matter of institutionalization, and he sought to standardize the rules of psychoanalytic training before the end of his term as chair of the Training Commission.

The Presidency of Moshe Wulff and Reorganization of the Palestine Psychoanalytic Society

Max Eitingon died in 1943. On December 11 of that year the Palestine Psychoanalytic Society held a plenary session to discuss its reorganization, draft new bylaws, and establish the modes of operation for the Psychoanalytic Institute in Jerusalem. This general assembly was decisive for the future of the Freudian movement in the country. Among those present were Ilja Schalit (chair), Gershon Barag (rapporteur), Moshe Wulff, Josef Friedjung, Anna Smeliansky, Erich Gumbel, Berta Grünspan, David Idelsohn, and Shmuel Golan. Ilja Schalit was reelected as treasurer and secretary, and Moshe Wulff was elected as president. Thus began a new era in the annals of psychoanalysis in Palestine and Israel.

Ilja Schalit opened the floor for discussion on the issue of psychoanalytic training, announcing that "the integration into the Society of a certain number of newcomers" had generated misunderstandings among members, which needed to be resolved. His meaning was plain: he was referring to the pedagogues and social workers who sought training at the Institute through the seminars for pedagogues organized by Fanny Lowtzky. Gershon Barag spoke first, proposing that only holders of a medical license be granted full membership and the right to treat adult patients. He argued that the psychoanalytic treatment of adults by non-physicians was highly questionable and subject to dispute. Wulff then took the floor to express his fierce opposition to any discrimination between physicians and non-physicians, arguing against the exclusion of lay practitioners from the Society. In response to Barag's remarks, he asserted that "we are a Society with a scientific mandate, not a medical institution." Erich Gumbel, who aligned himself with his mentor Eitingon, asserted that "only the International Training Commission is authorized to grant analysts the title of a didactician [supervisor], whether they are physicians or not" – a position supported by Wulff and Idelsohn.[546]

Wulff then took the floor again to propose a compromise, which a majority of the assembly accepted: pedagogues seeking to practice psychoanalysis would have to undergo didactic analysis under the close supervision of the Psychoanalytic Institute in Jerusalem. In delegating the exclusive authority for non-physician analytical training to the Jerusalem Institute, however, Wulff made a strategic error that proved fateful for the future of lay analysts. He should have granted such authority to the Institute in Tel Aviv as well. While he continued to serve as president (until 1952), non-physicians, and pedagogues in particular, could still receive psychoanalytic training in Israel; Anna Freud personally saw to this. But the dispute with opponents of lay analysis remained unresolved, and Gershon Barag continued to fight for his cause. In 1953 these adversaries were able to seize control of the Jerusalem Psychoanalytic Institute and the Psychoanalytic Society, and they hastened to put an end to the practice of lay analysis in Israel. Barag and other opponents of lay analysis continued to struggle against the inclusion of pedagogues in the Psychoanalytic Society and to call for the revocation of their status as analysts. Let us also bear in mind that from 1944, in accordance with a resolution of the Psychoanalytic Society, the Max Eitingon Psychoanalytic Institute in Jerusalem was run by physicians and had relative autonomy in its relations with the new president of the Society and the Freudian group in Tel Aviv.

As noted, the Jerusalem Psychoanalytic Institute enjoyed considerable prestige by virtue of Fanny Lowtzky's seminars and the training they offered for pedagogues referred by HaKibbutz HaArtzi and social workers referred by the Hadassah Medical Organization. There were no grounds for opponents of lay analysis to claim that the Psychoanalytic Institute would be discredited in the eyes of the country's medical authorities as a result of the importance it attributed to the analytical training of non-physicians. Moreover, there was no basis for the assumption that a lay analyst was less able to treat adults or children, in Palestine or abroad, than someone holding a degree in medicine or neuropsychiatry.

Nevertheless, after Israel achieved independence, professionals across various disciplines began to reorganize, establishing new institutions and laying down new operating guidelines. Opponents of lay analysis were intrigued by the prospect of administratively and institutionally restructuring the medical practice in Israel; they sought to forge new alliances with psychiatry, while redirecting psychoanalysis away from the path it had been following for many years – namely, pedagogy.

The Closure of the Psychoanalytic Seminar for Pedagogues

The country's extremely rapid population growth made it impossible for the psychoanalysts of the Israel Psychoanalytic Society (Chevra Psychoanalytit BeIsrael, as it was renamed after Israel's independence) to attend to the many requests they received to help immigrant children and their families who were facing hardship. We are familiar with the extensive work of Fanny Lowtzky in this regard: sought by teachers across the country and abroad, she became a source of inspiration and authority for the pedagogues of HaShomer HaTza'ir and leaders of Aliyat HaNo'ar. She was renowned for her contribution to the training of pedagogues and educators as well as *metaplot* (caregivers) and youth counselors. Educational and social service providers in Tel Aviv and Jerusalem recognized her invaluable role in improving the welfare of neglected children and abandoned immigrant adolescents. Why then did the administration of the Jerusalem Psychoanalytic Institute decide to expel her from the Israel Psychoanalytic Society? In 1952, after many long years of activity, the administration of the Jerusalem Psychoanalytic Institute decided to close the seminar run by Lowtzky and her students. With this decision, psychoanalysis in Israel was completely severed from pedagogy so that it could forge new alliances with medicine and psychiatry. To the best of our knowledge, this closure was not driven by legal concerns: the new obstacles posed before Wulff and his students as well as Anna Freud, who defended them, came from within the ranks of the Society. In the early 1950s the Seminar for Teachers was at the heart of a fierce conflict that erupted in Israel's psychoanalytic movement between proponents and opponents of lay analysis.

In 1952, at a general assembly of the Israel Psychoanalytic Society, its members voted to terminate the activities of the Seminar for Teachers and revoke the accreditation granted to pedagogues. Lowtzky was accused of being too lax, supposedly relying on pedagogical principles that were overly permissive and harmful to her students. But what "deviationist" attitude of Lowtzky towards psychoanalysis could justify a sudden decision by the Jerusalem Psychoanalytic Institute to issue a death sentence against her psychoanalytic training of pedagogues, considering how much it had enhanced the prestige of the Institute and of psychoanalysis during more than a decade? Why did the Institute or another entity not reorganize this training program, given that until then it was regarded as of central importance by the Berlin Psychoanalytic Institute, the Vienna Psychoanalytic Society, and the psychoanalytic establishments of Mandatory Palestine and the State of Israel during the presidencies of Eitingon and Wulff? Why did no one continue or even expand this remarkable Freudian enterprise that had operated so well during the Mandate era and early years of statehood? And even if they were willing to dismiss Fanny Lowtzky, why not continue the endeavor by drawing on other psychoanalyst members of the Society, given that there was no shortage of skilled, prolific specialists in pedagogy and education, such as Shmuel Nagler or Lizzi Rosenberg, or even physician analysts who had contributed to the development of the psychoanalytic Seminar for Teachers?

Barred from teaching at the Psychoanalytic Institute, Fanny Lowtzky remained in Jerusalem for a while, continuing to meet with patients and students. In 1956 she left Israel and resettled in Switzerland. She died on April 9, 1965, after being hit by a car in the streets of Zurich.

The dissolution of the Seminar for Teachers in 1952, the dismissal of Fanny Lowtzky, and the dispute between Wulff and Barag over lay analysis all played a part in the severe crisis that plagued the Israel Psychoanalytic Society after 1953.

By 1954 psychoanalysis in Israel had evidently surrendered to the medical establishment, after having formed new alliances with representatives of American psychiatry and psychoanalysis who came to Israel to establish a department of psychiatry at the Hebrew University and implement the modalities of psychoanalytic training and practice reserved exclusively for physicians. Thus the new administration of the Jerusalem Psychoanalytic Institute and some members of the Psychoanalytic Society relinquished the privileged place that pedagogues had granted to psychoanalysts within the field of education, leaving the latter open to various psychological schools of thought. Henceforth, non-physician analysts who were members of the Israel Psychoanalytic Society, without exception, had to limit themselves to the treatment of children; they were only allowed to treat adult patients if supervised by a physician analyst, and they could no longer serve as analysts for candidates undergoing psychoanalytic training. Experienced non-physician analysts such as Lizzi Rosenberg[547] and Shmuel Nagler, deprived of their status as "active members," essentially lost any influence in the Society. It was only thanks to the direct intervention of Anna Freud that Lizzi Rosenberg was able to remain a full member of the Israel Psychoanalytic Society and retain her status as a didactic supervisor recognized by the International Psychoanalytic Association and authorized to train psychoanalysts who treat adults. Some years later Anna Freud again intervened directly with the leadership of the Israel Psychoanalytic Society to protest measures aimed at depriving lay practitioners of their rights. She voiced her indignation, which colleagues of Gumbel conveyed to him, and he responded in a letter to Anna Freud in 1964[548] on behalf of the psychoanalysts participating in the Psychoanalytic Congress in Amsterdam that year.

The end of Moshe Wulff's term as president of the Psychoanalytic Society in 1953 also marked the brutal ending of one of the most beautiful episodes, lasting more than three decades, in the history of psychoanalysis in Palestine and Israel.

Alliances with University Psychiatry

For some years psychoanalysts occupied an important place in the field of psychiatry in Israel, although they never held high-ranking positions in mental health institutions. Beginning in 1953, the new leadership of the Psychoanalytic Society sought to consolidate its alliance with the country's medical establishment, and particularly with university-based psychiatry, where psychoanalysis occupied a privileged place. After years of waiting, the Hebrew University opened a faculty of medicine at Hadassah Hospital. That same year a department of psychiatry was finally opened and five psychiatrists – all psychoanalysts – were appointed as instructors. These included three Americans – Milton Rosenbaum, who was appointed department chair, James Mann, a member of the Boston Psychoanalytic Society, and John Mohrr of New York – as well as two instructors from Jerusalem – Heinrich Zvi Winnik and, to the great regret of Moshe Wulff, Shlomo Rothschild.

During the 1950s and 1960s, American psychiatry had close ties with psychoanalysis, and when Milton Rosenbaum took over the project launched in 1947 to create a Max Eitingon Foundation, he adapted it to the model of American universities: students who could not afford tuition would receive scholarships and loans. Towards this end, he sought assistance from large numbers of analysts in the United States to help finance psychoanalytic training for psychiatry students in Israel. It was agreed that financial aid candidates would be selected by a local committee composed of representatives of the Department of Psychiatry at the Hebrew University and the Jerusalem Psychoanalytic Institute.

The opening of a psychiatry department and Milton Rosenbaum's efforts to introduce psychoanalysis into the training of psychiatrists appealed to Jerusalem psychoanalysts and encouraged them to strengthen their ties with him and with

American psychiatry and psychoanalysis – all the more so given the severe economic crisis Israel was undergoing in the early 1950s. It is undoubtedly thanks to Rosenbaum and his American colleagues that through the Eitingon Foundation many psychiatry students in Israel were able to receive psychiatric training, which is costly and difficult to secure. The analysts of the Jerusalem Institute therefore had many reasons to welcome the opportunities offered by the Hebrew University's Department of Psychiatry, after some 30 years of fruitless efforts to introduce psychoanalysis. Would Freud – who above all else feared that psychoanalysis would be "swallowed up by medicine and confined to a few pages on psychopathology in psychiatric manuals"[549] – have welcomed such an alliance between the Jerusalem Psychoanalytic Institute and the new Department of Psychiatry? In any event, the Hebrew University decided to commemorate Freud in 1956, on the centennial anniversary of his birth.

I have no intention of casting aspersions on those psychoanalysts who aspired to be part of the academic world of psychiatry. Rather, the problem lies in the danger that psychoanalysis, once subjected to the medical establishment, would lose its uniqueness and autonomy and no longer be a discipline in its own right with authority over its private institutions, its modalities of psychoanalytic training, and all aspects of its regulation – in short, everything that Freud rightly considered indispensable for its survival.

"The Barricade Years"

Serious conflicts divided the leaders of the Israel Psychoanalytic Society during 1953-1956, which came to be known as the "barricade" years. The dispute between Moshe Wulff and his students, on the one hand, and Heinrich Zvi Winnik and Erich Gumbel, on the other, intensified, especially surrounding questions of how the Society was to function.[550]

In 1953 Wulff completed his ten-year term as president of the Israel Psychoanalytic Society. That same year, the very discreet Ilja Schalit died suddenly, at the age of 54. Schalit, one of the founders of the Palestine Psychoanalytic Society, had served as its secretary for nearly twenty continuous years. Erich Gumbel was elected as president of the Israel Psychoanalytic Society and held this position several times until 1973. He became director of the Jerusalem Psychoanalytic Institute in 1967.

At the Jerusalem Psychoanalytic Institute, which had become his stronghold, Gumbel was considered both Max Eitingon's heir and the "guardian of the golden rules of psychoanalysis." But unlike his mentor, rather than protect the status of non-physician analysts, he joined the opponents of lay analysis. His quasi-religious defense at the 1934 Congress in Lucerne of the "golden rules" of psychoanalytic training established by his mentor marked the start of a lengthy process of bureaucratization of psychoanalysis in Israel, which continued until the early 1980s. The process took a heavy toll: fierce disputes and a growing intolerance among members of the Israel Psychoanalytic Society, and the departure to the United States, during the late 1950s, of young candidates who had been rejected as analysts or were dissatisfied with the psychoanalytic training available to them in Jerusalem. This situation also fostered extreme dogmatism within the Society, particularly among candidates. The Society's leaders did not tolerate any breach of the Institute's rules of psychoanalytic practice; any deviation was punished by expulsion. They refused, for example, to grant psychoanalytic certification to Dr. Joseph Hess (who later became a renowned psychiatrist in Israel) simply because he had referred to the work of Melanie Klein during his presentation of a case study. In fact, during the late 1940s in Palestine, a resolutely Anna-Freudian environment, it was categorically prohibited to teach the works of Melanie Klein.[551] Only in the 1960s, with the immigration of South American analysts, were the works of this important psychoanalyst introduced into Israeli teaching curricula; prominent among these immigrant analysts was Yolanda Gampel, who arrived from Argentina in the late 1960s.

In 1954, after Winnik's appointment as professor of psychiatry at the Faculty of Medicine, relations between Gumbel and Winnik deteriorated completely. Although Erich Gumbel taught at the Department of Psychiatry as an adjunct professor, he made the Psychoanalytic Institute his sole bastion,[552] as did Margareth Brandt, who barricaded herself behind the walls of the Jerusalem Psychoanalytic Institute.

In 1957, disciples of Moshe Wulff (including Dov Alexandrowicz), who were also students of Winnik at the Faculty of Psychiatry in Hadassah Hospital, attempted to reconcile between these two titans of psychoanalysis in Israel. Their efforts failed: Wulff, Winnik, and other leaders of Society refused to relax their position, and no common ground could be found regarding the training and certification of candidates for the practice of psychoanalysis. Many young analysts left for the United States to complete their psychoanalytic training: Dan Hertz, for example, trained with Hélène Deutsch in Boston,[553] while Dov Alexandrowicz was urged by Moshe Wulff to go to the United States for training in child psychoanalysis.[554]

Moshe Wulff's successors in the leadership of the Israel Psychoanalytic Society accused him of committing transgressions, including deviation from the established rules for analytical training.[555] They sought to discredit him by circulating the claim, particularly among candidates in the Psychoanalytic Institute, that he was unqualified to serve as a didactic supervisor because he personally had no experience on the psychoanalytic couch. He was compared with Eitingon, who unlike him had undergone his first so-called didactic analysis with Freud, founded the International Training Commission of the International Psychoanalytic Association, and presided over it for many years. They further argued that Wulff could not be a good child psychoanalyst "because he himself had no children and had no experience of parenthood." Gumbel and Winnik went so far as to deny psychoanalytic certification by the Society to candidates who had undergone analysis with Wulff. They asserted that Wulff did not respect the rules of psychoanalytic training established by the Jerusalem Psychoanalytic Institute, even though Wulff's position in the Freudian movement in Israel speaks for itself.

Despite being ousted by the new administration of the Israel Psychoanalytic Society – which went so far as to invalidate the didactic aspect of analyses and Supervision carried out under his direction – Wulff continued to have considerable influence on the training of psychotherapists in Tel Aviv. Indeed, for many years the psychiatrists and psychologists he trained constituted the elites of psychoanalytically inspired psychotherapy in Israel. Among many others, they included Ruth Jaffe, Gottfried Bloch, Ephraim Libowsky, Henricus Weissenbeck, Julius Zellermayer Alexander Zeidel, Chava de Friess, Dov Alexandrowicz, Raphael Springmann, Micha Neumann, Bracha Gaoni, Lea Katz, Tzipora Shabat, Tirzha Cohen, Miriam Golomb, Gad Tadmor, Franz Brüll, Yehuda Fried, Avner Elitzur, and of course, Lizzi Rosenberg, with whom Wulff continued to cooperate, treating patients and supervising the work of many young psychiatrists at the Shalvatah Psychiatric Hospital, located to this day in Hod Hasharon, near Tel Aviv.

Thus this extraordinary man, one of the most important figures in the Russian psychoanalytic movement and later a leader – indeed, the foremost pioneer and the real architect – of the analytical movement in Mandatory Palestine and the State of Israel, was excluded from the Society of which he had been a founder. Nonetheless, until the late 1960s he continued to listen, behind his psychoanalytic couch, to future psychotherapists, physicians, philosophers, artists, jurists, literary scholars, and other Israeli intellectuals, who unanimously recognized their analyst as a clinician and an exceptional intellectual.

Thanks to Winnik, Wulff, and their disciples, psychoanalysis remained alive for some years within the realm of psychiatry in Israel. Yet its complete subjection to the medical establishment and to rules of training and practice that differed from those that had fostered its development, as well as the uncompromising implementation of those rules by the Jerusalem Psychoanalytic Institute's "guardians of the golden rules" and leaders of the Psychoanalytic Society, severely compromised the future of psychoanalysis in the country. Thus, in 1941 – only seven years after its founding – the Psychoanalytic Society impressively numbered 18 active members; by 1954 it had only grown to 23 active members and 8 candidates in various stages of training; and in 1975 it recorded a mere 41 members and candidates.

During the 1960s and until the late 1970s, the German language came to be regarded as the "official" language of the discipline, and in Israel psychoanalysis was perceived as a discipline of *yekim* (German Jews, presumably of a fastidious nature). Psychoanalysis thus came to be seen as highly elitist, hermetic, and even sectarian. As psychoanalysis became associated exclusively with a specific community, the general public began to view it as just one among many psychotherapeutic techniques, and in this sense it dug its own grave. Accordingly, by 1960-1970 Freud's work sparked far less public interest or curiosity in Israel than it had previously. The policies pursued in those days by the new administration of the Israel Psychoanalytic Society, which since the mid-1950s had distanced itself from Wulff, resulted in Freudian research becoming an "endangered discipline" by the late 1970s. This goes some way towards validating Freud's claim that the fiercest opposition to psychoanalysis always came, paradoxically, from within the discipline itself.

Since 1977, however, with the establishment of the Sigmund Freud Center at the Hebrew University under the directorship of British psychoanalyst Joseph Sandler,[556] there has been some renewed interest in Freud's work. The past two decades have seen a number of new developments, including retranslations of the writings of Freud and other psychoanalysts; attention to the works of Freud and Lacan in various university departments and faculties, including literature, theater, philosophy, history, and law; efforts to establish the first psychoanalytic journal in Israel;[557] and the formation of small study groups focused on psychoanalytic texts in English or the writings of Winnicott, Bion, Kohut, and Lacan. Do these developments perhaps foreshadow an end to the state of crisis in which psychoanalysis in Israel currently finds itself?

Conclusion

The history of psychoanalysis in Israel, as we have seen, cannot be read without taking into account the tragic fate of the Jewish people from the end of the nineteenth century until the years following the creation of the Jewish state in 1948.

The reception of new ideas proposed by Freud at the beginning of the twentieth century led to their integration into the Zionist project, making them part of a new secularized Hebrew culture (heir to the Haskalah), the resurrection of the Hebrew language, and the call to Jews to return to the land of their ancestors, its spearhead.

It was not until the arrival of the British in Palestine in 1918, and the establishment of the Jewish National Home, that Zionist aspirations for autonomy, freedom, and recognition among the nations could finally be realized, and that Freudian theory, in all its dimensions, could also find a first anchorage in this Middle East enclave.

The history of psychoanalysis in Mandatory Palestine therefore confirms, once again, that only in a country based on the "rule of law" (that is, a country that guarantees the democratic functioning of institutions, and respect for the liberties and rights of its citizens), can Freudianism find the conditions for its establishment.

Moreover, it could not have been established without the presence of those few figures of the Zionist world who were "bitten" by psychoanalysis and enabled this discipline to make its entry into the discourse of the Yishuv and its institutions. There is no chance that "Freudian science" and immigrant psychoanalysts would have been heard in the country's medical, social, and educational institutions without the incessant battles fought on their behalf by Montague David Eder and the tireless Aryeh Feigenbaum; by Siegfried van Vriesland and Andor Fodor; by the pedagogues Grete Obernik, David Idelsohn, Shmuel Golan, and Zvi Sohar (supported from abroad by Siegfried Bernfeld); and by influential figures from the Zionist world, friends of Freud and of psychoanalysts, such as Chaim Weizmann and Henrietta Szold. It is thanks to them that psychoanalysis acquired its titles of nobility in the Jewish society of Palestine; they are the true precursors and heroes of psychoanalysis in Jewish Palestine and later Israel.

The reception of Freud's work in a vast and rapidly expanding Hebrew cultural and linguistic universe – which extended beyond the borders of Jewish Palestine – could only take place from the early 1920s, with the restructuring of mass circulation and specialized press networks. The pages of these newspapers would present to Hebrew readers the texts of the great representatives of the new Hebrew culture – Ahad Ha'am, Bialik, and Chernikhovsky in particular – as well as translations of the great classics and the new masters of modern thought, including Marx, Nietzsche, William James, Bergson. . . and Freud.

However, it was undoubtedly from April 1, 1925, when Lord Balfour engraved in gold letters the names Einstein, Bergson, and Freud on the front of the "new temple of knowledge" of Mount Scopus, that Sigmund Freud's work became a major event in the history of Hebrew culture, Zionism, and the Jewish world in general.

As a result, Freud's life and work became a subject of great interest to these "fanatical" Zionist intellectuals of the Hebrew language, such as Yohanan Tversky, the first to translate and publish a text by Freud in *HaDoar*, the journal of the Hebrew intellectuals of America.

If in the 1920s, it was the work of Freud "the Jew of genius" that made an inaugural entry into Hebrew culture and the Zionist world, from 1933 onwards, it was the work of Freud the "Jewish victim of anti-Semitism" that would take the stage in the Yishuv. It was now Freud, the representative of "degenerate Jewish thought" who had been banished from the German language and culture by Nazism, who would benefit from privileged forums in the Yishuv press. Even the publication of his *Moses and Monotheism*, which aroused the fury of Orthodox circles against Freud "the heretic," the "poor senile old man suffering from assimilationist disease," did not prevent the formidable spread in Palestine of Freud's work, of which we have presented only very modest testimony.

The introduction of psychoanalysis in Palestine would not have been effective without the presence of psychoanalysts. And this pioneering task was fulfilled by Dorian Feigenbaum. He was the first to apply and transmit the principles of psychoanalysis in the field of mental health. He was the first to have transmitted the teachings of Freudian theory in the circles of avant-garde pedagogy and in the country's specialized Hebrew-language press. His presence in Jerusalem confirms one of the "structural invariants" of the history of Freudianism – to borrow from Lévi-Strauss – namely that the advent of psychoanalysis goes hand in hand with the development of psychiatric knowledge, that is, "a look at madness capable of conceptualizing the notion of mental illness to the detriment of any idea of divine possession."[558]

Although at first sight the failure to definitively establish psychoanalysis in the Yishuv might seem to have stemmed from a lack of pro-Zionist motivations on the part of Dorian Feigenbaum, this failure seems to us to be due, rather, to the strong tensions from which Palestinian Jewish society suffered from the beginning of the Mandatory era: to the painful passage of the traditional Old Yishuv (which shunned Freud's infantile sexual theories as presented by Feigenbaum), to a New Yishuv which advanced confidently towards the construction of a modern society based on universal and secular values, with Freudian doctrine as one of its pillars.

It was therefore from the early 1930s that, after the rise to power of National Socialism in Germany, the migratory flow from that country brought to Palestine Jewish psychoanalysts who, under the leadership of Moshe Wulff (who had arrived in Palestine earlier) and Max Eitingon, would inaugurate the golden age of the Freudian movement in Palestine.

Co-founder and former director of the Berlin Psychoanalytic Institute, former president of the International Association of Psychoanalysis, philanthropist and mentor of Palestinian artists, and a "faithful disciple of Freud," Max Eitingon brought to psychoanalysis in Palestine a not inconsiderable notoriety, which went beyond the borders of this small country. In 1943, one might have dreamed with Max Eitingon, if only briefly, that the Psychoanalytic Institute in Jerusalem was to become a "beacon of Freudianism" for Egypt, and perhaps even for the whole Middle East!

If the pages of this book seek to pay tribute to Max Eitingon's invaluable contribution to the institutionalization of psychoanalysis in Palestine, they also aim to deconstruct the myth long conveyed by the official historiography of psychoanalysis in Israel, which overstates the role of a Berlin heritage centered on the figure of Max Eitingon in Israeli psychoanalytic history.

However, the small village of Jerusalem was not the bubbling Berlin of the 1920s. And the Jerusalem Psychoanalytic Institute, much to the regret of its founder, did not count on the presence of great clinicians and theorists of psychoanalysis such as Karl Abraham, Ernst Simmel, Hans Sachs, Sandor Rado, Melanie Klein, Otto Fenichel, Reik, Bernfeld, Franz Alexander, Karen Horney, and many others, who gave the Berlin Institute and Polyclinic its national and international reputation. Nor were the premises of the Psychoanalytic Institute of Jerusalem offered by Max Eitingon, or the "golden rules" of psychoanalytic practice and training jealously guarded by his heirs, Erich Gumbel and Margareth Brandt in particular, what allowed psychoanalysis in Israel to flourish.

Even today, the survival of a living and innovative psychoanalysis cannot be achieved without the commitment of psychoanalysts capable of transmitting the principles of Freudian doctrine in all its dimensions: in the training of analysts and new disciples; through oral and written work; and finally, in its promotion in other fields of cultural science outside of the analytical clinic itself.

However, this was precisely the mission, as we have seen, that Moshe Wulff so wonderfully accomplished in Palestine/Israel over the course of nearly four decades.

The Eitingonian myth of Israeli psychoanalysis with a Berlin face is based on the denigration not only of Wulff's definitive work, but also of the extensive work accomplished by psychoanalysts trained in a "Viennese tradition" and recognized as such, namely that of Freud and his daughter Anna, that of "Laienanalyse" or lay analysis, of the free practice of psychoanalysis, also practiced by non-physicians.

Supported by Anna Freud of London, Moshe Wulff had to fight long, hard battles against Freud's opponents. The case of the Psychoanalytic Society of Palestine and later Israel does not escape another structural invariant specific to the history of the Freudian movement, that is, the conflicts surrounding the training and practice of psychoanalysts, conflicts that still today gnaw at and divide psychoanalytic societies from within.

As soon as he arrived in the country, and even before his arrival, Moshe Wulff understood that the spread of psychoanalysis in Palestine was inexorably linked to the cause of child and adolescent psychology. It was by training two generations of health and education workers in Freudian theory that – with the help of David Idelsohn and Martin Pappenheim, Shmuel Golan, and Zvi Sohar, Fanny Lowtzky, Bertha Grünspann, Shmuel Nagler, and Lizzi Rosemberg, among others – Moshe Wulff would provide the content for the most inspiring pages of the history of psychoanalysis in Israel.

The advent of psychoanalysis in Israel is therefore inextricable from its contribution to the field of child psychology. But which child? There was the orphaned child, abandoned, or in need of integration in Palestine at the end of the Ottoman Empire, consumed by poverty, desolation, and distress. There was also the immigrant child and adolescent who suffered the worst treatment and humiliation at the hands of anti-Semites during World War I, and who upon returning to the land of their ancestors embodied the promise and the image of the *halutz* – the new and valiant socialist Jew delivered from the "ghetto neuroses" or the flaws of bourgeois life imposed by capitalist society.

It was also because immigrant psychoanalysts were able to bring a singular and adapted form of listening to the unspeakable sufferings of these children and adolescents who had survived the Nazi death camps that the members of the Yishuv were more than grateful to them. Just as the pedagogues of HaShomer HaTza'ir who, thanks to Freud's discoveries and with their help, were able to develop in their kibbutzim an innovative model of collective education that gave birth, if not to the "Ideal Man of the kibbutz" announced at the dawn of their movement, then at least to citizens highly committed to the fight for a better society.

It is also thanks to his immeasurable contribution to the cause of the child of the Zionist dream, that psychoanalysis occupies a privileged place in the annals of Israel's history

Bibliography

A

Aichhorn, A. (1932-1933). "Khinukh Anashim Dissotziali'im" [The Education of Dissocial People], *Ofakim*, 3: 4-10 [Hebrew].

Aichhorn, A. (1935). *Wayward Youth*, New York: Viking Press. Aichhorn A. (1956). *No'ar Azuv: HaPsychologia BeTipul Khinukhi-Sotziali, Eser Hartza'ot* [Psychoanalysis in Educational-Social Treatment, Ten Lectures], trans. David Idelsohn, ed. Mordechai Brachyahu. Jerusalem: S. Zack. [Hebrew]. Freud's introductory remarks appear on pages 4-5.

Alkalay, A. (June-July 1935-1936). "Kitvei Sigmund Freud BeIvrit" [The Writings of Sigmund Freud in Hebrew], *Hed HaKhinukh* 7-10, n° 3: 61.

Atzeret Freud: LeYom Huladeto HaMe'a, 5 June 1956 [Freud Memorial: on the Occasion of His 100th Birthday, 5 June 1956]. (1957). Jerusalem: Magnes Press, Hebrew University [Hebrew].

B

Bakan, D. (1954). "Freud's Jewishness and His Psychoanalysis," *A Quarterly Journal of Jewish Life and Thought*, vol. 3, no. 1: 1-7.

Ben-Chorin, Sh. (5 May 1939). "Freud Al Moshe Rabenu" [Freud on Moses Our Teacher], *Davar*: 3-4 [Hebrew].

Bergmann, Sh. H. (25 September 1939). "Professor Sigmund Freud," *Haaretz*: 5 [Hebrew].

Bernfeld, S. (1916). "Die Kriegwaisen," *Der Jude* 2: 269-271.

Bernfeld, S. (1921). *Kinderhein Baumgarten: Bericht über einen ernsthaften Versuch mit nueuer Erziehung*. Berlin: Jüdischer Verlag.

Bernfeld, S. (1922). "The Hidden Languages and Codes Used by Children" and "Language Development among Children Who Grew up in Yiddish and Hebrew Culture" (translated titles), in "Anweisungen zur Sammlung von Material," *Korrepsondenzblatt der Jüdischen Institutes für Jugendforschung und Erziehung*, 7: 1-5 and 8: 1-5.

Bernfeld, S. (1925). *Sysiphos oder die Grenzen der Erziehung*. Leipzig and Vienna: Internazionaler psychoanalytischer Verlag.

Bernfeld, S. (1927). "Die heutige Psychologie des Püberät," *Imago*, vol. XIII, no. 1: 1-56.

Bernfeld, S. (1948). *HaAm VeHaNo'ar* [The People and the Youth], trans. Edna Kornfeld, afterword by Zvi Sohar. Merhavia: Sifriat Poalim and Shvilei HaKhinukh.

Bluhm, K. (1934). "A Case of Depression" in "Palestine Psycho-Analytic Society", in *International Journal of Psycho-Analysis*, vol. XV: 532.

Brandt, M. (1950). "The First Decade of the Palestine Psychoanalytic Institute," in *Max Eitingon in Memoriam*: 268-273.

Buber, M. (1957). *Moshe* [Moses]. Jerusalem and Tel Aviv: Schocken [Hebrew].

Bulletin de l'Association Internationale de psychanalyse. Conclusion du XIIIe Congrès International de psychanalyse, Assemblée Générale de la Commission Internationale de l'Enseignement, Lucerne, 30 août 1934. (1935). " *Revue française de psychanalyse* 3: 520-524.

C

Colonomos, F. (1985). *On forme des psychanalystes. Rapport original sur les dix ans de l'Institut psychanalytique de Berlin, 1920-1930*. Paris: Denoël.

D

Dash, J. (1979). *Summoned to Jerusalem. The Life of Henrietta Szold*. New York, Hagerstown, San Francisco: Harper & Row Publishers.

Doryon, I. (1939). *Mamlekhet Lynkeus: Tochnit LeYetzirat Mishtar Hayim Hadash, Takin VeEnoshi* [Lynkeus' New State: A Plan for the Establishment of a New Social Order on an Improved and Humane Basis]. Jerusalem: Reuven Mass [Hebrew].

Doryon, I. (1946). *Freud HaIsh VeMoshe* [Freud the Man and Moses] (Tel Aviv: Massadah, 1946) [Hebrew]. Doryon, I. (1971). *Freud et le monothéisme hébreu*, trans. H. Baruk and M. Weisengrun. Paris: éditions Zikarone.

Dotan, Sh. (1996). *Adumim be'Eretz Israel* [Reds in Palestine]. Kfar Saba: Shivna HaSofer Publishers [Hebrew].

"Dr. Mordechai Brachyahu, Zikhrono LiVrakha" [Dr. Mordechai Brachyahu, RIP]. In Freud S. (1959). *Pesher HaHalomot* [The Interpretation of Dreams]. Tel Aviv: Yavneh, vol. II: 15 [Hebrew].

Dwossis, J. (5 May 1936). "Freud: Al Tirgum Kitvav LeIvrit" [Freud: On Translating His Writings to Hebrew], *Haaretz*: 4 [Hebrew].

E

Eder, M. D. (1917). *War Shock: The Psycho-Neuroses in War Psychology and Treatment*. London: William Heinemann.

Eder, M. D. (September-October 1919). "Pikuakh Yetomim" [Supervision of Orphans], *HaKhinukh*: 107 [Hebrew].

Eder, M. D. (1945). *Memoirs of a Modern Pioneer*, ed. J. B. Hobmand. London: Victor Gollancz.

Eitingon, M. (1941). "From a memorial speech in the Psycho-Analytical Association," *Siegfried van Vriesland, May 2nd 1886 – December 4th 1939*. Collected Documents, Jerusalem: 70-71, Document No. S4-1-A291 [Hebrew and English], National Library of Israel, Jerusalem.

Ekstein, R. (1966). "Siegfried Bernfeld," in *Psychoanalytic Pionneers*. New York: Basic Books.

Etkind, A. (1997). *Eros of the Impossible: The History of Psychoanalysis in Russia*. Boulder: Westview Press.

Henry Ellenberger, H. (1970). *The Discovery of the Unconscious: The History and Evolution of Dynamic Psychiatry*. London, Allen Lane: The Penguin Press.

F

Feigenbaum, A. (5 May 1939). "The Medical Faculty in Jerusalem," *Palestine Review*: 43.

Feigenbaum, A. (1943). "The Faculty of Medicine at the Hebrew University of Jerusalem," *Medical Leaves*. New York, vol. V: 82-106.

Feigenbaum, A. (7 April 1943). "Ambulances. Palestine's Tribute to USRR," *Palestine Post*: 1.

Feigenbaum, A. (12 March 1969). "Our Age of perplexity viewed through Hells and Judaea," in *Opening Address read at the 7th Symposium of the Ophthalmological Society*. Jerusalem: The Israel Museum: 10.

Feigenbaum, D. (1924). "Palestine," *International Journal of Psycho-Analysis*, vol. X, no. 1: 100-101.

Feigenbaum, D. (1927-1928). "Problemot Psychologiyot SheBaYaldut U-BaBahrut BeYahasan LeKhinukh" [Psychological Problems of Infancy and of Adolescence in Relation to Education], *Hed HaKhinukh*, vol. I-II, no. 11: 180-183, and no. 17: 343-345 [Hebrew].

Fodor, A. (undated). *Nefesh HaAdam VeHayei HaDat* [The Soul of Man and the Life of Religion] (Tel Aviv: Yavneh [Hebrew].

Foucault, M. (1972). *Histoire de la folie à l'âge classique*. Paris: Gallimard.

Freud, A. (1931). *Mavo LeTorat HaPsychoanalyza* [Introduction to the Theory of Psychoanalysis] Jerusalem: Sifriat Hed HaKhinukh [Hebrew].

Freud, S. (27 March 1925). "To the Opening of the Hebrew University," *The New Judea*, vol. 1, *GW* XIV: 556-557.

Freud, S. (1926). Die Frage der Laienanalyse: Unterredungen mit einem Unparteiischen. *Studienausgabe* Ergänzungsband. Frankfurt am Main: Fischer Verlag: 271-349.

Freud, S. (1926). Die Frage de Laienanalyse: Unterredungen mit einem Unparteiischen. *Studienausgabe*, Ergänzungsband. Frankfurt: Fischer Verlag: 271-349.

Freud, S. (12 November 1926). "HaHitnagduyot LePsychoanalyza" [The Resistances to Psycho-Analysis], trans. Yohanan Tversky, *HaDo'ar*, 12 November: 20-21, and 19 November: 38-39 [Hebrew].

Freud, S. (1928). *The Future of an Illusion*, trans. W. D. Robson-Scott. London: Hogarth Press.

Freud, S. (1928). *Psychologia Shel HaHamon VeHaAnalyza Shel HaAni* [Group Psychology and Analysis of the Ego], vol. I, trans. Judah Dwossis. Jerusalem: Sifriat Hed HaKhinukh. [Hebrew]

Freud, S. (1934). "Al Hashkafat Olam Ahat," [On One Worldview] translation and preface by Israel Cohen, *Gilyonot*, vol. A, no. 3: 251-268 [Hebrew]. An article under the same title, translated by Shmuel Golan Sch. (1936). In *HaShomer HaTza'ir* . Cited in "Sifriat Poalim, Mikhtav LaMa'arekhet" [Sifriat Poalim, Letter to the Editor], *HaPo'el HaTza'ir* (20 May 1943), no. 36: 12, and reprinted in Freud S. (1943). *Culture and Religion*, ed. Zvi Sohar. Merhavia: Sifriat Poalim [Hebrew].

Freud, S. (1934). *Shi'urei Mavo BePsychoanalyza* [Introductory Lectures on Psychoanalysis], trans. Judah Dwossis. Tel Aviv: Stybel [Hebrew]. Source of English translation: Freud S. (1955). "Preface to Hebrew Translation [1930]". In *The Standard Edition of the Psychological Works of Sigmund Freud*, vol. XV. London: Hogarth: 11-12.

Freud S. (19 April 1936). Letter from Freud to Barbara Low. Reprinted in Montague David Eder, *Memoirs of a Modern Pioneer* (1945). London: Victor Gollancz: 21.

Freud, S. (1937). "Moses, ein Ägypter," *Imago*, vol. 23: 5-13; Freud S. (1937). "Wenn Moses ein Ägypter war," *Imago*, vol. 23: 387-419.

Freud, S. (2 April 1938). "Davar Al HaAntishemiyut" [A Word about Anti-Semitism], *HaPo'el HaTza'ir*: 13 [Hebrew].

Freud, S. (9 December 1938). "HaIsh Moshe VeAmo" [Moses the Man and his People], *HaPo'el HaTza'ir*, no. 20-21: 18-19 [Hebrew].

Freud, S. (9 December 1939). "Moshe HaIsh VeAmo" [Moses the Man and His People] (an excerpt from "Wenn Moses ein Ägypter war"), *HaPo'el HaTza'ir*: 18-19 [Hebrew].

Freud, S. (1939). *Totem VeTabu: Kama Te'imot BeHayei HaNefesh Shel HaPra'im VeHaNevrotikanim*. With a preface by Freud [Totem and Taboo: Resemblances between the Mental Lives of Savages and Neurotics], trans. Judah Dwossis

(Dvir). Jerusalem: Kiryat Sefer [Hebrew]. Freud, S. (1955). *Totem and Taboo.* London: Hogarth: xi.

Freud, S. (1940). "Al Milhama" [On War], *HaShomer HaTza'ir*, 8th year: 7-8 [Hebrew].

Freud, S. (1940). "Akhzavat HaMilhama" [The Disappointments of War], *Gilyonot*, vol. 9, no. 10: 354-357.

Freud, S. (1942; fourth ed. 1953). *Psychopathologia Shel Hayei Yom-Yom* [The Psychopathology of Everyday Life], preface by Max Eitingon, trans. Zvi Vislevsky. Tel Aviv: Massadah [Hebrew].

Freud, S. (1943). "Od Nakim Et Harisot HaMilhama" [We Will Rebuild What the War Destroyed], *Ofakim* 1: 2-3 [Hebrew].

Freud, S. (1943). "Halomo Shel Na'ar Yehudi" [The Dream of a Young Jew], *Ofakim* 1: 116-119 [Hebrew].

Freud, S. (1947). *Hayai VePo'alai* [My Life and Work], trans. Zvi Sohar and Shmuel Golan. Merhavia: Sifriat Poalim [Hebrew].

Freud, S. (1948). "HaPsychologia BeZikata LeSifrut, LeOmanut VeLaMada'im" [The Relationship of Psychoanalysis with Literature, Art, and Science] trans. Zvi Sohar, *Ofakim* 1: 2-5 [Hebrew].

Freud, S. (1948-1950). "Obsessive Acts and Religious Practices," in *Collected Papers*, trans. Joan Rivière. London: Hogarth Press and the Institute of Psycho-Analysis.

Freud, S. (1953). "Al Shum Ma Mehayekhet Mona Lisa?" [Why Is Mona Lisa Smiling?], *Ofakim* 7: 41-47 [Hebrew].

Freud, S. (1953). "Shalosh Massot" [Three Essays], trans. Shmuel Golan, published as part of the teaching and training curriculum of the Education Department of HaKibbutz HaArtzi, in *Psychologia Shel Gil HaNe'urim* [The Psychology of Adolescence]. Merhavia: Sifriat Poalim [Hebrew].

Freud, S. (1955). "The Uncanny." in *The Standard Edition of the Psychological Works of Sigmund Freud*, vol. XVII: London: Hogarth: 368-407.

Freud, S. (1959, 1974). *Pesher HaHalomot* [The Interpretation of Dreams], vol. I and II, trans. Mordechai Brachyahu. Tel Aviv: Yavneh [Hebrew]. See also the updated translation, Freud S. (2007). *Peirush HaHalom*, trans. Ruth Ginzberg. Tel Aviv: Am Oved [Hebrew].

Freud, S. (1962). *Three Essays on the Theory of Sexuality*, trans. James Strachey. New York: Basic.

Freud, S., Jung, C. (1974). *The Freud/Jung Letters: The Correspondence between Sigmund Freud and C. G. Jung.* Ed. William McGuire, Bolligen Series XCIV. Princeton: Princeton University Press.

Freud, S. (1978). *Moshe HaIsh VeEmunat HaYhud* [*Moses and Monotheism*], trans. with an epilogue by Moshe Atar. Tel Aviv: Dvir [Hebrew].

Freud, S., Eitingon, M. (2009). *Sigmund Freud – Max Eitingon Correspondance, 1906 -1939*. Paris: Hachette.

Freudiana. (1973). Jerusalem: Internal brochure from the collection of the Jewish National and University Library [Hebrew].

Friedjung, J. (1931). *Die Feihlerzeihung in der Pathologie des Kindes*. Wien: Verlag von Julius Springer.

Friedjung, J. (24 April 1942). "… un der 'Aufbau' des Menschen?". *Orient*, vol. III: 5.

Friedjung, J. (22 May 1942). "Reform der Erziehung?". *Orient*, vol. III, no. 8: 8.

Friedjung, J. (1946). "HaKhinukh Likrat HaSotzialism" [Education towards Socialism], *Ofakim* 1: 20-26 [Hebrew].

Friedjung, J. (1950). "5 Years Psycho-Analytical Educational Work among Jewish Youth Immigrants," in *Max Eitingon in Memoriam*. Jerusalem: Israel Psycho-Analytic Society: 256-267.

G

Ginor, I., Remez, G. (March 2012). "Her Son, the Atomic Scientist: Mirra Birens, Yuli Khariton, and Max Eitingon's Services for the Soviets," in *Journal of Modern Jewish Studies*, vol. 11, no. 1: 35-55.

Golan, Sh. (1932). "She'elat HaPsychoanalyza BaYaldut,". *Ofakim*, vol. 3: 109-113 [Hebrew].

Golan, Sh. (13 May 1947). "LeZikhro Shel Doctor Friedjung" [In Memory of Dr. Friedjung], *Al HaMishmar*: 8 [Hebrew].

Golan, Sh. (29 November 1963). "Keitzad Hitkhalnu" [How We Started], *Al HaMishmar* (Jubilee supplement in honor of Shmuel Golan): 58 [Hebrew].

Goldschein M. (Golan, Sh. "Milek") (2, February 1929). "Die Kinderheinde ‚Beit Alpha'," *Das Werlende Zeitalter*: 99-112.

Gothelf, Y. (1927). "Idea Khinukhit" [A Conception of Education], *HaKhinukh HaShomri*: 23-26 [Hebrew].

Grinstein, A. (1957). "Friedjung, Josef K.," in *The Index of Psychoanalytic Writings*. New York: International Universities Press, vol. II: 686-690.

Gröger, H. (1988). "Joseph Karl Friedjung," Vertriebene Vernunft II. *Emigration und Exil österreicshischer Wissenschaft. Jugend und Volk*: 819-826.

Gumbel, E. (1995). *Al Hayai Im HaPsychoanaliza* [My Life with Psychoanalysis]. Jerusalem: Gefen [Hebrew]. Published in German under the title "Über mein Leben mit der Psychoanalyse," *Jahrbuch der Psychoanalyse*, no. 34, 1995: 7-63.

H

Halamish, A. (2009). *Meir Ya'ari, Biographia Kibbutzit: Hamishim HaShanim HaRishonot, 1894-1947* [A Kibbutz Biography: The First Fifty Years, 1894-1947]. Tel Aviv: Am Oved [Hebrew].

Halpern, L. (1944). "Neurologie and Psychiatry in Palestine,". *American Journal of Psychiatry*, vol. 100: 777.

Heymann, F. (2005). *Un Juif pour l'Islam.* Paris: Stock.

Hoffer, W. (1965). "Siegfried Bernfeld and 'Jerubaal'". *Leo Baeck Year Book*, vol. X: 158.

Hirsch, E. (1948). "Al Dargot Rishonot Shel Activiyut HaYeled VeYozmato VeAl HaNezek HaNigram Al Yedei Shgi'ot BeKhinukh" [The Early Stages of Activity and Initiative of the Child, and the Damage Caused by Educational Misconceptions], *Ofakim* 4-5: 65-79 and 209 [Hebrew].

I

Idelsohn, D. (1929). *Hevrat HaYeladim BeBeit Alpha: Nisayon LeHanekh Yeladim LeKhinukh Hevrati Al Yedei Arba Shnot HaKiyum HaRishonot, 1926-1929* [The Children's Society at Beit: An Experiment in Social Childhood Education Based on the First Four Years, 1926-1929], typewritten manuscript, Archives of Jewish Education in Israel and the Diaspora, Tel Aviv University, Ron-Polani files, 5.184/3.

Idelsohn, D. (1932-1933). "Khinukh HaNo'ar BeBrit HaMo'atzot" [Youth Education in the Soviet Union] *Ofakim* 3: 127-130, and 6: 275-278.

Idelsohn, D. (1933). "Haiyav HaMini'im Shel HaYeled" [Sexuality of the Child], *Hed HaKhinukh*, vol. 15, no. 3: 81-85.

Idelsohn, D. (1937). *HaMachon HaPsychoanalyti Al Shem Doctor Eder* [The Eder Psychoanalytic Institute], typewritten manuscript. Tel Aviv: Archives of Jewish Education in Israel and the Diaspora, Tel Aviv University, 5/207/2179.

"In Memoriam – Dorian Feigenbaum, M.D. 1887-1937," (1937). *The Psycho-Analytic Quarterly*, vol. VI: 1-3.

J

Jones E. (1953, 1955, 1957). *Sigmund Freud: Life and Work.* London : Hogarth Press.

Jones E. (1959). *Free Associations: Memories of a Psychoanalyst.* New York: Basic Books.

K

Kaminka, A. (18 August 1939). "Milkhemet Freud Neged Moshe Rabeinu" [Freud's War against Moses Our Teacher], *HaTzofeh*: 7 [Hebrew].

Kettenacker, L. (1982). "The Anglo-Saxon Alliance and the Problem of Germany, 1941-1945," in *Journal of Contemporary History*, vol. 17: 453-458.

King P., Steiner, R. (eds.) (1991). *The Freud-Klein Controversies, 1941-1945*. London: Routledge.

Kloocke, R. (1998). "Mosche Wulff (1878-1971). Leben und Werk," *Luzifer Amor: Zeitschrift zur Geschichte der Psychoanalyse* 16: 87-101.

Kloocke, R. (2002). *Mosche Wulff. Zur Geschichte der Psychoanalyse in Russland und Israel*. Tübingen: Diskord.

Koch, A. (1974). "Siegfried Bernfeld Kinderheim Baumgarten. Vorassetzungen jüdischer Erziehung um 1920". PhD diss., University of Hamburg.

L

Lagerlof, S. (1994). *Jérusalem en Terre sainte*. Paris: Stock.

Laqueur, W. (1972). *A History of Zionism*. London: Weidenfeld & Nicolson.

Lask, I. M., (30 June 1939). "A Freudian Myth", *Palestine Review*: 169-170.

Les premiers psychanalystes. Minutes de la Société psychanalytique de Vienne. (1976). Paris: Gallimard.

Levy, N. (1998). *Prakim BeToldot HaRefua BeEretz Yisrael 1799-1978* [Chapters in the History of Medicine in Eretz Yisrael, 1799-1978]. Tel Aviv and Haifa: Hakibbutz Hameuchad Publishing House and the Bruce Rappaport Faculty of Medicine, Technion [Hebrew].

Liebermann, G. (2002). "Demeures freudiennes en Palestine-Eretz-Israël", *Les voyages de l'intelligence. Passages des idées et des hommes. Europe, Palestine, Israël*, ed. Dominique Bourel and Gabriel Motzkin. Paris: CNRS: 295-310

Liebermann, G. (2006). *Histoire de la psychanalyse en Israël. Des origines et de l'essor de la psychanalyse en Palestine britannique (1918-1948)*, doctoral thesis supervised by Élisabeth Roudinesco, University of Paris 7.

Liebermann, G, (2012). *La psychanalyse en Palestine 1918-1948. Aux origines du mouvement analytique israélien*. Paris: CampagnePremière.

Liebermann, G. (2014). *La psychanalyse à l'épreuve du kibboutz*. Paris: CampagnePremière.

Liebermann, G. (2015). "Max Eitingon in Palästina/Eretz-Israel (1933-1943)", *Luzifer-Amor. Zeitschrift zur Geschichte der Psychoanalyse* 55: 94-118.

Lubitsch, R. (1984). *Korot Shel Yedidut* [The History of a Friendship, translated by publisher as "The Movement of Friendship Israel-U.R.S.S. - 40 Years"]. Tel Aviv: Israel-USSR Friendship Movement [Hebrew].

M

Malinowski, B. (1929). *The Sexual Life of the Savages in North Western Melanesia*. London: Routledge.

Marcuse (Marcuza), M. (1942). "Sexualprobleme und Tradition," *Orient* 4: 9-11.

Marcuse (Marcuza), M. (1942) "Charakter und Gericht", *Orient* 7: 7-9.

Margalit, E. (1971). *HaShomer HaTza'ir: MiEdat Ne'urim LeMarxism Mahapkhani (1913-1936)* [HaShomer HaTza'ir: From Youth Culture to Revolutionary Marxism, 1913-1936]. Tel Aviv: HaKibbutz HaMeuchad [Hebrew].

"Marie Bonaparte. Griechische Prinzessin und Shülerin Freuds besucht Israel. Eine Freudian des jüdischen Volkes," *Aufbau*, 26 January 1962: 22.

Mintz, A., ed. (1993). *Hebrew in America: Perspective and Prospects*. Detroit: Wayne State University Press.

Mintz, M. (1995). *Havlei Ne'urim: HaTnu'a HaShomrit, 1911-1921* [Pangs of Youth: The Shomrim Movement, 1911-1921]. Jerusalem: HaSifria HaZionit [Hebrew].

Mühlleitner, E. (1992). "Josef Karl Friedjung," in *Biographisches Lexikon der Psychoanalyse*. Die Mitglieder der Psychologischen Mittwoch-Gesellschaft und der Wiener Psychoanalytischen Vereinigung, 1902-1938. Tübingen: Diskord.

Müntz, I. (1922). *Die jüdischen Arzte im Mittelalter*. Frankfurt am Main: J. Kaufmann Verlag.

N

Nagler, Sh. (1944). "MeHayei HaMa'ase" [A Life of Doing] *Hygiena Ruhanit* 2: 4-5 [Hebrew].

Nagler, Sh. (1948). "Al Avodato Shel HaHug HaAnalyti-Pedagogi" [On the Work of the Analytic-Pedagogic Seminar], *Ofakim* 6: 61-64 [Hebrew].

Nagler, Sh. (1998). *Ketavim* [Writings] (texts by Nagler and testimonies collected by Miriam Rick). Kfar Bialik: Ach [Hebrew].

Near, H. (1985). "Experiment and Survival: The Beginnings of the Kibbutz," *Journal of Contemporary History*, vol. 20, no. 1: 192.

O

Obermayer, H. (1942). "Uber Massenpsychologie," *Orient* 20: 14-17.

Obernik, G. (1918). "Was wir Jungen brauchen?" *Jerubaal*: 100-101.

Obernik, Grete, (1920). "Beit Talmidim" [House of Students], *HaPo'el HaTza'ir* 1: 15 [Hebrew]

Obernik, M. G. (1922). "Asefat Imahot Ba'Ir Ha'Atika BeYerushalaim" [Meeting of Mothers in the Old City], *HaGina*, 4-5: 27-28 [Hebrew].

Obernik, G. (1930). "Beobachtungen einer Kindergärterin," *Internationale Zeitschrift für Psychoanalytische Pädagogik* 2-3: 94-97.

P

Paret, P. (1992). "Sysiphos und sein Author. Eine Einführung," in Karl Fallend and Johannes Reichmayer (eds.), *Siegfried Bernfeld oder die Genzen des Psychoanalyse. Materialism zu Leben und Werk*. Basel-Frankfurt: Nexus/Stœrmfeld.

Pe'utot [Infants] (1935). Collected documents edited by Israel Rivka'i, published by HaVa'ada HaBein-Kibbutzit LeShe'elat HaTipul HaMeshutaf. The Inter-Kibbutz Committee on Collective Childcare [Hebrew].

Platek, Y. (1989). *HaMossad: Beit HaSefer HaRishon Shel HaShomer HaTza'ir BeMishmar HaEmek, 1931-1940.* [The Mossad: The First HaShomer HaTza'ir School in Mishmar HaEmek, 1931-1940]. Giv'at Haviva: Yad Tabenkin. [Hebrew].

Pomer, S. L. (1966). "Max Eitingon 1881-1943," in *Psychoanalytic Pioneers*. New York: Basic Books.

R

Reichmayr J. (1994). *Spurensuche in der Geschichte des Psychoanalyse*. Frankfurt: Fischer.

Reshef, Sh. (1985). *Khinukh Hadash BeEretz Israel, 1915-1929* [New Education in Eretz Israel, 1915-1929]. Merhavia: Sifriat Poalim [Hebrew].

Rolnik, E. (2012). *Freud in Zion: Psychoanalysis and the Making of Modern Jewish Identity*. London: Karnac Books.

Ron-Polani, Y. (1957). "Darko Shel Halutz Sotzial Pedagog" [The Way of a Pioneer Socialist Pedagogue], *Orim* vol. 12, no. 3: 193-196 [Hebrew].

Ron-Polani, (1961). Y., *HaNisayon HaRishon* [The First Experience]. Tel Aviv: Abouka [Hebrew].

Rosenbaum, M. (1954). "Freud-Eitingon-Magnes Correspondence," *American Journal of Psychoanalysis* 2: 315.

Roudinesco, É. (1994). *Généalogies*. Paris: Fayard.

Roudinesco, É. Plon, M., (1997). *Dictionnaire de la psychanalyse*. Paris: Fayard.

Roudinesco, É. (2014). *Revisiting the Jewish Question*. Cambridge: Polity Press.

S

Sabourin, P. (2011). *Sándor Ferenczi, un pionnier de la clinique*. Paris: CampagnePremière/.

Safouan, M. (1983). *Jacques Lacan et la question de formation des analystes*. Paris: Seuil.

Safouan, M. (2013). *La psychanalyse. Science, thérapie – et cause*. Vincennes: Thierry Marchaisse.

Schalit, I. (1941). "The Psychoanalytic Society in Palestine/Eretz Israel", in *Die Chewrah Psychoanalytith B'Eretz Israel gratuliert ihrem Präsidenten zum sechzigsten Geburtstag*, typewritten manuscript. Jerusalem: Chewrah psychoanalytith b'Eretz Israel.

Schneeurson, F. (1925). "Drakhim Hadashot LaKhinukh HaSotziali" [New Ways to Social Education], *HaKhinukh*, vol. 7: 1-11 and 22-31.

Simmel, E. (1950). "Aus: Zehn Jahre Berliner Psychoanalytisches Institut," in *Max Eitingon in Memoriam*. Jerusalem: Israel Psychoanalytic Society: 48-49.

Singer, M. (1975). *'Arba'at Pirkei Lekakh MiToldot Tnu'at HaPo'alim BeAustria* [Four Lessons Learned from the History of the Austrian Labor Movement]. Haifa: Mo'etzet Po'alei Haifa. [Hebrew].

Sohar, Z. (1932). « Khipous drakhim » " [The Search for the Path], *Ofakim* 3: 106-108.

Sohar, Z. (1953). "Sigmund Freud VeHaSotzialism" [Sigmund Freud and Socialism] *Ofakim* 2-5: p. 122-132 [Hebrew].

Sohar, Z. (1971). Remarks on behalf of the Psychoanalytic and Psychiatric Society at memorial event for Professor Moshe Wulff, typewritten manuscript. Givat Haviva: HaShomer HaTza'ir Archives, Zvi Sohar Collection, (4) 7.13 .95 [Hebrew].

Sternhell, Z. (1999). *The Founding Myths of Israel: Nationalism, Socialism, and the Making of the Jewish State.* New Jersey : Princeton Univ. Press.

Szold, H. (May 1935). "MiVa'adat HaPe'ula" [From the Actions Committee], *HaShomer HaTza'ir*: 26-28 [Hebrew].

S. S. (1942). "Yahaduto HaMudheket Shel Freud" [Freud's Repressed Jewishness], *Maaznayim*, vol. 14, no. 11: 317-319 [Hebrew].

Siegfried van Vriesland, May 2nd 1886 – December 4th 1939. (1941). Collected Documents, Jerusalem: 70-71, Document No. S4-1-A291 [Hebrew and English], National Library of Israel, Jerusalem.

T

Tidhar, D. (1956). *Encyclopedia LeHalutzei HaYishuv U-Vonav* [Encyclopedia of the Yishuv Pioneers and Builders]. [Hebrew].

Tidhar, D. (1960). *BeSherut HaMoledet, 1912-1960* [In Service of the Homeland, 1912-1960]. Tel Aviv: HaMerkaz Publishing [Hebrew]

V

Vaksberg, A. (1994). *Stalin Against the Jews.* New York: Alfred A. Knopf.

VeAhavata LeNefesh Re'ekha: Dr. Berta (Betty) Grünspan, Rof'a, Doda, Yedida, Adam [Love Thy Neighbor's Soul: Dr. Berta (Betty) Grünspan, Physician, Aunt, Friend, Human], a collection of eulogies delivered during her funeral and memories of family members, friends, colleagues, students, patients, and neighbors of Berta Grünspan at Kibbutz Yif'at. Merhavia, 1976.

W

Weiss, Lepopold – Muhammad Talal Asad. (2005). *Un Proche-Orient sans romantisme.* Paris: Editions CNRS.

Weizmann, Ch. (1951). *Masa VeMa'as – Zikhronot Haiyav Shel Nasi Israel* [Autobiography of Chaim Weizmann]. Jerusalem and Tel Aviv: Schocken [Hebrew].

Windhager, G. (2002). *Leopold Weiss alias Muhammad Asad. Von Galizien nach Arabien 1900-1927.* Vienna: Erschienen im Böhlau-Verlag.

Winnik, H. (1977). "Milestones in the Development of Psychoanalysis in Israel," *Israel Annals of Psychiatry and Related Disciplines*, vol. 15, no. 1: 85-91.

Winnik, H. (1977). "Sur l'histoire de la psychanalyse en Israël," in *La Folie. Actes du colloque de Milan.* Paris: 10/18 Union générale d'éditions: 356-373.

Wulff, M. (1946, 1949). *Nefesh HaYeled* [The Soul of the Child]. Merhavia: Sifriat Poalim [Hebrew].

Wyneken, G. (1913). *Schule und Jugendkultur*. Iena: Dierich Verlag.

Y

Ya'ari, M. (1927). "Tfisatenu HaKhinukhin" [Our Educational Conception] *HaKhinukh HaShomri*: 19 [Hebrew].

Ya'ari, M. (1972). *BeMa'avak LeAmal Meshuhrar* [Struggling for Liberated Labor]. Tel Aviv: Am Oved – Tarbut VeKhinukh [Hebrew].

Ya'ari, M. (1992). *Dyukano Shel Manhig KeAdam Tza'ir, 1897-1929* [Portrait of a Leader as a Young Man: Life Events, 1897-1929]. Merhavia: Sifriat Poalim [Hebrew].

Yerushalmi, Y. H. (1991). *Freud's Moses: Judaism Terminable and Interminable*. New Haven: Yale University Press.

Yitzhaki, Sh. (1976). "Al Gustav Gyneken" [On Gustav Wyneken], *HaKhinukh HaMeshutaf* 90: 47-55 [Hebrew].

Z

Zayit, D. (1987). *Yisud HaKibbitz HaArtzi, Haifa, 1-3 April 1927* [The Founding of HaKibbutz HaArtzi, Haifa, 1-3 April 1927]. Giv'at Haviva: Mekorot Publishing – Studies on HaShomer HaTza'ir [Hebrew].

Zeitlin, A. (4 August 1939). "Freud HaYehudi VeMoshe Ha. . . Mitzri" [Freud the Jew and Moses the. . . Egyptian], *HaTzofeh*: 6 [Hebrew].

Zweig, A. (1978). "Die Liga V," in *Der Briefwechsel zwischen Louis Fürnberg und Arnold Zweig, Dokumente einer Freunschaft*. Berlin: Aufbau-Verlag: 245-249.

Zweig, A. (1934). *Bilanz der deutschen Judenheit 1933. Ein Versuch*. Amsterdam: Querido.

Zweig, A. (1932, 1996). *Die Vriendt Kehrt Heim*. Berlin: Aufbau Verlag.

Notes

NOTES TO PREFACE

1   Guido Liebermann, *Histoire de la psychanalyse en Israël. Des origines et de l'essor de la psychanalyse en Palestine britannique (1918-1948)*, doctoral thesis supervised by Élisabeth Roudinesco, University of Paris 7, defended on November 23, 2007. The advisory committee included Dominique Bourel (Director of Research at the National Center for Scientific Research – CNRS), André Gueslin (Professor at the University of Paris 7 – Denis Diderot, chair), Patrick Guyomard (Professor of Psychopathology at the University of Paris 8 and Paris 7, rapporteur), Jacques Le Rider (Director of Studies at the École Pratiquedes Hautes Études – EPHE, rapporteur).

2   These facts have been explored and verified by other historians.

3   I was personally able to research aspects of this relationship thanks to Guido Liebermann's exploration of archival documents. See Élisabeth Roudinesco, *Retour sur la question juive* (Paris: Albin Michel, 2009), published in English as *Revisiting the Jewish Question*, trans. Andrew Brown (Cambridge: Polity Press, 2014).

4   Yosef Hayim Yerushalmi, *Freud's Moses: Judaism Terminable and Interminable* (New Haven: Yale University Press, 1991), translated into Hebrew by Dan Daor (Jerusalem: Shalem Press, 2006); Edward Said, *Freud and the Non-European* (London: Verso, 2003), translated into Hebrew by Yael Sela (Tel Aviv: Resling, 2005).

5   Eran Rolnik, *Freud in Zion: Psychoanalysis and the Making of Modern Jewish Identity* (London: Karnac Books, 2012), translated from the Hebrew edition (2007) by Haim Watzman. This book also addresses the history of psychoanalysis in Germany, particularly during the period that Ernest Jones collaborated with the Nazis, as well as the question of Jewish identity in the history of the psychoanalytic movement.

6   Alexander Etkind, *Eros of the Impossible: The History of Psychoanalysis in Russia* (Boulder: Westview Press, 1997), translated from the Russian edition (1993) by Noah and Maria Rubins. This thesis was reasserted in Mary-Kay Wilmers, *The Eitingons. A Twentieth-Century Story* (London: Verso, 2009).

7   See Roudinesco, *Revisiting the Jewish Question*.

8   Aharon Kaminka, "Milkhemet Freud Neged Moshe Rabeinu" [Freud's War against Moses Our Teacher], *HaTzofeh*, 18 August 1939, p. 7 [Hebrew].

NOTES TO CHAPTER 1

9   "Eretz Yisrael," in *Hebrew in America: Perspective and Prospects*, ed. Alan Mintz (Detroit: Wayne State University Press, 1993).

10   Rabbi Nathanael, *Anleitung zum Heile der Seele und des Körpers*, cited in Izak Müntz, *Die jüdischen Arzte im Mittelalter* (Frankfurt am Main: J. Kaufmann Verlag, 1922), p. 13.

11   Based on Nissim Levy, *Prakim BeToldot HaRefua BeEretz Yisrael 1799-1978* [Chapters in the History of Medicine in Eretz Yisrael, 1799-1978] (Tel Aviv and Haifa: Hakibbutz Hameuchad Publishing House and the Bruce Rappaport Faculty of Medicine, Technion, 1998) [Hebrew].

12 Walter Laqueur, *Histoire du sionisme*, vol. I (Paris: Gallimard, 1994), p. 75.

13 Deaconesses were Protestant women who typically resided with the community, devoting their lives to religious worship and charity. They first established welfare homes in 1836 in Germany and France.

14 Selma Lagerlof, *Jérusalem en Terre sainte* (Paris: Stock, 1994), p. 35 [translation by GL].

15 I have been working since 1994 in a psychiatric hospital in the center of the country. One of my patients was a young Bedouin man who had been hospitalized on occasion following brief hallucinatory or delusional spells. His father, the head of the tribe, saw his son's illness as a source of shame and a disgrace to the family. To keep the son hidden from sight, in consultation and active participation with tribal elders, the father would chain him in a tent. After he managed to escape, my patient went to a hospital some distance from the region of his family's residence; he knew that if he remained in the same area, the family might assassinate him.

16 Levy, *Chapters in the History of Medicine*, p. 23.

NOTES TO CHAPTER 2

17 Founded as the Zionist Organization in 1897, it changed its name to the World Zionist Organization in 1960.

18 Ernest Jones, *Free Associations: Memories of a Psychoanalyst* (New York: Basic Books, 1959), p. 239.

19 Ibid, p. 240.

20 Élisabeth Roudinesco and Michel Plon, "Chronologie," in *Dictionnaire de la psychanalyse* (Paris: Fayard, 1997), p. 1126.

21 According to Eder, his experience in the Andes inspired him to read the "remarkable book of Dr. Jung." Montague David Eder, *Memoirs of a Modern Pioneer*, ed. J. B. Hobmand (London: Victor Gollancz, 1945), p. 60.

22 Edward Glover, "Eder as Psycho-Analyst," in Eder, *Memoirs of a Modern Pioneer*, p. 215.

23 Montague David Eder, *War Shock: The Psycho-Neuroses in War Psychology and Treatment* (London: William Heinemann, 1917).

24 Letter from Zangwill to Eder, 25 October 1918, Central Zionist Archives, L/120/333.

25 Montague David Eder, "Pikuakh Yetomim" [Supervision of Orphans], *HaKhinukh*, September-October 1919, p. 107 [Hebrew].

26 Glover, *Memoirs of a Modern Pioneer*, pp. 99-100.

27 Joan Dash, *Summoned to Jerusalem. The Life of Henrietta Szold* (New York, Hagerstown, San Francisco: Harper & Row Publishers, 1979), p. 151.

28 Dorian Feigenbaum, "Palestine," *International Journal of Psycho-Analysis*, vol. X, no. 1, 1924, pp. 100-101.

29 The Rorschach test, developed by Swiss psychiatrist Herman Rorschach in 1921, relies on subjects' responses to ink diagrams. Clinical psychologists often use this test for diagnostic purposes, despite the controversy surrounding it.

30 Florence Heymann, *Un Juif pour l'Islam*, (Paris: Stock, 2005), pp. 95 ff.

31 Letter from Leopold Weiss to Dorian Feigenbaum, Frankfurt, 26 July 1926, Municipal Archives of Jerusalem, Aryeh Feigenbaum AF/700. See also *Lepopold Weiss – Muhammad Talal Asad, Un Orient sans romantisme*, trans. F. Heymann, ed. CNRS, 1924, as well as Günther Windhager, *Leopold Weiss alias Muhammad Asad. Von Galizien nach Arabien 1900-1927*, (Vienna: Erschienen im Böhlau-Verlag, 2002).

32 On the history of communism in Jewish Palestine, see Shmuel Dotan, *Adumim be'Eretz Israel* [Reds in Palestine] (Kfar Saba: Shivna HaSofer Publishers, 1996) [Hebrew].

33 David Tidhar, *BeSherut HaMoledet, 1912-1960* [In Service of the Homeland, 1912-1960] (Tel Aviv: HaMerkaz Publishing, 1960), pp. 92-94 [Hebrew]

34 Letter from Dorian Feigenbaum to Norman Bentwich (attorney general for Palestine under the British Mandate), 8 July 1923, Municipal Archives of Jerusalem, Aryeh Feigenbaum, AF/700, Dorian Feigenbaum.

35 Tidhar, *In Service of the Homeland*, pp. 92-94.

36 This loyal Stalinist agent was expelled from Palestine in 1935, imprisoned in the Siberian Gulag, and released sixteen years later, when he was permitted to emigrate to Poland and from there to Palestine. In his later years he became religious. He died in 1974.

37 Letter from Norman Bentwitch to Dorian Feigenbaum, 7 July 1923, Municipal Archives of Jerusalem, Aryeh Feigenbaum, AF/700, Dorian Feigenbaum.

38 Letter from Dorian Feigenbaum to Norman Bentwitch, 8 July 1923, ibid.

39 Ibid.

40 "M. D. Professional Record," Municipal Archives of Jerusalem, Aryeh Feigenbaum, AF/700, Dorian Feigenbaum.

41 According to an anonymous eulogy, "In Memoriam – Dorian Feigenbaum, M.D. 1887-1937," *The Psycho-Analytic Quarterly*, vol. VI, 1937, pp. 1-3.

42 "Experimental Psychology and Freud's Depth Psychology," The Unconscious," "Hypnosis, Sleep, and Dream," *International Journal of Psycho-Analysis*, "Palestine," vol. X, no. 1, 1924, p. 102.

43 See below, "Grete Obernik-Reiner, Spokesperson for Siegfried Bernfeld."

44 Deborah Kallen was as interested in pedagogy and psychoanalysis as her brother, the renowned pacifist Zionist and Pluralist philosopher Horace Meyer Kallen (1882-1974), who at the time was a professor of philosophy and psychology at the New School for Social Research in New York. Horace Kallen, a fierce defender of human rights and ethnic pluralism, came to Palestine in 1926 with the intention of opening a social research institute.

45 "The Interest of Pedagogic Circles in Psychoanalysis was Emphasized by the Appointment of Dr. D. Feigenbaum as Specialist-consultant in the Free School Conducted by Miss Kallen, Formerly of Boston," *International Journal of Psycho-Analysis, "*Palestine," vol. X, no. 1, 1924, p. 101.

46 See Pierre Sabourin, *Sándor Ferenczi, un pionnier de la clinique* (Paris: CampagnePremière/, 2011).

47 Aryeh Feigenbaum, "Our Age of perplexity viewed through Hells and Judaea," in *Opening Address read at the 7th Symposium of the Ophthalmological Society*, 12 March 1969, The Israel Museum, Jerusalem, p. 10; private archives of Naomi Belsitzmann (daughter of Aryeh Feigenbaum).

48 Gesellschaft jüdische Ärzte und Naturwissenschaftler für medizinisch-biologische Interessen in Palästina.

49   Freud had conducted his own analysis through correspondence with this colleague.

50   *Siegfried van Vriesland, May 2ⁿᵈ 1886-December 4ᵗʰ 1939*, Collected Documents, 1941, p. 25.

51   Judah Magnes, "Preliminary Report of the Plan for Care of Jewish War Orphans," 10 June 1919, and "40ᵗʰ Meeting of the Palestine Orphans Committee," 17 August 1920, Central Archives for the History of the Jewish People, Hebrew University.

52   Obituary for S. van Vriesland, 16 December 1939, Israel State Archives, Max Eitingon Collection, File No. P-5/2974. 72-52/1-70.

53   In a letter to van Vriesland dated August 3, 1927, Adolf Storfer acknowledged receipt of the text on behalf of the *Internationaler Psychoanalytischer Verlag* but said that the article could not be published in the upcoming August issue because that issue had already been finalized. Van Vriesland informed Freud of this shortly thereafter; the article was never published. Central Zionist Archives, van Vriesland files, 114/121.

54   Telephone conversation with Henricus Wijsenbeek, 23 October 1997, Tel Aviv.

55   Max Eitingon, "From a memorial speech in the Psycho-Analytical Association," *Siegfried van Vriesland, May 2ⁿᵈ 1886 – December 4ᵗʰ 1939*, Collected Documents, Jerusalem, 1941, pp. 70-71, Document No. S4-1-A291 [Hebrew and English], National Library of Israel, Jerusalem.

56   "Keren Siegfried van Vriesland," undated, Schocken Archives, Sch. A 844A2, vol. 8:9.

57   Tracing her biography was not a simple matter: the documents, no less rare than the testimonies I was able to gather, cannot be disclosed, and the story of her life as I was able to piece it together remains fragmentary.

58   Letter from Efraim Reiner (Grete Obernik's son) to Guido Liebermann, 9 July 2004.

59   This correspondence, housed in the manuscripts department of the National Library of Israel, is available for perusal but may not be published or quoted.

60   Telephone conversation with Rony Reiner, 24 June 2008.

61   Grete Obernik, "Was wir Jungen brauchen?" *Jerubaal*, 1918, pp. 100-101.

62   Letter from Martin Bergmann (son of Hugo Bergmann), now deceased, to Guido Liebermann, 8 November 1997.

63   Letter from Grete Obernik to Siegfried Bernfeld, 8 October 1920, Library of Congress Archives, Siegfried Bernfeld Papers.

64   Ibid.

65   Letter from Grete Obernik to Siegfried Bernfeld, undated, Library of Congress Archives, Siegfried Bernfeld Papers.

66   Grete Obernik, "Beit Talmidim" [House of Students], *HaPo'el HaTza'ir*, no. 1, 1920, p. 15 [Hebrew]

67   Margalit Grete Obernik, "Asefat Imahot Ba'Ir Ha'Atika BeYerushalaim" [Meeting of Mothers in the Old City], *HaGina*, no. 4-5, 1922, pp. 27-28 [Hebrew].

68   Letter from Aryeh Feigenbaum (addressee unknown), 4 October 1924, Municipal Archives of Jerusalem, Aryeh Feigenbaum 688/25. This letter also confirms that Grete Obernik married Markus Reiner while employed at Deborah Kallen's school in Jerusalem.

69   Letter from Grete Obernik to Siegfried Bernfeld and Willi Hoffer, undated, 1921, Library of Congress Archives, Siegfried Bernfeld Papers.

70 David Tidhar, "Reiner, Markus," *Encyclopedia LeHalutzei HaYishuv U-Vonav* [Encyclopedia of the Yishuv Pioneers and Builders], vol. 7, 1956, pp. 2850-2851 [Hebrew].

71 Letter dated 5 May 1925, Library of Congress Archives, Siegfried Bernfeld Papers.

72 Letter dated 22 October 1925, Library of Congress Archives, Anna Freud Papers, no. 24. Efraim Reiner confirmed that his mother was trained in psychoanalysis by Anna Freud, among others. Telephone with Efraim Reiner, 7 November 1999.

73 August Aichhorn, *Verwarhloste Jugend, die Psychoanalyse in der Fürsorgeerziehung*, (Leipzig: Internazionaler psychoanalytischer Bibliothek, 1925), with a preface by Sigmund Freud.

74 Grete Obernik, "Beobachtungen einer Kindergärterin," *Internationale Zeitschrift für Psychoanalytische Pädagogik*, no. 2/3, 1930, pp. 94-97.

75 August Aichhorn, "Erziehung-Beratungs-Seminar," in *Zeitschrift für Psychoanalytische Pädagogik*, vol. VII, 1934, p. 153.

76 Aichhorn, *Verwahrloste Jugend,* translated into Hebrew by David Idelsohn and published as a series of articles: "No'ar Azuv," *Hygiena Ruhanit*, no. 1, pp. 11-20; no. 2, pp. 31-40; no. 3, pp. 54-56; no. 4-5, pp. 85-102; no. 6, pp. 113-122; no. 7, pp. 134-144; no. 8, pp. 156-170; no. 9, pp. 177-198; no. 10, pp. 215 ff., 1948; later published as a book: *No'ar Azuv: HaPsychologia BeTipul Khinukhi-Sotziali, Eser Hartza'ot* [Psychoanalysis in Educational-Social Treatment, Ten Lectures], trans. David Idelsohn, ed. Mordechai Brachyahu (Jerusalem: S. Zack, 1956).

77 Letter from Moshe Wulff to Max Eitingon, 16 June 1933, Israel State Archives, Max Eitingon Papers, 1933-4/1939 (P-3/2970).

78 Letter from Efraim Reiner to Guido Liebermann, 9 July 2004.

79 Letter from Grete Obernik to Max Eitingon, 22 May 1934, Israel State Archives, Max Eitingon Papers, 6-1932-1943 (P-12/2973).

80 Letter from Grete Obernik to Max Eitingon, 1 June 1934, ibid.

81 Letter from Grete Obernik to Max Eitingon, 29 June 1934, ibid.

82 "Bulletin de l'Association internationale de psychanalyse," *Revue française de psychanalyse*, no. 3, 1935, p. 534.

83 Letter from Grete Obernik to Max Eitingon, 20 February 1935, Israel State Archives, Max Eitingon Papers, 6/1932-1943 (P-12/2973.

84 Max Eitingon, "From a memorial speech in the Psycho-Analytical Association," *Siegfried van Vriesland, May 2nd 1886 – December 4th 1939*, Collected Documents, Jerusalem, 1941, pp. 70-71, Document No. S4-1-A291 [Hebrew and English], National Library of Israel, Jerusalem.

85 *International Journal of Psycho-Analysis*, vol. XV, 1934, p. 470.

86 Grete Obernik, "Psychoanalytic Observation of the Individual Child within the Group and its Value for Collective Education," conference, 9 March 1935, reported in *International Journal of Psycho-Analysis*, vol. XVI, 1935, p. 393.

87 Letter from Grete Obernik to Max Eitingon, 3 March 1936, Israel State Archives, Max Eitingon Papers, 2/1934-1939 (P-2/2970).

88 Letter from Max Eitingon to Grete Obernik, 11 March 1936, ibid.

89   Letter from Max Eitingon to Sigmund Freud, 26 March 1938, *Sigmund Freud – Max Eitingon Correspondance, 1906-1939* (Paris: Hachette, 2009), p. 843.

90   Letter from Anna Freud to Max Eitingon, 22 January 1936, Library of Congress Archives, Anna Freud Papers, No. 24.

91   Letter from Dorian Feigenbaum to Max Eitingon, 22 January 1936, Library of Congress Archives, Anna Freud Papers, No. 24.

92   Max Eitingon, "From a memorial speech in the Psycho-Analytical Association," *Siegfried van Vriesland, May 2ⁿᵈ 1886 – December 4ᵗʰ 1939*, Collected Documents, Jerusalem, 1941, pp. 70-71, Document No. S4-1-A291 [Hebrew and English], National Library of Israel, Jerusalem.

93   Eitingon, "From a memorial speech in the Psycho-Analytical Association," ibid., collected documents by van Vriesland, eulogies, and memoirs of friends and colleagues, 1941, p. 83 [in English text] and p. 25 [in Hebrew text].

94   Letter from Aryeh Feigenbaum to Milton Rosenbaum, 28 December 1953, Municipal Archives of Jerusalem, Aryeh Feigenbaum, 687/Psychoanalysis.

NOTES TO CHAPTER 3

95   The reference here is to the psychiatric hospital of the University of Zurich, located on a forested hill in the southwestern part of the city and known by the name "Burghölzli" - meaning "madhouse" in the Swiss-German dialect.

96   Ernest Jones, *La vie et l'œuvre de Sigmund Freud*, vol. II (Paris: PUF, 1972), p. 34.

97   Conversation with Aliza Z. O., 21 June 1997. I am grateful to Professor Dominique Bourel and Jeanine Lazar for putting me in touch with a former patient of Max Eitingon.

98   This term, sometimes translated as simply "control" and introduced by Freud in 1919, refers to a practice systematized by the International Psycho-Analytical Association in 1925, which Eitingon made mandatory, as he did with "didactic analysis." Élisabeth Roudinesco, Michel Plon, "Psychanalyse (ou analyse) de contrôle ou supervision," in *Dictionnaire de la psychanalyse* (Paris: Fayard, 1997), pp. 194-195.

99   *Les premiers psychanalystes. Minutes de la Société psychanalytique de Vienne* (Paris: Gallimard, 1976).

100 Traumatic neurosis was identified as early as 1889 by the renowned German neurologist and psychiatrist Hermann Oppenheim (1858-1919). In 1919 Montague David Eder began treating "war shock" or "war trauma." The term "war neurosis" was adopted in 1920. See Élisabeth Roudinesco, Michel Plon, "Névrose de guerre," in *Dictionnaire de la psychanalyse*, p. 717.

101 Ernst Simmel, "Aus: Zehn Jahre Berliner Psychoanalytisches Institut," *Max Eitingon in Memoriam*, Israel Psychoanalytic Society, 1950, pp. 48-49.

102 Sidney L. Pomer, "Max Eitingon 1881-1943," in *Psychoanalytic Pioneers* (New York: Basic Books, 1966), p. 57.

103 Letter from Eitingon to Freud, 19 March 1933, in Sigmund Freud – Max Eitingon, *Correspondance, 1906-1939* (Paris: Hachette, 2009), p. 784.

104 Élisabeth Roudinesco, Michel Plon, "Eitingon Max (1881-1943)," in *Dictionnaire de la psychanalyse*, p. 247. See also the entry "Berliner Psychoanalytisches Institute (BPI)" in the same publication, pp. 103-104.

105 Ibid., p. 247.

106 Letter from Eitingon to Freud, 2 November 1933, in *Sigmund Freud – Max Eitingon, Correspondance, 1906 -1939*, p. 803.

107 Ilja Schalit, a former member of the German Psychoanalytic Society, was supposed to travel to Palestine with Moshe Wulff to provide psychoanalytic training for the educators of HaShomer HaTza'ir. As in the case of Anna Smeliansky, not many people know of the achievements of this loyal colleague of Eitingon in Palestine. Born in Riga in 1898 to a wealthy family of timber traders who were also loyal Zionists, he completed high school there and began a medical career at St. Petersburg Military Academy. After the October Revolution he left Russia and settled in Germany. He continued his medical studies at the University of Freiburg and from there traveled to Zurich to study psychiatry at the Burghölzli Clinic under the direction of Bleuler. Upon returning to Germany, he studied psychoanalysis at the Berlin Psychoanalytic Institute and began working with Moshe Wulff at the renowned clinic established and run by Ernst Simmel in Berlin, the Schloss Tegel. This was the first psychoanalytic clinic to treat psychotic patients, alcoholics, and drug addicts. In 1933 he settled in Haifa, where for five years he was the only analyst, until the arrival in 1938 of Austrian analysts, two of whom, Josef Karl Friejdung and Berta Grünspan, settled in the same city. Schalit passed away in 1953.

108 Killian Bluhm, Erwin Hirsch, Margareth Brandt, and Erich Gumbel were already in Palestine.

109 Letter from Eitingon to Freud, 2 November 1933, in *Sigmund Freud – Max Eitingon, Correspondance, 1906 -1939*, p. 803.

110 Palästinensische Psychoanalytische Gesellschaft. The official documents also bear the names Palestine Psychoanalytic Society and, in Hebrew, Chevrah Psychoanalytit BeEretz Israel (the Eretz-Israeli Psychoanalytic Society, also translated as the Israeli Psychoanalytic Brotherhood).

111 Part of this document as currently available to researchers is missing, presumably the part indicating the roles of Walter Kluge and Anna Smeliansky. Max Eitingon, Written Declaration of the Founding of the CPEI, 28 October 1933, Israel State Archives, Eitingon Files, P-4/2974, 72.52/1-69.

112 Alexandre Etkind, *Histoire de la psychanalyse en Russie* (Paris: PUF, 1991), p. 329.

113 "Reports," in *International Journal of Psycho-Analysis*, vol. XV, 1934, p. 383. This is indeed the first publication that mentions the names of the Society's founders: Eitingon, Wulff, Smeliansky, Schalit, and Kluge.

114 Letter from Eitingon to Freud, 2 November 1933, *Sigmund Freud – Max Eitingon, Correspondance, 1906-1939*, p. 804.

115 Letter from Ilja Schalit to Max Eitingon, undated, January-February 1934, Israel State Archives, Eitingon files, 2/2970.

116 Letter from Freud to Eitingon, 1 March 1934, in *Sigmund Freud – Max Eitingon, Correspondance, 1906-1939*, p. 809.

117 Erich Gumbel, *Al Hayai Im HaPsychoanaliza* [My Life with Psychoanalysis] (Jerusalem: Gefen, 1995), p. 16 [Hebrew]. Published in German under the title "Über mein Leben mit der Psychoanalyse," *Jahrbuch der Psychoanalyse*, no. 34, 1995, pp. 7-63.

118 Ibid., pp. 15-16.

119 Ibid. p. 28.

120 Wulff wrote to Gumbel that "medical practice – including analytic practice – is not possible without a license and diploma because the authorities forbid this. They do not permit anyone who is not a physician to practice analysis (such practice could result in legal sanctions). All that remains, therefore, is pedagogic analytical work." Ibid., p. 13.

121 Max Eitingon was the first president of the Palestine Psychoanalytic Society, from 1934 (the year of its registration) until 1943. Throughout this period he served as director of the Psychoanalytic Institute in Jerusalem. Moshe Wulff replaced him as president, from 1943 to 1953 (in 1948 the society was renamed and is now known as the Israel Psychoanalytic Society).

122 Killian Bluhm. "A Case of Depression" in "Palestine Psycho-Analytic Society", in *International Journal of Psycho-Analysis*, vol. XV, 1934, p. 532.

123 Letter from Freud to Eitingon, 27 May 1934, and letter from Eitingon to Freud, 21 July 1934, in Sigmund Freud – Max Eitingon, *Correspondance, 1906-1939*, p. 812.

124 "Bulletin de l'Association Internationale de psychanalyse. Conclusion du XIIIe Congrès International de psychanalyse, Assemblée Générale de la Commission Internationale de l'Enseignement, Lucerne, 30 août 1934," *Revue française de psychanalyse*, no. 3, 1935, pp. 520-524.

125 As noted, Dorian Feigenbaum had participated in the Salzburg Congress in 1924.

126 The original German term is "Heilpädagogik," which has no precise equivalent in English. It may be compared to pediatrics or child psychiatry (after World War II). Today it is perceived as a synonym of sorts for the term "Sonderpädagogik" (special education).

127 Max Eitingon, 28 August 1934, Israel State Archives, Eitingon files, P-4/2969 75.52/1-4.

128 "Bulletin de l'Association psychoanalytique international," in *Revue française de psychanalyse*, no. 3, 1935, p. 534.

129 Letter from Eitingon to Freud, 14 October 1934, in Sigmund Freud – Max Eitingon, *Correspondance,* p. 814.

130 Religious and conservative population groups tended to make greater use of the services of Fishel Schneeurson, Enzo Buonaventura, and other psychologists and pedagogues trained in academic psychology.

131 This remained the only psychoanalytic institute in Palestine until the inauguration of the institute in Tel Aviv in 1938.

132 Letter from Moshe Wulff to Erich Gumbel, 9 September 1933, in Gumbel, *My Life with Psychoanalysis*, p. 15.

133 "Bulletin de l'Association psychoanalytique international," in *Revue française de psychanalyse*, no. 3, 1935, p. 534.

134 In 1948, during the War of Independence, a shell landed on the roof of the Institute, causing severe damage to its structure and suspending its operation. The repairs, which were very costly, were funded by membership dues and a donation from Anna Smeliansky. In 1955 the Institute relocated to 13 Disraeli Street, in the neighborhood of Talbieh, where it still stands today. Erich Gumbel, *My Life with Psychoanalysis*, p. 43.

135 Ibid., p. 34.

136 Ibid., p. 16.

137 The Jerusalem Psychoanalytic Institute signed an agreement with the Histadrut Health Fund stipulating that it would provide treatment for immigrant children referred to it by the Youth Aliyah project.

138 Ilja Schalit, "The Psychoanalytic Society in Palestine/Eretz Israel" and Margareth Brandt, "Sieben Jahre Jerusalemer Psychoanalytisches," typewritten manuscript, *Die Chewrah Psychoanalytith B'Eretz Israel gratuliert ihrem Präsidenten zum sechzigsten Geburtstag,* coll., dactyl., Chewrah psychoanalytith b'Eretz Israel, 1941, National Library of the Hebrew University, Jerusalem, and Freud Museum, London.

139 Margareth Brandt, "The First Decade of the Palestine Psychoanalytic Institute," in *Max Eitingon in Memoriam,* pp. 268-273. The reports, organized by year and detailing the number of patients seen by each analyst, their pathology, the membership list, and more, are located in the Max Eitingon collection of the Israel State Archives (P-7/2971.72.52; P-12/2973).

140 "Deutschen-Allijah und Gesundheitsfüsorge, Jerusalem, 12 August 1933," Central Zionist Archives, "Association of German Immigrants," J14/31.

141 Schalit, "The Psychoanalytic Society in Palestine."

142 Ibid. See also Erich Gumbel, *My Life with Psychoanalysis,* p. 17.

143 I was unable to ascertain the trial's starting date or additional details.

144 Letter from Eitingon to Freud, 19 December 1938, in Sigmund Freud – Max Eitingon, *Correspondance, 1906 -1939,* p. 855.

145 For additional information, see Isabella Ginor, Gideon Remez, "Her Son, the Atomic Scientist: Mirra Birens, Yuli Khariton, and Max Eitingon's Services for the Soviets," in *Journal of Modern Jewish Studies,* vol. 11, no. 1, March 2102, pp. 35-55.

146 Letter from Eitingon to Freud, 22 November 1938, in Sigmund Freud – Max Eitingon, *Correspondance, 1906 -1939,* p. 850.

147 Letter from Eitingon to Freud, 12 December 1938, ibid., p. 853.

148 Like other Jewish intellectuals, Mikhoels was suspected of being a "Zionist agent" and was assassinated under Stalin's orders shortly after the war. See Arkady Vaksberg, *Stalin Against the Jews* (New York: Alfred A. Knopf, 1994), p. 213.

149 Arnold Zweig, "Die Liga V," in *Der Briefwechsel zwischen Louis Fürnberg und Arnold Zweig, Dokumente einer Freunschaft* (Berlin: Aufbau-Verlag, 1978), pp. 245-249. I am grateful to Dr. Alexander Zeidel for bringing this text to my attention.

150 In order to reconstruct this puzzle, and in the absence of sufficient documents, I had to deduce a number of inferences based on clues I was able to glean here and there.

151 After the British-Soviet alliance was sealed in 1941, the Mandatory government decided to grant legal status to the PCP. On the history of this party, see Shmuel Dotan, *Adumim: HaKomunistim BeEretz Israel* [Reds in Palestine] (Kfar Saba: Shivna HaSofer, 1996) [Hebrew].

152 The alliance between these two military superpowers was intended to thwart a potential German advance towards Asia, in the event that German armed forces were able to reach the Middle East through Palestine. In forging this alliance with the Soviet Union, Britain also sought to ensure that the Soviets' participation in the war would not threaten its hegemony over the Middle East. See Lothar Kettenacker, "The Anglo-Saxon Alliance and the Problem of Germany, 1941-1945," in *Journal of Contemporary History,* vol. 17, 1982, pp. 453-458.

153 Letter dated 15 March 1942, addressed to members of League V and signed by Dr. Mendelberg on behalf of the Council to Aid the USSR in Her War against Fascism. The

name Moshe Wulff (Woolf) appears among the membership list of this committee. The Pinhas Lavon Institute for Labour Movement Research,"League V," W-407-1-20.

154 Ruth Lubitsch, *Korot Shel Yedidut* [The History of a Friendship, translated by publisher as "The Movement of Friendship Israel-U.R.S.S. - 40 Years"], Tel Aviv: Israel-USSR Friendship Movement, 1984), p. 19 [Hebrew].

155 Arnold Zweig, "Der Liga V," p. 17.

156 Ibid., p. 397 ff.

157 "League V for Soviet Russia," Jerusalem, 15 February 1943, Stifung Archiv der Akademie der Künste, Berlin, file 20483.

158 Aryeh Feigenbaum, "Ambulances. Palestine's Tribute to USRR," *Palestine Post*, 7 April 1943.

159 *Orient*, an independent weekly edited by Arnold Zweig and Wolfgang Yourgrau, reprinted in *Exilliteratur*, vol. 14, ed. Hans-Albert Walter and Werner Berthold (Hildesheim: Gerstenberg Verlag, 1982), p. XV. This reprint was published in the former German Democratic Republic as part of a single volume containing all the issues of *Orient*, including an introduction and commentary.

160 Harry Obermayer, "Uber Massenpsychologie," *Orient*, no. 20, 14 August 1942, pp. 14-17.

161 Max Marcuse (Marcuza), "Sexualprobleme und Tradition," *Orient*, no. 4, 24 April 1942, pp. 9-11; "Charakter und Gericht", ibid, no. 7, 24 April 1942, pp. 7-9.

162 Ruth Lubitsch, The History of a Friendship, p. 49.

163 Letter from Hamdy Abdel Hamid to Josef Friedjung, 22 April 1943, Israel State Archives, Eitingon files, P-5/2974. 72-52/1-70.

164 Aside from the many works of Freud that he had already read (a long list that we shall not enumerate), Abdel Hamid claimed that he had also read works by Franz Alexander, Chifford Alle, Martin Peck, David Forsyth, Hans von Hattingberg, and Edward Glover. Ibid.

165 Letters from Eitingon to Zweig, 19 and 22 December 1942, Stifung Archiv der Akademie der Künste, Berlin, Arnold Zweig, 6643b, 6638. Eitingon's health began to deteriorate in December 1942. He was confined to bedrest for four weeks, followed by a long period of recuperation under the care of Dr. Julius Kleeberg.

166 Letter from Eitingon to Friedjung, 13 July 1943; private archives of Raphael Friedjung.

167 Ziwar returned to Egypt from Europe with the outbreak of World War II, after completing his studies and undergoing analysis with René Laforgue in Paris. His favorite book was Freud's *The Psychopathology of Everyday Life*, which he taught in Arabic to his students using examples from the Arabic language. After the war he returned to France, where he studied psychosomatic medicine, working closely with the Parisian Psychoanalytic Society. He then returned to Egypt, and in 1953 took an important position at the University of Alexandria. As a central figure in the world of psychology in Egypt, he had a great influence on his students, including Moustapha Safouan, the well-known disciple of Jacques Lacan. See Moustapha Safouan, *La psychanalyse. Science, thérapie – et cause* (Vincennes: Thierry Marchaisse, 2013), pp. 300, 303, 305, 310.

168 Letter from Ziwar to the "Director of the Psychoanalytic Society," 27 May 1943, Israel State Archives, Eitingon files, P-5/2974.72-52/1-70.

169 Letter from Ziwar to Eitingon, 23 August 1943, Israel State Archives, Eitingon files, P-1/2972.

170 Letter from Schalit to Ziwar, 19 September 1943, Israel State Archives, Eitingon files, P-1/2972.

171 This book cannot address all the developments covered in my dissertation, which explores the relationship between psychoanalysis and other disciplines before the founding of Israel. Nonetheless, I have endeavored to provide a general overview of the relationship between psychoanalysis and some of these disciplines insofar as it relates to the issues that concern us.

172 Heinz Winnik, "Milestones in the Development of Psychoanalysis in Israel," *Israel Annals of Psychiatry and Related Disciplines*, vol. 15, no. 1, March 1977, p. 85-91.

173 Letter from Dizengoff to the governor of the Negev District in Jaffa, 21 September 1927, Tel Aviv Municipal Archives, file aleph-gimel 04-4737. Unfortunately, it was not possible to locate additional documents indicating the measures Eder took to raise the necessary funds abroad.

174 Letter from Dr. Leibowich to the governor of the Negev District in Jaffa, 7 October 1927, ibid.

175 Letter from Dr. Leibowich to the governor of the Negev District in Jaffa, 7 October 1927, ibid.

176 See the declaration that appears among the photographs in this volume.

177 Lipman Halpern, "Neurologie and Psychiatry in Palestine," in *American Journal of Psychiatry*, vol. 100, 1944, p. 777.

178 Letter from Dizengoff to Sa'adia Shoshani and L. Esterman of the Commission for the Mentally Ill, 25 July 1933, Tel Aviv Municipal Archives, file 04-7735.

179 Letter from Rokach to Stricker, 4 October 1933, Tel Aviv Municipal Archives, file 4-4735 [German].

NOTES TO CHAPTER 4

180 Ernest Jones, La Vie et l'œuvre de Sigmund Freud, vol. III, Les Dernières années (1919-1939) (Paris: PUF, 1969), pp. 252-253.

181 Letter from Eitingon to Freud, 26 March 1938, Sigmund Freud – Max Eitingon, *Correspondance*, 1906-1939, pp. 842-843.

182 Letter from Jones to Eitingon, 13 May 1938, Israel State Archives, Eitingon files, P/2974.72.52/1-69.

183 Three of Freud's sisters, Marie, Pauline, and Adolfine, perished in the gas chambers. See Élisabeth Roudinesco, Michel Plon, "Freud Schlomo Sigmund, dit Sigmund (1856-1939)," in *Dictionnaire de la psychanalyse*, (Paris: Fayard, 1997), pp. 351-360.

184 Jones, La Vie et l'œuvre de Sigmund Freud, pp. 257-258.

185 Letter from Jones to Anna Freud, 20 April 1938, Archives of the British Psychoanalytic Society (ABPS), CFF/F01/04.

186 The Mandate authorities issued visas termed "capitalist" or "category A" for Jewish entry to Palestine. After the Arab nationalist riots of 1936, the British government imposed severe restrictions on Jewish immigration, precisely during this dramatic historical period when immigration was most vital to Jews. Anyone who wanted to immigrate, beyond the quota, had to demonstrate a capital of at least £1,000. See Walter Laqueur, *Histoire du sionisme*, vol. II, (Paris: Gallimard, 1994), pp. 733-741.

187 Letter from Jones to Eitingon, 6 April 1938, Israel State Archives, Eitingon files, P/2974.72.52/1-69.

188 Letter from Jones to Eitingon, 21 April 1938, Ibid.

189 Letter from Eitingon to E. Mills (Commissioner for Migration and Statistics), 17 May 1938, Israel State Archives, Eitingon files, 4/2974/72.52/1-69.

190 Letter from Jones to Anna Freud, 20 April 1938, ABPS, CFF/F10/04.

191 Other analysts and candidate members of the Vienna Psychoanalytic Society, who received assistance in fleeing Austria from Anna Freud, Ernest Jones, Marie Bonaparte, Max Eitingon, and Willi Hoffer, also sought to reach the shores of Palestine. Yet after a brief stay they left for other destinations. Their names are not mentioned here because – unlike the "migrant" psychoanalysts arriving mainly from Germany after 1933 – they did not take an active part in the Palestine Psychoanalytic Association.

192 Although today the terms "applied psychoanalysis" and "applications of psychoanalysis" are subject to dispute, or even regarded as nonsensical, in Freud's day psychoanalysts used them quite readily.

193 Letter from Anna Freud to Eitingon, 28 June 1938, Library of Congress Archives, Anna Freud Papers.

194 Letter from Eitingon to members of the Palestine Psychoanalytic Society, 19 October 1938, Israel State Archives, Eitingon papers, P-3/2970.

195 Hellmuth Gröger, "Joseph Karl Friedjung," Vertriebene Vernunft II. *Emigration und Exil österreicshischer Wissenschaft. Jugend und Volk*, 1988, pp. 819-826.

196 Elke Mühlleitner, "Josef Karl Friedjung," in *Biographisches Lexikon der Psychoanalyse. Die Mitglieder der Psychologischen Mittwoch-Gesellschaft und der Wiener Psychoanalytischen Vereinigung, 1902-1938*, (Tübingen: Diskord, 1992), pp. 109-110.

197 Ibid., p. 109.

198 Rather than list Friedjung's many and varied works in the field of pediatrics, we refer the reader to the following indispensable index: Alexander Grinstein, "Friedjung, Josef K.," in *The Index of Psychoanalytic Writings*, vol. II (New York: International Universities Press, 1957), pp. 686-690.

199 Hellmuth Gröger, "Joseph Karl Friedjung," p. 821.

200 Letter of Testament of Josef Karl Friedjung, Haifa, 16 February 1946, addressed to his socialist comrades, private archives of Raphaël Friedjung.

201 Mühlleitner, "Josef Karl Friedjung," p. 109.

202 Marriage license of Friedjung, private archives of Raphaël Friedjung.

203 Shmuel Golan, "LeZikhro Shel Doctor Friedjung" [In Memory of Dr. Friedjung], *Al HaMishmar*, 13 May 1947, p. 8 [Hebrew].

204 Josef Friedjung, "HaKhinukh Likrat HaSotzialism" [Education towards Socialism], *Ofakim*, no. 1, 1946, pp. 20-26 [Hebrew].

205 Élisabeth Roudinesco, Michel Plon, "Edouard Hitschmann (1871-1957)," in *Dictionnaire de la psychanalyse*, pp. 441-442.

206 *Les Premiers psychanalystes. Minutes de la Société psychanalytique de Vienne* (Paris: Gallimard, 1976), vol. II, p. 271 ff.

207 Ibid. See also Josef Friedjung, *Die Feihlerzeihung in der Pathologie des Kindes* (Wien: Verlag von Julius Springer, 1931). His best-known books include *Erlebte Kinderheilkunde*, 1919; *Die kindliche Sexualität und ihre Bedeutung für Erziehung und ärzliche Praxis*, 1923; and *Die geschliechtliche Aufklärung im Erziehungswerke*, 1926.

208 Mühlleitner, "Josef Karl Friedjung," p. 110.

209 Ibid.

210 Mendel Singer, *'Arba'at Pirkei Lekakh MiToldot Tnu'at HaPo'alim BeAustria* [Four Lessons Learned from the History of the Austrian Labor Movement] (Haifa: Mo'etzet Po'alei Haifa, 1975), p. 122 [Hebrew].

211 "Zeugnis-Bundes Polizeidirektion in Wien," 1938, private archives of Raphaël Friedjung.

212 Letter from John Mayer to the US Consul in Vienna, 29 June 1938, private archives of Raphaël Friedjung. In his letter, Mayer (a wealthy American businessman) requested permission for Friedjung to enter the United States, describing him as a great contributor in the service of science whose presence in the US would benefit the country.

213 As noted, Szold was a member of League V, along with Friedjung, Eitingon, Wulff, Zweig, Magnes, and Buber.

214 Henrietta Szold had planned to leave Palestine and return to the United States for good. But with Hitler's rise to power she decided to postpone her departure and devote herself entirely to helping Jewish children and adolescents in Europe escape the Nazi threat and flee to Palestine, which she never ended up leaving. Through her organization, thousands of children from Europe were able to escape the death camps and immigrate to Palestine. For more details on the origins of Aliyat Hano'ar, see Recha Freier, "The Beginnings of Youth Aliyah," undated, Central Zionist Archives, A 125/105.

215 As during the period following World War I, Palestine during the 1930s had many abandoned children who wandered the streets, engaged in delinquency, or fell victim to sexual slavery. Henrietta Szold provided care for these children, immigrants as well as non-immigrants. The children, generally from Jewish families with roots in Persia, Yemen, and other Middle Eastern countries, lacked the benefit of institutional care or schooling.

216 Henrietta Szold, "MiVa'adat HaPe'ula" [From the Actions Committee], *HaShomer HaTza'ir*, May 1935, pp. 26-28 [Hebrew].

217 Letters from Marie Bonaparte to Anna Freud, December 30, 1938, and January 3, 1939, Library of Congress Archives, Anna Freud Papers, A 14. Following this visit, Princess Marie Bonaparte, a disciple of Sigmund Freud and pioneer of psychoanalysis in France, returned to Israel in 1962. Regarding these visits and her meetings in Palestine and Israel, see Marie Bonaparte. "Griechische Prinzessin und Shülerin Freuds besucht Israel. Eine Freudian des jüdischen Volkes," *Aufbau*, 26 January 1962, p. 22.

218 Josef Friedjung, "5 Years Psycho-Analytical Educational Work among Jewish Youth Immigrants," in *Max Eitingon in Memoriam*, Israel Psycho-Analytic Society, 1950, pp. 256-267.

219 Singer, Four Lessons Learned from the History of the Austrian Labor Movement, p. 162.

220 Friedjung, "Five Years Psycho-Analytical Educational Work," p. 256.

221 Shmuel Golan, "LeZichro Shel Yosef Friedjung" [In Memory of Josef Friedjung], *Al HaMishmar*, 13 May 1946, p. 8 [Hebrew].

222 Friedjung, "Five Years Psycho-Analytical Educational Work, " p. 258.

223 Ibid.

224 See letter from Shmuel Golan to Hanoch Reinhold of the Jewish Agency, Central Bureau for the Settlement of German Jews, 7 September 1941, and letter from David Omiansky to Shmuel Golan, 24 December 1941 (in which Golan relates a conversation with Henrietta Szold regarding Friedjung), Kibbutz Mishmar HaEmek Archives, Golan G/3/9.

225 Golan, "In Memory of Joseph Friedjung."

226 Friedjung, "Five Years Psycho-Analytical Educational Work," p. 259.

227 Ibid.

228 Ibid., p. 261.

229 Ibid.

230 Ibid.

231 Ibid., pp. 263-264.

232 Ibid., p. 267.

233 Josef Friedjung, "… un der 'Aufbau' des Menschen?" *Orient*, vol. III, 24 April 1942, p. 5.

234 Ibid.

235 Ibid., pp. 6-7.

236 Josef Friedjung, "Reform der Erziehung?" *Orient*, vol. III, No. 8, 22 May 1942, p. 8.

237 Elke Mühlleitner, "Berta Grünspan," in *Biographisches Lexikon der Psychoanalyse. Die Mitglieder der Psychologischen Mittwoch-Gesellschaft und der Wiener Psychoanalytischen Vereinigung 1902-1938* (Tübingen: Diskord, 1992), pp. 125-126.

238 Conversation with Tamar Naveh, 27 October 1997.

239 Ibid.

240 See the remarks by Hanna Adar in *VeAhavata LeNefesh Re'ekha: Dr. Berta (Betty) Grünspan, Rof'a, Doda, Yedida, Adam* [Love Thy Neighbor's Soul: Dr. Berta (Betty) Grünspan, Physician, Aunt, Friend, Human], a collection of eulogies delivered during her funeral and memories of family members, friends, colleagues, students, patients, and neighbors of Berta Grünspan at Kibbutz Yif'at, Merhavia, 1976, p. 9.

241 Ibid.

242 Conversation with Tamar Naveh, 27 October 1997.

243 Mühlleitner, "Berta Grünspan," p. 125.

244 Letter from Eitingon to Schalit, 6 November 1938, Israel State Archives, Eitingon files, P-7/2971.72.52.

245 Remarks by Shmuel Nagler, in Adar, *Love Thy Neighbor's Soul*.

246 Letter from Eitingon to Schalit, 6 November 1938, Israel State Archives, Eitingon files, P-7/2971.72.52.

247 Remarks by Heinrich Zvi Winnik, in Adar, *Love Thy Neighbor's Soul*, p. 40.

248 Remarks by Shmuel Nagler, in Adar, *Love Thy Neighbor's Soul*, p .49.

249 Letter from Grünspan to Golan, 26 October 1941, Kibbutz Mishmar HaEmek Archives, G/3/9/.

250 Remarks by Rachel Manor, in Adar, *Love Thy Neighbor's Soul*, p. 50.

251 Ibid., p. 41.

252 Ibid., p. 50.

253 Ibid.

254 Victor Magal, "BeShnoteiha HaAkhronot KeRof'a U-KeHola," [Her Final Years as a Physician and a Patient], in Adar, *Love Thy Neighbor's Soul*, p. 33.

255 Ibid., p. 22.

256 Conversation with Tamar Naveh, 27 October 1997.

257 Letter from Nagler to Eitingon, 29 January 1939, Israel State Archives, Eitingon files, P-1/2970.

258 Shmuel Nagler, "Research in Children's Games, Its Methods and Results" [originally titled "Methoden und Ergebnisse der Kinderspielforschung"], lecture of 14 March 1941; "Analytisch padagogischeArbeit an verwahrlosten Kindern (Darstellung zweier Falle)," lecture of 27 December 1941, *International Journal of Psycho-Analysis*, vol. XXV, Israel State Archives, Eitingon files, P-8/2971 72.52. Letter from Eitingon to Schalit, 14 December 1941, Israel State Archives, Eitingon files, P-8/2971 72.52.

259 Letter from Anna Freud to Fanny Lowtzky, 4 September 1946, Library of Congress Archives, Anna Freud Papers, No. 60.

260 On the life and work of Shmuel Nagler, see Shmuel Nager, *Ketavim* [Writings] (texts by Nagler and testimonies collected by Miriam Rick), (Kfar Bialik: Ach, 1998) [Hebrew].

261 Shmuel Nagler, "Al Avodato Shel HaHug HaAnalyti-Pedagogi" [On the Work of the Analytic-Pedagogic Seminar], *Ofakim*, no. 6 (1948), pp. 61-64 [Hebrew].

262 Ibid., p. 61.

263 The texts, according to Nagler, were "Analysis of a Phobia in a Five-Year-Old Boy" (Little Hans), 1909; "On Narcissism: An Introduction," 1914; "The Ego and the Id," 1923, ibid.

264 Nagler, "On the Work of the Analytic-Pedagogic Seminar," p. 61.

265 Sigmund Freud, *Three Essays on the Theory of Sexuality*, trans. James Strachey (New York: Basic Books, 1962), originally published as *Drei Abhandlungen zur Sexualtheorie*, (Frankfurt am Main: Fischer, 1905).

266 Nagler, "On the Work of the Analytic-Pedagogic Seminar," p. 62.

267 Nagler, *Writings*.

268 Nagler, "On the Work of the Analytic-Pedagogic Seminar," p. 62.

269 Ibid., pp. 63-64.

270 Ibid.

271 Ibid., p. 64

272 Ibid., p. 63.

NOTES TO CHAPTER 5

273 Walter Laqueur, *Histoire du sionisme*, vol. I (Paris: Gallimard, 1973), pp. 436-437.

274 Elkana Margalit, *HaShomer HaTza'ir: MiEdat Ne'urim LeMarxism Mahapkhani (1913-1936)*[HaShomer HaTza'ir: From Youth Culture to Revolutionary Marxism, 1913-1936] (Tel Aviv: HaKibbutz HaMeuchad, 1971; ninth edition, 1985), p. 19 [Hebrew].

275 Margalit, *HaShomer HaTza'ir*, p. 34.

276 See Shlomo Yitzhaki, "Al Gustav Gyneken" [On Gustav Wyneken], *HaKhinukh HaMeshutaf* 90, October 1976, pp. 47-55 [Hebrew].

277 Gustav Wyneken, *Schule und Jugendkultur* (Iena: Dierich Verlag, 1913), cited in Yitzhaki, "On Gustav Wyneken," p. 48.

278 Yitzhaki, "On Gustav Wyneken," p. 48.

279 Ibid.

280 At Freud's recommendation, Bernfeld joined the faculty of the Berlin Psychoanalytic Institute in 1925.

281 Peter Paret, "Sysiphos und sein Author. Eine Einführung," in Karl Fallend and Johannes Reichmayer (eds.), *Siegfried Bernfeld oder die Genzen des Psychoanalyse. Materialism zu Leben und Werk* (Basel-Frankfurt: Nexus/Stœrmfeld, 1992), p. 16.

282 Yitzhaki, "On Gustav Wyneken," p. 48.

283 Siegfried Bernfeld, *Das jüdische Volk und seine Jugend* (Vienna, Berlin, Leipzig: R. Löwit, 1919). Three decades later, a Hebrew translation appeared: Siegfried Bernfeld, HaAm VeHaNo'ar [The People and the Youth], trans. Edna Kornfeld, afterword by Zvi Sohar (Merhavia: Sifriat Poalim and Shvilei HaKhinukh, 1948).

284 Yitzhaki, "On Gustav Wyneken," pp. 56-57.

285 YIVO Institute for Jewish Research, New York, Bernfeld collection, Series 4/25/152965.

286 Willi Hoffer, "Siegfried Bernfeld and 'Jerubaal'," in *Leo Baeck Year Book*, vol. X, 1965, p. 158.

287 YIVO, Bernfeld collection, Series 4/22/153003.

288 For further information, see YIVO Series 4/22/153003, 4/22/152965, 6/22/155942.

289 Bernfeld, *The People and the Youth*, p. 12; see note on page 223.

290 Ibid.

291 Rudolf Ekstein, "Siegfried Bernfeld," in *Psychoanalytic Pionneers* (New York: Basic Books, 1966), p. 427.

292 Letter from Meir Ya'ari, 27 March 1921, cited in Matityahu Mintz, *Havlei Ne'urim: HaTnu'a HaShomrit, 1911-1921* [Pangs of Youth: The Shomrim Movement, 1911-1921] (Jerusalem: HaSifria HaZionit, 1995), Appendices, p. 404 [Hebrew].

293 Siegfried Bernfeld, "Die Kriegwaisen," *Der Jude*, no. 2, 1916, pp. 269-271.

294 Hoffer, "Siegfried Bernfeld and 'Jerubaal'," in *Leo Baeck Year Book*, pp. 150-167; Peter Paret, "Sysiphos und sein Author," p. 19.

295 Siegfried Bernfeld, *Kinderhein Baumgarten: Bericht über einen ernsthaften Versuch mit nueuer Erziehung* (Berlin: Jüdischer Verlag, 1921), p. 34.

296 Annette Koch, "Siegfried Bernfeld Kinderheim Baumgarten. Vorassetzungen jüdischer Erziehung um 1920"(PhD diss., University of Hamburg, 1974), p. 124.

297 Yitzhaki, , "On Gustav Wyneken," p. 56.

298 See Bernfeld's articles "The Hidden Languages and Codes Used by Children" and "Language Development among Children Who Grew up in Yiddish and Hebrew Culture" (translated titles), in "Anweisungen zur Sammlung von Material," *Korrepsondenzblatt der Jüdischen Institutes für Jugendforschung und Erziehung*, no. 7, 1922, pp. 1-5; no. 8, pp. 1-5.

299 Koch, "Siegfried Bernfeld Kinderheim Baumgarten," p. 173.

300 Bernfeld, *Kinderhein Baumgarten*, p. 78.

301 Ibid., p. 73.

302 Siegfried Bernfeld, *Sysiphos oder die Grenzen der Erziehung* (Leipzig and Vienna: Internazionaler psychoanalytischer Verlag, 1925).

303 Hoffer, "Siegfried Bernfeld and 'Jerubaal'," in *Leo Baeck Year Book*, p. 151.

304 Meir Ya'ari, "Yamim VeLelot Me'al HaKineret" [Night and Days over the Kineret], in Meir Ya'ari, *Dyukano Shel Manhig KeAdam Tza'ir, 1897-1929* [Portrait of a Leader as a Young Man: Life Events, 1897-1929] (Merhavia: Sifriat Poalim, 1922), p. 62 [Hebrew].

305 Circular sent by Ya'ari from Beitania Illit to HaShomer HaTza'ir members abroad, partially reprinted in issues *Haszomer,* no. 1 (1921) and no. 1-2 (1922). This text was translated into Hebrew by Yosef Rav and printed in Mintz, *Pangs of Youth*, pp. 375-402.

306 According to a book by Aviva Halamish, Meir Ya'ari, *Biographia Kibbutzit: Hamishim HaShanim HaRishonot, 1894-1947* [A Kibbutz Biography: The First Fifty Years, 1894-1947 (Tel Aviv: Am Oved, 2009) [Hebrew].

307 Ya'ari, *Portrait of a Leader*, p. 31.

308 Meir Ya'ari, *BeMa'avak LeAmal Meshuhrar* [Struggling for Liberated Labor] (Tel Aviv: Am Oved – Tarbut VeKhinukh, 1972), p. 348 [Hebrew].

309 Ibid., p. 349.

310 Ibid.

311 Ya'ari, *Portrait of a Leader*, pp. 37-38.

312 Mintz, *Pangs of Youth*, p. 394.

313 Ibid., p. 245.

314 According to Matityahu Mintz, this letter, written between August and November, was published in the Polish *Haszomer*, no. 1, 1923, pp. 5-6.

315 Mintz, *Pangs of Youth*, p. 388.

316 Ibid., pp. 388-389.

317 Mintz, p. 389.

318 According to Ya'ari, *Portrait of a Leader*, p. 8.

319 Published in the daily *Al HaMishmar*, 8 February 1952, cited in Walter Laqueur, *Histoire du sionisme*, vol. I.

320 Letter from Meir Ya'ari to the leadership of HaShomer HaTza'ir in Lvov between August and November 1919, in Mintz, *Pangs of Youth*, p. 354.

321 Yehudit Dror, sister of Binyamin Dror.

322 Margalit, *HaShomer HaTza'ir*, p. 81.

323 Dorian Feigenbaum, "Palestine," *International Journal of Psycho-Analysis*, vo. X, no. 1, 1924, p. 101.

324 Mintz, *Pangs of Youth*, p. 347.

325 The play, first performed at the Haifa theater in 1976, was very well received.

326 "Al Hashkafat Olam Ahat," [On One Worldview] translation and preface by Israel Cohen, *Gilyonot*, vol. A, no. 3 (1934), pp. 251-268 [Hebrew]. An article under the same title, translated by Shmuel Golan in *HaShomer HaTza'ir* (1936), is cited in "Sifriat Poalim, Mikhtav LaMa'arekhet" [Sifriat Poalim, Letter to the Editor], *HaPo'el HaTza'ir*, no. 36, 20 May 1943), p. 12, and reprinted in Sigmund Freud, *Culture and Religion*, ed. Zvi Sohar (Merhavia: Sifriat Poalim, 1943) [Hebrew].

327 Regarding the debate between psychoanalysis and Marxism in Jewish Palestine, and specifically in HaShomer HaTza'ir, see Guido Liebermann, "Freudisme *versus* marxisme," chap. 1 in *La psychanalyse à l'épreuve du kibboutz*, part III "Entre freudisme et marxisme" (Paris: CampagnePremière/, 2014), p. 219.

NOTES TO CHAPTER 6

328 Shimon Reshef, *Khinukh Hadash BeEretz Israel, 1915-1929* [New Education in Eretz Israel, 1915-1929] (Merhavia: Sifriat Poalim, 1985), p. 11 [Hebrew].

329 Yehuda Ron-Polani, "Darko Shel Halutz Sotzial Pedagog" [The Way of a Pioneer Socialist Pedagogue], *Orim* vol. 12, no. 3, 1957, pp. 193-196 [Hebrew].

330 Ibid., p. 195.

331 Yehuda Ron-Polani, *HaNisayon HaRishon* [The First Experience] (Tel Aviv: Abouka, 1961), p. 100 [Hebrew].

332 Ernst Meumann (1862-1915) was a German psychologist from the School of Experimental Psychology and Pedagogy. He worked at the Institute of Experimental Psychology in Leipzig, was a disciple of Wundt, and worked as well with William Stern at the Colonial Institute in Hamburg.

333 Ron-Polani, *The First Experience*, pp. 100-101.

334 Ibid.

335 Bernfeld, *Kinderheim Baumgarten*.

336 Ron-Polani, *The First Experience*, p. 170.

337 Zeev Sternhell, *Binyan Uma O Tikun Hevra? Leumiyut Ve Sotzialism BeTnu'at HaAvodah HaIsraelit, 1904-1940* [Building a Nation or Correcting Society? Nationalism and Socialism in the Israeli Labor Movement, 1904-1940] (Tel Aviv: Am Oved, 1995, third printing, 1996), p. 263 [Hebrew].

338 Reshef, *New Education*, pp. 115-116.

339 Letter from Bernfeld to Bergmann, 22 September 1920, National Library, Archives Department, Hugo Bergmann collection.

340 Sternhell, *Building a Nation or Correcting Society?*, p. 312.

341 Letter from Idelsohn to Ron-Polani, 27 August 1925, Archives of Jewish Education in Israel and the Diaspora, Tel Aviv University.

342 Reshef, *New Education*, pp. 139-140.

343 David Idelsohn, *Hevrat HaYeladim BeBeit Alpha: Nisayon LeHanekh Yeladim LeKhinukh Hevrati Al Yedei Arba Shnot HaKiyum HaRishonot, 1926-1929* [The Children's Society at Beit: An Experiment in Social Childhood Education Based on the First Four Years, 1926-1929], typewritten manuscript, Archives of Jewish Education in Israel and the Diaspora, Tel Aviv University, Ron-Polani files, 5.184/3.

344 Milek Goldschein (Shmuel "Milek" Golan), "Die Kinderheinde ‚Beit Alpha'," *Das Werlende Zeitalter, Berlin*, no. 2, February 1929, pp. 99-112.

345 Idelsohn, *The Children's Society*, p. 4.

346 Bernfeld, *The People and the Youth*, pp. 14-16.

347 Ibid., p. 4.

348 David Idelsohn, "Al Avodati Bein HaYeladim YeHaYeladot" [My Work with Boys and Girls], in *The Children's Society*, p. 22.

349 Idelsohn, *The Children's Society*, pp. 5, 16.

350 Ibid., p. 6.

351 Ibid., p. 34.

352 Idelsohn, *The Children's Society*, p. 9.

353 Reshef, *New Education*, p. 160.

354 See Shmuel Dotan, *Adumim be'Eretz Israel* [Reds in Palestine] (Kfar Saba: Shivna HaSofer Publishers, 1996) [Hebrew].

355 During Passover (1927), members of four kibbutzim – Ma'abarot, Merhavia, Mishmar HaEmek, and Ein Shomer – gathered in a shack on the kibbutz based at Beit Galim and decided to establish a pioneering settlement network: HaKibbutz HaArtzi – HaShomer HaTza'ir. See David Zayit, *Yisud HaKibbitz HaArtzi, Haifa, 1-3 April 1927* [The Founding of HaKibbutz HaArtzi, Haifa, 1-3 April 1927] (Giv'at Haviva: Mekorot Publishing – Studies on HaShomer HaTza'ir, 1987) [Hebrew].

356 David Idelsohn, "Khinukh HaNo'ar BeBrit HaMo'atzot" [Youth Education in the Soviet Union] *Ofakim*, Warsaw, no. 3, 1932, pp. 127-130, and no. 6, 1933, pp. 275-278. See also David Idelsohn, "Yaldei Hefker BeBrit HaMoatzot" [Abandoned Children in the Soviet Union], ibid., no. 4, pp. 190-192.

NOTES TO CHAPTER 7

357 Ruth Kloocke, "Mosche Wulff (1878-1971). Leben und Werk," *Luzifer Amor: Zeitschrift zur Geschichte der Psychoanalyse*, no. 16, 1998, pp. 87-101.

358 Ibid., p. 89.

359 Cited in *The Standard Edition of the Complete Psychological Works of Sigmund Freud*, vol. XIII (1913-1914), *Totem and Taboo and Other Works* (London: Hogarth, 1955), p. 128.

360 Letter from Sigmund Freud to Carl Jung, 21 March 1912, in *The Freud/Jung Letters: The Correspondence between Sigmund Freud and C. G. Jung*, ed. William McGuire, Bolligen Series XCIV, (Princeton: Princeton University Press, 1974), p. 495.

361 Otto Schmidt (1891-1956), mathematician and director of the state publishing house, husband of Vera. See "Schmidt Vera, née Yanitskaïa (1889-1937)," in Élisabeth Roudinesco and Michel Plon. *Dictionnaire de la psychanalyse* (Paris: Fayard, 1997), pp. 951-953.

362 Ruth Kloocke, *Mosche Wulff. Zur Geschichte der Psychoanalyse in Russland und Israel* (Tübingen: Diskord, 2002), p. 169.

363 Ibid.

364 Roudinesco and Plon, *Dictionnaire de la psychanalyse*, pp. 951-953.

365 Ibid., p. 1103.

366 Letter from Sigmund Freud to Nikolai Ossipow, 23 February 1927, cited in Etkind, *Histoire de la psychanalyse en Russie* (Paris: PUF, 1991), p. 285.

367 Ibid., p. 286.

368 Anna Freud, *Mavo LeTorat HaPsychoanalyza* [Introduction to the Theory of Psychoanalysis] (Jerusalem: Sifriat Hed HaKhinukh, 1931) [Hebrew].

369 David Idelsohn, "Haiyav HaMini'im Shel HaYeled" [Sexuality of the Child], *Hed HaKhinukh*, vol. 15, no. 3, 1933, pp. 81-85; Shmuel Golan, "She'elat HaPsychoanalyza BaYaldut," *Ofakim*, vol. 3, 1932, pp. 109-113 [Hebrew].

370 *Pe'utot* [Infants], collected documents edited by Israel Rivka'i, published by HaVa'ada HaBein-Kibbutzit LeShe'elat HaTipul HaMeshutaf (The Inter-Kibbutz Committee on Collective Childcare), 1935, p. 111 [Hebrew].

371 The course was conducted at Seminar HaKibbutzim, opened by Shmuel Golan in 1933, and it continues to operate to this day in Tel Aviv.

372 Moshe Wulff, *Nefesh HaYeled* [The Soul of the Child] (Merhavia: Sifriat Poalim, vol. 1, 1946; vol. 2, 1949) [Hebrew].

373 Letter from Hedwige Gellner (government inspector for juvenile delinquents) to Shoshana Persitz, 9 October 1933, Tel Aviv Municipal Archives, A/Aleph, 04-2116.

374 David Idelsohn, Memorandum, 22 October 1933, Tel Aviv Municipal Archives, A/Aleph, 04-2116.

375 Letter from Gellner to Persitz, 9 October 1933.

376 David Idelsohn, Report on the Abandoned Children's Club, 2 August 1934, Tel Aviv Municipal Archives, B/Bet, 04-2116.

377 Ibid.

378 Footnote by Idelsohn to his Hebrew translation of August Aichhorn *The Youth and the People*, trans. David Idelsohn, ed. Mordechai Brachyahu (Jerusalem: S. Zack, 1956), p. 12 [Hebrew].

379 Letter from Idelsohn to the British Magistrate, Haifa District, 20 November 1934, Tel Aviv Municipal Archives, G/Gimel, 04-2116.

380 Letter from Idelsohn to W. H. Chinn (Probation Supervisor for the British Mandate Government) 17 March 1936, Tel Aviv Municipal Archives, A/Aleph, 04-2117.

381 In 1935 Idelsohn was appointed probation officer for juvenile delinquents in the Tel Aviv Municipality and the District of Jaffa.

382 David Idelsohn, "HaTipul BaYeled HaMuznah" [Treatment of the Neglected Child], Lecture, 8 June 1936, Archives of Jewish Education in Israel and the Diaspora, Tel Aviv University, p. 1, 5/206/2156.

NOTES TO CHAPTER 8

383 Margalit, *HaShomer HaTza'ir*, p. 145.

384 This took place during the assembly of May 2-3, 1928. Yitzhak Platek, *HaMossad: Beit HaSefer HaRishon Shel HaShomer HaTza'ir BeMishmar HaEmek, 1931-1940* [The Mossad: The First HaShomer HaTza'ir School in Mishmar HaEmek, 1931-1940] (Giv'at Haviva: Yad Tabenkin, 1989), p. 42 [Hebrew].

385 Shmuel Golan, "Keitzad Hitkhalnu" [How We Started], *Al HaMishmar* (Jubilee supplement in honor of Shmuel Golan), 29 November 1963, p. 58 [Hebrew].

386 Report of the General Assembly of Va'ad HaKibbutz HaArtzi, 8 May 1929, intervention by Zvi Sohar, HaShomer HaTza'ir Archives, Education Department, A/Aleph, (1) 1.4.

387 Platek, *The Mossad*, p. 42.

388 Shmuel Golan, "How We Started," p. 58.

389 Introductory brochure, Zvi Sohar Files, pp. 2-8, HaShomer HaTza'ir Archives, Zvi Sohar Collection [Hebrew].

390 Introductory brochure, Zvi Sohar Files, pp. 2-8.

391 Meir Ya'ari, "Tfisatenu HaKhinukhin" [Our Educational Conception] *HaKhinukh HaShomri*, Warsaw, 1927, p. 19 [Hebrew].

392 Yehuda Gothelf, "Idea Khinukhit" [A Conception of Education], *HaKhinukh HaShomri*, Warsaw, 1927, pp. 23-26 [Hebrew].

393 See Henry Near, "Experiment and Survival: The Beginnings of the Kibbutz," *Journal of Contemporary History*, vol. 20, no. 1, 1985, p. 192.

394 Letter from Zvi Sohar in Vienna to the Committee on Education Department Affairs, 22 February 1931, HaShomer HaTza'ir Archives, Zvi Sohar Collection, B/Bet (1) 1.4.

395 Siegfried Bernfeld, "Die heutige Psychologie des Püberät," *Imago*, vol. XIII, no. 1, 1927, pp. 1-56, cited in Zvi Sohar, "Hipus Drakhim" [The Search for the Path], *Ofakim*, no. 3, 1932, p. 106.

396 Sohar, *The Search for the Path*.

397 Ibid.

398 Ibid.

399 Ibid., pp. 107-108.

400 Zvi Sohar, "Sigmund Freud VeHaSotzialism" [Sigmund Freud and Socialism] *Ofakim*, nos. 2-5 1953, p. 125 [Hebrew].

401 Zvi Sohar, Remarks on behalf of the Psychoanalytic and Psychiatric Society at memorial event for Professor Moshe Wulff, typewritten manuscript, 1971, HaShomer HaTza'ir Archives, Zvi Sohar Collection, (4) 7.13 .95 [Hebrew].

402 Letter from Zvi Sohar to Eliezer HaCohen, 30 March 1930, HaShomer HaTza'ir Archives, Zvi Sohar Collection (8) 1.13.95.

403 Letter from Zvi Sohar to Paul Federn, 17 September 1930, HaShomer HaTza'ir Archives, Zvi Sohar Collection H (8).1.13.95.

404 The first issue of *Ofakim* evidently appeared in the summer of 1932, but unfortunately not a single copy could be found.

405 August Aichhorn, "Khinukh Anashim Dissotziali'im" [The Education of Dissocial People] *Ofakim*, no. 3, 1932-1933, pp. 4-10 [Hebrew].

406 Sigmund Freud, *Hayai VePo'alai* [My Life and Work], trans. Shmuel Golan and Zvi Sohar (Merhavia: Sifriat Poalim, 1947) [Hebrew].

407 Yona Golan confirmed this in a conversation on August 16, 1999.

408 Letter from Shmuel Golan to Yona Golan, 26 July 1931, HaShomer HaTza'ir Archives, Shmuel Golan, (1) 1.1-95.

409 Letter from Shmuel Golan to Yona Golan, undated. This letter was apparently sent around late November 1932 or early January 1933, ibid.

410 Arnold Zweig, *Die Vriendt Kehrt Heim* (1932; Aufbau: Verlag, 1996); see Hebrew edition, trans. Zvi Argon (Tel Aviv: Dvir, 1991). The novel deals with the life and murder of Jacob Israel de Haan.

411 Letter from Shmuel Golan to Yona Golan, undated, HaShomer HaTza'ir Archives, Shmuel Golan, (1) 1.1-95.

412 Bronislaw Malinowski, *The Sexual Life of the Savages in North Western Melanesia* (1927; London: Routledge, 1929).

413 Guido Liebermann, "Les douches partagées" chap. 4 in *La psychanalyse à l'épreuve du kibboutz*, (Paris: CampagnePremière/, 2014), pp. 196-205.

414 Letter from Golan to Sohar, 1 October 1933, HaShomer HaTza'ir Archives, Shmuel Golan, (1) 1.1-95.

NOTES TO CHAPTER 9

415 David Idelsohn, *HaMachon HaPsychoanalyti Al Shem Doctor Eder* [The Eder Psychoanalytic Institute], typewritten manuscript, dated 26 December 1937, Archives of Jewish Education in Israel and the Diaspora, Tel Aviv University, 5/207/2179.

416 Ibid.

417 Dov and Nathalia Pollack (who Hebraized their name to "Peled" after Israel was founded) joined Wulff and Idelsohn in enthusiastically supporting lay analysis (Laienanalyse). Dov was born in Palestine and studied psychology and pedagogy in Vienna and later at the Sorbonne, where he earned his PhD. He underwent analysis with Marie Bonaparte, while Nathalia underwent analysis with René Spitz. Conversation with Noa Melnik (Dov and Nathalia's daughter), 20 May 2001.

418 Idelsohn, *The Eder Psychoanalytic Institute*.

419 Ibid.

420 See Chapter 1, note XX, page XX [[84 in Hebrew]]. The Rorschach test was very popular at the time and psychoanalysts attributed much importance to it.

421 Idelsohn, *The Eder Psychoanalytic Institute*.

422 Ibid.

423 Kloocke, *Mosche Wulff*, p. 36.

424 Notice of a meeting of the Psychoanalytic Group in Tel Aviv, 17 October 1941, and letter from Gershon Barag to Shmuel Golan, 14 October 1941, informing Golan that the meeting would take place at Idelsohn's residence in Tel Aviv. Kibbutz Mishmar HaEmek Archives, Shmuel Golan, G/9/3.

425 Footnote added by Idelsohn to his Hebrew translation of Aichhorn, *Neglected Youth*, p. 121.

NOTES TO CHAPTER 10

426 The reader can find a complete biography and bibliography of Fanny Lowtzky in Nina Bakman, "Fanny Lowtzky (1873-1965): eine Pionierin der psychoanalytischen Pädagogik in Palästina und Israel," lecture presented at the 31 Symposium der Psychoanalyse, 2-4 March 2018, Berlin. This article is forthcoming in the psychoanalytic history review, *Luzifer-Amor, Zeitschrift zur Geschichte der Psychoanalyse.*

427 The term Pädagogenanalyse ("pedagogue-analyst") was already in use in the Vienna Psychoanalytic Society.

428 Shmuel Nagler, "Al Avodato Shel HaHug HaAnalyti-Pedagogi" [On the Work of the Analytic-Pedagogic Seminar], *Ofakim*, no. 6, 1948, p. 64 [Hebrew].

429 One can find a number of issues of *Hygiena Ruhanit* at the Archives of Jewish Education in Israel and the Diaspora, Tel Aviv University, and at the library of the Faculty of Medicine at Hadassah Hospital in Jerusalem. As with other pre-state publications, it is extremely difficult to access a complete collection. According to Heinz Winnik, the journal was discontinued when Mordechai Brachyahu retired. Heinz Winnik, "Sur l'histoire de la psychanalyse en Israël," in *La Folie. Actes du colloque de Milan* (Paris: 10/18 Union générale d'éditions, 1977), p. 371.

430 Shmuel Nagler, "MeHayei HaMa'ase" [A Life of Doing] *Hygiena Ruhanit*, no. 2, 1944, pp. 4-5 [Hebrew].

431 Erwin Hirsch, "Al Dargot Rishonot Shel Activiyut HaYeled VeYozmato VeAl HaNezek HaNigram Al Yedei Shgi'ot BeKhinukh" [The Early Stages of Activity and Initiative of the Child, and the Damage Caused by Educational Misconceptions], *Ofakim*, nos. 4-5, 1948, pp. 65-79, 209 [Hebrew].

NOTES TO CHAPTER 11

432 Otto Warburg (1859-1938), a professor of botany at the University of Berlin and later at the Hebrew University in Jerusalem, came from a wealthy banking family.

433 Although Britain had occupied Palestine since 1918, it did not receive a mandate from the League of Nations until 1922.

434 Chaim Weizmann, *Masa VeMa'as – Zikhronot Haiyav Shel Nasi Israel* [Autobiography of Chaim Weizmann] (Jerusalem and Tel Aviv: Schocken, 1951), pp. 235-236 [Hebrew].

435 Freud's relationship with Zionism (and his reception in the Zionist world) is beyond the scope of this discussion. It remains a topic for future analysis.

436 Sigmund Freud, "To the Opening of the Hebrew University," *The New Judea*, vol. 1, GW XIV, 27 March 1925, pp. 556-557.

437 Sigmund Freud, *The Future of an Illusion*, trans. W. D. Robson-Scott (London: Hogarth Press, 1928), originally published in German as *Die Zukunft einer Illusion.*

438 See Sigmund Freud, "Obsessive Acts and Religious Practices," in *Collected Papers*, trans. Joan Rivière (London: Hogarth Press and the Institute of Psycho-Analysis, 1948-1950).

439 Sigmund Freud, *Die Frage der Laienanalyse: Unterredungen mit einem Unparteiischen* (Frankfurt am Main: Fischer Verlag, 1926, republished in the compilation *Studienausgabe Ergänzungsband*, 1926), pp. 271-349.

440 See, for example, Fishel Schneeurson, "Drakhim Hadashot LaKhinukh HaSotziali" [New Ways to Social Education], *HaKhinukh*, vol. 7, 1925, pp. 1-11, 22-31; "Gil HaDor HaTza'ir HaIvri" [The Young Generation of Jews], ibid., pp. 38-40 [Hebrew].

441 Letter from Freud to Wulff, 26 June 1932, Library of Congress Archives. In his letter of recommendation, Freud wrote, "The intention of the Zionist Organisation to establish a chair for Psychoanalysis in our University at Jerusalem meets with one of my innermost wishes. I am already acknowledged that I think the choice of Dr. Wulff as representative of our young science a very fortunate one." Letter from Freud to David Baumgardt, 17 December 1932, Manuscripts Section, National Library, Hebrew University.

442 Letter from Eitingon to Freud, 2 November 1933, in Sigmund Freud – Max Eitingon, *Correspondance 1906-1939*, p. 803.

443 Wulff already had teaching experience at the universities of St. Petersburg and Moscow.

444 Letter from van Vriesland to Magnes, 21 October 1933 (typewritten).

445 Letter from Magnes to Freud, 27 November 1933, cited in Milton Rosenbaum, "Freud-Eitingon-Magnes Correspondence," *American Journal of Psychoanalysis*, no. 2, 1954, p. 315.

446 Letter from Freud to Magnes, 5 December 1933, in Rosenbaum, "Freud-Eitingon-Magnes Correspondence," pp. 313-314. Also available at the Jerusalem Municipal Archives, Aryeh Feigenbaum/Psychoanalysis.

447 Alphabetical Register of the Staff of the Hebrew University, dactyl., Jerusalem, 31 July 1940, p. 5, Jerusalem Municipal Archives, Aryeh Feigenbaum, 690/28.

448 Andor Fodor, *Nefesh HaAdam VeHayei HaDat* [The Soul of Man and the Life of Religion] (Tel Aviv: Yavneh, undated) [Hebrew].

449 "It is our honor to invite you to a meeting [to discuss] the question of psychoanalysis at the University. The meeting will take place on Sunday the thirteenth of Shvat (January 29) at 8 p.m. at the residence of Professor A. Fodor. Very Respectfully Yours, A. Even-Ze'ev, on behalf of the Secretariat," invitation to Aryeh Feigenbaum on Hebrew University letterhead, Jerusalem, 26 January 1934, Jerusalem Municipal Archives, Aryeh Feigenbaum/Psychoanalysis.

450 Letter from Eitingon to Freud, 21 July 1934, Sigmund Freud – Max Eitingon, *Correspondance 1906-1939*, p. 813.

451 Aryeh Feigenbaum, "The Medical Faculty in Jerusalem," *Palestine Review*, 5 May 1939, p. 43. Let us recall that thanks to Aryeh Feigenbaum, who invited his brother Dorian to Palestine, during 1921-1923 the physicians of the Jewish Medical Association were able to hear lectures on psychiatry, and Hadassah nurses received training in psychology and psychoanalysis from Dorian.

452 Aryeh Feigenbaum, "The Faculty of Medicine at the Hebrew University of Jerusalem," *Medical Leaves*, New York, vol. V, 1943, p. 101; private archives of Nomi Belsitzmann.

453 Only in 1956 did the Hebrew University appropriately honor Freud with an official tribute. *Atzeret Freud: LeYom Huladeto HaMe'a, 5 June 1956* [Freud Memorial: on the Occasion of His 100th Birthday, 5 June 1956] (Jerusalem: Magnes Press, Hebrew University, 1957), p. 112 [Hebrew].

454 I am grateful to Professor Shmuel Koteck, Director of the Department of the History of Medicine at the faculty of medicine of the Hebrew University for drawing this issue to my attention.

455 Feigenbaum, "The Faculty of Medicine at the Hebrew University of Jerusalem," pp. 82-106. The article as published does not include the critical remarks about religious authorities.

456 Gregory Zilboorg, "Psychology and Culture, in *Psychoanalytic Quarterly*, vol. XI, 1942, cited in Feigenbaum, "The Faculty of Medicine at the Hebrew University of Jerusalem," p. 105.

457 Ibid., p. 30.

458 The Commission on Medical Psychology, 28 May 1946, minutes of meeting, (in attendance: Buonaventura, Heilpern, Feigenbaum, Ben-David), Jerusalem Municipal Archives, Aryeh Feigenbaum/Psychoanalysis.

NOTES TO CHAPTER 12

459 They were preceded by Eliezer Ben-Yehuda, the man responsible for reviving Hebrew as a spoken language in Palestine during the late nineteenth and early twentieth centuries.

460 On April 1, 1925, at the opening ceremony of the Hebrew University, Lord Balfour, Britain's Foreign Minister, described Freud as one of the great intellectuals of modern thought, alongside Einstein and Bergson – three representatives of the "Jewish genius."

461 Sigmund Freud, "HaHitnagduyot LePsychoanalyza" [The Resistances to Psycho-Analysis], trans. Yohanan Tversky, *HaDo'ar*, 12 November 1926, pp. 20-21, and 19 November 1926, pp. 38-39 [Hebrew], originally published in French as "Les résistances à la psychanalyse," *Revue Juive*, no. 2, 15 March 1925, pp. 209-219, and soon thereafter in German as "Die Widerstände gegen die Psychoanalyse," *Imago*, vol. 11, no. 3, 1925 pp. 222-233.

462 Sigmund Freud, *Psychologia Shel HaHamon VeHaAnalyza Shel HaAni* [Group Psychology and Analysis of the Ego], vol. I, trans. Judah Dwossis (Jerusalem: Sifriat Hed HaKhinukh, 1928), originally published in German as "Massenpsychologie un Ich-Analyse," *Studienausgabe* IX, 1921, pp, 61, 65-134.

463 Freud's text was part of a large collection of books on pedagogy and psychology intended for teachers and parents, which were translated into Hebrew and published by Otzar HaMoreh, the publishing house of Histadrut HaMorim BeEretz Israel. See "Sfarim Pedagogi'im LeHorim VeLeMorim" [Pedagogic Books for Parents and Teachers], *Hed HaKhinukh*, vol. 6, 1928-1930, p. 71 [Hebrew]. The references cited include "Sikhot Psychologiyot LeMorim" [Psychological Conversations for Teachers], a 1923 translation by Nissan Turow of William James, "Talks to Teachers on Psychology and to Students on Some of Life's Ideals" (1899); *Psychologia: Sefer Limud LeMorim VeLeTalmidim* [Psychology: A Manual for Teachers and Students], a 1923 translation by Mordechai Brachyahu of Wilhelm Jerusalem, *Die Aufgaben des Lehrers an den höheren Schulen* (1912); *Nefesh HaTinok* [The Psychology of the Infant], a 1929 translation by Yitzhak Epstein of William Stern, *Psychologie der frühen Kindheit bis zum sechsten Lebensjahre* (1914), with contributions by Kurt Lewin and Heinz Werner; *Mahut Beit HaSefer HaAmlani* [The Foundations of the Work School], a 1929 translation by Judah Dwossis and Aryeh Ilan of the book by German pedagogue Georg Kerschensteiner, *Die Schule der Zukunft: eine Arbestischule* (1912).

464 Dorian Feigenbaum, "Problemot Psychologiyot SheBaYaldut U-BaBahrut BeYahasan LeKhinukh" [Psychological Problems of Infancy and of Adolescence in Relation to Education], *Hed HaKhinukh*, vol. I-II, 1927-1928, no. 11, pp. 180-183, and no. 17, pp. 343-345 [Hebrew].

465 Letter from Freud to Dwossis, 20 September 1928, Freud Museum Archives, London.

466 Appendix to Freud, *Group Psychology*, p. 84.

467 After translating *Group Psychology*, Dwossis translated *Introductory Lectures on Psychoanalysis* (1934) and *Totem and Taboo* (1938).

468 Judah Dwossis, "Freud: Al Tirgum Kitvav LeIvrit" [Freud: On Translating His Writings to Hebrew], *Haaretz*, 5 May 1936, p. 4 [Hebrew].

469 The book appeared under the title *Totem VeTabu: Kama Te'imot BeHayei HaNefesh Shel HaPra'im VeHaNevrotikanim* [Totem and Taboo: Resemblances between the Mental Lives of Savages and Neurotics], trans. Judah Dwossis (Dvir) with the permission of the author (Jerusalem: Kiryat Sefer, 1939) with a preface by Freud [Hebrew], originally published in German as *Einige Übereinstimmungen im Seelenleben der Wilden und der Neurotiker*, *Studienausgabe* IX, 1912-1913, pp. 287-444.

470 This description is from a letter from Freud to Judah Dwossis, 20 September 1928, Freud Museum Archives, London.

471 Letter from Freud to Dwossis, 15 December 1930, Freud Museum Archives, London.

472 Excerpt from the preface by Freud to the Hebrew edition of Sigmund Freud, *Shi'urei Mavo BePsychoanalyza* [Introductory Lectures on Psychoanalysis], trans. Judah Dwossis (Tel Aviv: Stybel, 1934), p. XVII [Hebrew]. Source of English translation: "Preface to Hebrew Translation [1930]," in *The Standard Edition of the Psychological Works of Sigmund Freud*, vol. XV, trans. James Strachey (London: Hogarth, 1955), pp. 11-12.

473 See Sigmund Freud, "Das Unheimliche," *Imago*, Bd. V. 1919, translated into English as "The Uncanny." in *The Standard Edition of the Psychological Works of Sigmund Freud*, vol. XVII, trans. Alix Strachey (London: Hogarth, 1955), pp. 368-407.

474 Letter from Freud to Dwossis, 15 December 1930, Freud Museum Archives, London.

475 Freud, "Preface to the Hebrew Translation," in Sigmund Freud, *Totem and Taboo*, translated from German by James Strachey (London: Hogarth, 1955), p. xi.

476 Letter from Freud to Barbara Low, 19 April 1936, reprinted in Montague David Eder, *Memoirs of a Modern Pioneer* (London: Victor Gollancz, 1945) p. 21.

477 Aryeh Alkalay, "Kitvei Sigmund Freud BeIvrit" [The Writings of Sigmund Freud in Hebrew], *Hed HaKhinukh*, vol. 7-10, 1932-1936, no. 3, June-July 1935, p. 61.

NOTES TO CHAPTER 13

478 Letter from Freud to Dwossis, 4 January 1935, Freud Museum Archives, London.

479 Sigmund Freud, "HaIsh Moshe VeAmo" [Moses the Man and his People], *HaPo'el HaTza'ir*, no. 20-21, 9 December 1938, pp. 18-19 [Hebrew].

480 Sigmund Freud, *Psychopathologia Shel Hayei Yom-Yom* [The Psychopathology of Everyday Life], preface by Max Eitingon, trans. Zvi Vislevsky (Tel Aviv: Massadah, 1942, fourth ed., 1953) [Hebrew]. This book was first published in 1910.

481 David Tidhar, "Zvi Vislevsky," in *Encyclopedia LeHalutzei HaYishuv U-Vonav* [Encyclopedia of the Yishuv Pioneers and Builders], vol. 2, (Tel Aviv: Hotzaath Harishonim, 1956), p. 1822 [Hebrew].

482 This preface appeared on pages 6-10 of the Hebrew edition.

483 Sigmund Freud, "Davar Al HaAntishemiyut" [A Word about Anti-Semitism], *HaPo'el HaTza'ir*, 2 April 1938, p. 13 [Hebrew].

484 Sigmund Freud, "Akhzavat HaMilhama" [The Disappointments of War], *Gilyonot*, vol. 9, no. 10, 1940, pp. 354-357.

485 Sigmund Freud, "Al Milhama" [On War], *HaShomer HaTza'ir* [later renamed *Al HaMishmar*], 8th year, 1940, pp. 7-8 [Hebrew].

486 Sigmund Freud, "Od Nakim Et Harisot HaMilhama" [We Will Rebuild What the War Destroyed], *Ofakim*, no. 1, 1943, pp. 2-3 [Hebrew].

487 Sigmund Freud, "Halomo Shel Na'ar Yehudi" [The Dream of a Young Jew], *Ofakim*, no. 1, 1943, pp. 116-119 [Hebrew]. This was a translated excerpt from *Selbstdarstellung* (1925), with commentary by Zvi Sohar on Reik's book *From Thirty Years with Freud* (London: Hogarth Press, 1942).

488 Sigmund Freud, *Hayai VePo'alai* [My Life and Work], trans. Zvi Sohar and Shmuel Golan (Merhavia: Sifriat Poalim, 1947) [Hebrew].

489 Sigmund Freud, "HaPsychologia BeZikata LeSifrut, LeOmanut VeLaMada'im" [The Relationship of Psychoanalysis with Literature, Art, and Science] trans. Zvi Sohar, *Ofakim*, no. 1, 1948, pp. 2-5 [Hebrew].

490 August Aichhorn, *No'ar Azuv: HaPsychoanalyza BeTipul HaKhinukhi-Sotziali, Eser Hartza'ot* [Neglected Youth: Psychoanalysis in Social-Educational Treatment, Ten Lectures], trans. David Idelsohn (Jerusalem: S. Zack, 1956) [Hebrew]; Freud's introductory remarks appear on pages 4-5.

491 Sigmund Freud, "Al Shum Ma Mehayekhet Mona Lisa?" [Why Is Mona Lisa Smiling?], *Ofakim*, no. 7, 1953, pp. 41-47 [Hebrew].

492 Sigmund Freud, "Shalosh Massot" [Three Essays], trans. Shmuel Golan, published as part of the teaching and training curriculum of the Education Department of HaKibbutz HaArtzi, in *Psychologia Shel Gil HaNe'urim* [The Psychology of Adolescence] (Merhavia: Sifriat Poalim, 1953 [Hebrew].

493 Cited in *Freudiana*, internal brochure from the collection of the Jewish National and University Library, Jerusalem, 1973, p. XX [Hebrew].

494 Sigmund Freud, *Pesher HaHalomot* [The Interpretation of Dreams], vol. I and II, trans. Mordechai Brachyahu (Tel Aviv: Yavneh, 1959, 1974) [Hebrew]. See also the updated translation, Sigmund Freud *Peirush HaHalom*, trans. Ruth Ginzberg (Tel Aviv: Am Oved, 2007) [Hebrew].

495 "Dr. Mordechai Brachyahu, Zikhrono LiVrakha" [Dr. Mordechai Brachyahu, RIP], in Sigmund Freud, *Pesher HaHalomot* [The Interpretation of Dreams], vol. II (Tel Aviv: Yavneh, 1959), p. 15 [Hebrew].

496 *Freudiana*.

NOTES TO CHAPTER 14

497 Arnold Zweig, *Bilanz der deutschen Judenheit 1933. Ein Versuch* (Amsterdam: Querido, 1934).

498 Letter from Freud to Zweig, 30 September 1934, in Sigmund Freud – Arnold Zweig, *Correspondance 1927-1939* (Paris: Gallimard, 1973), p. 129.

499 Letter from Zweig to Freud, 11 October 1934, in Sigmund Freud – Arnold Zweig, *Correspondance 1927-1939*, p. 131.

500 Pater (Father) Wilhelm Schmidt, a priest and an academic, both anti-Semitic and anti-Nazi, actually defended Jews, and therefore Freud did not want to anger him.

501 Letter from Zweig to Freud, 29 October 1934, in *Sigmund Freud – Arnold Zweig, Correspondance 1927-1939*, pp. 133-134.

502 Ibid. Franz Grillparzer (1791-1872), an Austrian writer and playwright, was regarded as the national poet of Austria. His play *Libussa*, though written in 1848, was performed for the first time in 1874, two years after his death. This was what Zweig meant when referring to "leaving *Libussa* in the drawer."

503 Arnold Zweig, "Freud's Moses," dactyl., 1941, Stifung Archiv der Akademie der Künste, (SAAK), Berlin.

504 Sigmund Freud, "Moshe HaIsh VeAmo" [Moses the Man and His People] (an excerpt from "Wenn Moses ein Ägypter war"), *HaPo'el HaTza'ir*, 9 December 1939, pp. 18-19 [Hebrew].

505 Sigmund Freud, *Moses and Monotheism*, trans. with an epilogue by Moshe Atar (Tel Aviv: Dvir, 1978) [Hebrew].

506 Letter from Eitingon to Freud, 16 February 1939, *Sigmund Freud – Max Eitingon, Correspondance 1906-1939*, pp. 861 ff.

507 Ibid.

508 Ibid.

509 Martin Buber, *Moshe* [Moses] (Jerusalem and Tel Aviv: Schocken, 1957), foreword to the first edition, note 1 [Hebrew].

510 Letter from Eitingon to Freud, 11 April 1939, *Sigmund Freud – Max Eitingon, Correspondance 1906-1939*, pp. 864.

511 Shalom Ben-Chorin, "Freud Al Moshe Rabenu" [Freud on Moses Our Teacher], *Davar*, 5 May 1939, pp. 3-4 [Hebrew].

512 Ben-Chorin is referring to two studies, the first by Delmachen, *Shem Elohim HaHindi VeToldotav* [The Name of the Hindu God and His History], published in 1889, and the second by Berdichevsky, *Sinai VeGarizin* [Sinai and Garizin], published in 1926 (after the author's death in 1921), which argued among other things that Joshua killed Moses (an updated edition of this book was published in 1962 by Moreshet Micah Yosef Publishers).

513 I. M. Lask, "A Freudian Myth," *Palestine Review*, 30 June 1939, pp. 169-170.

514 Ibid., p. 170.

515 Ibid.

516 Ibid.

517 See, for example, David Bakan, "Freud's Jewishness and His Psychoanalysis," *A Quarterly Journal of Jewish Life and Thought*, vol. 3, no. 1, 1954, pp. 1-7.

518 S. S., "Yahaduto HaMudheket Shel Freud" [Freud's Repressed Jewishness], *Maaznayim*, vol. 14, no. 11, 1942, pp. 317-319 [Hebrew].

519 Ibid.

520 Letter from Zweig to Freud, 8 August 1939, in *Sigmund Freud – Arnold Zweig, Correspondance 1927-1939*, pp. 225-226.

521 Aharon Zeitlin, "Freud HaYehudi VeMoshe Ha. . . Mitzri" [Freud the Jew and Moses the. . . Egyptian], *HaTzofeh*, 4 August 1939, p. 6 [Hebrew].

522 Ibid. (concluding lines of the article).

523 Ibid.

524 Ibid.

525 Ibid.

526 Aharon Kaminka, "Milkhemet Freud Neged Moshe Rabeinu" [Freud's War against Moses Our Teacher], *HaTzofeh*, 18 August 1939, p. 7 [Hebrew].

527 Ibid.

528 Letter from Raphael Da Costa to Sigmund Freud, 13 April 1939, Freud Museum Archives, London.

529 Ibid.

530 Letter from Freud to Da Costa, 2 May 1939, Freud Museum Archives, London.

531 Letter from Siegfried Wolff to Freud, 10 May 1939, Freud Museum Archives, London.

532 Nahum Perelmann, "Professor Freud VeTotzeret HaAretz" [Professor Freud and the National Product of (Jewish) Palestine], with an open letter to Sigmund Freud, 2 July 1939, Central Zionist Archives, Nahum Perelmann, A 279/10/1. English-language versions of this article and open letter, if indeed they were translated to English and published in the *Palestine Post* as Perelmann requested, could not be located.

533 Nahum Perelman, "Professor Freud and the National Product of (Jewish) Palestine," p. 2. The term "Luftmenschen" was used to describe the men of the Jewish ghettos of Russia between 1860 and 1897, most of whom had no well-defined jobs and survived hand-to-mouth. Zionist historian Walter Laqueur translated this term as "rootless and hopeless." Laqueur, *Histoire du sionisme*, vol. 1, p. 94, note 1.

534 Israel Doryon (1908-1992), who immigrated to Palestine in 1934, is also known by the pen name B. Einan. He was a pioneer of nutritional medicine and veganism in Mandatory Palestine and the founder of Einan Bread, which to this day is sold throughout Israel. He was also known for his efforts to promote the social and economic order proposed by Josef Popper-Lynkeus.

535 Israel Doryon, *Freud HaIsh VeMoshe* [Freud the Man and Moses] (Tel Aviv: Massadah, 1946) [Hebrew]. A review of this book appeared in the "Hebrew Bookshelf" section of *The Palestine Post*; see "Freud on Moses," *The Palestine Post*, 11 July 1947, p. 7.

536 Israël Doryon, *Freud et le monothéisme hébreu*, trans. H. Baruk and M. Weisengrun (Paris: éditions Zikarone, 1971).

537 Sigmund Freud, "Moses, ein Ägypter," *Imago*, vol. 23, 1937, pp. 5-13; "Wenn Moses ein Ägypter war," *Imago*, vol. 23, 1937, pp. 387-419.

538 Letter from Doryon to Freud, 15 September 1939, Freud Museum Archives, London.

539 Israel Doryon, *Mamlekhet Lynkeus: Tochnit LeYetzirat Mishtar Hayim Hadash, Takin VeEnoshi* [Lynkeus' New State: A Plan for the Establishment of a New Social Order on an Improved and Humane Basis] (Jerusalem: Reuven Mass, 1939) [Hebrew].

540 Doryon, *Freud et le monothéisme hébreu*, p. 56.

541 Ibid., pp. 33-34.

542 Ibid., p. 52.

543 Henri Baruk, preface, ibid., pp. 6-30.

544 Shmuel Hugo Bergmann, "Professor Sigmund Freud," *Haaretz*, 25 September 1939, p. 5 [Hebrew].

NOTES TO EPILOGUE

545 For further information on the training of psychoanalysts and the controversy surrounding lay analysis in the history of the psychoanalytic movement, see Sigmund Freud, *Die Frage de Laienanalyse: Unterredungen mit einem Unparteiischen* (Frankfurt: Fischer Verlag, *Studienausgabe*, Ergänzungsband, 1926), pp. 271-349 ; *La question de l'analyse profane* and "Postface de 1927" (Paris: Gallimard, 1985); Élisabeth Roudinesco and Michel Plon, *Dictionnaire de la psychanalyse*: "Analyse profane," pp. 41-42, and "Reik Theodor [1888-1969]," pp. 893-894; Fanny Colonomos, *On forme des psychanalystes. Rapport original sur les dix ans de l'Institut psychanalytique de Berlin, 1920-1930* (Paris: Denoël, 1985); Moustapha Safouan, *Jacques Lacan et la question de formation des analystes* (Paris: Seuil, 1983); Johannes Reichmayr, *Spurensuche in der Geschichte des Psychoanalyse* (Frankfurt: Fischer, 1994), pp. 99-106.

546 Some years later, while serving as president in the early 1950s, Gumbel completely reversed his position and joined Barag in defending the principle that psychoanalysis be solely the purview of physicians.

547 Lizzi Rosenberg, who became Wulff's most prominent disciple, held a central position in HaShomer HaTza'ir (initially alongside Wulff). As supervisor over the seminars for psychoanalytic training of *metaplot* and preschool teachers at Mishmar HaEmek and Tel Aviv, she was one of the leading experts in infant psychoanalysis in Mandatory Palestine and Israel. She was regarded as the movement's leading psychologist after Wulff. Born in Vienna in 1905, she underwent analysis in Zagreb with Stjepan Betlheim, and settled in Tel Aviv, where she met Wulff and with whom she underwent a second "phase" of psychoanalysis. She worked primarily in the field of pedagogy, and specifically within the kibbutz movement; she wrote a number of articles on psychoanalysis focused on infant psychology and education, and with Wulff, she co-authored a very important text devoted to the study of childhood schizophrenia, in which they described the psychoanalytic treatment of two preschool kibbutz children suffering from schizophrenia. At the end of World War II, like other child psychoanalysts in Palestine, she left for London to continue her training with Anna Freud, with whom she remained in contact for many years after the founding of Israel.

548 "Our colleagues returning from the last Congress told me about the unpleasant, even painful, impression created by our Society's decision to confine non-physicians to the practice of child analysis, as mentioned in the President's report. I feel indeed very sorry that this resolution has been taken, an unwise compromise, [which will] cause grief. I was told by Prof. Winnick that he explained to you the legal situation in Israel which contributed to this step." Letter from Erich Gumbel to Anna Freud undated, Anna Freud papers, No. 38, Library of Congress Archives, Washington D.C.

549 Freud, *Die Frage der Laienanalyse: Unterredungen mit einem Unparteiischen*.

550 I cannot be more specific: although Dov Alexandrowicz and Dan Hertz, with whom I spoke, were first-hand witnesses and recall the stormy debates among the Society's leaders quite well, unfortunately they could not accurately describe what the crux of the dispute between their mentors actually was. In my assessment, the arguments surrounded the issue of lay analysis.

551 I am unable to go into detail here regarding the views of psychoanalysts in Palestine on the dispute between Anna Freud and Melanie Klein during the period between the two world wars. On this matter, see Pearl King and Riccardo Steiner (eds.), *The Freud-Klein Controversies, 1941-1945* (London: Routledge, 1991).

552 Conversation with Professor Dan Hertz, 30 June 1998.

553 Ibid.

554 Conversation with Dov Alexandrowicz, 30 June 1998.

555 The deviation can, of course, only be assessed in relation to established norms and, in this case, to the rules applicable to candidate psychoanalysts and members of institutes affiliated with the International Psychoanalytic Association. This policy, particularly after World War II, proved to be a source of many problems. It hindered the spread of psychoanalysis to new spheres and thwarted risk-taking – two processes that are essential for innovation, creativity, and the further development of psychoanalysis, as well as the opening of the unconscious.

556 The Sigmund Freud Center, located on the Mount Scopus campus of the Hebrew University, continues to operate to this day.

557 The first issue of the *Israel Journal of Psychoanalysis* appeared in 2001, and the fourth and final issue appeared in 2003.

NOTES TO CONCLUSION

558 As Elisabeth Roudinesco rightly points out, after Michel Foucault and Henry Ellenberger. See Élisabeth Roudinesco, *Généalogies* (Paris: Fayard, 1994), p. 73; Michel Foucault, *Histoire de la folie à l'âge classique* (Paris: Gallimard, 1972; Henry Ellenberger, *The Discovery of the Unconscious: The History and Evolution of Dynamic Psychiatry* (London, Allen Lane: The Penguin Press, 1970).

Index of Names